MAKING A MARRIAGE:

A Personal Book of Love, Marriage,
and Family

MAKING A MARRIAGE

A Personal Book of Love, Marriage, and Family ❧

KEVIN AND MARILYN RYAN

Foreword by Andrew M. Greeley

ST. MARTIN'S PRESS·NEW YORK

Library of Congress Cataloging in Publication Data

Ryan, Kevin.
  Making a marriage.

  1. Marriage.   I. Ryan, Marilyn.   II. Title.
HQ734.R88   306.8   81-21480
ISBN 0-312-50662-7   AACR2

10 9 8 7 6 5 4 3 2 1
First Edition

To
Andrew M. Greeley,
for his special gift of friendship

Contents

Foreword

The family, we are often informed, is in trouble. Divorces are increasing; more people are choosing not to marry or to remain childless in their marriages; single-parent families are more frequent; more women are working and demanding economic independence; children are not being raised in the stable, traditional two-parent families. The "old" family, it is said, is being replaced by a variety of "new" modes—more flexible, more open, more concerned with personal fulfillment.

One would be well advised to remain skeptical. Childlessness is less common than it was at the end of the last century. Women have worked since the days when we were hunter/gatherer primates. Families are less likely to be broken by divorce today than they were by death a century and a half ago. The increase in divorces since the early 1970s is concentrated at the low end of the socioeconomic ladder and seems to be the result of free legal aid and inexpensive court actions. Chastity, always popular in theory, has never been easy in practice.

The family has always been in transition, and the "old" or "stable" or "traditional" family is mostly a product of the "good old days" (or, if one wishes, the "bad old days") fallacy of social commentary: a myth, created not from empirical evidence but from the imagination of the commentator, to prove the existence of a social change for which the data are hardly persuasive. Indeed, the Western European family as far back as we can trace it empirically (to the middle of the fourteenth century) is marked by structures that have been remarkably durable—rather late age at marriage, closeness of ages of spouse, relative equality of husband and wife, small family size, separate residence (from paternal or maternal family), and some kind of ideal of affection between the spouses. Within this constellation of structures there has been considerable variation as social and economic conditions have changed, but the serious historians of the family are hard put to find any simple, unidirectional, evolutionary pattern to these changes. Nor does it seem reasonable to think that the transitions of our own era are going to overthrow the basic patterns of family life in the North Atlantic world. The family seems to be remarkably resilient, durable, and flexible.

I do not deny that there are problems in family life, new, poignant, and seemingly intractable problems, but they are not problems of deterioration. They are, rather, problems of the revolution of rising expectations. We expect far more out of our marriages and our family life than we ever did before, but we have yet to acquire the skills, elaborate the wisdom, and portray the models that are essential to guide us toward the achievement of our expectations. The Ryans are engaged in just these tasks, not, indeed, with the hope of writing the definitive book on twentieth-century marital fulfillment, but rather with the intent to share their experiences toward the development of new wisdom, skills, and models.

Kevin Ryan is not all that much younger than I am, though he comes from the less civilized New York milieu; Marilyn is a product of a much younger generation. Yet the difference between Kevin's experience of marriage and that of my own contemporaries is enormous, and not merely because those of us who chose mates in the late forties and early fifties would hardly have looked in such an obscure place as Bellingham, Washington (what and where is it, anyway?). Nor is the difference to be explained by the fact that he is a distinguished university professor. Few of my contemporaries have produced (save for an occasional cleric who discovered a belated vocation to the academy) or developed marriages that are as happy and in harmony with the contemporary world as the Ryans. They have achieved this in spite of having an academic and a transcontinental marriage.

Probably more devastating than transcontinental and academic marriages is the quest for personal fulfillment, a concept for which neither the name nor the image existed in the decade after the Second World War. The personalistic revolution, when it finally came, came all at once. Combined with the demographic revolution, which has in the last century and a half quadrupled the duration of marriage (from twelve to forty-eight years), personalism has profoundly transformed the ambience, the climate, the milieu, the atmosphere of contemporary marriage. Minimally, as our colleague and friend Teresa Sullivan has put it, there has to be a lot more than four times as many fights and marital treaties than there used to be in marriage. In fact, it is about this personalistic revolution—the desire to be independent and yet fulfilled in marriage and in other aspects of their lives—that the Ryans have written so insightfully. They have done it with candor, wit, and wisdom.

I trust that one need not assert that these changes represent gain for humankind and for the church, which has always claimed that the union between man and woman is the closest image we have of the union between Jesus and His people. The Ryans' discussion of creative conflict—which shocked a number of theologians when they first presented it in the rarified air of an academic colloquium and delighted a number of married social scientists at the same time—would not have been possible even ten years ago. One theologian even suggested it was making a virtue out of deviancy! Yet anyone who has been conscious of his or her experience of love (of whatever kind) knows that anger is merely the other side of that powerful, delightful, messy, unruly, driving emotion—perhaps, as Mary Durkin and Joan Anzia have suggested in *Marital Intimacy* (Andrews and McMeel, Inc.,

1980), because we are (quasi) pair-bonded primates with the pair bonding dragging us towards loving affection while our primate nature frequently pulls us in the opposite direction.

The love affairs between God and His people and Jesus and His church have also been stormy, as one is informed in, for example, the book of Hosea. It is both theological and psychological progress to say that not only may we conflict with those we love, but that conflict, properly handled, can contribute to the growth of love, indeed is a routine method for growing in love.

The Ryans are tentative about the questions and cautious in their answers, even though they have had experience and are skilled in the "human sciences." They are not dogmatic about their prescriptions. The reader does not have to agree with their point of view. In fact, as their format illustrates, they do not always agree with each other. They have the academics' respect, even admiration, for diversity of opinion and life-style. Still, the Ryans deal with the core issues that plague love, marriage, and families: sex, money, children, and the routine of everyday life.

In their book and in their lives, the Ryans stand as evidence that not only is married love possible in our time, but it can be immensely rewarding; indeed, probably more rewarding for more people than ever before. It is precisely in these twin possibilities of marriage and love that the challenge of contemporary marriage is to be found.

Don't let anyone tell you different!

—ANDREW M. GREELEY
National Opinion Research Center
The University of Chicago
September 1981

Preface

No doubt about it! Being in love is the great state of being. Most of us are never more fully alive than when we have found and have been found by our life's love. Our daily chores take on a special vibrance. We have the feeling that half of the love songs were written just for the two of us. Finally, someone has discovered the essential us, our core goodness. And not just anyone, but someone unique. Part of the thrill of being in love is the new sense of specialness. It is as if you and your love have special vision that can see into one another's souls, while other people can only see you skin deep. It is a magic time.

In most cases romantic love goes in either of two directions: the pair falls out of love and they drift apart; or they marry. There are many who see these two developments as essentially the same. But while everyone celebrates love, few celebrate marriage. From Shakespeare to Updike, the picture that emerges from literature is one of disenchantment, sourness, and personal isolation. A major theme running throughout literature is the transformation from high romance to bitter marriage.

Wits and wags have always had a field day with marriage. "The days just prior to marriage are like a snappy introduction to a tedious book." "When a girl marries she exchanges the attention of many men for the inattention of one." "Marriage is a romance in which the hero dies in the first chapter." "All men are born free, but some get married." And on and on.

When one moves from literature and humor to social science, the picture of marriage does not brighten. Reports of happy marriages are few and reports of breakups are many. The statistics on marriage suggest that one out of two will end up in the divorce courts. And if 50 percent divorce, it doesn't mean the other 50 percent are happy and fulfilled. Hardly. The picture is grim. The statistical warning signs are there. But still, lovers come pouring down the aisle to the wedding altar. Each couple is convinced that they are different. Their fate will be different. They may have secret doubts about themselves or about their lovers, but these forebodings are not enough to stop them.

We went down that aisle, too. Like lambs into a dark chute. That was seventeen years ago. Somehow we have muddled through. So far, we have seen many of our good friends—good people, too—go down the altar and then down the drain. Some have done it twice. Having gone down the marriage drain, of course, has not been the end for them. Many of them are quite happy now. However, along the way they experienced and often caused a great deal of pain and suffering. Besides wasting years of their lives in marital—and then legal—wrangling, the emotional scars on themselves, their spouses, their children, their parents and in-laws have been great. Many who have gone through this experience seem to be better husbands and wives the second time around. They're basically the same people, but they seemed to have learned some things about themselves and how to be married. And while we're happy for them, we are often left with the question, "Was this trip necessary?" However, the damage has been done, the books and records divided, the homes and the rest of the property settled. And in many cases, new households have been started. But why couldn't they have learned what they've learned without all this trauma? Probably because they are like most people—married and not married—who think one doesn't learn about marriage. One simply *does* marriage.

We, too, believed that. Even though both of us have been trained as teachers, we never looked at marriage—ours or others'—as a thing to be learned. It was experienced. Marriage, of course, was talked about and, in a sense, something may have been learned along the way, but marriage was not seen as something one seriously studied and learned how to do. We went a long time with that attitude, which is akin to strolling through a mine field and every once in a while hearing an explosion and seeing a puff of smoke where the couple across the street used to be, and then another indicating where the friends down the street used to be. We were frightened by what we saw going on around us. At times we became scared about what we were feeling. But we never thought to stop and study the terrain, let alone get a mine detector.

About five years ago we moved to a new community. One of us is a university teacher, and we asked to be part of a marriage preparation given by the Newman Center, one of the campus religious centers. Teams of people put on weekend workshops, usually three times a year, for university students who are contemplating marriage. We were apprehensive about getting involved in this for many reasons. For one, we were sure that our marriage was far from the Christian ideal we had heard preached from various pulpits. We were quite aware that our marriage was far from the one we had set out to have. Nevertheless, we decided we would go to one weekend workshop as observers. We heard an array of couples and a few divorced persons speak with searing candor about their experiences as married people. We discovered that what we thought were our own dirty little secrets and failures were quite common in marriage. These accounts of other flesh-and-blood people enabled us to talk more freely about our own experiences. We felt we had gained a great deal and decided to join the marriage preparation team.

It was as if we had a new agenda. We began to talk more about our marriage, about what each of us was experiencing. We began discussing it, as we had once discussed movies or politics. Sometimes the impetus was a workshop talk we had to give. Sometimes it was just our growing curiosity about some marriage-related topic. We began confronting the realities of our relationship in a new way. We sometimes uncovered problems we had conveniently swept under the rug. Somewhere along the line we got into the habit of working on our marriage.

Three years ago we were invited to be part of a study team, composed of social scientists and theologians, examining the topic of marital intimacy. We began to sense a need for a frank look, warts and all, at what happens to lovers when they marry. We thought, too, that it would be useful to others to pull together what we had learned and what others had shared with us. Right at that point, a wise and generous friend, Andrew Greeley—to whom this book is dedicated—gave us the encouraging shove we needed. At that point we began thinking of this book.

As we began our book, we had an attack of nerves. We were not at all sure that our experience of marriage was like anyone else's. Granted we wanted a personal book (rather than a textbook or treatise), but we did want it to be connected to the marriage experience of others. We decided to hold a series of semistructured interviews with a cross section of married people. We ended up interviewing six couples, a few of whom were old friends, a few from our marriage preparation team, and a few who were relative strangers. These interviews, which in truth turned out to be long conversations, were fascinating to us. With each couple, we were quickly able to get below the clichés and chitchat and get to the pains and pleasures, the sweetness and sourness of their marriages. We learned much from these generous, sharing souls, but most important, we discovered that we were on the right track. We found that our experience was unique, but not that different. Our struggles and inner strains were theirs. Their defeats and private joys were ours. In short, we learned that we had something to say.

This book has been three years in the making. It has been

written on three continents, wedged in between classes and meetings, between braiding a child's hair and doing the marketing. In the midst of it, our snug family of four became, to our surprise, a fullsome five. (No family-planning manual this!) While one of us was helping Justin Thomas Patrick Ryan enter the world, the other was in a waiting room birthing the first draft of the chapter on children and parenting. The story of his early and underweight arrival and his struggle to remain in our family and in this world is a story in its own right and must wait for another time. The three years have been a rich period for us in more than "a family way." Before we started this book, the two of us knew little about marriage in the abstract. We knew even less in the concrete about our own marriage. We have read much about marriage but talked to one another even more. We have been shocked to find disagreement where we were sure there was agreement. And happily surprised to find accord where we were convinced we differed.

As a flip through these pages will reveal, we have used three typefaces to represent what are, in fact, three authors: the two of us together and each of us individually. While the mathematics may not be clear, we have ended up with three voices, each with its own typeface. While this may initially confuse some readers, our intention is to tell a further story, to allow more room for our individual experiences and thoughts, for our personal views.

Although writing and rewriting this book has been time consuming and an added pressure in our already harried and frayed lives, we have no regrets. Because of it we know one another better. We appreciate one another's views more. We have a clearer sense than we did three years ago of the marriage we are making. Even if no one else reads our book, for us it already has been a success.

KEVIN AND MARILYN RYAN
SEPTEMBER, 1981
COLUMBUS, OHIO

1

Choosing a Mate

Love, like a punch in the stomach, takes the breath away. Love is oceans of emotion. Love is a grand exaggeration of the difference between one person and everybody else. Love has its own symptoms which turn every season into spring. Love affects mind and body; a chemical magic occurs which increases the heartbeat and interferes with the ability to concentrate. The desire to be with the beloved over distance and time is such a powerful force that reason is abandoned, at least temporarily. Women who function normally with their jobs find themselves reduced to daydreaming; men who usually sleep like babies find themselves lying awake at night. Articulate people sometimes cannot find the words to adequately describe a loved one. People falling in love, whether for the first or fifth time, are overwhelmed. We are so wrapped up in each other and the new learning about ourselves that we don't want the feeling to end or the music to stop. Even if we know full well that we've been this way before and the feeling is in part self-discovery, still we smell, taste, feel alive in a miraculous moment. We are Gene Kelly in Paris dancing through puddles, singing in the rain, not caring if we get soaking wet. It used to be said that love was wasted on the young; more accurately, love makes people feel young— splashing in the rain—and very happy.

Science on Love

Love, love, love. We grow on it; we mourn over it; we worship it; we run from it. This age, like ones past, is intrigued with love. So much that the word needs adjectives surrounding it: divine love, committed love, free love. Now even the cold eye of science has turned its gaze on the bubbly, champagne quality of love. Scientists have asked some questions and come up with some answers. Do people have only one all-absorbing love? They tell us we can love several times as happily and as completely as the first love. We can even love two people at once, though if we are committed to one, we do not let the other one flower. Are fear and hate the antithesis of love? No, it turns out that fear sometimes precedes love. Somehow, to have bodily passions—whether in excitement, fear, or ecstasy—aroused at all gives cause to love, which explains how hostages fall in love with their captors (defined as the Stockholm Syndrome) and women fall in love with their doctors, psychiatrists, and priests. Turned on its side, love involves elements of fear and vulnerability. We are sometimes angry with those we love most. They have reached us as no others have, and they threaten us where we live.

People who once had an all-consuming love can fall in love and marry again very happily. Neil Simon deals with this second-love thesis in his play and movie, *Chapter Two*. A man who loses his first wife in the bloom of love, falls again, but has to resolve the conflict he feels over what he thought was the only great love of a lifetime.

Can everybody love? Some people have not been taught to love by their parents. They have never experienced it and therefore may never learn to give and receive it. Others are too narcissistic to care enough about someone else outside themselves.

Is love incapacitating? Does the lovesick person go into a trance, unable to carry on without the object of that love? Some do, surely, but the very opposite is more true. Love gives us energy and creativity. We can accomplish more and create with inspiration. As one great chef remarked to his cooks: "The more you love the people you cook for, the better you will cook."

But regardless of what scientists can tell us about being in love, knowing when someone we love is the right person to marry and cook for is another matter. No one can deny the attractions that occur when we gaze at a good-looking body or when we are stimulated by an inquiring mind. We are flattered by attention from a new and appealing stranger. Attraction is a pulling, magnetic feeling, but it is an initial response and not one necessarily to act upon. Feelings of love are the next stage, but sometimes even they are not to be followed. Furthermore, these attractions and infatuations do not stop once we are married. We are inclined to dismiss them, however, as we focus on the mate and come to understand the meaning of lasting attraction and love.

Like participants in an ever-changing jigsaw puzzle, we are all pieces of sky looking for a matching piece of blue. Some people are looking for a reflection of themselves, a reflection of their tastes and sensibilities. Others are looking for a missing link to complete their adult makeup. Still others want someone to challenge them. In searching for the matching piece for our sky, some of us want an electric thunderbolt. Others look for a gentle breeze. In the days of courtship and dating, we want someone to step out who makes us feel very special; someone who makes our hearts beat faster than anyone else; someone who strikes the talkative ones dumb and the shy ones into song.

Reasons for Choosing a Mate

While falling in love is scarcely a rational event, we have our own reasons—often hidden from ourselves—for selecting a particular mate. When asked, few people articulate their motives for choosing a mate. Many give reasons that suggest their choosing a mate was a very casual decision: "He looked at me like no one else," or, "He was steady and calm, while I was frivolous and silly," and, "She reminded me of my mother, and she baked pies." For some people the puzzle of their lives needs a missing piece. Something is lacking which they hope to find. They give their reasons: "Bill's family background was so different from mine. They were settled people. Mine moved around like nomads. He liked me because we had lived in different places." The mirror-image mate holds appeal because, "He fit in our family. He had good manners, and I liked the way he looked." Or, "Most of all, he was smart." Often people reflect the feeling of comfort: "I was nervous around women, but then she just made me feel comfortable."

Most of the reasons for choosing a mate don't seem like reasons at all. They are more like responses . . . but somehow the speaker knows the reasons were good ones. The desire to marry someone is based upon attraction and fear. Attraction is visible; fear is deeply hidden. The fear is that once someone has touched the core acceptance of ourselves, we will lose that person. He will go away, marry another, find a fluffy cloud for his sky.

After all the searching for love, for many marriage comes to mind. Love and marriage, said one of the lyricists, go together like a horse and carriage. Love and marriage don't always go together, nor do they "go" for always. And how will we know which love is for marriage? Most of us love the idea of love. It feels good. We are surrounded by notions of romantic love, conveyed by movies and music.

Chances are we will love several people before and after marriage. But we marry only one. At least we hope so. "People should mate for life, like pigeons and Catholics," Woody Allen declared in his confession, acknowledging that he had used up one marriage. Pigeons have their own complexities to deal with, but we Catholics seem to be catching up with the rest of the population in divorce statistics. We are not much better than non-Catholics at keeping our relationships polished.

Falling in love appears to be the easy part; staying in love with the same person—now there is a worthy challenge—is often another set of realities. Sociologists point to the pressures of modern life, of rising personal expectations that lead people to marry again. The supermarket variety of people available to meet and fall in love with only adds to the confusion.

Falling in love is simple. Designing a marriage is the elaborate task. The parents of many of us married because it was in the natural sequence of their lives, and it was expected. As single people, they didn't ask if they were fulfilled, or if there were more self out there to be discovered first. They married because someone asked. And maybe there weren't so many options.

There is a time for mating. At a certain juncture in our lives, usually between ages twenty and thirty, we have added up our mutual myths of romantic love and pledged our plight to another person. We are often so ready to marry for love or sex or both that at times it seems we are saved from a bad decision only by some trick of fate. The event of graduation from high school or college puts strong pressure on people to marry. Many girls conveniently graduate from school with a diploma in hand and an engagement ring on the finger. It is both a time to graduate and a time to set up housekeeping. Men typically wait until they have a good job. Often after earning regular money for a while and too many nights with just the boys, they begin to look around.

We believe that each of us could be happy with many people, but timing determines the choice of a mate. A recent song suggests this complication: "Where were you when I was falling in love?" When the time was right, why wasn't the right girl there? A young woman we know was convinced she had to choose between two men and rejected the advice that perhaps neither was right for her. The time was right and pressure so strong to commit—to one or the other. She reasoned that she could be in love with two men, but she could only marry one. Delaying marriage is most difficult under such emotional pressure, when the time is right. But a little delay was necessary, and she did marry one in a year. Commitment to the idea of marriage is so demanding that some couples go ahead with the ceremony, even if one or both know privately they are marrying for the wrong reasons.

Romance is in our blood. We are convinced of the possibilities for love. We begin as children in search of a mate. We dream of princes or princesses to come and carry us away in chariots or Corvettes. Little ones learn that marriage is as much a part of their destiny as their anatomy. They talk and dream about getting married. Little girls "marry" their best friends, their brothers, or their daddies. One eight-year-old we know very well said she got married in her dream, to her six-month-old brother. "That way," she explained, "I won't have to sleep alone."

But we grow up and begin to realize what mating is all about. We practice models from various households; we copy the attempts of others to pair off. We begin early to find a best friend. If we don't have a boyfriend in the fifth grade and all the other girls seem to have one or two, we decide to pick one just because everybody else is doing it, even if it makes no sense. We tease the girl with red hair, hoping to get her to sit with us all the way home on the bus. From grammar school throughout the teens and twenties, we practice relationships with the opposite sex, pairing off for a time with one or another who suits our fancy. Symbols of the commitment are exchanged: friendship rings, silver footballs on chains, fraternity pins, engagement rings, and finally wedding bands. We are convinced that finding a mate is an event, that falling in love is a quest, and that our happiness will be greater once we are comfortably paired off. Often our parents are so eager to marry us off that we come to believe we are incomplete without the wedding ring. We are convinced that somehow we are meant to come in pairs, like gloves—and often regardless of the fit.

MARILYN:

*Like other young women of my age and background, I
was the marrying kind. There was never any real question
that I would marry. In my family it was as inevitable as
college and would take place in proper time. Whether one
married into a trap or a new life was the issue for me. How
could I know ahead of time how the future would fall out?
Would he make all the major decisions about where to live,
which house to buy, and how we would spend Sunday
afternoons? Caught in the protocol of dating, the man asked
for the date, he proposed marriage, the life-style. I accepted
or didn't. That was the script.*

*There were my private fears about marriage. I had seen
young wives drained by baby after baby. I feared the tubs of
soiled diapers and half-finished kitchens waiting for weekend
carpentry. I had seen mothers stirring (not sautéeing) dinner
(probably out of a can) with an infant on the hip and a
toddler scribbling on the walls. Conversation with these
mothers disappeared in favor of developmentally detailed
reports on the children. First one's figure and then one's
mind could be lost in a few years of such a life.*

*Furthermore, there was my deep fear that all the fun in
the relationship would be lost once the chase was over.
Conquest and love were synonymous. The movies I grew up
with were full of the love chase, just as they now deal with
the "relationship," another word for "the chase." Clark
Gable charmed and badgered his way into the arms of a
variety of leading ladies. He often had an adversarial
relationship with women. In the beginning of the movie he
couldn't stand the dame because she was so independent, or
she loved someone else. Scarlett O'Hara couldn't get
another man out of her head in time to keep him. Stewart
Granger and Jean Simmons conquered in period costume;
Bogart and Hepburn battled down jungle rivers; Grace Kelly
and Claudette Colbert both married the same man twice*

(which was clearly better than repairing the house every weekend). In one movie, Let's Make It Legal, *Miss Colbert left Macdonald Carey after eighteen years of marriage when she learned that he had won her in a crap game. She was recaptured in the end after discovering that he had weighted the dice. I knew those scripts by heart.*

The young men I knew were set on conventional marriages. They were often imaginative in the chase, but they would settle into traditional roles after marriage. Perhaps some graduate school would be thrown in for the "little lady," if it didn't interfere with their ambitions. I would live in a pumpkin shell. The chase would be over, and so would the fun.

I married before I was ready because I was afraid this man would get away. He didn't promise what he had not already proven. Others promised houses hanging over California cliffs (the future revealed how wise I was not to fall for those dreams); or two homes, city apartment and a country farm; or the comforts of marriage to a corporate lawyer. This man was different. He didn't send fourteen valentines or buy me a coat I had admired or send flowers. He didn't have a party supply of delicatessen cold cuts delivered when I was home sick, nor did he supply me with an antique paisley purse containing ten dollars in dimes in case I needed to call. He didn't send my sister baby-doll pajamas and nightshirt identical to ones given to me at Christmas (how better to get them past parental censorship). He didn't phone for three hours all the way across the country every Saturday night. Courtship seemed to be the art of impressing a girl with material things and clever games. This man was different.

He was known for taking dates to Manhattan Night Court (admission free) and for rides on the Staten Island Ferry (five cents in those days) and to neighborhood diners (chili sixty-five cents). He didn't believe in currying favor with girls by taking them to expensive restaurants in fancy cars. He believed in spending little money before marriage to the girl (picnics along the beach, a walk in the woods, Shakespeare in Central Park), but, as I learned later, he believed in indulging her after marriage. He seemed more interested in getting to know me than trying to impress me. Whatever the reasons, ambitions, or dreams we marry for, it was clear early that this was the right man for me. At less romantic moments I believed I could be happy with any number of men, but clearly this was the right one for me. It wasn't just that he loved me (others had, or said they did), but what I felt for and with him. All my private worries temporarily took flight. Nothing else seemed as important, and we wanted to be together. He was the older man waiting for the right girl.

KEVIN:

I was thirty when I met her. I felt ready for marriage. Perhaps it is more accurate to say I was ripe for marriage. In fact, I was so ripe, I was getting gamy. I had been seriously searching for a wife for about five years. In retrospect, my attempts to secure a mate look a little dubious. I had seen and read about romances where the man and woman were swept off their feet and then the marriage went into the dustpan. I wanted her—wherever she was out there—to know me and to love me for what I was—warts and all. And there is no doubt about it, I succeeded magnificently in not sweeping anyone off her feet. Looking back at it, it seems I had what psychologists call the will to fail. In those five years of serious hunting (stalking?) I met several lovely women. And, in fact, there was much romance in my life. While no one quite broke my heart, I had my ego cracked a few times. I became what we used to call "serious" about three or four women in that period. But something always held me back from getting "very serious." There was a pattern. After several weeks of dating a particular person, I would start thinking about the possibility of marriage. But then the same question would arise. "OK, she is a fine person and you are having a good time, but do you really want to spend the rest of your life with her?" And while I rarely got clear "no's" for answers, I never heard back a strong "yes." And after a while things would stumble and stagger to some awkward ending.

I was beginning to think I was being foolish and totally unrealistic. I believe now what I believed then, that many of the girls and women I knew would have made me marvelous wives. That is, if I could have persuaded them to marry me. But something held me back.

Getting on to my thirtieth year, I was becoming rather discouraged. Everyone I took out seemed somehow to be someone I had met before. The sense of romance, which I had enjoyed so much, was never quite there. While I was still interested in finding a wife, I wasn't enjoying the hunt much.

Under the questionable theory that misery loves company, most of my friends were actively trying to get me married. When the wife of a fellow teacher told me that she had just met someone I "just had to meet," I had my doubts. With a mixture of optimism and ennui, I said, "Sure," and dutifully took down the name and telephone number. I called Marilyn that night, and even though we set up a date, I wasn't particularly excited. She sounded very "peppy" and "sorority girlish." I pictured her as very young and in her I've-come-east-to-see-the-world stage. (In fact, she was all of those things.) So, putting the phone down, I decided to show her the inside of my favorite greasy spoon. I wasn't going to take her to some dark roadhouse where I couldn't see her, let alone talk to her. Doing that could take me two or three dates to find out if she were a mushhead. And what I knew about sorority girls suggested that it would probably be a short evening. So, the Spring Valley Diner.

A few nights later when I rang her doorbell and she answered it, I knew immediately I had made a big mistake. Also, I sensed that something special was going on here. Nevertheless, in a slightly stunned state, I took her to the diner. What was supposed to be a very short date turned out to be quite long. Since we both had to teach the next day, I finally got her home shortly after twelve. By then I was sure something different had happened, but I didn't realize what deep trouble I was in until I went home and tried to go to sleep. I kept thinking one thought, "I want to marry this girl. This is it. Finally! I want to marry this girl!" Then I felt like a fool. Here I was, a thirty-year-old man who had just met for a few hours a kid fresh out of college—and a sorority girl at that—and I was thinking about marrying her. I felt decidedly irrational. As I tossed and turned, I gave myself several very stern lectures about not acting like an adolescent, love-struck kid. Finally, I gave up and started to plan how I would ask her to marry me . . . and then I fell asleep.

MARILYN:

That spring we were both teaching school outside New York City. Our first date was in a diner, the second in church on Palm Sunday. After that, we saw each other nearly every night for two months (once a few other entanglements were taken care of). Concentration on grading papers vanished, replaced by daydreams. I didn't have to tell anyone what was happening to me. Apple blossoms burst out that year like never before. Barbra Streisand was singing about people who need people—as the luckiest people in the world. Every song was written for us. When school was out for summer, he took a teaching job at Officer Candidate School in Newport, Rhode Island, and I moved to a magazine job in New York City. We saw each other only on weekends, and stormy ones at that. Just as we had met, he had been accepted in the Ph.D. program at Stanford University, so at the end of that turbulent summer, he left for the West. He lived in California for three months before I moved west. The early blossom of love found maturation difficult. We loved each other, but we were running aground as we attempted to chart two courses as one. It is serious business settling two separate lives, two sets of dreams and ambitions, into one life rhythm.

We had our recurring fears to encounter. Did I want to marry a teacher? Was I ready to give up my life in Manhattan? Would I be stuck with a baby a year? Could I make him happy? He wanted to do good, not do well; he would not settle for a life of corporate comfort. I was worried when he quoted French novelist Leon Bloy: "There is only one unhappiness, not to be one of the saints." How did saints live from day to day—in sackcloth and ashes?

KEVIN:

I was just plain scared. I knew I loved her, but I was afraid I wouldn't be able to keep her. Off and on I would convince myself that while I really loved her, to her I was only the latest crush. It seems the way I dealt with it was to come up with weird and pompous quotes, like the one above. All the time I was asking myself, "Can I make her happy? Does she love me for what I am? If she knew me as I am, would she still want to marry me? Will she be happy as a teacher's wife?" With all of these questions swirling around in my head, thirty years old seemed very young to be getting married.

Plaguing fears and uncertainties about marriage are not uncommon among people who are realistic about the chances of a good marriage. Both Marilyn and I had them, long after I had proposed to her. About ten months into our relationship (I would give anything for a better word!), we were both feeling very uncertain about making a permanent commitment. And the fact of being uncertain caused more uncertainties. Just when things were most confused and tense, some wartime friends of my family came from London to visit in San Francisco. We were living (in separate domiciles, mind you) nearby in Palo Alto. This lovely elderly English couple treated us to an elegant meal, and afterwards the host invited me out for a short after-dinner walk. After some pleasantries, he asked, "Are you going to marry her?"

I was stunned but somehow managed to reply, "I don't know. We've had some problems, and we're trying to work through them."

He paused and said, "Well, I think she is a fine girl. Do you love her?"

"Yes. Sure, yes."

"Then there is no further question, is there?" I don't remember answering, but I do remember at that moment my world turned on its axis. The words and setting were less important than the impact. He was right. There were no further questions. That evening Marilyn's uncertainties dissolved, too. Shortly after, we announced our engagement and wedding date. Probably we would have worked things out and gone ahead with our plans without that particular evening. That friendly nudge, the reassurance coming from an older, wiser person, someone who knew me and my family, was very important to me during the moments of doubt.

MARILYN:

While Kevin was out on his walk, the wife spoke to me. And with similar results. We began planning our wedding, and at that point all doubt disappeared.

One clear blue day in June the proposal that had been made a year earlier was vowed again before man and God. During our dream-sequence wedding ceremony, I was jarred out of my mist by a painful pressure on my ring finger. To remind me of the difficulties ahead, he squeezed my hand so it would hurt and I would feel the pressure of those vows at this moment and remember the bittersweet moments of the proposal.

Asking someone to marry you is an enormous request. To marry means to commit life and belief, body and mind.

—strong desire to raise children
—loneliness
—ability to share things in common
—regular sex
—an ironing board and someone to iron for
—financial security
—a roof, a fireplace,
—and to get the damn thing settled!

To argue the case for rational decision making about marriage is to be a voice in the wilderness. Many people just aren't ready to reason when they are in love. Their heads give them one message, while their bodies whisper—sometimes scream—another. But the old advice still holds. Keep your eyes wide open before marriage and half-closed afterwards. This advice suggests that people should keep their heads when getting married and giving their hearts away. One should not run down the aisle to exchange wedding promises; two should move slowly and thoughtfully down the aisle. The great French actor and lover Maurice Chevalier once said, "Many a man has fallen in love with a girl in a light so dim he would not have chosen a suit by it." The same, of course, can be said of women. If the reasons for marrying are not good ones, there will be other people to love.

Love is only one element in the decision to marry. Difficult as it may be, the decision to marry, like any other path taken, must be based upon reason. And we do decide to marry. We decide to commit to another person for life. It is better, therefore, to commit to someone who shares our interests and concerns. The more we match in various compartments of our lives, the better it usually works out. If we are both athletic, both bookish, both like to dance, or refinish furniture, or fish or hike; if we both like to eat and make love, we have fewer adjustments. It is sometimes said that opposites attract. In magnetic fields, perhaps, but for people who are going to marry, to spend their lives together, it is the likenesses that are truly significant. We can and will learn new attitudes and interests because of our mate. But if one likes the opera and the other listens only to country and western music, there will be static. If one of us likes to be alone much of the time and the other requires constant companionship, if one huddles indoors and the other only feels alive outdoors, if one likes to read quietly and the other needs to be on the move, these can be serious differences. It is preferable to have the same tastes, religion, and politics, particularly if these are firmly held attitudes. Likenesses in these areas indicate shared values. Differences in taste can change (and they do change), but beliefs and values are stubbornly held.

Choosing a mate is probably the most serious choice of one's life. Our past, present, and future are at stake. Our mental and physical health are affected; our finances and families are changed. To be married means losing one's past and redefining oneself in the present. The past is seen dimly because the present is all shiny and new. And the future will be unlimited if we marry well.

Health and Marriage

Mental and physical health are strengthened or weakened by our choice of a mate. If we don't live happily ever after our marriage—we at least live longer than unmarried people. People who are happily married gain a tranquilizing influence, a buffer against stress, from the companionship of marriage. Dr. James J. Lynch, in his book, *The Broken Heart: The Medical Consequences of Loneliness*, notes that unmarried people not only visit physicians more often but also stay in hospitals longer than do married people with similar illnesses. People actually die of loneliness when they have no one who cares for and about them.

Happiness is greatly affected by marriage. In surveys, the strongest predictors of happiness in life are social factors— marriage, family, friends, and children. Although at the same time that large numbers of people are getting divorced and questioning the viability of marriage as an institution, research reveals that married people, overall, are happier than single people. Love is the single most important element in happiness. People without love nearly always list it as important—even though poor people do not always say that money is the secret of being happy. Love is equally important to men and women, according to Dr. Jonathan Freedman, a Columbia University psychologist, in his book, *Happy People*. "Lots of money, a good job, health, beauty, marriage and even sex do not make up for a lack of love." (Our mothers could have told us this, but still it is reassuring.) Unhappy marriages add to the stress level, so we hope to have a good one.

Picking a mate is a time of high self-interest. We are looking for someone who makes us feel special, someone who challenges and develops us. We are looking for someone we can grow with. Choosing a mate is the one time that one's self-interest should really take the reins.

Self-interest is something of which most of us have an excess. For many of us, being in love with another person is the first great step out of ourselves. We learn to come fully in contact with another human being. We learn to give, and to give generously. Our self-interest may be at the lowest ebb when we are in love. And, therein, lies a danger. Being generous to another person is one thing. Devoting your life to his or her rehabilitation is quite another. For one thing, it is hard enough to change ourselves when we want to change, let alone try to change someone else. For another, devoting your life to improving someone else is a sure way to guarantee that he will end up hating you. We are sure that there is a parallel in marriage to the saying about one of our aunts, "She devoted herself to others. You can tell the others by their hunted look."

Love isn't exactly blind. It's myopic. It distorts the beloved, the object of love. Our strong attraction to the other blurs his defects. It magnifies her strengths. We want the search to be over. We want this to be the one. We want this dream to be true. That's a powerful force, that love, but we can be foolish and deceive ourselves because of the sheer thrill of being loved. Indeed, love often makes the mate stronger in her virtue or helps to rid him of weakness. In full friendship, the marriage relationship offers the best conditions for personal growth. This partnership matches us with a person whose self-interest is vitally caught up with our best interest. We have a loving critic-in-residence, someone who knows our strengths, our moods, and our imagination.

One function of marriage is the personal growth and self-development of two separate people. What two people learn about themselves and each other in the courtship period should continue through their lives together. Dating is the time to practice self-expression and adaptation to another person.

All too frequently the quality of a couple's relationship is confused with "how they get along." Learning a process for dealing with our feelings is more to the point. If two people never had a fight before marriage, they must wonder what will happen when the first one comes along. If one is a dominant personality, we want to ask how that person maintains dominance. Does he allow for expression of others' desires and ideas? Is she certain she is always right or knows the best way to do a job? Has he kept silent to keep peace, or is he lazy in communicating his opinions and thoughts? What style of communication will develop after they are married?

It is in our self-interest to ask ourselves these questions before we choose a mate. "Does he listen to me?" "Can I make this person happy?" "Will he make me happy?" "Do we *like* and *admire* each other as well as love each other?" "Does she want what I can't give?" "Does he love me, or his image of me?" "Will she be satisfied with my salary and the possible promotions and sacrifices of my job?" These are things to look for, questions to ask ourselves, which may cut through the romantic haze that is part of being in love.

Compatibility may be a major concern to couples before marriage. Couples talk of things in common: similar tastes, interests, and their needs for space. Sociologists and psychologists are studying which marriages are compatible. (If they don't, anthropologists may soon have to look for traces of marriage along with bits of bone, cooking vessels, and shards from ancient man.) When researchers talk about compatibility, they mean what makes people stay together and be happy together.

MARILYN:

When I was growing up, "compatibility" was a code word for "sexual." Compatible didn't mean "did we like the same books," but it did mean "did both people like sex." By and large, sex was something men liked and women put up with. Sometimes the women even liked sex eventually, but since they had managed all these years without it, it was probably no big deal. It seemed to be on men's minds all the time. The sexual explorations of dates were something of a bother. In my more gloomy moments, I thought perhaps that was all there was and that one just closed her eyes, picked a husband, and then the wife would learn to have strong sexual feelings. In my mind, sexual adjustment ("compatibility") was a matter of the woman adapting to her man's desires. I didn't know much about sex, and particularly woman's sexuality, then.

It was, and still is, puzzling for me to hear about people who made love before they were married and maybe even with two or three different people. How, I wondered, did they know with whom to select the bed linen and kitchen pans, let alone which to marry for better or worse. There were lots of dates in my growing up who were fun to joke or dance or swim with, ones who gave intelligent gifts or ones who would have promising futures, but finally it came down to one man for life. How could a woman test her true feelings if she were already sexually involved with a man? If the sex was good, maybe she would think everything else would settle into place in the marriage; if the sex was only

OK, or disappointing, would she reject an otherwise "good specimen" of malehood and husbandry because the earth didn't move in that early phase of their sexual life together? If she wanted this one man, it was all settled, and the decision was made, then maybe under certain circumstances it would be permissible to have sex. But it still wasn't a good idea since one could never discount the possibility of last-minute reversal of events. It was, however, sex—or, at least, sexual attraction—that finally determined my choice of a mate.

My litmus test for readiness for marriage was that I wanted to be in bed with this man. I had never really felt that way before. Once when I was very nearly swept away by the romantic justice-of-the-peace, spur-of-the-moment proposal, I thought about being in bed with him that very night; then I came to my senses. When I met the man I married, there was no doubt in my mind that I wanted to share my life and everything else with him.

But for us, sex was like a present: Do not open before marriage. Since neither of us had had other sexual partners, we had nothing and no one to compare each other with. We were ready for each other. There was no confusion ever whether we would be sexually fulfilled, because we had the learning to do together. We weren't pressured by the need for one of us to have "experience," since we had waited for each other.

Through much of the dating period, the tension exists between finding someone who attracts us sexually and someone who makes a good companion. In my mind the resolution to commit to one man for life was the product of examining intellectual and aesthetic interests, of measuring and explaining our religious and personal values, and then testing emotional and romantic responses. Some inner voice whispered "You're frightened, but it feels so right."

There is a human tendency to reorganize our personal histories so that everything turned out for the best. We reassure ourselves that we did the right thing. We assume that the way we ordered our lives is the way our children and friends should probably settle theirs. However, over time trends change and new patterns emerge. We didn't live together before marriage. We didn't sleep together. Much as we may have wanted to, that was not part of the rules we grew up with. If the people we knew had sex before their weddings, they kept it a great secret.

Living Together

From the first date to the altar stretches a period of getting to know one another. We think, "This is it!" We want to be together. We want to become intimate. We think we can learn nearly all about each other. We want a time of high contact. Couples want to learn as much as possible about someone they might marry. Some couples choose to have sex and to live together. For some, living together is their way of gaining what they see as a more realistic view of each other. They have made a rational decision to move in together. However, it seems to us that it must be much more difficult to be rational about breaking up. There will be broken hearts over the dissolution of these living arrangements. People get hurt when their love and commitments were deeper than their partners'. Or they are disappointed when this central person in their lives was found wanting. It is never easy or painless to end a romance with a fiancé or someone for whom we care deeply. Some aspects of the broken relationship seemed just what we had always wanted. Some qualities were just perfect. But when it is time to break up, it hurts. The physical intimacy comes to an end. We have to start from scratch. How difficult it must be to break off the living arrangements! In addition to all the heartache, there are the niggling questions of who gets the rest of the subscription of *Newsweek*? Who gets the cat?

While we see certain values in the current trend, we feel that it is safer and wiser to wait until marriage to bed. Like some of the important things, though, it is a matter of conscience. It is not a decision to be made out of convenience. It is not a choice to be made with one's body. We should listen to the authorities in our life, the people whose judgment we trust. Once we have put that all together, giving passion and style their just measure, then we can make a choice. We are sure, though, that casually playing house is no preparation for marriage. As we said, we are more comfortable with the pattern we followed because we feel that delaying such intimacies as sex and living together allows the conditions for marriage to be more fully developed. (And besides, it's a lot easier on one's family.)

At least one million unmarried people are currently living together. Many are living together as a way to test compatibility, so that they do not make a mistake marrying someone with whom they cannot meld their lives. Through living together, these couples hope to discover that theirs is a strong and viable relationship or to uncover crippling incompatibilities. But divorce statistics show that people who lived together before marriage are no more likely to stay together than those who didn't.

For us, aside from the fact that there is no comparative advantage to living together, the trial marriage has some unresolved questions and issues. For one thing, there is the question of how good a test of marriage a trial marriage actually is. Do real incompatibilities come out during the trial period? Of course, there is the possibility, if not the certainty, of superficial differences and irritations coming to the surface. He leaves the bathroom a mess and his socks under the bed. She cannot cook a decent egg and spends money casually. But most wives are confident (at least in the beginning) that they can improve their husbands' sloppy habits. Most husbands do not judge their wives' failures as cooks because the first months do not produce excellent cuisine. Most wives do not determine their husbands' ambitions and futures on the basis of the first year's promotions and earnings. To what degree, then, are these early issues a good basis for judgment of compatibility and suitability?

Another question has to do with the nature of this marital test. How much of a test is living together when the individuals know they are on trial? Are the individuals natural when they know the other is judging them and still deciding if this is the partner with whom they wish to spend the rest of their lives? What is the effect of being on trial in bed, in the kitchen, and in the sharing of possessions? If one is really in love with the other and wants to have that other for the rest of his life, there may be a very strong tendency to be on his very best behavior.

There is also the question of the effect the partial commitment of a trial marriage has on the relationship. There is the strong possibility that at times, or continually, the lack of full commitment to the other will be felt as a partial commitment. And this lack of commitment will itself feed the fires of incompatibility. "This is a nice comfortable arrangement of his, but I don't sense he is really committed to me."

And, finally, there are the victims of living together, those individuals who have given three or five years to someone, and all of a sudden it is over. They have given someone what they see as some of their most "eligible" years, if not their best years, and all they have is an empty place in their lives. Of course, this happens in marriage, too. But at least divorce requires serious deliberation, and the victim has a court settlement to ease the pain and, perhaps, redress the real injustices.

Compatibility in marriage is a crucial and important issue. Trial marriage, if seriously undertaken, may be a new form or stage of courtship and marriage that society will evolve to and adopt. All the evidence isn't in yet. For us, though, the case looks weak; the arrangement dicey. To us, sweet reason and romance look better.

Those two, reason and romance, should also combine to tell us why we want to spend our lives with this person. But the pace of modern life—where the hurried telephone call has replaced the thoughtful letter—gives us few opportunities to think the matter through carefully.

Modern technology allows such rapid communication that the moments with one another are less reflective than romance requires. For most couples, the dating period is intense and the two are in close proximity. They want to know a great deal about each other and their families. Some fastidious persons even look up the bloodline of the intended before agreeing to marriage. (These are truly rational people who could call a halt to their love affair upon learning that one had come from the gene pool of Simon the Stupid or Winona the Witch.) The careful couple, furthermore, experiences separation to reflect on the relationship; the careful couple applies words to paper or tape to explain their feelings for each other. The definition of love is a useful habit. Explaining a love relationship is both beneficial and reassuring. We have a right to know the reasons why we are marrying each other. We deserve the explanation of those feelings. No one is ever so secure in love that he doesn't want the expression and communication of love.

No one can tell us exactly who is the right person for us to marry. But our friends can tell us who is not the right person. If nearly all our close friends say this is not the person for us, then we ought to carefully reexamine the relationship before continuing it. We can always get out of the engagement, even if the invitations are ordered and the church reserved. A little public embarrassment is far better than a life of boredom or unhappiness, or both.

MARILYN:

In the old days (the sixties) it was accepted that the Richards would beat the Ellens at tennis. The Ellens of those days even expected to be outrun or outjogged or outskied. They expected their men to be stronger and smarter than they were. Sometimes women even hid their intelligence in order to "get a man." Over the years, however, women have tired of playing dumb to get a husband. They refused to settle for warnings that men didn't make passes at girls who wear glasses. Actually, the glasses had nothing to do with it. It was the matter of being smart enough to require glasses and using one's eyes for close work other than gazing transfixed at the closest passing male. A number of us went on walking into street signs, squinting at friends, and smiling at strangers all because we wouldn't wear our glasses.

Now that the revolution has begun to come, many women have discovered that they are smart, strong, athletic. But they still want a smart man. In fact, finding an intelligent companion is a significant endeavor. The emotional and physical attractions are not the whole face of love. We have an intellectual side of our lives. The petite cheerleader will lose her ability to cartwheel and the rest of her girlish litheness. Even if she turns us on for a time, will this feeling endure? Being swept off our feet by a football hero is not the proper balance for marriage.

We can't all marry a Rhodes scholar or find a brilliant trial lawyer who comes home every night for dinner, but we can tune our appreciation to the person who uses his head. A good mind abhors boredom. We should look for a smart mate, someone who stimulates our brain cells as well as our pituitary glands. After all, the mate's mind is the organ that will most affect our life together; the mate's judgment, prudence, clear thought, intuitive senses, and intelligence will be with us for the life of the marriage.

Love Tradition

A good deal of the modern idea of romantic love comes from medieval times. The modern version of romantic love, however, is something of a perversion of the art of courtly love, dating from the twelfth century. Courtly love gave women an exalted place in the world. Such romance was a novelty for the courts of Europe. The main idea of medieval love was that for every fair lady (and, of course, they were all fair) there was bound to be a gentle knight who desired to serve her in all respects. If sometimes the lady was married to another, it was a complication but not uncommon. Medieval knights fell in love after marriage, not before. This vision of love was carried by troubadours throughout Western Europe in song and lyric poetry—just as the message is carried on to this day in popular music. There was one major difference: The message of medieval love, idealized as it was, required a foundation of personal goodness. Virtue, charity, and chastity were highly prized. Love came to those who endeavored to follow the right path. Modern troubadours scarcely consider goodness in their prerequisites for love, except in physical terms. Then there is the problem medieval lyricists left us with: Their songs were often about unrequited love. These lovers never settled into an apartment or mortgaged a bungalow. Everybody knows unrequited lovers never had to wash diapers, force green things down a child's throat, endure the NFL season.

The love conventions of the twelfth and nineteenth centuries were opportunities for the male to approach the female; love in our day and in this country, conversely, has become a demand of the female, who is in the position to extend or withhold sexual favors. Her own sexual desire probably somewhat lessened by cultural repressions, she can use such favors to reward or stimulate emotional expression. Increasingly, females demand sexual satisfaction for its own sake, especially as they are less likely to be "caught" with unwanted pregnancy. Keeping sex and true love, both strong drives, separate is a struggle in any romance. They blur our vision. Modern love appears not identical with romantic love and is based more on ego demands than on ideal demands.

But whatever form love takes, it is rarely the only condition upon which marriage is contracted. Rather, love is one selective factor operating within our culture. Other factors are age, race, religion, ethnic origin and class, and regional proximity. These factors are only vaguely in the mind of the lover in hot pursuit, but they can be inhibiting factors, nonetheless.

Our parents warned us of the company we should keep. They were worried that we would be influenced by a crowd who liked smoking dope or wild drinking parties. If we hung out with one type of teenage kid they didn't like, they feared we would imitate those kids and pick up bad habits. That process of imitation and adaptation continues with the mate we have chosen. Whether we recognize it or not, we are going to become more like the person we marry than we suspect. Some couples we know even come to look alike over the years together. Mainly, though, people reflect and imitate each other. Therefore, we must find someone whom we wish to emulate and whom we can admire. Not only should we love this person we are choosing, but we must like that person very much. Advice sometimes given to new brides goes: "Don't think you can make him over." This advice is partially true. We do make each other over, but not always consciously. We become different people as a result of living together and shaping each other.

If the romantic poets of the middle ages taught us anything, it is a message frequently overlooked. Their songs about love conveyed the importance of goodness. If those poets are to be trusted, the emphasis should not be lost on us. We know we can love someone who isn't a good person; we can be infatuated by him or her but know he wouldn't make a good husband, she a good wife. Part of our role will be to encourage the goodness, but we should begin the marriage relationship with deep respect for each other so that our love can be nurtured.

Six Reasons Not to Marry

In choosing a mate, a few practical considerations leap out. The first of these is: Don't decide to spend the rest of your life with someone you haven't known for more than three or four months. And if you're being pressured to rush to the altar by someone you've known for a short time, ask yourself, "What is the reason behind the rush?" If he truly cares, he will give you time to be sure.

Second, don't marry anyone you don't like. It's one thing to be in love with someone. It's another to have a deep liking and admiration for him or her. If you can't respect the behavior and values of your potential mate, rethink the situation. What will it be like with this person once the haze of romantic love fades?

Third, if people who know you well and care a great deal about you—parents, teachers, and *wise* friends—are counseling you against this marriage, pause. Although they may not know your potential spouse as well as you do, their vision may not be as blurred as yours. At the very least, give yourself plenty of time to make sure that your major doubts are resolved.

Fourth, don't marry someone in whom there are signs of really unstable behavior. If your beloved needs to be drunk or to have drugs to have a good time, you have a serious cause to worry. If he or she has had several different jobs in the last year, find out why. Can't he get along with coworkers? Can't she stand the responsibility? Is the discipline of work too much for him?

Fifth, if your primary drive for getting married is an overpowering urge to have—or to continue to have—sex with this individual, stop. Sex is of immense importance in a good marriage. It can provide the glue for marriage, but it can't provide the substance. Better take up jogging for a while.

Sixth, don't decide to marry someone just because everyone else is getting married. There are times in our lives when it seems that all our friends have found companions and are getting married. Marriage is in the air around you.

Marriage means more than partial commitment; it demands more than half-time dedication. Marriage requires the full share of our mind and body. It requires maturity. As Eric Fromm said, mature love contains the elements of "care, responsibility, respect and knowledge . . ." That just about sums it up. The ability to love one person before all others is part of the human capacity, and it is deeply in our nature to nurture such a relationship. It is in our own self-interest and part of our personal growth to be the husband or wife who is both loving and loveable.

In choosing this unique person for our mate, this combination of history and charm, this merging of flesh and brain, we are looking for the lifetime love that will sustain us. But as we have come to understand, genuine love is not a free gift but an earned achievement.

Falling in love and choosing a mate are the first steps of what is for most of us the great adventure of our lives: a marriage in which we continue to redefine the nature of love. If we, like pigeons, plan to mate for life, we must know that we do not fall in love as though it were a spasm. Perhaps we catch love (when it comes our way) like a virus, but finally it is up to us to learn how to grow in love.

2
How Am I Doing?

There is nothing like going to your high school reunion—preferably twenty or twenty-five years out—to discover not only that there *is* life after high school, but also that human change does occur. These nights are occasions of confirming expectations and jolting shocks. There are the predictables, of course. The head male cheerleader is still the slightly frantic life of the party and remembers the names of everyone in the class. He now is some sort of a success in advertising. The girl voted Most Beautiful is still a knockout, if not more of a knockout. The president of the student body became one of the youngest judges in the history of the state. What are really interesting, though, are the shocks—and not just the bald heads and massive redistributions of weight. The class greaser who roared around town in his hot rod frightening all the mothers and most of the girls with hot stares now owns a string of garages and last year was elected president of the PTA. Then there is the girl voted Most Likely to Succeed, who dropped out of college, is on her third marriage, and came to the reunion with a snootful. And there is the class semitramp, known to the boys as Red Feather because she had the community chest. She married, has four children and a thriving part-time real estate practice, and seems to be the happiest person there. And the night is filled with reports and rumors of long-ago names and the successes and failures of those who did not—for one reason or another—show up. All those you meet, though, are certainly different, but some seem strikingly different. There are some who seem to have gained strength over the years. They are more quietly confident and seem to have their lives under control. Some others seem not to have developed or fulfilled their potential. They seem prematurely beaten, less confident, and somehow they have narrowed their world. They don't appear comfortable with themselves.

We have been responding to their self-concepts, the sum of what each of us thinks of himself or herself, what we value, what we stand for, who we are. Self-concept is, of course, an abstraction, a construct. It is used to explain why we behave the way we do. One self-concept theorist claims that preserving intact one's perception of one's self is the prime motive of all behavior. That includes the behavior of getting married.

When we marry someone, whether we are aware of the mate's self-concept or not, that self-concept is the most important part of the bargain. For a wedding is the marriage of two self-concepts—for better or worse, for richer or poorer, for sickness or health. Nothing in the Western world prepares us properly for the marriage of two selves. We are taught about the freedom of "I" and the safety of "We," the loneliness of "I " and the intrusiveness of "We." Increasingly we are aware of the selfishness of "I" and the burdens of "We." Nowhere do we hear about the development of the making of "We." The individual's self-concept mushrooms, prompted by incidents and experiences collected in memory. Not often is it suggested that we could be the helping hand or silver tongue of encouragement for someone else.

KEVIN:

Twenty years ago when I was a graduate student at Columbia University, I took a course from the great teacher and literary critic, Mark Van Doren. In fact, because of retirement, it was the last course he was to teach. Approximately 250 students sat in rapt silence scribbling down the words of the great man. After starting us with the Greek poets and taking us on the run through the modern American playwrights, he came to the end of his final lecture. After a pause he said, "The question that unites all of these great works of art and that runs through all great literature is not, 'Is there a God?' or 'What is the true nature of man?' or 'What is reality?' The real question is," and here Van Doren paused and looked out at the audience and said, "'How am I doing?' That's the question Man tries to answer." One felt, listening to this distinguished scholar, that he, too, at that moment was sharing his own concern to know "how he was doing."

During our years in college, we, of course, had what we now refer to as a self-concept, but we did not talk about it as much. We dealt with it in a less direct way than we do now. One phrase we did use, however, is "inferiority complex." "Inferiority complex" is one of those phrases that has gone out of fashion; perhaps because it is so very general. Reserved people, introverts, late bloomers were often said to have "inferiority complexes." It was not uncommon for a close friend to blurt out in moments of great candor that he or she "had a terrible inferiority complex." However, if the words have gone out of style, the idea that stands behind it hasn't.

In those days we talked a great deal about personality. "He has no personality." "She has a terrific personality," and this was inevitably followed by "but" and the revelation of some maiming defect like "Pizza complexion" or "elephantine legs." But we saw personality as a fixed entity. It was a composite of what we had become, not a sense of self that was in the process of becoming. Our personalities were set and subject to change in a very limited way. Now, we seem to exist in a different psychological landscape. We have to discover our feelings, deal with the process of self-development and constant change. Adapting to mobility and novelty, needing stimulation, we think not so much about personality (and outward manifestation) as self-concept and our inner state.

Another difference between then and now is that having "an inferiority complex" or what-have-you is no longer a life sentence. We also now see that the symptoms surrounding an "inferiority complex" are situational, and many people come and go. We now speak of a person having a poor self-image or a negative self-concept. And we have much faith in human change and development. Still, though, the idea of playing with one's personality is relatively new. As undergraduates, we didn't get doses of Carl Rogers applied to ourselves, nor did we have the human-potential movement prodding us on to higher levels of self-realization and development. We were not finding ourselves, or "getting in touch with our feelings." In the same vein, there was very little understanding and even less direct talk about sex. Perhaps the closest we came to it was to say that there was a "chemistry" between a certain man and a certain woman. And we thought that the proper chemical attraction was a necessary ingredient to a good marriage. But actually, to say about someone that "there is real chemistry there" was to say pretty much the same thing as "she turns me on."

Still, we didn't talk about these areas much. We submerged many of these feelings and concentrated on developing our minds, largely through literature and philosophy. And, of course, there was the most universal concern for a job and for a wife or husband.

A person's self-concept is not a constant. Our sense of self changes as a result of many forces and events in our lives: our achievements and failures; our encounters and experiences with parents, friends, and associates. Each of these forces and events in our lives adds a little or takes away something. Our self-concept is the product of these pluses and minuses, the secret doubts and secret prides, the public blemishes and public beauty marks.

In the making and maintaining of a self-concept there are two elements at work: one, habit; the other, fluctuation. By habit, we are referring to the regularities, the usual way we think of ourselves, such as: "try-hard-but-make-too-many-mistakes-fair-dealer, friendly-but-oh-so-disorganized-me"; or the "hard-driving-impatient-very-lonely-me-who-no-one-understands." The habitual part of self-concept is the regular reoccurring aspect of our picture of self.

But then there is the fluctuating part of self-concept. Most of us vary a great deal. The two of us certainly do. Sometimes, when we add up the pluses and minuses, we get a plus. The next time, a minus. There is a situational, time-bound factor that is hard to predict. However, we found that our self-concept is predictably affected by the weather, by what we have recently gotten done (accomplished) or what we have not gotten done, by whether or not we have had much physical exercise. That may seem odd, but how we feel about ourselves seems to be very closely related to whether or not we have run or engaged in some heavy, physical exercise. At any given moment, then, our self-concept is the interplay of our habitual image of self, plus the product of the moment.

KEVIN:

Perhaps it is to state the obvious, but the one we choose to spend our life with, our spouse, becomes a major agent in the development of our self-concept. More than anyone else in our adult life, our spouse answers this question for us, "How am I doing?" And he or she tells us, "for better or for worse." Not only do we spend a great deal of time and have a great number of exchanges together, there is also the value or quality of the spouse's judgment. This "other person" thought enough of me to spend her life with me and to take perhaps the biggest risk of her life. By the time we were married, she knew me better than anyone besides my parents. As such, she is in the prime position to tell me the answer to, "How am I doing?" If I look into Marilyn's eyes and I see disappointment or annoyance or indifference, my self-concept is affected. If she tells me—either with words or actions—that I let her down or never developed the way that she had hoped or that upon closer scrutiny I turned out to be shoddy merchandise, my self-concept withers. If, on the other hand, she tells me, "Hey, you turned out to be a good deal," or, to use Debbie Boone's line from a song of a few years ago, "You light up my life," I grow. If she tells me (and in what I believe to be a normal pattern in marriage) that I'm doing fine in A, B, and C but X, Y, and Z need a little attention, then my self-concept grows and I know the direction in which, at least, my caring critic-in-residence wants me to go.

MARILYN:

We thought we had much in common when we were first married. That's why we married in the first place. We had great, long conversations. We liked to do the same things, and we had similar reactions to art and theater. We liked to play sports, to talk about books and politics. Our values were similar. We wanted a family, but not immediately. We expected to finish graduate school and travel. We had come from close families, and we both liked our parents. We had come from different coasts of the country and had had very different upbringings, but we had much to share with each other. We knew what we wanted and how to get there—vaguely. We read Mary McCarthy, J. D. Salinger, and J. F. Powers; we watched Barbra Streisand and Bob Dylan become stars; we watched a growing horror of a Vietnam War. We learned to live without the Kennedys. We adapted to urban life on the South Side of Chicago. These were forging experiences that we shared.

We have discovered there is more to molding into marriage than we once believed and what we have experienced together. Our independent self-concepts have grown toward each other. We are like two trees planted side by side which bend together in the same wind and, gnarled by the same winters, reach together for the same sun and sky. We believe we are different people now because we have lived together. What was once magic, though, is now sometimes managerial. But instead of making a decision on the basis of our own preference and convenience, we decide after discussion and accord. The end result of forging and molding is that we are different people than we were. We have changed towards each other, shaping ourselves in new patterns. The content of these patterns has also changed. The girl who once swam away the summers now spends them on the tennis courts; the man who ate in late-night diners and greasy spoons now loves French cuisine; the man and woman who slept late on weekends and stayed up late on weeknights now rise together to jog or to have some early-morning quiet together or change baby diapers.

I am what Kevin sees in me. I am becoming what he wants me to be. Kevin is becoming what I want him to become. If this sounds narcissistic, it is also fearful. Over the months and years together, I can see what has advanced and what has retreated from the self I once was. I see a reflected self in what I have become and in the changes I see in Kevin. I think I am a better person having lived with him than I was without him. In my parents' home, I was dreamy and disorganized and undirected. In the time we have been married, I have become, I believe, what he wanted. This may sound like a submissive surrender of self to the other, but it is not. For one thing, we have both done it, defined a new self. We both changed "I" for "We." In effect, what happened back there when we decided to get married is that we also decided to be what the other wanted and needed. While I don't believe we've lost ourselves, our unique identities, we have almost unconsciously moved toward what the other desires.

Our experience tells us that how we think and feel about ourselves, how we value ourselves, depends on the other person. From this perspective, our spouse is a major factor in our own mental health. If the mate believes in us and supports us and can give us help when we wander off target or a loving nudge when we stray from the path, we gain energy and confidence from that. We have a strengthened self-concept. If, through nagging or ignoring or ridicule, we come to believe that the mate knows us but finds us wanting, then it is hard to have a favorable view of ourself. Sometimes our spouse is our own worst enemy. Some men are known to make fun of their wives to embarrass them, a social game with the guys. There are women who work out their angers by belittling their husbands in the presence of other couples. A friend told us recently that a couple we had known in Chicago finally divorced. They had been married for twenty years, and the split came as a shock to many people. But our friend was not surprised. "Mrs. S. said to me on more than one occasion: 'You know, Nelson isn't very good in bed!'" Surely Mrs. S. couldn't have been among the surprised when old Nelson finally took up with a younger woman.

MARILYN:

Our sense of self is very fragile. Even if we have constructed a self-image that is impervious to petty attacks, or if we show little reaction to the comments people make about us, most of us salt those remarks away for moments of self-doubt. My husband isn't a great help if he complains about the faded chair cover, thinning carpet, or reminds me of the bad meals. Everyone has bad-meal days or lapses in the housekeeping or days that sales fell through or research did not come together. If our concern as a mate is such that we understand the off days and try to support and compensate, then we are both further ahead.

We think we have made changes in our thinking and feelings. It came as a great shock to me to return to my hometown of Bellingham, Washington, and to meet again one of my old friends from high school. "You haven't changed a bit," she said. I was stunned. I thought that I looked different. I felt different. I thought that I had been learning about myself, about physical well-being, about the world, and that all this knowledge would show. My former classmate may have been trying to pay me a compliment, but I was disappointed. Like the lady in the Clairol advertisement,, I wasn't getting older, I was getting better. Or so I thought. What I knew about life's passages, behaviorism,, and Chinese art didn't come through. That I was unlocking my inner self and had developed a respectable tennis game was unseen. I had become a wife, a mother, a graduate student, and none of it showed!

We are all more aware of self these days. Part of the new consciousness of self is healthy and important. The young people we meet seem less dreamy and more realistic than my friends and we were at the same age. They seem more savvy, more worldly wise. They seem to know their way around and how to take care of themselves. This has not been an unmixed blessing, though. In the last ten or fifteen years in this country, there has been a quiet but definite shift in values from loyalty to family and group to a new consciousness and concern for self. Today the superstar is the individualist, rather than the team player. People seem to be paying to see the extraordinary soloist, rather than the coordination of many different talents. Our baseball heroes have shifted from the Jackie Robinsons to the Reggie Jacksons.

Ten years ago we were urged to do our own thing. We began to find where we were "at." Since then, we have seen the evolution of self-serving slogans into life-styles and then into book titles. We were told consistently that, "We're only going around once. Make the most of it." "Nice guys finish last." "Winning isn't everything, it's the only thing." Not long ago, *Looking Out for Number One* was high on the best-seller charts, followed, of course, by another focus-on-self book. What some call the "me" generation is not confined to a particular age group. "Me-ism" or "the new narcissism" is like a virus that many of us have contracted. We feel—and are reinforced by our notables and gurus—that if we don't look out for ourselves, no one else will.

Perhaps we are simply reflecting our own legitimate worries about ourselves, but we see this self-preoccupation, this love affair with self, in so may modern trends: the married couple not having children because they don't want the responsibility; they would rather get a new sports car than a secondhand station wagon; they would rather go on the Club Med vacation than spend the money on maternity clothes and bassinettes. It is seen in the extraordinary sacrifices for their careers and financial success that men make, such as leaving child raising totally to their wives and hardly getting to know their children; in the subtle methods of control they put on wives to keep them tied to home and stunted in their development. We see it, too, in women denying their responsibilities to children and husbands in their efforts to get out of the house or further their careers.

It is seen in our picking friends strictly on the basis of how they can help or satisfy me and my ambitions, rather than what we can exchange or what I can offer them.

What all of this means to us is that to love one's neighbor as thyself is getting harder and harder, and so is loving one's wife. It is becoming a truly counterculture activity. But we remain convinced that our successful futures—and that of the race—depend upon our finding some balance between the questions, "How am I doing?" and, "How are you doing?"

But still the question, "How am I doing?" is a central and important one. Again, our own self-concept is based in large part on the answers we receive to the question, "How am I doing?" Am I living up to my ideals? Am I living up to the expectations of my family and friends? Am I the kind of person I set out to become? Many people give us many answers to these questions and on a daily basis. We're listened to or not listened to. We're complimented or ignored. People let us know that we're important in their lives or they don't. We're not invited to a social event. A dinner to which we have given special thought and preparation gets rave compliments.

One's children get complimented for good manners. Another gets cut from the team. Out of this mix of messages, a self-concept has been forged and continues to develop.

KEVIN:

We have found that there are two aspects of the self-concept that come into play regularly in marriage. They represent both passive and active aspects of the self. The passive is the vulnerable self, the self exposed to judgments, belittling, and rejection. Then there is the active or the "calls-for-help" self. Both come into play on an almost daily basis in our marriage. Let me illustrate. When I come home from having taught a bad class or from a day when I think I accomplished nothing, I feel reduced. As such, I complicate matters by failing at my aim of "bringing happiness home at five o'clock." And instead come in asking for first aid. Old self-doubts arise. I'm running out of ideas. My hoped-for self has never materialized.

On the other hand, Marilyn has had a day of Lysol, peanut-butter sandwiches, and folding laundry. She feels that she is getting no time to read and her brain is turning to soggy cereal. Her usual political activism works into writing a letter to Battle Creek, Michigan, complaining about the four hard raisins found in a box of Raisin Bran. She fears she is being turned into some stereotype of a suburban housewife. Daylight is fading, and instead of enjoying this day, we feel as if we have been run over by it. What we each want is solace, comfort, and uncritical love. What we want and what we get are not always the same. Part of the problem is that we don't always know how to say, "Hey, I'm hurting. Can you help me?" The other part is that we are often so preoccupied with our own psychic wounds that we don't think that the other one needs help. This setting is a perfect one for a fight. Add a few wrinkles like screaming children or notification of a bounced check, and the odds are against us. It is right at this moment when understanding of the active and passive aspects of the self-concept are important. If Marilyn can say, "I had a boring day. I need to get off the Johnson's Wax treadmill. Please tell me something interesting from the real world," then that's a start. If I can say, "I'm discouraged about myself. My private worry machine has started up," then it's a beginning. I have been honest with myself and my mate, and she hasn't laughed or rolled her eyes in revulsion. If we can expose our vulnerability to one another and ask for help, we've done half the job. Just doing that is helpful. Being able to say how we feel at that moment somehow eases the burden.

The second part, the more active part, is to be a counselor-friend. This is the more creative and more demanding part. It means forgetting your own agenda, your own score card of wins and defeats, and seeing how you can help the other.

Millions of words have been written telling us that husband and wife should help one another grow in spirit and in mind. Little, however, tells us how to do it. When we were first married, we found ourselves with a goal, the desire to be supportive to one another, but we didn't know how to reach that goal. We didn't have the habits. In effect, we wanted to be good to one another, we wanted to be virtuous husband and wife, but we didn't know how we could become that person. Long ago, Aristotle spoke to the question of how someone acquires virtues, such as courage. He said a man becomes virtuous by doing virtuous acts. He becomes brave by performing brave acts. He becomes kind by doing kind things. While that Aristotelian message helped, it didn't take us far enough. We needed some more concrete skills.

Ten Skills Needed for a Marriage

Along the way, we have picked up some skills that help us be a better counselor-friend to one another. Some few of these we brought with us to marriage, and some we discovered from our friends. Father Tom Ryan and Dr. Naomi Meara have taught us a great deal here. Ten skills that we have found particularly helpful are the following:

1. Honest Praise. People need to hear when they are doing something well. Given all the negative messages we get from inside and outside ourselves, it is important to be reminded of our good points. Sometimes it takes thought and imagination to give honest praise to those who are depressed or disturbed about a current problem. They may have failed to get a job that they wanted, or seen a project fall through. The last thing that they need is phony praise. Maybe the most important thing they need is to get back in touch with their strengths. And we can help by reminding them.

2. Praise Early and Often. We have never met a person who was suffering from too much praise, acceptance, or support from those around him. Our own experience, and what others have shared with us, suggests that the majority of people feel chronically underappreciated, occasionally rejected by family and friends, and often that they are floating around totally unsupported. We both have been surprised that simple compliments have meant so much to the other. We thought surely the other person knew how much we valued this or that aspect of him or her. We have come to believe that all of us are struggling in an impersonal world and are plagued by self-doubt. We need to be told about our strengths and the things we do well. And we need to be told early and often.

3. Make Yourself Available. When we get in trouble with one another, it's often because we haven't been giving one another the time that a marriage demands. We quietly slip into our own life and block the other out. We need to remind ourselves consciously that to build anything as elusive and fluid as a good marriage takes time, and it takes time on a regular basis.

4. No Guilt Trips. While many disagree with this, we believe that a little guilt is a good thing. Unfortunately, most of us have much too much of it. We seem to have it about crazy things like keeping our floors scrubbed because our mothers did, or going out on "school nights" years after you are out of school. It is very easy for the mate to tap into our guilt reservoir. When you are losing an argument it's a great temptation for the mate to say something like, "I wish your mother could hear you now."

5. Help the Other to Say "No." We know many people who find it very hard to say "no." In certain situations, we're that way, too. Perhaps it relates to the guilt we spoke about above. Many of us feel that in some vague way we aren't doing "our share," and so when asked, we almost automatically say "yes." And then we are mad at ourselves. We are overcommitted already. We feel weak. We feel put upon. We get angry. Seeing this, the mate can help by strengthening us and giving us determination to say "no." "Listen, love. You are a wonderful and generous person, but you are not indestructible. Enough already. Tell them 'no.'"

6. The Empathy Habit, or Getting Inside the Other's Skin. When one of us gets annoyed at the other, the normal temptation is to say, "I don't like what he or she is doing to me," or to pass some negative judgment on what the other is doing. We find it's helpful to stop and try to think through what the other is experiencing. What is behind his anger? What kind of a day has she had? What could I or the children have done to lead up to this? And most important, "What's it like to be her right now? What's she experiencing?" This approach we have found especially helpful. However, it takes time. It's a mental habit at which one has to work.

7. Respond to Calls for Help. Many people have a habit of continually putting themselves down. They are always

making reference to the fact that they can't do this or that as well as other people. Then in a discouraged fashion they will talk about how dumb they are or how disorganized they are. To us, that seems like a call out to the world for help. Many of us, while not making a habit of it, do call out for help. We may become withdrawn after a disappointment. We may become irritable. We may just want to get more and more sleep. We may, and this we find very common, begin complaining about ourselves. Probably each of us has our own way of signaling that we need help. The spouse to whom I act annoyed may be calling out to me for help, asking for reassurance, asking that I dispel his self-doubts. We need to learn to listen to those messages and those calls for help, and be ready to respond.

8. Say Your Mate Is Worth It by Actions. Often, the greatest thing we can do for our spouse is make his or her life easier. It can be something simple, like cutting the grass for him or making a dinner for her. Or making some calls the other has been dreading to make, or balancing the check book. What it shows is that you care enough to buy him a little space or to move some odious chore out of her path. This has special meaning when it is not expected of you and it comes as a surprise.

9. Don't Compete. Cooperate! We live in a very competitive world. Most of us have been pushed to excel individually and have received very little help in learning how to cooperate. It is difficult, therefore, to change these habits as we enter into marriage. As a result, couples often find themselves almost unknowingly competing for the affection of their children, or in social gatherings competing for the attention and affection of their friends. We know of no easy solution to this except to recognize the habit and break it.

10. Unacceptable Feelings. For many people, certainly us, marriage has fostered and uncovered strong feelings and

emotional states that we have found both surprising and disturbing. We find ourselves repelled by an individual, possibly an in-law, we should love. We realize that one of our children has been getting on our nerves lately. We find ourselves becoming resentful to our mate. Often, the feelings are followed by guilt and depression. If our mate can't come to us with those feelings and be accepted, we have failed him and complicated the problem. If we do accept those "unacceptables," we strengthen trust and provide a means for the feelings to work themselves out.

These, then, are a few of the skills of affirming that we have admired in our friends and have borrowed from them. To some few, these come naturally. Most of us have to learn them. We have to make them part of our daily interaction one with the other. Behind a very common marital complaint of being "taken for granted" are the habits counter to these affirming strategies that we have suggested. Part of becoming accustomed to people is a slight numbing to their good and bad qualities. We get accustomed to their dazzling smile or their generosity. Or we think because they have some imperfection or annoying habit that they are incapable of changing. These skills help us break through.

Contrary to what we have been saying, we don't see marriage as primarily therapy. In our view, it would be a mistake to get married in order to make oneself better or to polish up a diamond in the rough. Still, though, all of us need help to grow in marriage and to grow as people. None of us is a finished product as an individual. None of the marriages we know is perfect. Certainly, not ours. Our marriage, like our self-concepts, is continually in the process of becoming. We can't rest. We can't stand still. We are like the existentialist philosopher Sören Kierkegaard, who claimed, "I am not a Christian. I am a person struggling to be a Christian." So with us. We are two people struggling to make a marriage.

Nice People Fight . . .
and Talk

❧ Katharine Hepburn recently observed, "Sometimes I wonder if men and women really suit each other. Perhaps they should live next door and just visit now and then." Behind this light comment is the sobering truth that melding two lives together can be tough work. It is often a jarring surprise to newly married couples who are very much in love to discover their differences and disharmonies. It shouldn't be, though. Taking two individuals with different histories, and with different sets of needs and desires, and transforming them into a complementary and smooth-functioning unit in which both individuals are happy and fulfilled is no minor accomplishment. The word "challenging" is overworked in human affairs, but to say that making a good marriage is a truly challenging task is to understate.

Human beings are goal seekers. We are driven by this need and that dream. If we are blocked from achieving it, we quickly become frustrated. Each of us comes to marriage with our stated or unstated needs and dreams. If the spouse turns out to be standing in the path of our goal, we experience frustration first and then anger. People respond to being blocked in two ways: confronting and avoiding. Both are manifestations of anger. Since two people trying to work out their daily lives together are bound to stand in one another's way, each develops a pattern of dealing with being blocked. Some develop a pattern of becoming angry and confronting. Others back away form the mate and solve their problems by avoiding him and going around her. Confront or avoid. Open anger or silent anger. The two of us have done some of each, but on the whole, we are confronters.

KEVIN:

Eight years into our marriage, Marilyn and I became scared. In retrospect it seems that all the time we were together was devoted to building up to a fight, fighting, or getting over a fight. We were scared because our fights were becoming more frequent and more painful. Weekend after weekend would disappear in a puff of verbal smoke and the chill that followed. We were also sobered by the experiences of a number of close friends and professional acquaintances who were calling it quits and getting divorces. Both our fights and the marriages around us led us to the same question. Would this happen to us, too? Would we make it? The questions were not only unsettling to us, but shocking. We were not the "divorce type," and besides, we were, after all, Catholics!

Marilyn was raised on a farm amid a bucolic world that would make the setting of "The Waltons" seem fast and slightly depraved. Although one set of Marilyn's grandparents had been Catholic and there were churchgoers sprinkled around her family, her parents were not religious. Nevertheless, they could out-Christian any of the anointed I had known. They were understanding and supportive when she called them long distance and told them that she was preparing to marry a New York Catholic and to take up his religion. So family solidarity and a shared faith had supported this then eight-year-old, two-childed marriage. I couldn't find the cause there.

For me, marriage was like birth or death. I got only one. Indeed, so impressed was I by the permanence of marriage that I dared not take the step off the matrimonial ledge until I was past the threshold of the thirties. Not only did it have to be something special, but it had to last.

For the first twenty-one years of my life, or until I went into military service, I was warm in the bosom of the church. The suburb of New York City where I grew up was so Catholic that I thought there was something wrong with our family since we had only four children. My education from first grade through college had been in Catholic schools. In general, my childhood was quite serene, with generous helpings of love and support from my parents.

With varying degrees of intensity, I looked for ten years for "the right mate." I was at the brink of career bachelorhood and despaired of ever finding the "right girl," when I met Marilyn. Looking back on it, we had so much to talk about that we had to get married. Marriage was the best way I could think of to keep the conversation going. Besides, I couldn't keep my hands off the girl.

We married when I was at the beginning of my doctoral program. Marilyn worked first for a publishing company, and then again as a high school English teacher. With my studies and her work, we had a great deal of time pressure and little time to talk. Still, we had a rich social life, characterized by wine parties and endless academic arguments with our circle of graduate students and fellow newlyweds.

Once out of graduate school and as a young professor in a research-oriented university, there was a little more time, but there was more pressure. The pressure was first to publish, then to get promoted, and then to get to the top of some imaginary judge's imaginary list of "tops in the field." In this particular university, such neurotic motivation is the very octane that keeps the engine chugging along.

Marilyn, too, had her pressures. One was the loneliness of coming to a strange city. Another was the birth of our first child, a birth that she underwent without family or friends. Then, discovering that the life of an academic wife was only a little like that of Mrs. Chips and a lot like that of Mrs. Bush.

Somewhere in those early years, a sourness crept in. We still had much to talk about, but we also had a good deal more daily business to transact, business about the carburetor and the carpenter, and lists of names for the cocktail party and of items for the tax man, and her suggestions on the draft of a paper I was writing. Every night before the intimacies, there was a pile of messages to exchange and pieces of paper to get out of the way. In retrospect, it seems that we got to the intimacies with decreasing frequency.

We had from the beginning argued and occasionally fought. What was new was a lingering sense of discontent that could build to a fight quite rapidly. At the same time, we were conscious of the fact that we really had nothing to fight about. Both of us had gone—and were going—farther than we had ever planned or dreamed of. Although there was much that we didn't have, we lived modestly and had no crying—or even whimpering—material needs. And clearly we were in love with one another. That is, when we weren't arguing or sulking.

Even though we didn't seem to have anything to fight about, still, we were inventing. We had cutting fights that slashed at the other for this selfish motive and that self-serving performance. We had brittle little exchanges where the thrusts were at the psychic jugular. Then these exchanges were followed by the S & S, the sulks and silences. These could go on for hours, consuming entire weekends, and, even after makeups, would leave a residue of ill feeling. While Marilyn was quicker with the tongue, I was quicker with the sulk. Her rapid recovery from what I saw as a devastating blowup only confirmed to me (in the pit of my self-pity) that I had married a woman who lacked real "depth of feeling" or some such rot. My haughty silences convinced her that I had not made a proper transition from adolescence.

What was most upsetting to us about our fights—even

more than all time they took—was that these fights violated our expectations of a good marriage. Clearly we were failing. We hadn't known people who fought. We were convinced that nice people didn't fight. For instance, neither one of us had ever seen our parents quarrel. We saw our fighting as a clear and definite sign of failure. And we felt as if we were being sucked into a vortex, and there didn't seem to be much help. There was help out there, but we couldn't quite connect with it.

All this time we were still in the church. At first we went regularly to a large urban parish on the edge of the University of Chicago. During this period, seven or eight years into our marriage, we were both moving rather fast. Beside the fact that the late sixties and early seventies were times of intellectual ferment and changing attitudes, my career was in high gear and we here having a second child.

We, like others, were undergoing personal revolutions of rising expectations. Marilyn wanted to be a wife and mother, graduate student in political science, gourmet cook, contributing member of a women's group, active in civic affairs, and a good tennis player. I needed to spend much time and energy as a teacher and researcher. But I also wanted to be at the top of the university's squash ladder (even though my nearly forty-year-old legs only snickered at such a goal), involved in political campaigns, a writer of children's stories, and the jack-of-all-repairman our large and aged home demanded. Many of these personal desires kept us from the close relationship Marilyn and I needed and thought we would have.

The role of the church in our attempt to break this pattern of angry fights and to establish some personal intimacy is difficult to ascertain. On the one hand, teachings of the church, as I understood them, were an intellectual block toward acknowledging and solving our problem. On the other hand, our membership in the church provided us with some sense of stability. First, the church gave me a very one-dimensional and somewhat crippling view of the anger I was feeling. The church, or what one novelist recently called "the nun in my ear," taught me that anger is a deadly sin. It is a weakness and clearly a human failure. In the face of my frustration and mounting feeling of anger, I was to be humble and long-suffering. The only anger that I was allowed was that confusing anger of Christ's when he cleansed the temple: righteous anger. I could show anger to the fat cats (rather than the little people) if they were perpetrating some abomination that didn't touch me immediately. I could be angry at the poor education provided on the South Side of Chicago, but I could not be angry that a colleague had slandered me or saw to it that I did not receive a research grant. I found this confusing, not only because it brushed aside the psychological reality of anger, but also because the lesson about righteous anger was not quite clear. Both Christ and Moses exercised some righteous anger. Christ flipped over the money tables in anger, and Moses smashed the tablets. Unfortunately, though, Moses was punished for his deed by never being allowed to see the Promised Land. What all of this boiled down to was that my very real feelings of anger just added to my sense of failure. Said another way, the church gave me a set of ideals, but not a sense of psychological reality. Good husbands, like good people, do not get angry. A husband or wife does not feel used or threatened or thwarted by the other. They engage in rational discourse. They do not fight. To be angry was to be a sinner. Or at least that was the way I had put things together.

On the other hand, the church was clearly a positive and stabilizing force. I had learned much from a Catholic home about the rules of fairness and reasoned behavior, and the rules applied to marriage just as much as to other areas of life. I had learned to be cared for and, I believe, to care for in return. But more immediately, Marilyn and I could never go to church angry, as we did often, and stay angry. There was something in the gospel admonition to forgive your brother before worship that always brought us back to our emotional equilibrium. We found that it was impossible to give one another the kiss of peace with rage in our hearts. And so, somehow, every Sunday before communion we surrendered to one another, or at least called a loving truce.

There was another avenue of help that was in effect cut off from us. That was psychotherapy or psychological counseling. It's not that it was forbidden, but in the Catholic culture in which I grew up, it just "wasn't done." Psychoanalysis and psychotherapy and other related arts were looked upon with deep suspicion. They were seen as the sort of processes that eliminated personal guilt and urged self-indulgence. While both of us knew many people we liked and admired who were undergoing some form of counseling, we both gave it a wide berth. Our attitude was reinforced by the fact that during this same 1971–1973 period, three of our psychologist neighbors (and one a close friend) split from their wives. The physicians didn't heal themselves or theirs very well that season.

As we experienced it, then, the church was not helping our imaginations to find new depth in one another, to learn how to work together, to develop individually in ways that did not threaten or freeze out the other.

So what all of this meant for us was that the church, which we did not need to fall in love, was not helping us as we struggled to stay in love. But that, after all, may be asking too much from a church.

Then there was the family. We have both heard statements about the tremendous pressures being put on the nuclear family, and undoubtedly we had wagged our heads in agreement. We hadn't, however, understood the concrete manifestations of that abstraction in our lives. We were living in Chicago, eight hundred miles from our nearest relatives. We were raising our two children without the presence and advice of their grandparents, without the support and social-ization of uncles and aunts. Establishing a sense of family in our children involved constant reference to faraway people. It was as if we were involving them in a myth, the faraway family myth. Since few of our neighbors had views similar to ours, the total burden of supporting and disciplining our children fell to us. Our young children in no way belonged to our urban neighbors.

Marriage as an Act of the Imagination

During this distressful period we had a night out with a couple, the Arthur Manns, who were ten or so years older than we and for whom we had a great deal of respect and affection. The talk turned at one point in the evening to the number of our mutual friends that were splitting up. In words I shall never forget, Arthur said rather casually, "A good marriage is the ultimate act of the imagination." That remark lingered with us. It suggested that good relationships were no accident and helped us realize that good marriages just didn't happen. Marriage is not simply the luck of the draw, or something that we get involved in which just unfolds before us like a long movie. Good marriages, like good individual lives or good art, are conscious creations. They are made. But while this idea was helpful and reassuring, we did not seem to know how to start or exactly what to do—particularly about our fighting.

KEVIN:

And then, almost by accident, a solution came. While browsing in a bookstore, I came across the title, *How to Fight Fair in Love and Marriage,* by an author I had never heard of and whose name I have forgotten. As far as I was concerned, it was a silly "how-to" book. However, I was intrigued by what I thought to be the conflict in the title. Why would anyone tell someone else how to fight in marriage? I thought the only message to give was "Don't!" or perhaps, how to stop fighting. So I bought the book, took it home, and read about four or five pages. That was enough. The message was clear and simple. Just about everybody fights in marriage. It doesn't mean one's marriage is a failure. It doesn't mean we will never feel love for each other again. There are reasons for the anger that leads to fights. There are ways of dealing with it quickly and efficiently. There are rules to follow that will keep the fighting within bounds and that will aid in making something constructive out of it. Learning that simple message was a tremendous relief for both of us. We began to talk about our anger, but more importantly, we were able to head things off before they became severe. We were able to get through fights quickly. We were able to make up quickly. We were able to move from anger to humor or sex in a matter of minutes.

We relaxed about "our problem" more. Although we still fought, we fought with more purpose and more economy of emotion. We had begun learning the art of controlled conflict.

Quarreling

The first quarrel between lovers ends in grateful, even tearful, reconciliation. Then, later, the prickly sense of being unjustly wronged begins to be felt. "How could she treat me this way?" Or, "He is turning out like his father, after all!" Still later and with growing concern, "Why did I get myself into this situation? Maybe marriage just isn't for me. Maybe I'm not the marrying kind!"

Few young married people anticipate quarreling with the someone we love. We are twice hurt by fighting: once to have quarreled at all, and twice to have estranged ourselves from the one we care about most. He has the power to hurt us like no other. She was once a stranger in a crowd, and we have empowered this person both to please us and hurt us like none other. In the beginning he pleases and reassures us. Later the question arises, "Was our love an illusion? Does this friction of living together reduce this great romance to the business of everyday survival?"

Anger and fear, which go hand in hand in marriage, often arise from a fear of needing someone so much. Anger comes from our disillusionment that the great dream of the perfect partnership has gone awry. "Not only was I sure that I would be a different person with this great love, but he, too, would be different. For a time we were more generous with one another and stronger in our selflessness. We were willing to sacrifice some of our individual desires for the beloved. Then the old selves began to reemerge—mine, which is familiar, and his, of which I had only hints." When one or the other demands too much or shows too little concern, the bubble is pierced and we are deflated and hurt. Frequently, the disillusionment is with ourselves. We see our own inadequacies, and we need the reassurance that this person has given us. "She sees in me my potential. . .or at least she saw it once." "He also points out my inadequacies—and sometimes in rapier fashion."

Our rage, then, comes from multiple emotions: disappointment, disillusionment, depression. We know in our heads how it should be, but our fantasy never matches reality. Then suddenly this blind rage fills us up, and we aren't sure where it came from. Some little incident occurs, and something inside breaks. Words leap from our mouths that we hardly recognize. Accusations and suspicions that we were barely conscious of tumble out. Words spoken in strange and harsh tones cascade over us. How could that simple incident cause this emotion from someone pledged to love us? In turn we shock ourselves with the words we say. We want to reach out and stuff them back in our mouths. But it is too late. They have hit the mark, only to provoke a stronger response. And the anger gains strength and rolls on. Before being married, we never experienced anger like this. Why can this person I am supposed to love move me to such a precipice? We are baffled. We do not understand our anger. We have provoked it in our partner, too. If we aren't feeling the same anger, we are the object of it.

So great is our fear of high levels of emotion that we

wonder: Is there an irreparable rip in the marriage? Can we ever find calmer waters? What damage will there be after the storm? Can we patch up the sails and move forward again?

Women are harder to please in marriage. They express greater dissatisfaction than men do. One explanation is that women expect more from the marriage. In a sense, they have been preparing for marriage all their lives. From the time they played with dolls, helped mother fold the laundry, and helped take care of the new baby of the house, they have been practicing their adult role. For some, this is the only role for which they are prepared. Job is not so often "career" for women, and they tend to find less ego satisfaction outside their homes. Women expect more from the marriage partnership and are sensitive to the limits they encounter. They are socialized to be aware of human interactions. As girls, they worried more about being popular and "getting along with the group." Girls are taught to be good and nice and thoughtful to others. They are typically more sheltered, and their period of dependency insulates them from real hostility.

Many women never experience deep personal anger until they are married. Their education and their jobs in the past were less competitive. As a consequence, when they quarrel with their fiancés and husbands, they feel threatened. More than one newly married woman has said, "When Joe and I had our first fight, I thought that was it, that we would be getting a divorce!" Women's concepts of love and anger are often cloudy. They think of those emotions as two poles. The opposite of love is hate, of passion is frigidity. Much of their personal distress comes from being so new to anger.

Men, on the other hand, have more experience with hostility. The upbringing and general socialization of boys brings them into closer proximity to anger. It comes in school yard scuffles, in sports, and in the general expectation that boys must be ready to become warriors and defend the country. The man works more often in competitive environments where tempers may be close to the surface—controlled, but close to the surface. As a result, the man may come home from work having held his tongue and temper all day. He is like a tightly wound alarm clock, waiting for the signal to go off. Without even knowing it, the new housewife gives the signal—a mild request that he balance the checkbook or take out the garbage. The signal, of course, is not about the checkbook or the garbage. What the husband has heard is that someone else is trying to get him to do something, someone else is criticizing him. He is not free from it even in his home. And anger erupts. Soon anger follows anger, and they are teaching one another.

Seven Flash Points

A delicate balance exists in any marriage arrangement. Avenues for anger are under construction all the time. At times it seems that crews of people work at opening up the lines for a blowup. Flash points is a military term meaning danger zones, areas for potential conflict—like the Middle East, a perennial flash point. It's more than likely that each couple encounters its own original version of flash points, its own Middle East, but here are some general, even typical, minefields that arise in even the most civilized marriages.

1. Choice of Friends. Choosing friends is a private bestowing of affection. The bonds may be old ones, from a former neighborhood or grammar school. The bonds may be ones from memory, attachments unclear to a wife or husband. Old friends are a great comfort, and we hope to keep them after we are married. But our friends aren't our spouses'. When two friends from work, one who has married a steel worker and the other a stockbroker, get together, they should not expect their husbands to be friends. They have no history to share and probably little in common. Nights together are awkward and boring for the husbands. Or she is home, visiting her parents, and wants to spend several nights out having dinner with her high school best friends. They read over

their yearbooks and laugh over their crushes and senior proms. He doesn't know the girls, and he has no history of their years together.

2. Working Spouses. Avenues for anger occur because working people, especially with children, have problems establishing a fair balance of work in and around the house. In reality there are two people and three careers. Both have work pressures, demands on their energy and time, which take them away from time spent running the home life. Their roles multiply, and they have trouble coping. Easy anger erupts. The shirts aren't back from the laundry. Dinner is a drag and there is nothing for dessert.

3. Parents/In-Laws. Problems and disagreements occur around parents and in-laws, particularly if there is a disparity of affection on one side. Parents may place pressures on a daughter to be with them for family dinners on Sunday or to take a vacation in Mexico with them. Unbalance occurs when one spouse is expected to come round and repair the leaky faucets for his mother, or her family wants the baptism done the way their family has always done them. Parents sometimes take one side in the marriage. They are protective of their daughter, especially if they think she has married someone who can't provide for her material needs the way they did, or he is away on business too often to suit them.

4. Decision Making. One is the Take-Charge Type. He makes all the decisions, from where the honeymoon will take place to what car and furniture to buy. His work dictates much of the style and standard of living, but he makes all the decisions about the household as well. Or she runs a tight ship, takes the housekeeping on as a career. She commands the schedule, runs the children, the garden, the social life. He comes home and feels like something between an administrative assistant and a flunky.

5. Inside/Outside Time. Some people see themselves as community organizers. They need to be active in Little League, soccer team, business clubs, PTA, churchmen's groups. All the time devoted to outside organizations is time away from the family. If the wife gives her time and energies to the clubs, then he is forced to cover the domestic scene. The one left behind may also feel the mate is trying to be away from home. Quarreling begins over "you don't have time for me." Or, "he needs stimulation away from us."

Expectations for the amount of time spent together cause adjustment problems. Unconsciously, the patterns of our parents' interactions play themselves out in our lives.

MARILYN:

Kevin and I come from different family backgrounds, on separate oceans. Any couple mixes two diverse cultures when they marry. They, like us, bring expectations from the world of male and female and roles from their family of origin. How our parents worked out their togetherness greatly affects our expectations. Some families spend a great deal of time with each other; others spend little time in shared tasks and hobbies. In some families, togetherness is the only way to go. In others, privacy is granted in large doses.

My parents own a farm. They have worked together for forty-four years. When my mother wants something built or repaired, my father does the job, often with her help. In my youth there was a good deal of sitting around the kitchen with a glass of milk and a sticky bun and talking things out. There was also high demand that everybody in sight should pitch in and help move the irrigation pipes, pick strawberries, or dry dishes. There were few "male" or "female" tasks. I came to marriage with the attitude that two people did most things together. (Our personal research indicates that the ultimate test of whether two people will stay together is wallpapering a bathroom—particularly on a stifling July night in Chicago. Folk wisdom has it that if two people can finish, they can weather any crisis in their marriage.)

Kevin's father commuted two hours in and out of New York City every day for fifty-five years. His mother disciplined the children, made sure that his dad's shirts were ironed for business, packed the school lunches for twenty-eight years, and saw to other family needs. His father never so much as changed a light bulb and was a stranger to the lawn mower. He never knew the inside of a diaper. Men didn't change diapers, nor did they clear the table. Men made the drinks. Kevin's parents' most visible time together was over the evening cocktail. That finished, they went back to their individual roles.

6. Free Time and Extra Money. If one of the partners spends all the discretionary money on his hobbies—the gambling casino, sports cars, the local watering hole, antique weapons—or she lunches brown-bag style with the staff, buys shoes and handbags only on sale, and spends free time with a book from the public library, then this imbalance can easily become a source of friction.

7. Alienation of Affections. (Otherwise known as temptations of the flesh, lust in the mind, the wandering eye—or additional parts of the anatomy—and the biological itch.) The flash point ranges from flirtatious husbands to ones who are sleeping with someone or several at once. The French have their own solution—the man keeps a woman and a wife, separately. One has a temporary lover and a permanent mother-manager. Since the French solution isn't particularly fair or realistic in our culture, we just have to find another solution. Temptations of sex with new partners exist for both husband and wife. The issue of extramarital sex is present in many marriages. Deep anger results from sexual affairs. The question is

how to handle sexual attraction to someone new. When temptation is high, the best solution may be to try new positions, rather than new partners.

While many marriages thrive and seem most healthy when they are in balance on most issues, there is a quality of accommodation that goes a long way. If one person spends most of the money and the other doesn't much care about using discretionary money, then in the desire to please each other, a trade-off is made. In lieu of spending the money, the mate is relieved of balancing the checkbook or calculating the income taxes. Maybe he isn't the most tidy person to live with, but he offers quality time with the children or helps with the meals. However, marriage isn't a balancing act and doesn't operate on a trade-off mentality. Rather, it thrives on the spirit of trying to please each other, to make the other happy. But our anger—given and received—takes its toll on this good impulse and many of the other joys of married life.

Avoiding Anger

The confrontation of anger is the first way we respond to being frustrated and blocked. The second way is more subtle and more hidden. We avoid confronting. We retreat and find a way around the spouse. We do not deal openly with the reality we are experiencing. We submerge the anger of disappointment we have been feeling. Some learn "to handle" their mates. "When she starts sending negative messages about my bowling nights out, I change the subject and then ask why we always have Sunday dinner with her folks. That shuts her up." Whenever he starts in about how expensive the Hawaiian vacation I want is going to be, I begin mentioning how tired I'm getting of my job. A little threat to the second income that is supporting so many of his precious hobbies and toys, and he clams right up about my Hawaii." "When she starts withholding sex from me or giving me too much of that 'I'm too tired' routine, I just start talking about how sexy her girl friend Gladys is, or about how fun-loving the girls at work are, and she lays right down." This manipulating may get results for a time, but it sows the seeds of resentment. The one manipulated knows that she is being treated unfairly. She knows, certainly after a while, that her desires are not being dealt with directly. The manipulated know that a game is being played and that they are the losers. The balance in the relationship is perceived to be gone. The mutual goodwill that is the foundation of their marriage is being washed away. It also sets a pattern for the one who has been manipulated to follow.

Another avoidance response is to simply and quietly go your own way. "Ask her? Why hit her head-on and be guaranteed another fight? The hell with her. I'll just do it anyway." "I want children now and he doesn't. Well, I will just start forgetting the pill or what time of the month it is." Or, "I don't want kids now and he does. He doesn't have to know that I'm taking the pill." "She is always taking up my free time and never leaving me any time to read by myself. Well, I'll just hide for an hour or so a day." "He knows I don't want to have sex all the time. I'll turn him off by letting myself go and making myself unattractive." Besides all the ugly consequences that can follow from the spouse discovering how he or she is being thwarted, there are personal consequences. A meanness sets in. "Why must I resort to indirection, to deception? Why is this person making me be dishonest? My wishes are legitimate, so why this! If I were really loved and respected, I wouldn't have to act this way."

These patterns of handling, skirting, and avoiding bring on disappointment, and silent anger builds. They eat away at respect and the desire to be with the other. We almost unknowingly begin to disengage contact from the other. "Why ask for trouble? Why the hassle? Better I go out with the guys more or become a serious student of the National Football League . . . and every other sports event on the tube." "Maybe it would be better if I just faced facts and took sex whenever and wherever I can get it." "Why try to get blood from a stone?" "He is not the man I thought I was marrying. Better I throw myself into my family." "He's a good provider, but just not a true companion. I'll settle for this 'limited partnership' and get my romance from soap operas . . . and maybe sometime someone will come along. . . ."

Besides the silent anger, then, what avoidance often leads to is marital boredom. The frisky, energetic kitten of courtship turns into the dull, lazy house cat of married life. The avoidance of the other and the real issues robs the relationship of emotional authenticity. Even the searing jolt of rage is better than this boredom. Boredom is dangerous on many counts, not the least of which is that it leads to "maybe sometime someone will come along." Behind much sexual infidelity is not the spilling over of a deeply passionate nature or unquenchable sexual appetite, but boredom. Simple garden-variety boredom. We are bored with the mate and with being boring to the mate. Something in us is wounded at being taken for granted, at being upstaged and continually put off in favor of the children, at being found less attractive or less interesting than Howard Cosell. And then amid the loneliness and the unspoken insult of being judged no longer interesting comes a stranger. By word or deed, the stranger tells us we are still attractive, we are still loveable. "She is no Loni Anderson, but she has picked me out of the crowd. She finds me desirable. She listens to me. She laughs at my jokes. I don't care if it is wrong. It feels right to me. I was drowning and she saved me." So long, boredom. Enter, heavy trouble.

One of the great moments in the movies occurs in the film, *Cool Hand Luke.* Paul Newman has led an unsuccessful break from a southern, backcountry work farm. The until-then gentle and ineffective warden assembles all the prisoners and has Newman, handcuffed, ankle-braceleted, and beaten, brought before him. The warden looks at Newman imploringly and says, "What we have here is a failure to communicate," and then clubs him to the ground insensible. "Failure of communication" is not insoluble, if we don't beat it to the ground. We may feel we are incapable of communicating effectively, but we can improve, we can learn. Few people enter marriage with the kind of skills needed to live in the close physical and psychological proximity demanded by the married state and to be so interdependent with another person—materially and emotionally and every other way. The strains and ruptures we have described do develop, but we are not permanently bound to this condition of victim and perpetrator. The solution is a four-letter word: talk.

Communication is currently a more popular word than talk. It is also a more inclusive word, taking in looks, gestures, and, yes, chilling silences. At its core, the word "communication" has the word "union," the coming together of minds and spirits, and the mutual understanding that arises from that activity. We prefer the word "talk," though. Couples are always communicating, but they do not always talk to one another. The aim, though, is the same: union.

When most of us marry, we are ready for several aspects of life. We are ready to work, ready to take on responsibilities, and, oh indeed, we are ready for sex. Rarely, though, are we ready to talk to another person in the ways demanded by marriage. And this silence catches us off guard since we felt we had so much to share. Conversation seemed so easy before. Or conversation didn't seem so important since we just enjoyed being with one another. We later discover how little we really know of the other. And some of us realize that there were many aspects of the mate and our relationship that we avoided. We may have been vaguely aware of them, but we skirted them. While, on initial reflection, that may seem cowardly, it is possible that if couples knew all about one another before their wedding day, marriages would drop off precipitously. T. S. Eliot once wrote, "Human nature can stand just so much reality." On the other hand, most of us are suckers for wishful thinking, particularly at mating time. We can't seem to keep the eyes open when we want this person.

But amid all these human differences and marital frustrations, there are two people who want to succeed. They have in their favor their will and their imagination, the brawn and the brains of their marriage.

Will is something more than wanting to talk. That is

important, but more important is giving—or willing—time to it. Will means setting aside a time for an undistracted, intimate talk. For one partner, will involves the discipline of shutting out the echoes of the day and listening carefully to the other. Or it may involve not monopolizing the conversation and encouraging the other to express his views. Or will may involve forcing oneself to risk and share inner thoughts and feelings. And, too, to learn to replace conversations that evolve into fighting or avoiding takes persistence and readiness to try again, even after failures.

Imagination comes into play in numerous ways, initially in finding topics to talk about—topics that transcend the shopping list, topics that will be of interest to the other, topics that will not deteriorate into hurt feelings and anger. "What was your childhood like?" "Did you always believe you would marry?" "What kind of relationship did your parents have? Was it always that way?" "If you hadn't become a businessman, what do you think you would have become?" "How would you like our life to be in ten years?" "What is some secret ambition you have never told me about?" "What worries you most?" "What is something about you that you are sure I don't know?"

Appreciating Each Other

Some communication manuals and marriage-preparation checklists suggest that we explore questions such as, "What are three things about me that most disappoint you?" "If you had it to do all over again, would you still marry me? If not, why not?" This is sheer madness, bound to drive a couple into dark, narrow alleys of hostility. Just the opposite tack should be taken, avoiding topics that are unnecessarily provocative and doing everything possible to make the experience satisfying and positive. We have heard of a couple who set out to learn to talk with one another, and, not surprisingly, they found that their early efforts were not particularly successful and personally were not much fun. Still, though, they

believed it was important, so they decided to reward themselves for their efforts. Since they both loved dining out, they
seized on a plan to reward themselves with a romantic dinner
out every time they completed six days in a row of half-hour
talks. With that encouragement, they kept at it and developed
the skill of talking with each other.

But we need the imagination to find the words, the
subjects, and the styles of exchange which will give the
marriage this saving tool: the ability to open oneself up to the
other, to share all—success and failure, secret pride and secret
shame—the capacity in times of hardship and difficult choice
to be honest without wounding and to make decisions without
suspicion of self-interest.

We need imagination to look at our mates and see into
their lives—to look into their eyes and at the set of their
mouths. We need imagination to read the statement about
themselves they are making with their clothes and their hair.
We need imagination to order the many moments of contact
and to see the new patterns as they are emerging. We need it
to guide us with love and sensitivity into the lives of our
spouse.

The key, then, to getting past the angers and frustrations
and disappointments is to learn to talk and then to stay at it.
We know of no two people who habitually converse who have
split up. On the other hand, the best marriages we know are
those in which the two talk regularly and intimately.

Whether we choose confronting or avoiding probably
depends on our past history and the skills we have developed
in childhood to deal with frustration. In effect, we are doing
what comes naturally to us at this point in our lives. We do
not think through the issues and decide on one pattern or
another. We just do it. It does not have to be that way,
though. We do not have to be victims of doing what comes
naturally. As will be seen throughout this book, we believe
that there are things we can do to counteract nature or
whatever it is that leads us into marital troubles. There are
skills we can learn to replace the negative skills that eat away

at our marriages, such as angrily confronting or avoiding. We do not have to be passive victims of some marriage-crushing force. We can take control of the direction of our marriage. We can stop fighting—at least in a destructive way—and we can learn to talk together.

Nine Strategies for Dealing with Anger

Most of the skills and strategies that follow have come to us from our friends. We offer them not as *the* list of skills, but as a list, expecting and hoping the reader will go beyond what is here. Also, it is important to realize that old skills and patterns were not learned overnight. It is difficult to repress old response patterns and substitute new ones. There will be failures and false starts. But if you have ever learned to ride a bicycle, you know that.

1. Have Some Fighting Rules. Most married people fight. It can be healthy. It may indeed be inevitable. Nevertheless, it is important to fight by some set of rules. Do not live with the possibility of unlimited warfare every time you cross one another. Each couple should make their own rules, of course. These are offered by way of example only:

   Don't get physical. Besides being a deep affront to the other, "the laying on of hands" has an escalatory quality. The finger jabbing leads to the push, which leads to the shove, which leads to the slap, which leads to the punch in the stomach, which leads to the whack in the mouth, which leads to the knee in the groin (which does indeed slow things down considerably), which leads to armed combat; sticks and stones, which we all learned years ago, will break your bones, while words will hurt only the psyche.

   Don't leave the house. Running home to mother is for kids. Running to the bar is escapism. Even though you are mad, stay in proximate contact.

Always sleep in the same room. No sleeping on the couch. Isolation feeds isolation. And being near the scene of your sexual intimacies and pleasures drains anger and seems to heal.

No sandbagging. Stay on the topic of the fight. Don't use a fight about who is spending the most money as a time to remind your husband that his mother hasn't paid back the two hundred dollars she borrowed. Sandbagging with your favorite topic will just lead to your mate sandbagging his favorite topic.

These, then, are just some possible rules for your consideration. The important idea is to have *some* rules and to stick with them.

2. Get Help. Quite often couples get themselves into the kind of trouble that no amount of their own talking seems to solve. Every time they calmly and rationally set out to talk about their problem, things fall apart. They need an outside set of eyes and ears. They need the objectivity of someone who has no history with them and is not involved in their lives the way a friend or relative is. Fortunately, today there are a large number of trained counselors around. Many people connected with churches have been trained as marriage counselors. It is important, though, to find someone in whom both have confidence. So do not try one person, become dissatisfied, and then give up on counseling. Try until you find who and what you both need.

3. Care-fronting. This is a technique for avoiding serious fights and breakdowns by confronting issues at an early stage in a caring manner. We credit Father Tom Ryan, a Paulist priest living in Montreal, with this technique. Instead of allowing one's annoyance with the other to go unchecked until he is mad at the other, the technique of "care-fronting" deals with the issue directly. First, the complainant, in as calm a manner as he is able to muster, identifies the behavior that is bothering him and

states what he would like done about it. For example, instead of letting the spouse's habit of leaving socks and underwear on the bedroom floor go unchecked until frustrated rage takes over and then letting the spouse know that you think he's a roaring slob, care-fronting advocates a different approach. First, one identifies the offending behavior; second, states how it makes him feel; and third, suggests what he would like done about it. "When I find your dirty underwear and socks on the floor, I feel as if you have no concern or respect for me. I would really appreciate it if you would put your dirty clothes in the laundry basket. I know it's a little thing, but I'd feel much better." The technique is very simple, but it's part of a larger stategy for couples (and others) to not let little things escalate into big, overpowering, choking issues. In other words, keep the small things small.

4. Nonavoidance. Care-fronting may cover many of the feelings and frustrations experienced by couples. However, some issues, such as your feeling you are being continually manipulated, may not fit easily into that format. A low-key but direct approach is recommended here. First, realize that the other may not have been fully conscious that he was manipulating you, that she has been getting her way by subtly maneuvering you this way and that. Give the other the benefit of the doubt. Second, in the least hostile words and manner possible, explain how you interpret events and how you feel about them. Third, give the other an opportunity to state his side of it, to give her interpretation. Fourth, decide together what you will do if you feel you are being manipulated.

5. Talking Together. Andrew Greeley's recent research on marital happiness suggests that there are five key predictors: one, the ability to talk to one another; two, emotional satisfaction; three, sexual fulfillment; four, the

ability to communicate love and affection; and five, the ability to express disagreement without threatening the relationship. Three out of five of these characteristics of marital happiness directly depend on a couple's ability to maintain an open and honest dialogue. For many, though, this level of communication is a totally new experience. For one thing, time must be given to it Second, if fighting has been a problem, initially stay away from the topics that inflame. Third, make sure there is dialogue, not monologue. Fourth, talk about yourselves—your childhood and adolescence, your reactions to events, your hopes for the future, your private fears and worries. It may be difficult at first, but even the awkwardness may be fruitful grist for the conversational mill. Fifth, find ways to make sure that talking has positive consequences, that it is a rewarding experience.

6. Empathetic Listening. We've learned the value of empathetic listening to help one another and establish a more intimate relationship. This approach is based on therapeutic-counseling principles developed by the counseling psychologist, Carl Rogers. It comes into play when one partner is troubled or angered by something. The other takes his mate on, not in a sympathetic conversation or a back-and-forth, first-listen-then-give-my-advice manner. Rather, one tries to give his total attention to the other individual and establish what Rogers calls an environment of unconditional love. In such a condition, one does not judge or give advice or interrupt. Rather, one tries to listen empathetically, to experience the problem of the issue the way the other is experiencing it. He limits his comments to "reflective statements," which are paraphrases of what the other is telling him. "What I hear you saying is . . ." or, "Am I hearing you correctly that . . ." What Rogers asserts, and our experience confirms, is that empathetic listening establishes a climate of human intimacy, and that in itself has a powerful healing effect.

7. Learning Together. It is a rude shock to realize that we do not have nearly as much in common as we thought when we decided to get married. Now the differences look staggering. He likes to hunt, and she likes to dance. He is mad about current events, and the only use she has for the paper is to wrap the garbage. She likes novels, and he likes television. Instead of just reading this as an indication of incompatibility, first find out if the other will teach you what he knows, and you him. Chances are, though, the reason he never learned to dance is that it didn't attract him, and trying to teach him may not change his mind. Second, pick out something you both want to learn about or be able to do, and set out learning it together. Gardening, skiing, a book club are all possibilities. Another aspect of learning together is consciously setting out to share things sure to be of interest, such as cutting out articles from the newspaper she might have missed, or going to a good movie together. The point is to build common ground on which you can both stand.

8. Systematic Enrichment. Many couples have discovered that planned weekend retreats or regular meetings with other couples help them get their hostilities out in the open and address them in a constructive way. These special comings together also help the couples break through the summer-reruns quality of their marriages and deepen their understanding of and attachment to each other. One form of couple support, sponsored by churches, is Marriage Enrichment. Couples go away for a weekend that is devoted to exploring and expanding their communication. The pair goes through a series of exercises designed to get at dimensions of communication. The follow-up research on Marriage Enrichment has been very positive.

9. Brief Vacations. Everyday life has a way of stifling intimacy. It presents a married couple with a seemingly

endless supply of routine matters to discuss or takes each in directions away from the mate. A related problem is coordinating free time. When she is free, he is in the midst of changing the oil in the car. When he is cleaned up and ready, she is in the midst of a washing cycle. Simply wanting intimacy is not enough. Of course, some intimate moments surprise us, but more often we have to create opportunities, create the conditions. We call these moments brief vacations. They are times when we consciously block out the world—telephone, television, day-to-day affairs. We get up early for a special private breakfast. We go for a late-evening walk and talk over something about which we have been waiting to get another's views. We go off for a drive with no intentions other than to reestablish contact.

Brief vacations provide avenues for new construction in the relationship. New territory is sometimes opened up, and old ground is often recovered.

Conflict and communication are bred into marriage. They exist without permission. One channels the other. Areas of accord and conflict are unearthed when we communicate. Expressing our delight and sorrow, anguish and embarrassment, are ways we share ourselves with our spouse. Most of us have to learn how to handle these expressions of feelings as we learn each other's sensitivities. When we unveil our private selves, we allow anger to come forth, and we need to learn how to manage strong emotion. We try to share depth of feeling in artful ways.

4 🌿

Semiprivate: Sex

🌿 People talk about this era as one of sexual liberation. We are surrounded by sexual information, sexual stimulation, and sexual opportunities. While this may be true, it is also an era of sexual misinformation, confusion, and intimidation. We were both raised at a time of sexual silence and now live amid a sexual cacophony. While we wouldn't trade today for yesterday, the noise for the silence, easing back on the volume control and getting rid of the distortions would help.

We are not sex specialists or scholars. We are experts only on our own sex lives. The rest is from reading and a little bedroom hearsay. We have talked to one another a good deal these last few years about our sex lives and our attitudes toward and perception of what is going on in this corner of our marriage. Before beginning this chapter, we attempted to nail down our views on sex and marriage. While we were satisfied that we had clarified what we believe, we wondered whether our ideas and reactions were simply the reflection of our lives and, therefore, not generalizable past our own skins. So we decided to test our views. We asked for help from six couples; some we knew well and others we barely knew. Two couples have been married longer than we have; the others a shorter time than we. All were middle-class types like ourselves, but there was a good deal of variety in background and experience. We were, quite frankly, fascinated by these long conversations. They were open, graphic, and humorous.

Although we learned a great deal, our overriding impression was one of similarity of attitudes and views. While we all had our own personal experiences, and clear differences in sexual intensity and appetite were evident, there was a surprising and—to us—reassuring congruity of views.

The Experience of Sex

Having sex with someone is a semiprivate act. It begins with an invitation, often unspoken by one, and the acceptance, often tacit but clear, by the other. It is semiprivate in that the pleasure of sex is one's own, but the quality of the pleasure depends on what the other does. In sex, one is both a giver and a receiver of pleasure. One part of the mind is absorbed with savoring the sensation and anticipating the culminating sensation of climax. The other part of the mind is the doer of sex. This corner of the mind is concerned primarily with the stimulation it is giving to the mate. It is occupied with the intimate craft of sex. "Where is my love now, and what can I do to advance us or keep the pleasure high?" Or, "Where am I at this moment, and what do I need? Am I moving too fast toward climax? What can we do to reach that peak together?" Both minds, the receiver's and the giver's, move through the sex act speaking to self and occasionally to the sex partner. The receiver's mind briefly acknowledges the sensual delight being given by the other. The message is a spillover of joy, an announcement of high sensation, a sign of passionate appreciation. The receiver's mind may signal to the partner that he is close to climax, or that she is not ready for what he is doing. But these words and signals are few. Part of the individual concentrates on his pleasure and on what he is doing, and part of the individual is given over to his or her experience of pleasure.

Sex is often referred to as communication, and there is certainly much that goes on. But it is more like a dance in which two individuals move together in a patterned and highly interdependent way. And as they move through it, they have little to say to one another.

Sex is not only semiprivate, it is also staged, in the sense of going through successive stages. Indeed, it is like a suspenseful play that captures one's attention as the curtain goes up and moves from act to act, holding each in a pleasurable state of tension until the final scene, the resolution, the solution, the completion. Sex is staged or patterned in that a couple finds ways to enhance the enjoyment of the partner. Each has or develops needs for particular pleasures to take him or her to the next stage. For some, the patterns are rigid, with certain fondlings and touchings needed at particular times in set sequences. For others, the stages are there, but they can be reached through many different acts in different sequences.

These stages can be gone through quickly or slowly, depending on many factors. Sometimes the two just want to have the intense pleasure of climax and then get on to the next thing in their life. Or they may want to linger over it, drawing it out, slowing it down, enjoying and savoring the sensual delight of each move. Often, problems develop because the individuals have different sexual scenarios in mind. One may be planning a brief and intense encounter and then on to sleep, while the other is expecting an hour or two of sensuous reveling. One has invited the other to dance, but while he is hearing disco, she is gliding into a slow waltz.

Whether there are five stages or fifteen, we don't presume to know. We don't even know for ourselves, let alone others. And we don't want to become so self-conscious that we start counting. We know, though, that there is a stage of invitation, a point of uncertainty whether or not the journey will be taken. There are stages for various zones of the body: the mouth, the breast, genitalia. There is a stage for penetration and a stage for climax, and there is a stage of savoring afterglow when the individuals emerge from their semiprivate stage. (In case you don't recognize this one, this is where in the old movies he lights up a cigarette and they start the serious dialogue.) Each stage has its pleasures and needs.

Each stage has its possible mistakes and disappointments. To be good for the other, we know we must learn these stages, coming to know the other's in relation to our own.

Sex and Learning

While sex between consenting man and woman may be the most basic of natural acts, it does not just happen. Or at least it did not just happen to us. Sex is a learned behavior. Again, the dance may be the best analogy. Two people can stumble around the floor and call it dancing, or they can make themselves highly skilled performers.

KEVIN:

To say I grew up in a time of sexual silence is not quite true. Most of us didn't learn about procreation until the seventh or eighth grade, and then it was a matter of swapping the most outrageous half-truths and distortions. At twelve, I had a fistfight with my best friend, Peter Walsh, because he claimed my father was dirtier than his father. After all, my father had done "it" to my mother four times (once for each of the four Ryan children), and his father had only done it twice (once each for the two Walsh children). Although I fought with all I had, I couldn't get my heart into it, knowing my father was so flawed. Indeed, he had done it four times, as anyone could plainly see.

There was a lot of hushed talk about it during those early adolescent years. Most of it was the Peter Walsh variety. It wasn't until my fifteenth summer working as a stockboy in a large New York department store that I met two people who had actually done it and who talked about it (almost incessantly) from experience. One was Morris, a career stockboy of thirty-five: small, beady-eyed, sullen, and with great tufts of hair escaping from his ears. He lived for little else than his annual two-week vacation, at which time he went straight to Montreal and checked into a bordello for two weeks and lived among what he claimed were the most beautiful and free women in the entire world. When I would ask for details, his eyes would glaze and he would murmur, "Those girls will do anything. Anything! They'll do anything to you for five bucks." Very fascinating and most effective in setting my imagination aflame. But as far as guiding knowledge, I had learned only that "it" had different forms, and that five dollars traveled further and in more interesting directions than I had anticipated.

My second teacher that summer was a stockboy, too: a dark, handsome fellow of about nineteen. His name was Carlo, and he lives in my mind vividly even to this day. For Carlo had experienced every male's fantasy. At thirteen, he had been walking along the street near his home in "Philly" when two girls from a nearby private women's college drove up and offered to give him a lift. He got in, and they drove him into a suburban woods. There they seduced him. This became a weekly event for Carlo for the next three years. I gathered that life was sexually good to Carlo after that, but, we both suspected, never that good again.

Although I never learned much about the actual details of "it" from Carlo, I walked the streets of my hometown for many years eagerly awaiting a car to pull up alongside with two voluptuous college girls in it, beckoning me inside.

That summer in the stockroom made for great fantasies but little reliable data about "it." By the time I was sixteen, one was supposed to know all about "it" from, so to speak, stem to stern, and therefore no one was free to ask how one actually did it. Most of our locker room conversations consisted of swapping details we had picked up about Montreal-style "anything." Most of us went to our wedding beds knowing what "it" was and with visions of sexual sugarplums dancing in our heads, but also with profound innocence of the how and when and where of it.

If there is anything we believe about sex it is, as we said above, that sex is a learned behavior. To be good at sex, to

enjoy it fully, takes skill. Some people initially may have
talent or interest than others, but that changes. We
about our own bodies and our partners' bodies. We learn
they like and need, and what we like and need. We learn
to establish a mood, how to respond to the other, how
move in a certain way. While sex is among the most physi
of human acts, there is little doubt in our minds that the bra
is the most important sex organ of them all.

It is quite easy to understand why sex is a big problem i
many marriages. On the one hand, the popular culture (from
Reader's Digest to *Redbook*) tells us that sex is great and each
of us should be delirious with sensual pleasure. On the other,
few couples are initially very skillful at sex. Different individuals have different sexual tastes, drives, capacities, knowledge,
and skills. If two people are each having their first experience
of intercourse together, there is bound to be an awkwardness.
Often, there is disappointment with oneself and with the
partner, and an "Is that all there is?" reaction.

Sex and Self-Concept

The couples with whom we have talked confirm our own
experience: that the first sexual encounters were hardly a
roaring success. For the two of us, those beginning weeks
were a study in ineptness. However, the memory of them has
been softened over time. What was, during those first weeks, a
source of confusion, frustration, and embarrassment now
seems rather humorous. In fact, it has a positive value to us; it
is something we overcame together—like getting through an
obstacle course or sailing through a heavy storm.

It is surprising, though, that there is so little recognition
that sex is largely a matter of learning. People getting married
know that learning to cook well is a carefully developed art.
They know that to have a decent garden takes knowledge and
effort. And, perhaps, closer to sex, they know that to play
tennis or dance well together takes practice, coordinated
effort, and smooth, effective communication. But it seems

that the message that a good sex life needs learning, care, and feeding has not gotten through. The subject of sex is supercharged so that people build up expectations of almost immediate success: fireworks, rockets, the earth moves, and so on.

There is probably no better way to learn about sex than through experience. However, experience alone is no guarantee of developing a satisfactory sex life. In fact, experience has taught many people that sex is not for them. A woman whose new husband makes little effort to bring her to sexual arousal before he reaches climax will find little joy in sex and may begin to think that she has a low capacity for sex. On the other hand, the husband, seeing his wife's lack of satisfaction and ever-increasing reluctance to have sex, may blame himself, concluding that he just is not sexually attractive. Their mutual disappointment and embarrassment can easily lead to sensitivity and reluctance to talk about what has been happening to them. Sex, when it does take place, becomes a joyless ritual. Each has learned, but it is negative learning. Given the widely reported incidence of frigidity, male impotence, and so-called sexual incompatibility, we surmise there is a good deal of this type of negative learning going on in marriage. In what is becoming an increasingly sexually oriented culture, it may be too easy to reach the conclusion that *we* are the problem. Nude bodies engaging in explicit sexual acts stare out at us from the racks of drugstores and bookstores. Television parades before our eyes beautiful, sexy people. Few of us compare with them in physical attractiveness. Therefore, our private dialogue may be telling us, "It is just me. If there were more of me here (or less of me there), then I'd have more of a chance at sex."

Earlier, we wrote about self-concept and our hunger to find out over and over again, "How am I doing?" If we get positive messages back, our self-concept is strengthened. If we find out that we are not doing well, then our self-concept is weakened. Our sexual satisfaction has a strong relationship to our self-concept. Some years ago the psychologist Havelock Ellis said,

"Sexual pleasure, wisely used and not abused, may prove the stimulus and liberator of our finest and most exalted activities." Whether it is a new energy flowing from sexual pleasure that leads to the achievement or the enhanced self-concept one has knowing he or she is both a successful giver and receiver of sexual pleasures, we don't know. We believe, though, that a married person's self-concept is strongly affected by his or her sex life.

KEVIN:

My mother, closing in on eighty with a bounce in her step and a keen interest in the world, laughingly chided her children and their spouses at a family get-together recently. After a particularly explicit and frank discussion of sex, she said with an amused shake of her head, "You all sound as if your generation had invented sex!" Be that as it may, I remain convinced that sex is playing a bigger part in people's lives today. Better health and contraception, more knowledge about sexuality, fewer taboos, more assurance in planning, more leisure time, all point to the potential for more and better sex. And while this, if correct, is a real advance for people, the sexual revolution has its costs, too. Those who are not satisfied or do not satisfy are continually reminded of this condition. They get the message that many people are having a rich sex life, and they are on the sidelines. For many, then, sex is an area of failure and disappointment, and it is difficult to hide from this problem.

Gloria Steinem, the feminist writer and leader in the women's movement, has said that marriage is the last adventure open to the middle class. I very much doubt it. But adventure it is. Few of us do great things and have the thrill of fame and adulation. We live in the shadows of the great and famous. But many of us experience the high adventure of loving someone and being loved in return. The sensation of being thrilling to someone else is a peak of our lives. Someone has freely and knowingly chosen us and given us his love. Someone has been ready literally to throw her life away on me. What is more ego boosting! What is more enhancing of our self-concepts! To have another human being's heart quicken at the sound of my voice or the touch of my hand! What a satisfying sensation! The only problem is that we damned mortals cannot fly forever. We cannot maintain the peak. We "adjust." We adjust even to passionate romance. We cannot maintain the state of bliss. Even if our partner is still infatuated with us, we get used to it. Normally, though, we come down from the peak of intense romance and establish a love relationship that allows us to give a little attention to our work and those others around us. In effect, we settle into our love relationship.

Sex, though, has the almost magical quality of bringing two lovers back to the full flush of their romance. It relives or reinstates their mutual infatuation. They are again standing on the peak. That is, of course, if the sex is mutually satisfying; those who don't find it satisfying have more difficulty in recapturing and refreshing their love. For many, the flatness of their sexual lives leads downward into less frequent and less pleasurable sex. A brittleness creeps into their relationship. Silences and resentments grow. A grayness often settles in on their marriage and their lives. But as they walk around in their gray world, they have the memory tucked away in a corner of their minds of that marvelous experience of being in love. That memory may drive them to efforts to correct what is wrong. Or it may lead them away from their spouse. And as they go about their lives and mingle in the crowd, some pair of eyes may catch theirs. Someone may step out of the crowd again and let them know, "You are special. I want to be with you." And the high adventure may start again.

My mother, who has radically different views about these things than Ms. Steinem, is fond of saying that sex is the cement of a good marriage. In the last few years, I have seen the marriages of a frighteningly large number of our friends and acquaintances fall apart. From what I have been told directly or heard secondhand, the problem for many of them has been "the cement." It was never there or melted away.

Sex Cycles

Each life passage and each age has its merits. We are told as much by those who have been there ahead of us. So with sex. Each stage has its rewards. Sexual gratification is a basic biological need for both sexes in each age. There are, however, major differences between men and women and their basic sexual drives. Much has been written in the late seventies on the new woman, the sexual tigress, the predator female. Earlier, we thought sex was a stronger drive for men. Now we know that women have some later biological peaks than men. And sex is one of them.

The social pattern of marrying older men is the result of economic factors, not basic biological drives. An older man can provide economic stability in a male-dominant society. But the economics of marriage have little bearing on biological compatibility. Between the ages of eighteen and sixty, men and women move toward opposite poles of sexual drive that reach an extreme at about age forty. At eighteen, men and women are quite alike; then they move apart in every way in their twenties. In this period, men and women begin to differ in sexual capacity and availability for sex, in social roles that are often massively different and in personality characteristics. By the late thirties and forties, the sexual matching game has the greatest distance to cover. By their fifties, men and women slow up, and in general their sexual appetites and profiles begin to converge.

It is widely known that the male reaches his peak sexual capacity at about age eighteen. At this age, he is able to respond quickly and repeatedly to sexual stimulation. Ten minutes after the first orgasm he can be ready again with full erection for the same sex act. The true sexual potential of the eighteen-year-old girl is as yet unrecorded. Suppression of the young female's sex drive has been fundamental in stabilizing cultures around settled family life. But having a baby a year for twenty years is also not the way to run a marriage or a society. Fear of pregnancy and prohibitions in our culture have suppressed any real understanding of the female nature. Only recently have women of this generation been willing to talk about the sexual intensity they felt in their teens.

At the age that young men and women are discovering their bodies, they are alike in many characteristics, such as the need to break away from parents and begin their adult lives. They are, however, insecure, inexperienced, and as yet not firmly established in social and vocational roles.

Enthralled as much by what they are learning about themselves as by what they are learning about someone else, young lovers lose their egos in each other as if they were a layer of dirt in a soapy hot tub. This self-absorption and accompanying definition is perhaps why first love is so hard to give up.

Hot-blooded young men in their twenties frequently marry and have an outlet for their ardor; meanwhile, young wives are still learning the nature of sexual response. This is followed by the disruption of pregnancy and small children. At this point, men are in the career or professional sorting system; some women are in the juggling act of both the career system and minding the babies. Men in their late twenties have already experienced the sexual acme of their lives.

After completing childbearing at about age thirty-five, the woman is at her fullest sexual availability. Women seem to lose their inhibitions, particularly if they have resolved to limit their family. Also, they are usually at their sexual peak. Their capacity for repeated orgasms is greatest during this time. The period of greatest response most often occurs during the last fourteen days of the menstrual cycle. This sexual receptivity is greatest in women who have already borne children, due to the high levels of vasocongestion resulting from childbirth. The female erectile chambers have the capacity to refill immediately after every climax and thus recreate sexual tension by engorging the pelvis with a supply of blood and fluid. This means more pleasure. The woman's receptivity is one of the most striking differences between men and women, and between women and other primate females.

It is a biological fact of life that, as the years pile up, the male erection capacity goes down. The gradual human physical slowing down is not so easily offset in a man by a new sexual experience, the way it often is for a woman, primarily because the man has fewer sexual inhibitions to give up. On the contrary, for men midlife is when inhibitions are likely to trouble them for the first time.

This difference in the male and female sexual cycles would appear to spell trouble for married couples. However, what biology has dictated to the sexes is still subject to the actions of the actors. The divergent pattern of sexuality can be the opportunity for mates to help each other sexually, as they have in other aspects of their marriage. Where the male is the initiator in his twenties, the woman, if she has not lost interest in sex, may become the initiator more and more in her thirties and forties. Males are often on a renewed sexual quest at this period, partly to offset fears of impotence.

Just as the chronological sex cycle differs for men and women, so the peaks may follow a different pattern. The pattern of arousal itself is not the same for both sexes. Men go from being disinterested to being interested in sex very easily and quickly. But men talk of two states of sexuality: one, not consciously wanting sex, and two, very much wanting sex. The first is a state which enables men to carry on their other functions in life despite the sexual attractions and possibilities which surround them. In this state men have learned to curb their sexual needs or to displace them for another time. The second state means that a man needs sex to reduce the level of physical tension and usually pursues his mate in a fairly direct manner. When he is aware of his needs, that is. Most of us become fairly adept at denying or delaying what we need, though. We have learned to delay gratification of many needs, particularly sexual pleasure.

For women, awakening to sexual interest is slower but sustained longer. It is usually women who say: "If we hadn't been taught about sex, would we know what to do?" The physical factors alone differ greatly between men and women. Women are not so often confronted with their primary organs. As sexual learning develops, women are not often willing to give it up and may find that fantasy takes on an important role. Further, women in their thirties and forties who experience a declining sexual response from husbands, or who find themselves between husbands or lovers, often discover their sexual needs crying out for fulfillment. Perhaps this is why sex and the single person has become a major topic among liberated women.

This basic outline distinguishes male and female. There are areas of their outside lives which fill in as men and women enter the different stages and roles of their lives. The man, for example, pursues the professional or business goal; sometimes his energies are directed for a sustained period of time toward landing that contract or expanding the merchandising or becoming a supervisor. He may be up for promotion at the plant; his tenure may be under consideration at the college where he is teaching. Under these circumstances, his interest in sex may diminish. On the other hand, while the man is fleshing out his career goals, the woman may be bearing children. Her energy level falls during pregnancy. All the women we interviewed found that their sexual interests dwindled due to the fatigue caused by the demanding care of small children. Night feedings, the explosive energy of toddlers, carpooling the preteens all demand women's energies and leave them wanting to use their beds for rest, not recreation.

The great sexual desert for women seems to be in the late twenties when their children are small. Healthy young women approaching the prime of their lives find themselves overwhelmed with their offspring. Those whose husbands take some of the burden of child care or can afford to hire outside help, or have a parent or friend who takes the children, find this period less frustrating. Those women who have to cope with several small children without any of these supports find mothering a draining, lonely experience. If depression sets in during one of these down cycles, sex is affected.

As one woman said: "I would love to be available for lovemaking every couple of nights, but when I know I have to get up to care for small children at six A.M. or for night feedings, I just don't have the energy for it. Motherhood can be exhausting!"

MARILYN:

Literature is filled with stories of first loves who never had to deal with disillusionment. Movies of the fifties were riddled with people who loved each other in an uncomplicated way. There were a few thirties and forties films with unhappy love: Ingrid Bergman leaving Casablanca without Humphrey Bogart for the sake of dedication and commitment; Rhett Butler walking out on Scarlett O'Hara because she could not get her first love out of her mind in time. But these movie lovers did not have children with problems, divorces, job demands, bitterness, or prior commitments of their own to deal with. Even those of us who believe we have good marriages are at a loss for movie or literary role models, because these old films never took us beyond the marriage or remarriage (never because of divorce, mind you). Contemporary films seldom find themes of constancy in marriage; their topics concentrate on exploring self and new relationships. Never do they picture couples working out their dilemmas and resolving to stay together. The new themes are breaking away and starting over.

Even in our most sober reflections on marital union, we are seldom prepared for the day-to-day, humdrum quality of existence. We just weren't trained for the job of marriage. Who was ever told that the Cinderella fable was untrue because the sweeping and dishes really began only after marriage? Even princes who whisked us off to large Georgian mansions had no idea what bills and hours of removing old plaster or sanding floors would be required. How did we know that babies would lose half of every feeding, leaving us with a wardrobe comprised of blouses with yellow shoulder stains? Where did we learn to pick up roots and rugs and move with the company every three years? Weren't we taught that a mind is a gift to be used— but on brownie meetings and sorting socks? Where were men scripted to roll out of warm beds to beat the traffic to boring, repetitive jobs? What evolutionary shifts prepared them for abandoning the hunt in the jungle in favor of the assembly line or the meeting room? Then suddenly they are expected to be the animals back in the bed again.

No wonder sexual disillusionment comes after the first years of marriage. We married for love and affection, not for fixing the overflowing toilet.

Admittedly any relationship has its peaks and valleys, and so, too, the private sex life of married couples. In the first year of married life the novelty of sex is high. There is an old wives' tale claiming that if during the first year of marriage a couple puts a penny in a jar every time they have intercourse and from the beginning of the second year takes a penny out each time, the jar will never be empty. While we suspect that these were very old wives, our couples did report that as frequency of intercourse declines, the quality increases dramatically. Many are willing to adjust to this pattern. But there are variations.

One of the couples interviewed had experiences opposite from the old wives' tale. Their first year was much less sexually satisfying than later years. Over the intervening time they have found both quantity and quality intensifying. For all these couples, the new frankness and awareness of sexual behavior was liberating. For them, sexual peaks have come with experience and learning about each other.

Since we noted that a good deal of learning about sexual intimacy needs to go on, we are aware that learning each other's preferences and self-discovery take years of testing and practice. To attain peak experiences frequently requires periods of learning and new stimulation. On the other hand, personal pressures and physical limitations can interfere with these stages of learning and with genuine sexual pleasure.

Couples interviewed about their sex lives report that they experienced dramatic changes in sexual interest depending on other pressures in their lives. Even relatively newly married couples admit to prioritizing their sex, as they would other demands in their lives. Sex gets put on a hierarchy of needs along with sleep, food, work, recreation. But they acknowledge that sex comes after the other needs. States of anxiety detract from sexual satisfaction. Depression, job stress, fear of pregnancy, or the insecurity of not getting pregnant all create valleys for sexual satisfaction.

With the crunch of biological cycles and social pressures, the permanence of the union of men and women may appear to be on a disaster course. Their sexual cycles and highs and lows just do not mesh. Their needs for challenge and stimulation do not occur at the same time. However, biology may not have abandoned the sexes altogether. Despite varying arousal patterns, cycles of sexual intensity, and capacities for multiple orgasm, most people are willing to dedicate themselves to some new learning about their sexual needs. Couples who have a physical history with each other tend to know how to stimulate each other. Just as they learn to cheer the depressed mate, they learn the physical needs of the other. In healthy marriages, sexual satisfaction can increase with the duration of the relationship for the very reason that two people know how to please each other. They have learned the most powerful seats of eroticism for each other—something a casual sex partner could never master in a weekend tryst.

Five Misconceptions about Sex

We write our own poetry for love affairs. What powerfully attracts one mating pair means little to another couple. Other people's rhymes and rhythms don't work for us, but sometimes our own attitudes don't help us out when it comes to understanding our bodies and our needs for love and sex. Our adventure begins with what exists in our heads. For all the ideas we have tucked away, there are often distortions, misconceptions, half-knowledge. For all the abstractions and graphic details about sex, some popular myths take hold. Here are a few misconceptions.

1. "Sex is easy. The biological need to couple is so great that we will emerge from the marriage bed with glowing satisfaction." "Wanting" and "getting" do not always go together. Even while we want this creature, learning about making love to her or him will require some practice and experiment. This period of adjustment requires a relaxed atmosphere. Pressured into sexual performance, one or the other can easily turn off.

2. "The way sex is now is the way it's going to be tomorrow." Sex of this present moment will not be this way again. As love finds new definition when we grow together, so sex finds new expression. Somehow its pleasure is never quite the same again. Even if the stages of arousal are familiar, the peak changes, or the source of stimulation leads to surprise. It is the experimenting that makes sex a new pleasure, that hitches its gratification to the future pleasures, as well as to the moment.

3. "People are either sexually compatible or incompatible." Since men and women are not given a set sexual capacity from the start, there is rarely a physical reality that makes people "incompatible" partners. Most sexual dysfunction is psychological and can be corrected with experience or help. A few physical difficulties are possible as two people become accustomed to the act of sex. Appetites and sensitivities will be learned but cannot exist fully developed in the early stages of marriage. Incompatibility may be learned, just as compatibility is learned.

4. "There is one perfect and sexual person waiting for me.

This special person exists in my head, and I will know him or her by the sexual attraction between us." The danger in this misconception is that we fool ourselves because some of the symbols are right in this person. She is pretty and she has large breasts, or he is going to devote himself to healing the sick and also making a good income. We meet someone and "just know" he is the right person by sexual attraction and before examining the other important characteristics or faults he may have. We are likely to overlook the disturbing qualities simply because we are convinced the right person has come along. We *feel* this is the right person. Let us examine our relationships with clear eyes, since the fault, as Cassius says, "lies not in the stars."

5. "Sex is primarily a physical event, not a complex psychological encounter." This misconception accounts for much insensitivity to the difficulties one or the other partner may experience from time to time. Those who would confine intercourse to a basic biological drive overlook the intricate involvement sex has in marriage. For some, sex can be a gratifying physical release, but in marriage it is a complicated psychological event.

Layers of learning about sex have been acquired, and some of it is confusing. Sometimes we only partly understand fragments of things we have heard or we really never understood at all. We only thought we did. We once learned that our dad and mom did "it" four times, producing four children. We were told that we will have strong feelings for only one person who will be mutually monogamous. Television presents us with physical perfection, and we are always trying to measure up to that standard. No one prepares us for what marriage is really like. So much fragmentary learning confuses the person who encounters her first feelings of jealousy or attraction to another person. She is afraid someone will steal away her mate, the object of her sexual desire. He is attracted to an old girl friend at a party. We hear that sex is the cement for marriage, and then we meet people who look outside their marriages for sexual gratification. One day Mr. Charisma comes along, and we wonder how to handle his attention. An office acquaintance uses us for confidences, comes to depend on the relationship, and finds us the most interesting man she has ever met. Or we have lunch with someone in our graduate courses who likes our company. Then there is the outright flattering proposition and the temptation to try it just once—out of town, during a boring conference, or after work when the spouse thinks we are working overtime. We get involved before we know it. We are troubled because of the morality we were taught and we wouldn't want our friends to know, but we are both excited and affirmed, all the same. Whatever the scene and the lead characters, romance and sex find their way into our lives, sometimes in spite of prior commitment.

None of these vignettes are imaginary. They are all from the lives of real people. Chances are, we will find ourselves attracted to someone other than our spouse in the course of the marriage. As a character in Piers Paul Read's book, *A Married Man*, says: "Women always want to be with the men they sleep with and that's what breaks up families." How we handle these events becomes the issue, because sex is not just an isolated physical act, as some would like to believe.

Rules of the Game

Some people marry for the express purpose of having regular sex. Marriage becomes the arrangement that legitimizes sex. For a great many, too, sex becomes the mystery of married life. Its intensity and shared pleasure draw us together in a mystical way. The power of sex focuses us on each other and away from the cares and seductions of the other pockets of our lives. Even if there is discord from other corners of the house or disagreements over the dinner table, sex is a chance for vital renewal. But its mystery and renewal require open lines for communication. It's a powerful communication, the language of sex. Body language speaks to us through physical intimacy. It is this language that allows us to laugh over the hostilities of an earlier hour and renews our energies for the difficulties that might lie ahead.

There are rules to observe about this language of sex, as with any other language or communication. There are probably more than two rules that apply, but these are evident.

1. Don't play games of reward and denial with sex.

The powerful language of sex urges a sense of play. With this erotic communication the players are able to uncover what they can do, what is imaginary and what is possible. Husband and wife play games different from the games of courtship days. They may even repeat the earlier dating games in order to keep the dance alive. At some point, however, the couple has dropped the games surrounding the denial of physical attraction. Prohibited behavior of an earlier period becomes the ritual of the sexual dance. No one would suggest that all games and play be given up, but the games of withholding sexual favors are cast aside. The unwritten rule of the boudoir is that sex is never used as a weapon. There are times when one or the other may not be in the mood for sex because of various hostilities from other corridors of their lives, and sex is delayed. But sex is never to become the battleground.

2. Don't fake sexual response.

Whenever people fake pleasure or orgasm, trouble is surely ahead. Perhaps it is the problem of masking true feelings, denial of true intimacy, or the beginning of some dishonesty, but as surely as men and women are drawn to each other by sexual attraction, pretending to have an orgasm causes a falling apart. As a common phenomenon, female orgasm is a recent discovery. It is a product of lots of tinkering. How all that tinkering and

steamy breathing made headway in the erogenous zones
was the result of examining true feelings.

Pleasure should be the goal of both partners. If one says, "It
wasn't good for you last night, was it?" the only answer is an
honest one. Shading the truth to make him feel better is
deception. Furthermore, the partner cannot determine what
to change in his approach if she is pretending last night's
intercourse was among the "all-time top ten." Speaking about
the sex of last night is about the appropriate distance. There is
no point in spilling your guts immediately after he has spent
himself, or sighing, "It isn't the way it's supposed to be."
There is always tomorrow or even this afternoon to look
forward to, if egos are still intact. We both know when we
have reached a great peak, and any deception is inappropriate.
A sex partner must wonder if she will tell a white lie about
this, what must be the boundaries of her honesty or his
capacity for intimacy.

Intimacy grows from honest feelings that are shared.
Sexuality, to be energetic and developing, requires intimacy.
Sexual experience and genital sex are contexts for a young
adult's development of intimacy. As sexual maturity is
reached, one's capacity for intimate sexual exchange with a
loved one is developed and stabilized. Often before this
maturity is reached, sex is of a self-seeking, identity-hungry
kind; each partner is really trying to reach himself. Or it
remains a kind of genital combat in which each tries to defeat
the other. Even more significantly in marriage, sexual self-
abandon requires letting one's defenses down in the presence
of another. Sexual intimacy opens into a larger reservoir, the
capacity for abandoning oneself to sexual and sensational
feelings in a union with one who is both a partner to the
sensation and a guarantor of one's continuing identity.

Genital sex, however, is neither necessary nor sufficient for
the unfolding of intimacy. Either sex or intimacy can exist
without the other. It is easy to confuse one with the other in
early sexual explorations. It's possible to think that if the

sexual power is there, the intimate communication is present as well. Often sexual love is used as the metaphor of human intimacy, but both require development. The rituals of lovemaking and orgasm dramatically highlight elements common to other experiences of intimacy—the impulse to share oneself with another, the anxiety of self-revelation, the affirmation of being accepted, and the delight in the give-and-take. When intimacy and sex come together, no finer communication exists than between lovers. Every movement, every glance, every thought, and every shadow strike emotion in the heart of the lover. As we come to know each other better, the communication of sex is our most powerful language. Quite literally, unveiling our body allows us to reveal our innermost self. Repeated mutual pleasure in sex gives the couple a positive sense of self—that someone revels and takes pleasure in our body gives us the security to be the revealed person. Then we meet together in all our nakedness.

Sex as an Art Form

Roses fade. Wines sour. Blossoms wilt. Soufflés fall and passions dissipate. Does it necessarily follow that a couple's sex life pales after time? Experiences vary. The chances of remaining seductive to the same person for forty or fifty years are not all that great, without enormous determination. Some couples say their passions only truly develop over time. But in looking to those couples whose sexual interest intensified, we find that a certain quality of attention has been paid to sex. It is treated as an art form.

MARILYN:

Preservation of intimacy is the prerequisite for continued good sex. Some couples have learned to cue each other in advance when they want to have a night of lovemaking. An arching of the eyebrows, the presence of a heart-shaped pillow on the bed, a pat on the backside in the kitchen, a furtive fondle when the children aren't looking, a particularly ardent kiss when the other comes home from work, a special meal and candlelight are all calls that one wants or needs the intimacy and physical release of lovemaking. A marriage partner learns to read the cues that the other wants to settle the physical demands of his or her body. These prerequisite cues develop as an art form.

Keeping the sexy in sex has kept many couples interested in the refinements of lovemaking. For some, the choice of exotic nightwear (warmth and comfort must sometimes be abandoned in favor of the diaphanous, the plunging neckline, or the innocent lace) is worth the expense. Flannel nightgowns may be cozy but less than alluring to the man who has just perused a copy of Playboy. *Gowns suitable for cooking morning eggs or bedding down the children are not necessarily conducive to seduction. Sex can be looked at as a question of who is going to seduce whom first.*

A woman's selection of bed linens and other bedroom furnishings can dictate whether or not it is a place of romance. (Heavy-duty permanent-press white sheets lack the tactile qualities of satin or the innocence of wildflower designs.) Keeping the bedroom a comfortable temperature (in the age of energy crises) heightens the interest in removing clothing. An intimate but cold hand is less seductive than a warm one. Having responded to our recent energy crisis, I was accused by a visitor of practicing birth control with the thermostat. He understood the warm-hand phenomenon.

The mood for sex and affection can be maintained beyond the decor. Problems are left at the bedroom door. The boudoir is not the psychiatrist's couch nor the business office. Even if it has been used as a study by day, it is the chamber for intimacies by night.

Seduction and stimulation come in many forms: fantasy, looks, words, clothes, books, magazines, accoutrements, mood, language, music. Fantasies past and present are central in arousal of the brain for many people. Fantasies are sources of stimulation instrumental both before and during lovemaking. To help themselves become aroused and to reach climax, some people recall past sexual experiences; others fantasize about suggestive settings, other partners, or about what is coming. Several couples report the use of sex magazines or *The Joy of Sex* as sources of stimulation for their own lovemaking. (We have always doubted the claim that no girl was ever seduced by a book; some of us are seduced by magazines.) Some couples use music, candlelight, and different settings from sofa to backseat of the car. One couple frequently used candlelight at bedside for their nightly romancing. They were amused when their small child made them another candleholder in the form of a heart in art class. Somehow the child caught the mysteries of the bedroom.

All the senses come into play in romance. Animal instincts are triggered by scent, among other things. Human scents are carefully washed away, and we spend billions creating new scents for ourselves. Perfume and makeup applied before bedtime or a vase of fresh flowers in the bedroom are sources of sensual stimulation as well as visual pleasure. Whatever the legal factors surrounding marijuana, it is reportedly a boon to sex. Many people privately admit to being more easily aroused with a small amount of grass. Alcohol is sometimes used to reduce inhibitions and anxieties. While alcohol may reduce stress, sexual performance frequently is less satisfying due to delayed reactions and the onset of fatigue.

Stimulation and seduction are the introduction to foreplay. But foreplay varies from couple to couple. What turns one on may turn another off. The signaling and stimulation may be imitation of animal-like behavior. Some people make animal-like sounds, a me-Tarzan-you-Jane type exchange. Some engage in playful wrestling or intimate dancing. The chase observable between birds and four-legged animals is sometimes a method of sexual signaling for humans, too. Often in sex actions speak louder than words. An occasional word of encouragement may be enough. Some people say that a word at the wrong time can turn off their mood for sex. If that word is a subtle put-down, then the urge for intercourse may vanish for the evening.

In this age of assertive females, some men are put off by overt aggressive behavior, while others like to fantasize that they are being forcefully seduced, if not raped. It seems that many married men would like their women to be more aggressive. They report having to be the seducers all the time with women, when they would like to have a seductress.

Even in an era when the world seems ready to self-destruct over sexual fantasies and sexual expression, it is still sometimes difficult for couples to begin their commitment to stimulating each other's bodies. What we were taught as teenagers was taboo is suddenly required behavior. Years of modesty were swept away with the drop of a negligee. As one woman confessed: "When you said 'I will,' that meant you were going to have to." But these are inhibitions women give up in favor of pleasure.

Not everyone adjusts to sex and differences in style and timing in the first months of honeymoon bliss. Not every wife is ready to adopt new styles of sex. Adjusting to each other's presence takes experience and often tolerance; sometimes the adjustments become a pattern and sameness. New fears and insecurities crop up with each age. Women may feel they don't have breasts as attractive as girls of eighteen; discomfort with displaying one's body may increase with middle-aged spread. A man may think he isn't as adept at lovemaking as the guy his wife was once engaged to. One woman said, "I know I'm overweight, but it's important to me that George tell me that I'm beautiful to him."

We were tempted to label this section "What Jogging Books Never Tell You," or "Should You Have Sex Before the Big Game?" There was a frequently heard smug tale that those who "got more" exercise during the day "got less" at night. Coaches told their athletes not to have intercourse the night before the big game or tournament. More recent findings seem to indicate that performance on the field or the court or the track is not lowered by performance in bed.

New evidence suggests that those who jog or are physically fit do not enjoy sex less (nor less sex) but that they enjoy it more. Those who are physically fit, so the reports go, are proud of their bodies and less hesitant to unveil them. They have made their bodies objects of concern and training and feel like having sex more. Also, they are more elastic when it comes to the acrobatics of lovemaking. They can simply accomplish more. Fit people tire less easily and often report that they are "never too tired for sex."

Whatever the mode of stimulation, it is the attention and desire to please that convey caring and affection. Who can resist the mate who has taken special efforts to be alluring for us? There are and will be times when even the most highly sexed couples need titillation. Stresses of job and marital life make the act of lovemaking all the more important for keeping a couple's focus on each other. Depression, decline of self-worth, job dissatisfaction, personal crises, and childbirth are events that cause us to delay pleasure. But these are times when physical pleasure is most needed and most reassuring. The bedroom can be the haven from outside distractions and disappointments. It can ease the passages and repair the sense of self-worth.

What seems to be the most natural and desired engagement of each other, then, can be fraught with small disasters at any time, from the honeymoon to old age. The art of loving is the way in which each makes the other feel he or she is the most desirable creature in the other's world. It takes a lifetime to convince someone.

5

The Great Parenting Hoax

Someone has given kids a bum rap. Children are usually viewed as dirty, disruptive, and demanding. So far as we know, no one has polled the popularity of children alongside congressmen, clergy, or professors, but if behavior of adults is an indicator, it certainly appears that children have moved rather dramatically downhill in public opinion. If the population growth statistics in this country are an indication of the interest people have in children, they are clearly less appealing to many adults than roller skating and white-water canoeing.

Not only is the interest in giving birth diminishing, but other segments of the population are deciding to exclude children from their lives. Adults don't want babies crying in their apartment complexes; retired folks don't want children in their condos and retirement villages; teachers are retiring earlier to get away from children.

The idea of getting married to have children is often greeted with responses ranging from tongue clucking to outright contempt. "Why bring another kid into this crowded, rotten world?" "Why burden the earth with another energy waster, especially an American who will use five times more energy than an Asian!" "Why throw your life away raising kids when there are so many significant things to do?" "Let's face it. You only go 'round once in life, so you have to grab all the gusto you can" (with apologies to Schlitz beer). Kids just get in the way. And so it goes. But of course this is an overstatement. Many people thinking about getting married are excited about having children, but they are a shrinking minority.

In 1960, the birthrate in the United States was 23.7 per 1,000 people. The average family size was 3.33. In 1978, eighteen years later, the birthrate was 15.4 per 1,000; the average family size was 2.81. This change has not resulted from war, famine, or pestilence, but conscious choice. We in this country, and increasingly around the world, have undergone a massive attitude change about a fundamental human experience: having children. We have changed and changed rapidly.

As we talk with people about getting married and the child-rearing years of marriage, certain ideas and attitudes about children reoccur. One is the no-more-like-me attitude. People claim they wouldn't, couldn't, and even shouldn't put up with a child the likes of them. While perhaps said in jest, there is often deep seriousness, and presumably deep self-hate, behind this view. Intimations of not just hell raising and hijinx but of perversity come from the most angelic lips. Perhaps this no-more-like-me view is combined with a sense that the world is more difficult to grow up in now. But for whatever the reasons, the idea of bringing "replicas of self" into life is abhorrent to many.

A second attitude of rejection of children is based on a combination of popular views about the population explosion and the ecological limits of the earth. While this joint attitude is passionately and often righteously held, the rational basis for the view seems shallow. The individual holding—or, more appropriately, haunted by—this view conjures up slogans, isolated statistics, and a short hideous scenario, but not well-developed rationales. While deeply concerned about the balance between resources and population, they fail to see how people they might bring into the world could contribute to the solution. In their enthusiasm to make life better for others, they want to deny the possibility of bringing life to the world, to them, and to their spouses. One young woman we know had come to believe in her enthusiasm that zero population growth meant she and her husband should have zero children.

A third and very different rationale is the economic argument. A hundred years ago, having several children was for many married people the only insurance policy they could afford against a lonely and impoverished old age. Also, because of poor health conditions, one had to have six or seven children to insure two adult children. In effect, a family could not afford to have no children. Now the argument has completely reversed itself. A few months ago, when we discovered that we were to have our third child (an announcement that in itself caused much eyebrow raising—being one over our quota and all) we were assaulted with the news of how expensive it would be to feed, clothe, and especially to educate the little intruder. Estimates ranging from one hundred thousand to a million dollars were shot at us. When you add news like this to round-the-clock morning sickness, a seemingly endless winter, and the ravages of inflation, it makes the heartbreak of psoriasis seem like chicken feed. But underneath all the inflated figures there is a kernel of bad news for the budget-conscious: kids cost money. They will cause a shifting in financial priorities. They cut deeply into one's discretionary funds. And they may not be as good an investment as common stocks or South African gold mines.

KEVIN :

I don't know where I got the idea that being a parent would be a drag, but it was there. I saw children as an invasion into the privacy of my marriage, my union with Marilyn. Although I never thought seriously about not having children, it was viewed as just something one did. A slightly more benign inevitability than death and taxes. I figured, and still do, that it is the responsibility of married people to replenish the earth. However, I saw the probability of having children as an obligation. It was paying one's dues to society.

I don't recall how or from whom I picked up the idea that being a parent would be like a long trip to the dentist, but it was there. Being a bachelor into my early thirties, I had plenty of opportunity to observe married friends and their children. I heard about their colicky babies who wouldn't stop crying and their floor walking brought on by earaches and nightmares. On visits to married friends, I experienced the inability to carry on a conversation because of disruptions, distractions, and general mayhem. I'd had my usually indefatigable appetite dulled by full-to-overflowing diapers. Occasionally I sat on my hands to keep from strangling whining, nagging children who were bedeviling their parent for cookies, Cokes, and car keys. Perhaps I developed my attitude by a simple process of osmosis, but it was there.

When, three years into our marriage, Marilyn announced what I had already guessed, I quietly braced myself. Our turn had come. And, in fact, as the months went on, I did get more interested. I thought, though, that it was nothing more than kidding myself into the great parenting hoax. But still, I thought I'd go with the flow. I did become quite wrapped up in one respect, one over which I had no control whatever: the sex of the child. As the months rolled by, I developed a deep intuition—an Irish sense—that the baby would be a son. It was more than wishful thinking: I had an uncharacteristic assurance that "it" was a "he." As I sat in the father's waiting room I fantasized about basketballs and jump shots, about training for competition and readying for law school, and how I would need to learn how to fish for our fishing trips. When an unfamiliar nurse strode through and, without breaking stride, mechanically said, "You've got a daughter. Wife's OK," I was literally stunned. But, still stunned and before any sense of disappointment set in, I was told to come into the hall. "There she is," another strange nurse said, pointing to a covered glass cubicle on wheels. I peered in and saw this scrawny, angry little thing with tiny fists clenched in rage and a look of helpless fury on its—her—face. What happened to me then has made it easier to understand the instantaneous conversion of Saul of Tarsus into Paul the Apostle. Almost literally, my heart went out to her. I felt as if I were being picked up and carried away on a wave of strong emotion. Uncontrollably and from nowhere the words formed, "Kid, you need me." Then quickly the nurse reappeared and whisked her into the nursery. As I started after her, I thought "How lucky to have a daughter!"

MARILYN:

Today as I was putting blue satin ribbons on the wicker bassinette in preparation for a third child, I realized how much the eight-year span between the last two babies has changed the concept of parenthood.

A fourth reason for the anti-kid sentiment can be traced to the late 1960s and early 1970s and accumulated resentment. During those high-energy, electric years, one of the most vocal sentiments was "Don't trust anyone over thirty." On the other hand, the unstated but long-held view, "Don't trust anyone under thirty" held by the over-thirty folks was confirmed and deepened. Antagonisms between young and old, child and parent, were out in the open. The term "generation gap" appeared in sociology texts and was splashed across television from sit-coms to talk shows. The true meaning was experienced by many families who struggled with real and imagined differences which were being continually fueled by events outside their home: the war, civil rights struggles, the popularity of drugs, new sexual attitudes, new attitudes toward roles for women. All these and more kept the family pot boiling. While tempers have cooled in recent years, there is a strong residue of hostility. In many families, mention of children, particularly with the prefix "flower," at the dinner table causes wincing or worse. People having grown up during these times have absorbed firsthand, or certainly through television, a view that being a parent is somewhere on the scale of unpleasantness between athlete's foot and migraine headaches. But for whatever reasons, the opinion molders have done a fine job of persuading us that children are a nuisance or a self-indulgent luxury. The severe negative social consequences of a sharply declining birthrate are just now beginning to be discussed in professional journals. However, we are more concerned here with the reader appreciating the personal loss and loss to a marriage if children are not a part of it.

MARILYN:

Maybe it just isn't "fun" to have children anymore. Or perhaps we parents don't communicate what pleasure is derived from rearing a family. Maybe we need to do a better job of expressing the joys of being a parent. I don't think anyone told me it was great to have a child. Yet the happiest day of my life was giving birth to my first child, and then again when the two others were born. No postpartum depression, but a postpartum high each time.

Hearing about another's experience of childbirth in no way truly prepares a woman for her own participation. In all probability my children will learn that making love, being married, and parenting are fun in the same way we learned about it; by doing it. But the current preoccupation with lovemaking minus the following stages of parenting leads one to question what values our society is stressing.

The great malaise over children is of concern. It may be the current unpopularity of children that leads comfortable communities to reject school bond issues time after time. It may be this attitude that allows children to be brutalized by parents. But for me, children are their own reward. They are wise, sweet, and caring; they can be dirty, disruptive, and demanding as well, but they are my link in the chain of being, and they are my fire and flesh.

KEVIN:

The only surprise I have had in life has been being a parent. Sex, the experience of victory or defeat, the loss of a parent, being married, intense fear—all were familiar experiences that I had somehow anticipated. I had been told or had read about them in advance, so that when they came, there were no surprises. Newness, yes, but no real surprises. Not so with being a parent, being a father.

MARILYN:

When we anticipated the birth of what turned out to be our first daughter, we more or less did what couples were expected to do: procreate. That was twelve years ago. By the time we had our second daughter, the notion of limiting one's family was firmly ingrained. By the time the third was expected, we knew it was a "he" months before birth, due to the developments in medical technology. Even then what our parents did by natural evolution, we were doing by desire and decision. Now people don't just automatically have babies. They decide if, when, and how many. The "if" looms larger all the time. Young couples have come to space and organize their childbearing. Now one can hear them saying: "We are going to have a baby by next fall" or "We will start a family immediately after grad school." General Motors planning has reached the bedroom.

Becoming a Parent

The growing resistance to being a parent is not completely wrongheaded or groundless. Raising children is not easy. It is trying, frustrating work, and it lasts for a very long period in one's life. The horror of abused children is testimony to the strain that parenting places on some people. For most of us it means changes, many of which seem unpleasant. We no longer have as much time to spend as we choose. The baby, the family, gobble up Saturdays as if they were Oreos. Not only do children cut into one's discretionary time, but also into discretionary money. Sports cars get traded in for strollers and swing sets. Romantic vacations are switched to trips to grandparents. For the devoted consumer, children mean postponing or doing without.

The coming of children means a change of pace. A couple cannot decide at eight on a Wednesday night to hit a movie or go dancing. Planning ahead becomes essential. Baby-sitters or arrangements with other parents become a staple of life. The couple with children is in effect hemmed in, perhaps as they have never been before. For some this is a special strain. Some find the new sense of being depended upon particularly stressful. Giving up the free and easy independence of single life was one thing, but being at the beck and call of a baby or a small crowd of little ones is more than they can bear. They feel closed in and pinched. On the other hand, many jobs or preparation for jobs demand the same things as raising children: they consume all free time; they impose severe financial sacrifices; they tie us down, keeping us on a short rope; and, in a slightly different way, they choke off our independence, making us servants to the job.

Becoming a parent, then, is more than sacrifices. It is also more than joys—of which there are many. It cannot be captured by adding up the pluses and minuses. Rather, it is a different state of existence with different feeling levels, different rewards, and different demands. The fact that there are special terms and titles, like motherhood, fatherhood, parenthood, is no accident. Although they have lost much of their special meaning, they refer to a special state of being. Parents are different from others. Whether it is reacting to the sight of passing babes-in-arms or to the screech of car brakes, parents feel and behave differently.

One of the slogans-to-live-by of our times is "developing the human potential." Like most slogans it can be interpreted in numerous ways, from devoting one's life to the improvement of living conditions for the poor all the way to making sure each muscle of one's body is exercised and bulging to its limits. The term human potential directs our attention to what we can become, to full development of our personhood. While there are many roads to this development, parenting has special paths to aid in our growth. There is something in the very fabric of parenting that calls out to people to transcend themselves. The needs of our children for attention, for nurturing, for protection come to us in a voice that makes it more difficult to listen only to ourselves. Their presence in our lives makes it difficult to be continually asking and worrying about the question, "How am I doing?" While marriage often dulls the awful loneliness of self-concern, parenthood makes it a luxury. The gift of our love to our partner is just that: something given. The love we give to our children is not a gift. It is a need. It is a demand. They need it like they need mother's milk. And it is in this giving to them that we become different, we become changed.

We change in another way, too. Having children centers us on fundamentals. Life is no longer something that we as individuals are experiencing. We are no longer just passing through life, but passing it on. Questions like, "What are the effects of food additives or nuclear radiation or volunteer versus universal draft," have a larger context than one's own body and space. All of a sudden, we seek answers more seriously, because the stakes are higher. We are no longer dabbling on a small space, but painting on a larger canvas. We are called—even pulled—to a better self.

KEVIN:

I spend my days differently now that I have children. And I like it this way. Some of the best parts of my days and weeks are with the children. "Dad, will you come out and shoot baskets?" "Dad, listen to my new piano piece!" "Dad, you said you were going to plant the vegetable garden with me and you haven't yet. How about now?" "Dad, will you put down that book and feel my muscle? Is it growing, or what?" All this distraction from the serious work of the world and in

security one gets from owning property. Or it can be the happiness one gets from being thought well of by others. Or it can be the private sense of satisfaction derived from doing one's job well. It goes without saying that all values are immensely important. Our values shape our lives precisely because they dictate to us what is important. There is an old saying, "Be careful what you hope for because you surely will get it." This strikes us as the psychological equivalent of, "You are what you eat." For example, if we decide that our own individual happiness is foremost, the give-and-take of marriage may not be for us. If we decide we want to enter a profession, we have to be ready to spend the energy and make the sacrifice to acquire it.

Usually one's values can be determined by his or her actions. Or, rather, you can tell a person's true values by his actions. Take the case of the man who claims he loves history and, when asked about television, says it is a waste of time. One would expect, if the man were presenting an honest picture of himself—that is, being true to his values—that his free time would be devoted to reading history or being a part of a reenactment group or some such activity. And, further, that he would rarely have his television set on. If the opposite were true, we should wonder about the man's honesty or his level of self-knowledge. In any event, we can tell much about our own values and those of the people around us by viewing how we spend our free time.

After the basic desire we all have to provide our children with food, shelter, and the other requirements for health, our primary concern is with their values. Most of us want to pass on to our children those values, those intangible clusters of attitudes and interests, which we prize. We want our children to respect themselves and others. We want them to prize justice and fairness; we want them to value hard work, and human kindness, and peacefulness. And we want them to strike some comfortable balance between being able to compete with others and cooperate with others. Unfortunately, though, it takes more than wanting. It takes more, too, than being a good person and having admirable values. Abraham Maslow, the famous psychologist, has said, "Wonderful people do not always make wonderful parents." Our own experience regularly bears out this observation and, we must add, the opposite axiom. We have seen husbands and wives who possess a high degree of self-discipline and who have worked hard all their lives allow their children to become whining and self-indulgent oafs. Occasionally we have seen a gentle, thoughtful child come out of a family with parents who seemed to be continually rehearsing for the parts of George and Martha in Who's Afraid of Virginia Woolf. But on the whole, the old adage, "The apple doesn't fall far from the tree," is true. Children mirror in varying degree their parents' values. That happens because parents are a child's main teachers. We have at our children from their birth to our death. We have at them, as they say about voting in Chicago, "early and often." We tell them what we think is right (eating vegetables, helping your sister, developing a plan to get a summer job) and what we think is wrong (trying to exist exclusively on Coca-Cola, jabbing your brother with a number-two lead pencil, selling your blood to make a down payment on a motorcycle). And they find it hard to ignore our values and our insistence that they acquire our value system or something close.

We are primary sources of approval for our children, and we have to work very hard to squander their trust in our judgment. There are, of course, other influences on their values. There are the very strong influences on a child's values of school, church, friends, and, increasingly, television. But for all the strength of these other authorities, most educators, clergymen, child psychologists, and medical experts acknowledge that the family has the real power in the shaping and development of values. That power can, of course, be used positively and negatively.

KEVIN:

Our children have the most annoying memories. They can forget a request to clear the table before it is out of Marilyn's or my mouth but remember past events with photographic detail. And these memories are so selective. The carefully planned family picnics and Christmas mornings are never recalled, but our displays of human frailties are forever dancing in their heads. Once on a family outing, my brother and I and our four children went out to fire a toy parachute rocket. While my brother claimed this was his son's hobby, I have long harbored the suspicion that it was Dad's toy. We needed a large open space, so we went to an abandoned military airfield. There were several signs up around the entrance warning us that we were trespassing on military property and that violators would be prosecuted, but we figured that there was no one around and we'd risk it. When our children, young guardians of morality that they are, called the signs to our attention, we mumbled that they were old signs and that the war was over. As soon as we drove out on the runway to launch the rocket, a police car came roaring toward us, siren screaming and lights flashing. The policeman came up alongside, rolled down his window, and asked if we'd seen the signs. My brother and I looked at one another and said, "Signs? What signs? Have we missed some signs? You mean we shouldn't be here, officer? Certainly! We'll leave right away. Thank you for letting us know we were trespassing." And off we drove or, rather, slithered.

Since that time I have often wished we had thrown ourselves at the feet of the policeman, admitted our premeditated crime, spent a fortnight or whatever in the slammer. That punishment would have been nothing compared to the hell of never knowing when or in whose company our children in cherubic voices will tell in microscopic and interminable detail how Dad and Uncle Bob lied to the policeman "right to his face." I'm sure, too, that in the future when they become cocaine runners for the Mafia, groupies for the 1990s equivalent of rock stars or heavy-duty shoplifters, they will tell the judge, "Well, Your Honor, it all started when I was very young. My father and my uncle took us out to shoot off this rocket and. . ."

Our firmly held convictions are not always mirrored by our offspring. Too much passion over an issue sometimes has a negative effect. Confessed one mother: "I am very opposed to guns. Gun control is a major political issue with me. No toy guns were ever given to my son. At age fifteen my son is a gun collector."

The mother who is opposed to pets turns around to find her child kissing all the gerbils in the classroom. The parents opposed to religion discover their child heavily involved in a Christian youth group.

No one has perfectly acceptable and unconflicting values. Unclear and imperfect values are equally as much a topic for discussion. Parents need not wait until their values make them proud before communicating them. Dealing with changing attitudes and conflicts is part of their responsibility.

When should the couple start discussing their values? Now! Starting is the important part. Counselors tell families to begin where they are. Values discussions can take place in various settings: over the dinner table, viewing television (particularly during the commercials!), on the family camping trip, watching a sunset, anywhere families arrange to be together.

The values transmission side of parenting may appear ephemeral and obvious to the new parent. It all seems so easy when one is holding the first infant. Marriage itself was a sorting process. Man and woman looked for each other through a filter of shared values and interests, of similar standards and appreciations. That process of searching for a mate winnowed out people who simply didn't measure up.

Perhaps values training comes easily with the first child. The first is often closer to our value system. But children strive for independence early. Certainly each child tests his parents in the teenage years. But some kids are just more difficult; they experiment with independence: they smoke marijuana, they live with unmarried partners, they reject the church.

Suddenly the parents wonder where they went wrong. Where did they lose control? What the parent sometimes fails to notice is how his own values shift—gradually or dramatically but surely—and by the time there are children, the parents, themselves, have adopted other concerns.

The Problem

One source of the problem of transmission of values is our own contradictions. Our observable behavior does not always fit the words we have pronounced. We are people of conflicting behavior. For example, we say that we love Daddy but argue with him over an issue the meaning of which is lost on the children. What they understand is that we violated their understanding of love. In this case, perhaps, an explanation of the nature of love and conflict can help them. Often the children interpret a disagreement as a quarrel. All too often there is no follow-up explanation of conflicting values or some differences of opinion on vital matters.

Values Transmission

If our contradictory behavior seems confusing to our children, it is frequently confusing to ourselves. It is probably wise to point out our own contradictions and conflicts. Adult life is full of contradictions: we get angry with those we love; we feel lonely in the midst of a crowd of our friends; we finally find a solitary moment but discover we waste it away. A singular act (unable to made good use of the time alone) does not mean that we don't value the principle of having private time. We may not have found the time to read what we think are the good books, but we still place high value on reading.

We think we should have a more spiritual life, but we don't seem to be able to bring it off. We know that the values we hold dear are not always immediately achievable. That is part of adult living. We don't always get what we want, nor are we always able to do what we think is important.

Another source of the problem is the deliberate distortion of values, or bad example. What we do speaks louder than what we say. One set of parents we knew briefly seemed to have fine sons. But the boys told us of their family ploys once, when the parents were away. It was a game of how to beat the system. The boys were enthralled with this game. Cotton balls were stuffed in the Con Edison electric meters to slow the revolutions of the recording mechanism. When it was time for the meter reader to appear, the cotton was removed. Another trick was to save flip tops from beverage cans for use in parking meters. The tops were then the same size as coins required to fill parking meters. A large box was used to collect the tops, and as a driver was leaving the house, he would grab a handful to use around the city. One wonders if those boys grew up to become corporate embezzlers or were charged with failure to pay income taxes. To them, the rules applied to someone else, and the system that attempted to impose order on public life was there to be outwitted.

Fairness is in the eye of the beholder. We think we treat our children fairly and equally. But what we consider fair treatment may be lost on our children. Fairness is important to them early on. They are forever practicing legal skills or games of logic with their parents. "That isn't fair!" they protest. Equal treatment and equal reward; they count our errors of fairness in their own logic.

Parent logic bears explanation. Parent logic means that I try to give each child equal amounts of attention and material goods, but not necessarily at the same time. By fairness children usually mean: "I want as much as my sister got, right now." The first child seems to get more. He is older and receives the larger portion; she gets the clothes the first time around when they are new; he comes to expect that it is "fair" for him to receive more.

In reality, we don't treat any two people equally. We can't. Our behavior is tempered by space, time, and judgment—and sometimes by quick passion. Any attempt to equate treatment of children is doomed to failure. There is no way of equating life's gifts and parents' rewards from one child to the next. If one child is invited to vacation in Florida with another family, there is no way to compensate that event for the next child. If the next child is given a new skirt or a pair of shoes as an attempt to equalize, the first child is offended. "But I was *invited* to go to Florida, I should still get new shoes," goes the argument. Parent logic has it differently. We add in unequal units and do it over the years. But it never comes out equal to them. The best we can do is pass on to them John Kennedy's reminder, "No one ever said life is fair." But we must endlessly explain our logic to our children. "You received this special event in your life [ballet lessons, splash party], so later, at the right moment, your sister will get something special."

Just as children are quick to point out inequalities in our treatment of them, they keep track of our violations of parental morality. They are their own legion of decency and the economy-sized arbiters of justice.

We took our children to see the movie *Hair*. The music was still vivid (although we had forgotten such tunes as the one which celebrates masturbation) and we thought they would like the choreography, since we were unable to remember much story line. One daughter sat in shocked disbelief as the hippy band danced on a wedding feast table and discussed the probable parentage of an expected baby. When it came to a nude swim-in in Central Park, she summed up all the indignation possible for twelve years and announced in a loud whisper, "That shouldn't be in a PG-rated movie." Meanwhile, her younger sister giggled all the way through the movie.

Children like nothing better than to find cause to parrot their parents' teachings back to them. In our lives books have high value. Returning books late to the library and incurring a fine or losing them for four months is too frequent an occurrence. As a result, our family is in some constant relationship with the library. Either we wait for a book in high demand, or we are searching for the volume we borrowed but didn't manage to read by the due date. We have nightmares about the house being raided late at night, and amid the red flashing lights and confusion comes the librarian's voice over the bullhorn, "OK, Ryans. We know you are in there. Throw the overdue books out first, and then come out with your hands over your heads." Our friends give and loan us books. The children have been given books for each birthday. One such book, *Rain Makes Applesauce*, was given to one of them by a well-meaning friend. She was even a friend of the library, having purchased this book at a library book sale. The library envelope was still in the book. Children's memories are notoriously short at times. They remember the book, but neither its giver nor the reason for the library envelope and plastic cover. Every so often they look at this book, then eye us accusingly and declare: "You stole this book from a library in California."

Put simply, parents are teachers, and as such they ought to teach as consciously and effectively as possible. There is no doubt, however, that in our society the role of the parent as teacher is shrinking. In earlier times, when such activities as food preparation took great chunks of each day and when getting the laundry clean and dry was a many-stepped operation, a mother spent much time instructing her daughter in how to maintain a home. Fathers did the same for sons, showing them how to farm, carpenter, or run a store. That way of life has largely passed away. Jobs have disappeared or been simplified. Also, schools have taken over in areas such as home economics, drivers' education, and manual auto (shop), which formerly were the province of parents. But while there has been a dramatic decline in the parent passing on skills to children, parents still have a large and crucial role as teachers of value.

As in classroom life, there are two kinds of value teaching that parents engage in: teaching by word and teaching by action. Conventional wisdom has it that teaching by action or example is the more powerful of the two, and we have no reason to dispute this. This view is captured in many folktales and stories, such as the one about the man seeking the secret of life. As he traveled far and wide talking to whomever he thought would have answers, he heard about a wise man living on a peak in Tibet (and as we all know by now, the Tibetan peaks are crawling with gurus and holy men). After weeks and weeks of traveling by land, sea, and air, he reached the top of the mountain. There was the wise man, surrounded by adoring disciples, dressed in silks, being fanned and eating sweetmeats. The traveler told the wise man his purpose, and the wise man immediately began to lecture on the secrets of life. After listening for a few moments, the traveler got up and started to walk away down the mountain. "Why are you leaving?" asked the wise man. The traveler turned and said, "What you are speaks so loudly, I cannot hear what you are saying."

Our children are looking almost unknowingly for the secrets of life, those values that they can admire and that they hope will bring them happiness. As such, children are observing our lives and the others' around them. Almost imperceptibly they will begin to mirror our values. It seems, however, that parents become aware of this system only when it breaks down: such as the very traditional parents whose daughter leaves home to live in a commune; or the son of blue-collar parents who becomes a rabid Republican. We are shocked when children take on values different from our own; we take it for granted that they will have similar attitudes. Just as they copy our speech cadence and our way of approaching a problem situation, we think they will probably copy our values. If we prize loyalty or family peace at all costs, most likely they will, too. It is normally not a matter of conscious decision on their part. They are seeking, and we, people from whom they want approval, are right there. (Of course, the opposite sometimes occurs, where the offspring consciously goes in the opposite direction from the parent.) They come to act like us and to think like us quite naturally. It is a marvelous life-sustaining process when the values are positive ones. The process keeps our society moving forward. However, when parents' actions reflect get-ahead-at-any-cost values or pleasure first last and always, the individual children and the society are in trouble. So the fact that our daily actions speak louder than our words cuts two ways.

The second approach, transmitting values by words, is under a cloud these days. To accuse someone of moralizing is considered a put-down. Behind this distorted criticism is something to the effect that, "Who are you to tell me what I should value?" or to complain, "You may be right, but you certainly are heavy-handed." While these are usually criticisms of form, sometimes the statement means, I disagree with your values or your system of morality. Few, however, would deny the need of the older generation to help the younger generation develop a set of values to guide their lives.

There seem to be three ways we can transmit values by our words: through stories, by questioning the child, and by revealing our own values. The stories that survive, like the "Three Little Pigs" and "Snow White and the Seven Dwarfs," survive because parents feel that they incorporate values they want their children to possess. "Don't be a time waster. Be industrious, and plan ahead like the third little pig." "Be good and virtuous like Snow White, and you will be rewarded in the end. Good triumphs over evil." On the other hand, stories like the German folktales or "Struwwelpeter" by Heinrich Hoffman, have slipped dramatically in popularity. These tales of little girls playing with matches who burn their homes down and in the process immolate themselves, and of bad boys whose fingers are snipped off, are simply too harsh for these times. They project the picture of a crueller world than most of us will accept. Nevertheless, these fairy tales and stories, along with books we put in older children's hands and TV programs and movies we allow them to see, are values carriers. The choices need our attention.

The second approach is through questioning our children about what they value. "What do you want to be when you grow up?" "Who is your best friend? Why?" "If you had been in your teacher's place, what would you have done?" "What do you think would happen if everyone acted as generously as your Uncle Mick?" "Besides being funny, what do you like most about Mork? What can earthlings learn from him?" And so on. Just as important as asking the question is listening to the answer, respecting it, and not using it as a launching pad for one's own views or a little sermonette. We also need to be mindful that this value questioning can of course be overdone to the point that it is counterproductive, to the point where one's kids and spouse are ready to scream. However, done sensibly, it lets children know that you are interested in their views and, more importantly, that they should be thinking about these issues.

The third approach is talking about one's own values, either in response to a child's question or by simply letting him know where you stand. "I realize that it is nice that you were invited to the Redfords' for Thanksgiving, but we are a family. We're together for holidays." "I know we have the oldest, rustiest car on the block. I'd rather spend our money on books and tennis lessons." This does a number of things. It helps the child see past your actions, into the workings of your mind and into your values. It helps children fix you in space. Perhaps most important, it demonstrates that you are a valuing person.

Times of crisis or transition are the obvious ones for clarification of values. There are specific moments when parents feel the need to clarify their own values: when a baby is expected; when the last child enters kindergarten, approaches puberty, or goes to college; when the family moves. These periods trigger thoughts about personal values mainly because the adults have to adjust their relationship with the child. He is no longer the child; he has made the transition. But the major step often is the parent's: letting the baby, teenager, college student move to the next stage until he is autonomous, until he is free of you. The values we pass on to them are a large part of their roots. And with the right values, parents don't have to worry as much about their children.

The values we have taught our children, consciously and unconsciously, are up for the test from one stage to the next. Trusting what has been taught earlier requires parents to exercise restraint. Growth is not linear; the child takes two steps ahead and a step back.

A broken window was spotted near a baseball field. A teacher telephoned the parents of the boy whose name came up. The mother said: "Funny he didn't say anything. Usually if he has done something wrong, he tells me about it."

When the son arrived home that evening, the mother told him of the call. "I was surprised," she said, "not that I didn't think you could break a window, that doesn't surprise me at all. But you didn't say anything about it."

"I didn't want to be responsible," he confessed. Dejectedly he said, "What can I do now?"

"If I were the teacher, I would appreciate a phone call," said the parent. The boy phoned the teacher and apologized. "What did he say?" the parent asked. "He said he appreciated the phone call."

There is one unique and incontrovertible aspect to the parents' role as values transmitters: parents do not have a choice. They can choose whether or not to give their children dancing lessons or a good education. They can decide to raise their children in or out of the church. They can decide to lavish gifts and goods on their children or raise them with few luxuries. They cannot, however, make a choice whether or not to transmit values to their children. Values transmission can be done well or poorly, but it cannot be stopped. It is inevitable. Our only choice is whether or not we will do it well.

We are part of an evolutionary species. We are child, teenager, parent, adult in stages. We are in a dual relationship with our children. We are parent with them in the stages of infancy and youth; we are adult with them as adults.

The two of us are only halfway through this process with our children. The other half is still to come before we know what kind of product we have turned out. From birth the process of independence grows. In the normal course of events, a sense of self begins to emerge at about three months. The infant shows he is reacting to specific events or faces; he smiles or cries. He distinguishes between mother and the rest of the world very early. At age one and a half, the growth process accelerates away from mother. It's a fascinating world; there are so many things to see and touch and know, other than mother. The self is becoming more and more conscious.

The need to feel basic trust in life is essential for babies as well as for adults. The first demonstration of social trust in the baby is the ease of feeling, the depth of sleep, the relaxation of bowels. The child has begun to trust his mother, to relax; he doesn't have to keep awake to be sure she won't go away. "The infant's first social movement, then, is his willingness to let mother out of sight without undue anxiety or rage, because she has become an inner certainty," writes Erik Erikson.

From this stage of infancy/dependence, our children develop a symbiotic nature. But this symbiosis is a mutual relationship, as the parent shares mutual attachment to the child. The welfare and integrity of one person becomes tied up with the welfare of another. We become interdependent with our children and involved in their ego development.

We don't know, of course, how to tell when one stage of life ends and another begins. We seem to be constantly dealing with past responses. Even when our children are in sight and underfoot or on our minds, we are always behind them. Even as we look at them, our psychological view is made up of what they were, not who and what they are at this moment. As a result, they are a continual surprise. Just when we think we have a hold on the preschooler, she is off to her ballet lessons. You expect them to stagger toward you, and they cartwheel away. You think they have simply been consuming carbohydrates and vegetating, and suddenly they come out with some sophisticated observation about human nature. They are packing their belongings for an overnight, when they become young women.

Teenage years are eruptions. The symbiosis of infancy and lower school is strained by the trial independence of the teens.

Teenagers dent the car, they wear their hair in lengths and in fashions we don't like; they ignore our warnings about the crowd they hang out with.

Watching these parent-teenager struggles, we get the feeling of predictable biological events at work. It is as if some children and parents cannot separate, that the children cannot become full adults, without this painful tearing away. Other children, even in the same family, appear to gently, quietly become independent. It would be easy to say that the harsh and combative separation is bad and has A and B ill effects, and that the smooth separation is good and has X and Y positive effects. But we don't know this, either from reading or from personal observation. Nor do we have much in the way of advice for ourselves or others about dealing with the traumas of teenage rebellion and separation. It does seem, however, that the long view is important here. There should be no unforgivable sins. The prodigal son (and daughter) should always have buried in their minds that the father (and mother) are waiting to put on a banquet on their return.

One day they leave home for good. They are independent of their parents, but we parents are still responding to the past. We often act as though our children can't negotiate their own lives. But now the parent must trust in the job he has done. He must let the child be the adult.

At the time the son or daughter leaves home, the parent does not cease to be parent. But it is time to trust in the civilizing of the child. The parent is no longer needed as a corrective, a disciplinarian, an advice giver. The son or daughter on his own wants support, but not advice. If he wants advice, he asks for it. As the Beatles told us, it is a long and winding road to adulthood. But once our children are there, we should follow more of their advice and let it be.

Trade Secrets

Shortly after the birth of our first, we took her to be inspected by her maternal grandparents. She passed. At one point during the inspection visit, her grandfather got a very different look in his eye and quietly said, "Enjoy it. It goes very fast." We didn't appreciate it then, but now that our first is fourteen, his advice and warning have particular urgency for us. They are babies and toddlers and kids and teenagers for a brief time. Children are so ever present during the early years that we are lured into thinking they will always be with us. "We'll read that story together next week." "Not now, but one of these days Daddy's going to take you along on one of his trips." "As soon as this rush at work calms down, you and I and the children should start spending more time together." "My mother taught me how to bake. One of these days I ought to teach Michele." It must be very painful to have an emptied house and few memories.

More important than our memories are the irretrievable moments in the lives of children. They need us during most of their youth, and they need a different quality of guidance from us at different moments and different stages. Psychologists have long pointed out the importance of childhood to satisfactory adult development. But where do we learn to be present for our children? And where do we learn the tricks of the parenting trade? Social engineers have been lamenting for years that anyone can become a parent and permanently maim several children. And, they argue, if we license possession of guns and control of an automobile, why not license parenting? Along with these views is often a scheme to make the individual seeking a parent license go to school, take a special course, and pass a minimum-competency parenting test. The difficulty of implementing such a plan is relieved only by the potential humor from such a scheme: You are in the bathroom trying to take a bath and/or shower. Your three-year-old toddles into the bathroom and stares wide-eyed at your private parts. You should:

A. Plunge into the tub and/or shower as quickly as possible.

B. Forget the bath and/or shower and sit down, taking this as a clear sign that your child wants to know about sexual intercourse.

C.   Tell the child in a very firm voice, "Bug off."

D.   Forget the shower, cover up your "nasty bits," and call a child psychologist.

E.   Do A, C, and D, above.

While we would deplore the idea of the state issuing parent licenses, we are quick to admit that when our child was born, we weren't ready. We had a great deal to learn and unlearn. Books and magazine articles have been important and helpful to our learning, but not nearly as important as our friends and relatives. They have been for us a source of what might be called Trade Secrets. Some of these trade secrets we have incorporated successfully into the flux and flow of our family. We have tried to adopt others, but they never took. They seem to be out of sync with the particular rhythm of our family. We value them. We would like to do them, but we simply cannot.

Escapes from the Ordinary

A Chicago couple we know, whose girls are launched into the world and who are clearly works of love and art, once said to us that when their girls were young the family knew every swimming hole in the fifty miles of Northampton, Massachusetts (their home then). That casual comment, made with satisfaction, has been a very evocative one for us: the family scooping up towels and bathing suits and heading for the car; the drives to find a new lake; the swims and toweling off in the late-afternoon sun. But more than that, the wonderful separation of it; getting away from the phone, the television, the neighbors—big and small; getting away from the routine of the house, those crushing patterns that keep us bound up in the everyday.

These swimming hole explorations are the kinds of inventions a family needs to escape from the imprisoning isolation of the ordinary. What is at the core is the family adventuring together, doing something together that all enjoy. It could be cross-country skiing, or playing music together, or picking blackberries, or collecting seashells. On the one hand, it is a sense of specialness, of being something that *our* family does, that is important. On the other hand, it is the feelings of acceptance, of anticipation, of shared concern that count. It may seem odd to suggest that parents and children need to go on an adventure to find one another, but it works.

Getting in Touch with the Family History

We have another friend from Chicago, a carpenter, who anticipated the roller-skating rage by forty years. His family ritual was a trip with wife, daughter, and son to the roller rink. In the mid-sixties, he changed this, though. It was the time of the sit-ins and freedom marches in the South. Although having lived as a black all his life in the Chicago area, Tom sensed early that something very special was happening in the small southern cities, Selma, Birmingham, and the others. He knew, too, that he could help—not as an organizer or negotiator, but as what he was, a carpenter. So every other Thursday night or so he filled his car with blankets, sandwiches, and coffee and headed south for the Mississippi Delta to spend the weekend constructing sleeping quarters for this group of marchers or putting up latrines for that outdoor meeting. It was both unglamorous and dangerous, driving those long miles into small hostile towns. Often Tom brought his son Michael, who at the time was in the middle elementary grades. When it came out in conversation that Michael had been going along on these trips, we asked him why in the world he would risk it. He said simply, "That's Michael's history. I want him to be part of it. I want him to know his father was part of it, too."

Tom was, of course, showing his son during these moments—and, more to the point, for the rest of his son's life—what his father believed in. What we learned was the need to weave a child into his history. So many forces in our lives try to make us all the same. Television and the other mass media want and, in turn, create a common consumer audience. They do not want to develop programs for people who see themselves as romantic Irish-Americans or Kentucky mountaineers or German-American farmers. The communications industry, plus the schools, are busy making us one people with one national culture. Although there are advantages and merits to this plan, it denies the fact of who we are as individuals and as a nation. It is left to parents to tell the child more personally and precisely who he is, whose blood is running in his veins, and what stories he is a part of. "Little House on the Prairie" and junior-year American History won't do it. We need to share our own family stories and to find ways of showing our children who they are.

Controlling Television

We have some friends from the period shortly after we were married. Both couples have worked hard to maintain our friendship, which for most of these years has been at long distance. Recently we have been living about two hundred miles away from one another, and we usually come together twice a year. Both couples have children about the same age who have become friends, so when we get together, everyone has a companion.

One striking difference about their home and consequently their family life is the absence of the television. As long as we have known them, they have never owned a set. On the other hand, the family has many games. Instead of watching the tube, the parents and children play together or pursue some private activity like the piano or reading. The children, poor, deprived souls, are growing up without intimacy with the Fonz or with Charlie's pneumatic Angels. The family is being deprived of in-depth discussions of, "I always watch your programs and you never watch mine." Their children are growing up without a sense of the language. They fail to link words like heartbreak with psoriasis, champions with a cereal, and be sure of yourself with being well deodorized.

On the other hand, these children know their parents well, they know how to play, and they can entertain and educate themselves.

We, like many parents, know the anguish over our children's use of television. There is something very unsettling about how long they can be motionless, transfixed by the glowing tube. They seem like large zucchinis baking in the light of the sun and growing in unknown ways. Although we have always acted as content censors, only in recent years have we tried to limit television to one hour a day during the week. That seems to work well and gives us time in the evening for long talky dinners and sometimes games. It is a little upsetting, though, to realize your daughter is throwing the backgammon game because she has a date at eight with Mork.

KEVIN:

The Family Talent Hunt. The idea of children performing for their parents and one another has taken root in some of the families we know. They set aside evenings for family entertainment, a large part of which is the performance of children. There are many different and competing reasons, besides the rarely acknowledged hope we all have that from our loins another Shirley Temple will bloom. Some of them are negative reasons, reflecting the limited opportunities children have to stand on their feet and speak before others. The recitation method, which hauled many of us to our feet to bear the scrutiny of our fellows and teachers, has all but passed from our schools. On the other hand, television brings to our living rooms a continuing stream of highly polished performers. A generation ago when families had to create their own entertainment, it was not uncommon for children to be called into the living room to play their latest piano piece or recite "Twas the Night Before Christmas" or some other seasoned work before dinner guests and other visitors. While these classroom and living room practices may have left the occasional scar on our psyches, many of us value what was learned from the experience. For one thing, children develop a sense of presence on their feet, of it being natural to stand up and to speak before others. For another, children learn standards. They come to know how hard it is to play a piece flawlessly or get through a demanding recitation without a flub. They learn how far they have come and how far they have to go.

Finally, these performances bring the isolated members of the house together for an event of their own imagination and making. These in turn become part of the tapestry of their family. "Do you remember the time Dougie recited 'Twas the Night Before Christmas' in front of the entire family—the whole crowd, aunts, cousins, grandparents, the works—and he was only four years old!" "Once when the girls were young, they put on a skit for the Barkers and us. It was so hysterically funny Mrs. Barker actually wet her pants!" Ah, the stuff of family history.

Telling the Family Story

Both of us have old snapshots at home of our childhood: a girl, dressed in Sunday clothes, smiling in front of a farmhouse; an eight-year-old boy with a bat in hand, crouched in a slugger's stance for the camera. There are pictures, too, of young married couples, our parents, on the beach and at picnics. While we cherish these pictures and only wish there were more, they leave us with many questions: Who are those people—really? What was that little girl like? What sorts of things were happening in her world? What dreams were running through that boy's head? And those people who became Mom and Dad, what were they like at the time? What was happening to them and what were they thinking? Who are these people?

We want to know because of our own curiosity, but also, as we've said, we want to get our children in touch with their own stories, instead of those provided by ABC, NBC, and

CBS. To recapture our histories, we have used these approaches: tape recording, photographs, and letters.

Some of the most fascinating times we have spent with our parents have been our recorded interviews. While everyone was initially self-conscious when we brought out the tape recorder and plunked it down in the middle of the table, that didn't last long. Once one of our parents got engrossed in the story of how he and Machine Gun Jeanie (an aunt noted for her rapid staccato speech, not her Mafia connections) went off to school in New York City in trolley cars. Awareness of the tape recorder all but disappeared, except for the punctuation in the conversation brought on by the need to change the cassettes. Stories we had never heard were resurrected; details and names were added to familiar stories. Fragments of stories that we had heard over the years were ordered and put into perspective for us. These hours were precious in themselves, to say nothing of the fact that we have them on tape. And they make for much richer family get-togethers than those dominated by some dreary Banana Bowl Game and the accompanying holiday fare of commercials.

What Kodak Never Tells You

We take pictures, too. Our enthusiasm is somewhat tempered, though. We try to take stills of special events, like birthday parties, Christmas, visits from old friends, dance recitals, and the odd picnic or cross-country skiing outing. And we cherish our pictures, ordering and preserving them in albums. Pictures freeze a moment in time and space, but they can also hold feeling and return memories to us like old songs. We love them, but we've paid the price, and not just the cost of camera, film, flash bulbs, developing, prints, enlargements, frames, and albums. Those costs are real and growing daily. There are other costs, like the interruption of an event itself to capture a slice of it on film. The spontaneity is squelched as the photographer rearranges the principals, too many of whom are now more accurately called actors. Getting the scene set. The lights right. Getting Marybeth to stop looking like a manic-depressive and Timmy from looking like Howdy Doody. Finally, the perfect moment, and then the baby spits up. Or you are sure people blinked. Then, tired of family pictures of what seems to be a one-parent family, you turn camera over to some seemingly rational person, only to have your capacity as a judge of human nature brought severely into question. "Dad, why did Uncle Bob take all those pictures of us with the lens cap on? Huh, Daddy, why?" "I appreciate the fact that you like candid shots, but why did you take four while we were all straightening ourselves up and I was busy zipping up John's fly?" "Oh, now really, stop crying. Accidents will happen. Anyway, you didn't mean to drop it." Then there are disappointments when the pictures return. In all the pictures of your mother-in-law you have cut her feet off, and she can't believe it was unintentional. You shoot a whole roll at your son's birthday party, and he's only in two; one from the back and the other where he looks like a complete nerd. But there are more mistakes: those once-in-a-lifetime affairs. It's a perfect day for your daughter's First Communion, and you have a special brunch for the family. You shoot two rolls, send them off to be developed, and when they come back blank, you discover your light meter is broken. . . . You want to cry, but you are too busy figuring out how you are going to break the news to the family. Photographs can break your heart in more ways than one.

Letters for Tomorrow

Writing letters to one's infant children who are often a few feet away as you write may strike some as slightly bizarre. We started doing it, though, on an impulse. When we discovered that we were to have a baby, we just wanted to share the moment and its special meanings with what turned out to be a "her." The same was true when the baby was born. We wanted Hilary to know what was going on in the world when she came into it. We wanted her to know her parents' hopes and fears for her, and something of our lives. We wanted her to know that the country was involved in the Vietnam War and a civil rights struggle, and where we stood and what we were doing about it. We wanted her to know our special joy at her entrance into the world. When her first birthday came along, we wanted to tell her about it; what she could do as a one-year-old and the highlights of her first year. From then on we've been hooked. When the other children came along, it seemed like the natural thing to do. What it means is that on the children's birthday (give or take six weeks!) we sit down and have an adult conversation with—or, more accurately, send a yearly report to—our child. It takes about an hour per year per child, and then we file the letters away to be delivered to them on their twenty-first birthday. The letters are intimate and honest and probably wouldn't be of interest to them until they are adults. Never having heard of anyone else with this idea (although we are sure that others do it, or something like it), we have no idea how it will be received. But independent of that, it seems a good idea for us. It forces us to think through where we perceive our children are, where we are, and where we are going. In a way these letters are our yearly review and explanation of how we are and where they are.

On Being Available

Max Lerner, the political commentator, said once that he felt he had very good communication with his teenagers and college-age children. When pressed by the audience as to just how he was able to accomplish this, he responded, "I use the late-night refrigerator method." Lerner went on with something like the following: "It is very difficult to have a private or very sustained conversation during the day with the young people in my home. So I make sure I'm up and near the refrigerator on weekend nights when my children come home from movies or dates. Whatever, eleven, twelve, one or two in the morning, they head for the kitchen and I manage to be there. We do our serious talking over milk and cookies or

scrambled eggs and coffee." The Lerner approach demonstrates for us the two ingredients for successful parenting in
the last fifth of the twentieth century: imagination and time.
We need our imagination to break through the canned and
planned childhood worlds of television and school. We need
all the imagination we can muster to make sure we really
encounter our children and make sure they encounter us. We
need our imagination to seize the everyday aspects of life with
children and turn them into family picnics.

Time is increasingly viewed as a commodity that is in short
supply. Few of the people we encounter have any sense of
time lying on their hands. This is certainly true for us. The
problem is one of options. What will I do with these few
hours? Read a book; watch television; make love; go to the
gym; get to some household tasks; get a start on our tax report;
garden; run; dance; shop; or just putter. Even the choosing
takes up much time! It is as if the major business in our
modern society is selling us ways to spend our free time.
Advertisers and others are trying to sell us on this option or
that, so that we are in a state of tension described by Alvin
Toffler as "overchoice." While this probably beats lying
around in a damp sod hut staring at a peat fire, it may have
some derogatory consequences for parenting. Giving time to
our children may not seem as satisfying an option as many of
the others out there. While certainly not the entire cause in
itself, it is probably a contributing reason why many married
people are not having children. This concern for time also
affects how parents live with their children. In a free-time
world of attractive options, putting down an engrossing novel
and peeling our children from the television for a long walk
may not seem very attractive. When one is tired from a long
day of work and when you have fed, clothed, and provided
safe, warm shelter for your children, it is hard to get out of the
easy chair and give your cherished free time to the kids. The
only problem is that you cannot do the job without giving the
time. If we want to be well read, we must read. If we want to
be good at golf, we must play the game. The same with

parenting. We must give time to it, and while there is a great deal of routine nose-wiping time involved, some of the parenting time is the best time of our lives.

Growing and Parenting

Much of what we know about parenting has been learned from friends, books, and to some degree course work. There is valuable information and insight out there in the general culture, and we have a sense of security knowing the information is there and available to us. We have also found however, that much of what we have learned has come from on-the-job training. Much of this knowledge is unique, resulting from the interplay of our own personalities and clusters of strengths and weaknesses. Often these private learnings force us to reassess our views.

MARILYN:

The marriage bed separates children from adults. It is the most significant graduation into adulthood; more of a change than reaching eighteen or twenty-one or being able to vote and drink. At the same time, this transition is often the least discussed aspect of adulthood. As the mother and daughter prepare for the wedding day, they spend their words on the choice of china and crystal, on linen supplies and the management of home and work, but they rarely discuss sex or childbearing.

My Mother, Myself (which made best-seller lists for a considerable time) developed the thesis that mothers are incapable of acknowledging sexuality in themselves or their daughters. Therefore, they don't communicate about a major part of adult life. Sex, while it may not be the only part of adult life, is a very important part. Without good sex, the marriage may crack; without good sex, one of the chief pleasures of being married is lost.

To be sure, a few mothers discuss sex with their daughters. Some simply trot their daughters off to the gynecologist for birth control pills before marriage or an affair. But those are few. Most mothers don't engage the issue. Even those who deal with sex openly frequently fail to deal with the next stages of sexuality: childbirth and child bearing. Remarkable as it seems, many parents never discuss many passages in life with their children. As a result, young girls think the best years are the ones in school, and that life is over after high school or college. I had some clue to this line of thinking when I reflected on my daugther's comment after I had dressed carefully to go out for an evening.

"Gee, Mom, you look nice. You don't look pregnant or married or anything."

"Ah, yes," I said to myself, "the old life-is-over-when-you-get-married syndrome." I had experienced it myself. I have occasionally given in to the thought that my life was at its prime when I was a teenager. Only now do I prefer not to relive the teenage years and instead prefer life on the other side of thirty. The nice part was to discover that life was only really beginning when I married Kevin. But I thought life had improved. Moms have more fun now. The Moms I know and admire take good care of themselves; they go back to school or careers; they ride horses and play tennis; they buy clothes and calculators; they have jobs and give parties; they devote themselves energetically, often passionately, to causes. It didn't seem such a bad life. Besides, it seemed a lot more fun than turning out for sixth-grade basketball, visiting the orthodontist, and spending Friday nights watching "The Incredible Hulk."

This same daughter has peeked at the other side of life. When I brought home a tiny pink and blue bundle in the form of a baby brother, she whispered, her brown eyes wide, "Oh, Mommy, you're so lucky to have a baby."

KEVIN:

People say that with marriage comes a loss of innocence. I don't know about that, but I do know that becoming a parent means the loss of ideology. Before I became a father, I was quite confident that I knew how to raise children. I was a psychology major in college, had been a teacher, and done graduate work in education. I was familiar with the major theoretical approaches to child raising. I was quite enamored with B. F. Skinner's views, alternately called behavior modification or behavior analysis. This view advocated finding what the child experienced as pleasurable or reinforcing, and then reinforcing those actions or behavior which you decided were desirable. It was to work very simply. For instance, when the baby cried for no legitimate reason such as hunger or a jabbing safety pin, he should not be picked up until he stopped (not crying being a desired behavior). Once he stopped, you picked him up and cuddled him (a presumed reinforcement). If he were foolish enough to cry while being cuddled, he was plopped back in the crib (withdrawal of reinforcement). The same procedure applied to a whole range of negative behavior such as punching, throwing Jello from a high chair to the floor, playing with sharp objects, not doing homework or cutting the grass, and dating career surfers.

My efforts to successfully apply this theory to the raising of my first two children, two girls, have been roaring failures. The girls seem OK, but, as suggested earlier, I have no solid sense of their real state. However, my confidence in the theories, particularly behaviorism, has been shattered little by little. There was one bright and shining moment for behaviorism when our first child was four and hard set on her thumb. Having heard unsettling stories about the high cost of orthodontists—"It's college education or braces, parents, take your pick," rumors which I discovered six years later were only slightly exaggerated—I was eager to have Hilary stop sucking her thumb and thus moving those tender teeth around as if they were so many loose pieces of Chiclets. In a flash of insight, the solution came. I quickly hustled her down to a candy store—an illicit palace whose existence we were trying to keep hidden—and took her to the lollipop counter. Although we had been trying to keep the existence of candy a secret, she knew she was looking out at the world's true riches. Seizing this moment of near ecstasy, I said something on the order of, "All this will be yours, if you keep that dirty thumb out of your mouth." I told her that if she promised not to suck her thumb, I would let her pick out thirty lollipops, and she could have one after dinner every night if she hadn't sucked her thumb that day. Although I knew she was hooked, I wanted some backup insurance. After she had picked out the lollipops, I took her to a special display of giant rainbow-colored lollipops, some clearly larger than her head. I told her that if she stopped sucking her thumb completely, she could have whichever of these lollipops she wanted. She could choose it now, take it with her, and have it (at this point she almost swooned) when she had finally stopped sucking her thumb. She chose the biggest and the brightest, and with the thirty smaller lollipops (all totaling $2.50), we made our way home. I tacked the giant lollipop high (out of reach—a saint she wasn't) on the kitchen wall, but in a most conspicuous place. Well, it worked. Except for one day of backsliding (and, thus, no lollipop that night), she has never sucked her thumb. Even this victory of application has been diminished over time. For one thing, my daughter has become a candy junkie, and for another, when her second teeth did come in, we had her wired up and gave up thoughts of financial solvency.

And that's the way it has been for us. Many theories and approaches—such as parent effectiveness training, cognitive developmental views of childhood, Haim Ginott's approach—exist, but they have limited utility. For one thing, most theories of behavior contain some truth but cannot explain all behavior. They are partial truths, and when applied, their limitations really show up. For another, the kids, even very young ones, learn the theories fast. They learn the rules of application and learn how to subvert the system in their favor. There is a special sting to having your five-year-old say to you, "What I hear you saying is that you want me to go to bed now, so you can have the TV to watch 'Masterpiece Theatre.'" Or, "It makes me feel angry when you give me gunkie lima beans three days in a row." All of which leaves parents with few theoretical lighthouses on the stormy seas of parenting.

The Drip-Drip Approach

We find ourselves, then, with no great illuminating theory or map to guide our parenting voyage. However, we do have something of a theoretical lighthouse to help us keep our bearings when the trip gets especially rough. Our theory—and it is a low-level theory at best—is the drip-drip-drip Chinese-water-torture approach to child raising. Behind the theory stands the view that civilizing a child is very tough and draining work which yields to no quick and dirty solutions. It also takes the better part of two decades before you can step back and say, "Well, that's all I can do with that one." In brief, the role of parent-torturer in the drip-drip-drip approach is to hang in there and outlast them. In the parlance of boxing, it means being a jabber, a counterpuncher, someone not looking for the big knockout but someone trying to wear down his opponent by never letting up.

The parent drip-drip approach has its own famous slogans. Most parents know them by memory—from our own minds or lips.

"Parents are people, too!"

"Don't spit milk back into the glass!"

"I've told you a hundred times to hang up your pj's. Here goes a hundred and one."

"Do not—repeat do not—refer to your brother as a turd."

"When was the last time you held a toothbrush?"

"I know it's your favorite shirt, but twelve days in a row is enough already."

"Con Edison is not our family charity. Turn out the lights when you leave a room."

"Don't store half-eaten sandwiches under the bed."

"Now I know why makeup is called grease paint; take some of it off."

"Just what crop are you growing for the Jolly Green Giant under those fingernails?"

"You don't have to tell the man on the phone just exactly what Daddy is doing!"

"No, thanks, I don't particularly care for ice cream soup."

"Just because it's green is no reason why you can't just try eating it once."

"If you can drown in a thimbleful of water, why does it take you *forty-four gallons to take a bath?*"

"I don't know why God made your little sister. Maybe he has a sense of humor."

"No, I can't package your dinner for the 'starving children in Africa.'"

"Now that you have a thousand-dollar smile, why do you hook your lip that way?"

"Even with X-ray vision, Superman, you can't see the vitamins in your beans."

"Because I said so."

If this approach seems harsh and oppressive, so be it. Most serious historians acknowledge that civilization as we know it came into being and continues thanks to the unrelenting and heroic efforts of picky parents.

Children enter and leave our lives, the products of our genetic and moral codes and our particular brand of behavioral psychology. Sometimes we are pleased with the results of our training (drip-drip or whatever), and sometimes we are discouraged and disappointed. But we assume the responsibility for the product: we don't say "the schools ruined him" or "his friends tore him away from us": we usually blame ourselves for the negative qualities and seldom take due pride in the good things in his development.

Rearing children is the most significant task most of us will ever tackle. It's more difficult than running a business, teaching a class, identifying bacteria, or suturing a wound. Shaping another life has us so frightened and involved that we sometimes continue the job long after we should have transferred the responsibility to the person himself.

We witness both pleasure and pain as our children go through the stages from infancy to adulthood. While there is an interdependence as long as both parent and child live, the relationship is more intense at certain stages. We experience symbiotic bonding with our infants. They need their parents for the fundamentals of life itself; later they need their parents for advice and support. Bonding is based on need. The one who needs us commands our commitment. The infant learns to trust the world through his parents.

The period of dependency of the infant gives way to physical and emotional development away from Mother and Daddy. Brothers and sisters become more important; later, playmates and best friends and teen groups take over much of our child's attention. Mom and Dad let go little by little.

For some parents the exodus of the child—now young adult—causes anxiety. The product we've been molding for so many seasons—we are so proud of—always needs a few more touches. We would like to add or correct a few more things: a habit of being late or failing to communicate by wire or mail; being sloppy about clothes or spending too much money. He is our child, he is terrific—but he is not quite finished. A lawyer we knew said he had set up a trust fund for his son to use as an adult. The father kept changing the time for release of the funds from eighteen years, to twenty-one years, to twenty-five years. The father said the son would get the money when he was grown up, "if that ever happens."

The process of becoming a grown-up, of course, takes more than eighteen or twenty-one years. It sometimes takes half a century. The parents must exercise restraint. They must trust that their job is done. They are needed, surely, but mainly for support and confidence building. If the drip-drip method (or whatever) hasn't left its mark by then, it is too late. From the teachings of home, the child is now left to learn by going on his own pilgrimage.

A good friend of ours has a poster in his office that summarizes all this: "The best things parents can give children are roots and wings."

6

Great Families,
Good Friends

Our beginning and our end involve family. Our inheritance, both physical and material, comes from generations of a bloodline. The blood relationship is said to be stronger than the ties with friends, or even marriage partners. Families you always have with you; your friends change and go away. At the heart of our lives, what we believe and value comes from our family. What we pass along to our progeny is born of our tradition.

Generations of families worked at the upbringing and survival of our ancestors; they, in turn, worked at ours. Somewhere along the way we came upon the idea that civilization rested upon the institution called "the family." That is, each generation would be civilized and trained into proper young men and women by conditioning within the confines of two parents and a split-level dwelling. As a result of this idea, the major chore of the parents of *our* era, once they decided to take on that function in their marriage, was to calmly and rationally cajole offspring into unnatural habits that conformed to some adult standard of behavior. Manners, thoughtfulness, generosity, and a litany of other virtues would be learned within the domicile—just the way we became the way we are. What worked pretty well for centuries was based upon an extended family; that is, there were more than two people to carry out the training. Gradually relatives became more distant. Then suddenly a whole generation blamed their parents for what they personally found lacking in themselves once they began to visit a psychiatrist twice a week. A reversal had taken place: instead of the training ground to be adults, the home became a place of oppression, criticism, and over-dominance. The family became the focus of heavy attack from left and right. Everyone wanted to tell people what to do with their families. Subject to continuous cross fire from the radical and the righteous, beset by snipers from alternative life-styles, infiltrated by government agents (disguised as social workers), and threatened by insurrection from within, the nuclear family seemed to many to be on its last launching pad.

A clear case of "damned if you do and damned if you don't" appeared on the horizon. "The death of the family" has been pronounced with satisfaction by psychiatrists such as David Cooper, whose book argues that the conventional family destroys initiative, stifles personal growth, and tramples upon solitude. R. D. Laing holds the view that schizophrenia—insanity, to the layman—is typically the product of a family plot against its most troublesome or vulnerable member. ("One against all and all against one.") Further, sociologist Richard Sennett berates the family as a trap which effectively seals off its members from vital relationships with the outside world. From the other line of attack, there are social scientists who blame the family for abandoning its traditional authority through a kind of permissive default to outside "peer groups," mass media, and assorted social agencies. André Malraux claimed, "The denial of the supreme importance of the mind's development accounts for many revolts against the family." Perhaps that explains the criticism of the family in recent years.

If civilization is hedging its future on the products of the household, some of us are gambling in the market. Many of us involved in raising young children would be hard pressed to claim that family was the root of civilization. The family dinner, to be sure, is reminiscent of King Henry tossing bones under the table for his dogs. Brawling, scrapping, boisterous exchanges are more common than most of us care to admit. Perhaps civilization was never promoted at the dinner table. The plate of butter that ends up shattered on the floor and the second glass of spilt milk in one meal are usually enough to fray tempers. The daily green-things debate (for those who have color-coded foods they won't eat) erodes the determination to have "civilized conversation" with the children. Then there is the shattered *House Beautiful* image that goes with unmade beds, warm-up suits, and old socks stuffed under the unmade bed. What civilization was ever known to feed itself on anything with peanut butter, or spend its gold on boxes of peanut clusters so Disco Blue Birds could go to the zoo? What barbarism there is in being told that one child would rather live with the dynasty next door because their mom and dad don't fight, immediately after staging a siege with her sister. Everyone knows civilized is whatever the seventh graders are doing, or rather, what they are wearing: docksiders, designer jeans, eye makeup.

What are the accoutrements of this civilization? Curling irons, record albums, computerized games, and food processors. But this look at contemporary society is superficial. Underneath the circle pins and jogging shoes, we find the real family artifacts: baby books, scrapbooks, silver cups, ceramic pots from second-grade art class, puzzles with missing pieces, and photos from birthdays and christenings.

Like it or not, we are all products of a family. We have no choice. Our own set of social concerns are bound up with family life. Sometimes we have more family than we want or less than we hoped for, but they are part of us from infancy to old age. Those who would bear the bumper sticker "Nuke the Family" (it doesn't exist so far as we know) may have had enough of the nuclear family, or may even choose to stay clear of it, but they are still part of a clan. We are all part of a clan, and we all need one because we are human. We didn't come from nowhere. We aren't formed from Adam's rib.

Even if we live alone, even if our solitude is chosen and ebullient, we still cannot do without a clan. We are taught what Malraux said on another occasion: "Without a family, man, alone in the world, trembles with the cold."

We are born of a tribe. From a distillation of emotional and physical characteristics, we bear resemblance to our forebears. We carry a genetic code; we are the product of a biological drive that may or may not have desired our presence. Usually, though, we were welcomed with joy and expectation into our clan. We are told we reminded an uncle of our maternal grandmother with our fair hair, or we looked like Uncle John or have a sense of whimsy like Aunt Susie. Our family pulls at us, keeping us close when we stray; we probably become more like them as we grow older.

Marriage signals a new constellation of family clusters. A new branch is added to the family tree. We are paid the supreme compliment when we are asked to "meet the family" and then join the family. The marriage itself becomes the merger of two families, and therefore it is sometimes disappointing for a young couple to realize that the wedding is not their private and personal ceremony so much as a family event. The wedding party is for the family. It is the meeting and mating of two families and the chance for each clan to celebrate its wholeness.

There are tides, high and low, in the tribal life of most of us. There are pleasant childhood memories of Thanksgiving gatherings when everyone debated the choice of a vice-presidential candidate or the Middle East situation. There are family feuds that sometimes go on for years over obscure differences and long-forgotten details of a hurt. For most of us a family is a network of aunts and uncles, some honorary ones; godparents and grandparents who wrote in our baby books and witnessed our graduations and our weddings. They waved to us from parade routes and took to the bleachers when we played on the football team; they read our student columns written for the local paper; gave us books they thought we should read; worried when we put on weight or when we were too thin. They drove great distances to trot their fifty-year-and-over legs around baseball diamonds for family reunions or to watch one of us play a tournament.

They lent their opinions, whether we asked for them or not. They surveyed the current stock of boyfriends hanging around or the likelihood of our being elected to student-body office; they treated us to ice cream or wisdom; they invited us to stay with our cousins so we could see what their school days and friends were like; they were always there for Sunday dinners. They told our parents of their fears for us if we went with a certain crowd or if we traveled far away. They let us know if they didn't agree with our eating habits and our politics. And they ask for us and our well-being all the days of their lives.

It has been said that a friend loves you for your intelligence, a mistress for your charm, but your family's love is unreasoning: you were born into it.

Marital Health

Somewhere we read a psychological theory that claims that the happy moments of childhood act to support mental health in adult life. The function of the family, then, should be to supply the child with a storehouse of happy memories with which to do battle in later life. Surely this or some other theory is needed to explain the energy and imagination mothers devote to the yearly creation of a family Christmas: the months of ferreting out what each child needs and wants, tracking the items down through canyons of department stores, dragging them home, wrapping them, and then having to come up with a safe hiding place. It must be this same hidden drive that has fathers working overtime at Christmas and up late on Christmas Eve to assemble tricycles and dollhouses.

Besides those special moments of birthdays and holidays that we store up, there are the regularities and rituals that can add to our emotional attics.

KEVIN:

Whenever I think of my family of birth, some part of my mind touches on Sunday-night dinners. Monday through Friday nights we had sit-down dinners with my father's talk of business predominating, and school coming up as a distant and somewhat unpleasant second. I cannot remember Saturday-night dinner. It was probably an informal, everyone-fend-for-themselves affair. But Sunday night was different. It was open and free and filled with laughter. It was the night of the family stories—about Aunt Jean (Machine Gun Jeanie) and the time she tried to reform the boys when our parents went on a week's vacation and she stayed with us. Or my mother would tell tales of her girlhood at school with Angela Quinn, her best friend and my godmother. Or Dad, who had begun working at sixteen for two eccentric antique dealers and years later bought their business, would recount tales of his adventures with these elderly oddballs. My older sister was a great laugher, and once she got started she often lost control and had to run out of the room to regain her composure. My older brother was the undisputed family wit, and he would be the unofficial master of ceremonies on Sunday night, calling up the stories and linking one to the other, adding detail here and there, gently nudging a newcomer into the spirit of things.

Sunday-night dinner always had extra plates for friends, relatives, and the latest romance. Mickey Gibbs, Mary Ellen McLaughlin, Gene Doherty, Ray O'Hara—just the names bring back waves of memories. Sunday night was the time to pass our "latest" by the family for inspection. The others of us, of course, took full advantage of these occasions, pulling out pictures of the brother or sister with other romances, or of our sister when she ballooned up thirty pounds over her normal weight. Or telling the date, "Gee, you have hair just like Jane Marr [our older brother's ex-girl]." Or seeing how many times we could weave the name "Jane" into the evening's conversation. The humor was often broad and, when tried by us little ones, not very skillful. No one seemed to mind, though.

Then there were the practical jokes, usually reserved for newcomers. A rather ghoulish favorite was a grotesque plastic finger (rather, half a finger) that was very lifelike and always seemed to end up in the fruit cup of the guest. Once when we tried this on a newly ordained and very earnest young priest, his first words—after he got his dinner under control—were to speculate what the Church's Canon Law would dictate. Should the finger be given a Christian burial on the possibility that, one, the owner was a Christian; and two, was dead? He was so engrossed in the theological niceties that we dared not let him in on the joke. But, oh, those Sunday dinners. Sometimes we could hardly eat, our sides ached so much from laughing. To say the word "family" is to hear the laughter again and feel the warm joy of it.

Some athletes run miles or hit millions of balls before they realize they were living out family goals. They wanted to be good for their families. Chris Evert Lloyd confessed it took years to realize that she played tennis to please her father. She wanted him to be proud of her. As the first important male in our lives, we never quite get over our fathers. All the same, we finally hit the ball, change the baby diapers, or set the broken bones because it pleases us. We can live on great family expectations only part of our lives. Yet we always want that appreciation.

It is precisely this great expectation and affection, this closeness, that leads us into trouble with our clan. We want their approval for what we have chosen to do, or how we've turned out, or just the reassurance they will always care for us. It is this same bond that leads them to overcome their better judgment and give us their opinion, anyway. Because they cared for us in such a long-term and meaningful way, they feel they must tell us what their advice would be.

Then there are times when our family expresses outright

disapproval of our 1) ambitions; 2) choice of a mate; 3) use of drugs or alcohol. They make us feel guilty if we don't spend every vacation traveling home to see them, or if we didn't phone when we were there, or omitted a name from the Christmas card list.

The problem we run into with families is that they frequently consist of meddlesome elders who live too close, or they are too far away to be called on in emergencies. Our blood kin are often too remote to ease us from our Tuesdays to our Wednesdays. For this we must rely on our family of friends. If our relatives are not—or do not wish to be—our friends for whatever reasons, then by some complex alchemy we transform our friends into relatives.

Too many ebbs in family tide lead a couple to choose new allegiances and new families. If a newly married couple has moved away from blood ties, they are likely to want to celebrate the traditional holidays with someone close to kin; or at least with friends who also need a family atmosphere.

These new families, to borrow the terminology of an African tribe in the Cameroons, consist mainly of friends of the road, ascribed by chance and place, or friends of the heart, achieved by choice. Friends of the road are those we go to school with, work with, or live near. They know whom we saw last weekend and whether we have a cold. Just being around gives them a provisional importance in our lives, as we have one in theirs. Maybe they will still matter to us when one of us moves away; quite likely they won't. Six months or two years will probably erase us from each other's daily thoughts, unless by chance and effort they have become friends of the heart.

Friends of the heart we never give up. Distance, time, and interests don't dent the armor of such friendships. But they are rare. And they take time and energy. Wishing to be friends, Aristotle wrote, is quick work, but friendship is a slowly ripening fruit. He quotes an ancient proverb that reads: you cannot know a man until you and he together have eaten a peck of salt. A peck, a quarter of a bushel, of salt is quite a lot of salt—more than most married couples ever have occasion to share. The only way to share so much salt is to sit together at the table as much as we can. We must hold each other's eyes and hands through enough storms and calms that sooner or later it crosses our minds that one of us, God knows which or with what pain, must one day mourn the other.

MARILYN:

Some of my friends of the road and of the heart are quite literally from the road where I grew up—Ten Mile Road. Theirs was not the only house on the road, but they became friends of the heart very early. They were known as Circle K in the years when we were bent on a Western motif and renamed our farms into ranches; we wore cowgirl hats and shirts made by my mother; we paraded about with guns blazing. Roy Rogers and Gene Autry were our heroes. I was four or five, and Circle K had a girl who also wore braids and was just three years older than I was. I would walk down the road nearly to their house, closer each time, then turn and run all the way home. One day I made it as far as their porch, with a view through the kitchen window. Pressing my nose and forehead against the glass, I refused all invitations for entry. Ran home again. The next time I made it to the porch they offered me a piece of chocolate cake (calling me "Snydar," because they had no other name). My fear fled. In the years to come they repeatedly told the story that I sat down and silently eyed the cake. My first words were: "It isn't a very big piece."

The childhood stories grew. There was the time the green beans were thrown into the Saturday-morning wash by brother who took things into his hands when his sister Tammy and her friend's lunch consisted of green and brown things we couldn't possibly want to swallow. In those days green and brown items had to be eaten before rich, moist desserts. There was a time my friend and I went bathing in the creek, pretending as always at ages six and nine to be film stars. As the stars of St. Tropez or Cannes today, we removed the bottom halves of the suits and left them on the plank bridge to dry. When it was time to go home, we couldn't find the suits and had to walk home—down Ten Mile Road—half-clad, much to our embarrassment. We weren't punished this time, though we usually were for removal of clothing. Nudity was not tolerated in our childhood, not even for film stars.

In my grade school it was customary to have an ice cream bar after lunch—for five cents. The even more important ritual was to buy an ice cream for one whose favor we were seeking. (In later years we spitefully bought them for female teachers whom we knew to be on a diet.) Boys usually bought ice cream bars for girls. I made a collection of ice cream sticks with the boys' names scrawled on them. One day Tammy wanted to buy one for Buzz, her current fifth-grade passion. She asked her mom for two nickels that morning. On the way home from school in the bus, I asked if she had given the ice cream to Buzz. "No," she blushed, "I lost his nickel."

I became part of their family as their girl, Tammy, became part of ours. We would call each other in the morning and meet halfway down the road to plan the day. We ravaged attics for costumes for local parades. One year we were Queen of Hearts and Little Miss Muffett on a homemade float built to resemble an old shoe where there lived the woman who had so many children she didn't know what to do. We won first prize. We selected which family to eat with by virtue of whose menu proved more to our liking. We ran away—to each other's houses; we played dolls and house. We traded valentines and Christmas cards from our collections. We picked strawberries and took piano lessons together. We practiced water ballet performances that would threaten Esther Williams. For a time we even had the same boyfriends, since I thought whatever Tammy did was worthy of following. I am left-handed because she taught me to write. We went to the same high school, the same college,

and pledged the same sorority. We were in each other's
weddings. It should be no great revelation that our husbands
are very similar, in stature, coloring, and profession, though
they are from opposite sides of the country.

When I go home now, she tries to come home also.
There is sometimes a phone call asking if I can come and
play, and we meet halfway down the road.

Bonding is the key element in identifying our clan. With
blood families the bond is sometimes weakened by necessity
and the lack of choice. Yet they are valuable to us, our
families. They perform several functions in our lives. First,
they give us affection. Our families are a main source of
physical affection. They touch us and dry our tears; they hold
and rock us; they write and phone to connect with us. They
cluster around, gathering to celebrate and laugh. Second, our
families also educate us. Sometimes they give advice we can't
hear, but they persist, anyway. They teach us through shared
experience and stored memory the history of their seasons.
They know how babies should be handled; they have solved
the problem of dripping faucets and overflowing toilets; they
have studied the winds and the damage from a silver thaw.
They know which shrubs to plant in our soil, and they know
how to cultivate the spring earth. They have home remedies
and world solutions. They remind us where we have been so
we can discover where we are going.

Elements of Good Families

There are common elements in most great families,
according to Jane Howard, who spent considerable time
studying them. It seems to us worthwhile to investigate what
families have to offer the new family formed by marriage.

Good clans have a sense of themselves as family. Tradition,
ritual, and story are woven into the fabric of a good and
healthy clan. The sense of identity is consciously adopted. We
know this identity from our names: we are a Ryan or a

Prewitt. We identify with the name and assume certain characteristics because of the family name. Furthermore, members of the clan seek us out because we are part of it. Another identity is ethnic—an extension of clan. Businesses and shops are manned by ethnic groups. In South Water Street markets in Chicago, on Pike Street in Seattle, in the heart of Montreal, and on South Ninth Street in Philadelphia people identify themselves with ethnic ties, and they come to the marketplace because of their ethnicity.

The family is formed not for survival of the fittest but for the weakest. It is not so much an economic unit as an emotional one. It is not a place where people ruthlessly compete with each other but where they work for each other.

"The whole street is family,"says Paul Giordano, about South Ninth Street Market. "It wouldn't work without family. Family you can pay cheap and tell them they'll inherit." Italian or Chinese markets are a long tradition from grand-father to uncles. "Everybody here is a Giordano. It is unlikely that if you didn't have the Italian connections you would be able to work on Ninth Street. I'd say sixty percent of the street is Italian, though there is a Jewish contingent up the block, but they sell clothing. Everybody else sells food."

Great families have a sense of their own history, which resides with the elders. A family tree and photos from great-great grandparents preserve the sense of a dynasty. In some families there is a historian who keeps the records or, better yet, writes a family history. It has become the avocation of some families to spend their holidays tracing their lineage to County Clare, or the Austrian Alps.

Good clans honor their elders while they are being educated by them. Elders are to be indulged, pampered, and written to and telephoned. Their memories are the stuff of our beginnings, and we require their recollections to pass on to our children. The letters they wrote us in college or penned in our baby books, the music boxes and diaries they gave us, comprise our material history.

Families usually have a sense of place, which these days is not achieved easily. A ball field in Cornwall Park, Bellingham, Washington; the beach at LaPush on the Pacific; a balcony in Bird Island, Minnesota; and the Pavillion in Manor Park, Larchmont, New York. Sometimes it is the sense we had of the place more than the location itself that keeps us committed to geography. Affection remains for the sandy hill where we plunged toy trucks to move mountains and tin soldiers for battle. The lake where we swam at night and watched colored lights dance on the water or the store where we spent dimes for forbidden candy recapture our sense of place. A few of our hometowns still have the dance halls where our parents courted each other and where engagements were announced. We remembered the glamour of their names: Coconut Grove, The Palms, The Aragon and Crystal Ballroom. Our families danced even as they carried us in their wombs. The dreams of their romances and our first attempts at the fox trots still play in our heads.

Most people know they are "eastern," or "midwestern," or "from California," from the soil where they were very young. Values and characteristics are ascribed to the region itself and to those who were nurtured there. We may think we took on qualities of the mountain peak in whose snowy shadow we rode our bicycles or the erect New England houses where we pushed a lawn mower. Our family could not live for generations by the mountains or in the sun without taking on some attributes from them. A rare beauty, a physical quality lures us back. The rhythm of ocean waves or the whisper of the wind in the pines speaks to some inner mood we held as children. We come to know that much of our formation took place in those years, even though graduate school or a stint in the military may have done more to change the direction of our adulthood. We may even live in communities we like better than the ones where we grew up, but the heart will always know where home is.

Traditions Begin at Home

Each family, blood or otherwise, has its traditions. Tradition is, after all, tradition and should not be subject to the whims of parents. There is no use having a tradition if it's going to be abandoned because the family has decided on a trip to Florida instead of a home Christmas. Children like traditions and come to expect them never to change. They like the sense of repeating what has become cherished. We like the idea of vacationing in the same town by the ocean or returning to our hometowns each year. We always cut down our own Christmas tree. Even years when there is no time to drive for an hour each way to a tree farm, we make the trip. The tree is the most important Christmas symbol for us, mainly because it's usually ten feet tall and covered with ornaments, each carrying its own memory. Our ornaments date to a time before we were this family. Some are from Germany on a college trip. Some of them are from end-of-summer holiday browsing on Nantucket (a papier-mâché angel); others are seashells collected from beach vacations and raffia rice spoons from a Korean student who lived with us one year. A few remain of the California walnuts we painted gold when the graduate student budget permitted no other adornment.

MARILYN:

When my father was growing up, the son of immigrant parents in the Northwest, his family was quite poor. They were not poor in the relative way, like belonging to a yacht club and not having a yacht, but in a real sense of having scarcely enough to eat. At Christmas his family had so little to spare that the only gift he and his brother and sisters received was an orange or a potato with a dime stuck in it. A good year produced an orange; a bad year, a potato. When I was a child, my mother placed the orange or potato (with accompanying pieces of silver) out on Christmas Eve, along with the dozens of packages we received. It was a small reminder of a more humble time and what could lie ahead should mother fortune reverse herself.

Traditions are not tied to blood families; families of the heart devise their own rituals. They gather to commemorate the fifteenth showing of *The Wizard of Oz*, cackling, "Who stole my ruby slippers?" Someone carries a yellow basket with small scottie dog and murmurs: "Oh, Toto, will we ever get back to Kansas?" Others gather to watch every Humphrey Bogart movie or Ohio State versus Michigan game.

MARILYN:

My sister and I are believers in a baking tradition which comes down through our family of European immigrants. All the aunts and Grandmother made potecia, a yeast bread filled with nuts, raisins, dates, and sometimes cherries and shaped into a tight circle, so that when it is raised and sliced, layers of filling are displayed. This Austrian bread is for us what petites madelaines are for Marcel Proust. It is our own past. . . .". . . the past is hidden somewhere outside the realm, beyond the reach of intellect, in some material object (in the sensation which that material object will give us)," Proust wrote. Potecia gives us a connectedness to our custom and heritage. The recipe crossed the Atlantic in the mind of our grandmother, who left her home as a young girl with no knowledge of people or language in America. In addition, the yeast bread was a focus of considerable family attention during our growing up and has given us reassurance in our constancy.

Our grandmother was not what you would call a gourmet baker. She was definitely not a good cook, that simply being out of her range of necessity. She was known to make cookies that contained a solitary raisin in the center. We were given one when we went to visit her. That her potecia should be the object of so much attention was beyond our scope of understanding. Hers did not have nearly the amount of nuts or dates that our aunts or our mother put in theirs. If the truth were known, some years the flour she used was somewhat stale. But all the same, year in and

holiday out, our father and uncles fought for "Ma's
potecia," to determine who would take it home. They would
begin by hiding it the moment she arrived for the family
gathering. One of the boys would find it and carry it about,
passing it like a football, through bedrooms, in and out of
doors. Our grandmother laughed and laughed. It pleased
her enormously, which is, of course, why they continued
the game through so many seasons. It became for us,
watching the spectacle, a source of satisfaction. It was clear
to everyone that we still honored our elders and that we had
a head of the family (even when she was a widow). For once
and not again often in our lives, the prize was paid, not to
the best but to the eldest; the ritual was dedicated, not to
excellence but to endurance.

We have our family traditions and a few borrowed ones.
Our family has Brownie Night. Children become impatient
for Christmas. With school and home preparations, the
tension builds up during Advent. Small children and even a
few adults like to have an early present. For years the
Brownies ranked insignificantly alongside Hanukkah, which
supplied our Chicago neighbors with eight presents on as
many nights. But the Brownies help deal with anticipation.
About a week before Santa Claus is scheduled to once more
squeeze his oversized self down our blackened chimney, the
Brownies come by and leave a small package. Just a little gift,
maybe a dime store whistle (wise Brownies learn, however,
never to give whistles or drums or pea shooters) or a tree
ornament and a candy cane. The Brownies are unpredictable;
sometimes they leave the present on the bed or by the
fireplace or at the breakfast table. Sometimes they come in the
morning and sometimes at night. If we are traveling, the
Brownies know enough to adjust their deliveries to suit family
plans.

We borrow from the imagination of other families. Traditions become established simply by doing them. One family
we know sets aside a covey of decorative cardinals from the

rest of the Christmas ornaments. The cardinals are kept until grown family members return home for the holidays. As each arrives he places his cardinal on the tree as a symbol that he has come home to the nest for a while.

The ancient Druid ritual now known as Halloween is a family time. Costumes are necessary for everyone from Mom to infant. Just because one isn't going to a party is no reason not to dress. Mom sometimes answers the door for trick-or-treaters in a witch costume with bizarre music from a darkened background. Poisoned apples are, of course, treats. Baby goes dressed as a king. Budding adolescent dresses as a housewife, mascara smudges under the eyes and penciled-in wrinkle lines, pink rollers in her hair, motheaten bathrobe covering a drooping slip, and a wash pail on her arm. We all dress as something we aren't.

If we are tempted to doubt that holidays are the cement of family life, we need only remind ourselves that children are given to sighing after Christmas, "because there isn't anything else to look forward to," and old people wait until after their birthdays or New Year's to die.

Our family wants to be a great family. We talk about family; we discuss each other's current problems or triumphs; we share confidences. We gather for holidays even though we live far apart. We like to be together. In our case sisters married brothers, so we have a connectedness and double cousins. That way there are fewer birthdays to remember, let alone preferences and sizes. We have a female head of one side of our family—she looks a little like Rose Kennedy. For her, family always was and is first. With her rose-colored glasses, she thinks all her children and their spouses are smart, beautiful, sensible, and talented. She thinks we should all become rich and famous and appear on the "Donahue Show." She gives advice and asks if we need money. She has pithy bits of wisdom like: "You have to spend money to earn money." Or: "After the baby is born, go out and buy yourself a new dress." Or: "The French never waste a thing; what isn't eaten at one meal is soup the next." On our first Christmas as a married couple, she sent us silver candlesticks because she couldn't bear the thought that someone on the invitation list had not sent them as a wedding gift. She comes by her generosity from years of example. She was married for fifty years to a man who accumulated little money in his early life because he could never refuse a request for help from someone close to him.

Like any good colony, our family has its workers. The other set of parents invented work. They function as a team where there is a garden to be planted, a room to be painted, or a garage to be organized. They lend both money and energy, even though they think we are profligate in spending both. They replenish the tools when one is lost or left to rust in the yard; they make birdhouses and Santa Claus suits. And they take their grandchildren for a month each summer. Everybody is busy in good clans. Paint is spattered on eyeglasses, basketball games are weekend entertainment; person-to-person calls come in at all times of the night from Montreal and Phoenix. Ballet slippers, overdue library books, tennis balls, and other signs of extrafamiliar interests are everywhere.

Good families are both open and closed. During the troubles, the family closes around the one who is ill or in unhappy straits. Since no family is without its share of problems—bankruptcy, divorce, battiness—the healthy clan closes in to support their own. These difficulties which at sometime plague nearly every clan are never regarded as insurmountable, and therefore the burden of calamity is lightened. It is at these times of trouble that the family is closed; these events (custody battles, losing a job) are considered "family business," and not for general village knowledge. If such events later seep out, it is no matter, since by then the family members have made their adjustments to a new reality (spouse, job, move) and are free to admit to the past.

If loyal families are sometimes closed, they are more often open and hospitable. They give out honorary memberships in their family to those whom they urge to come early and often and stay late. The open clan, by blood or by choice, is flattered when the honorary members ask favors because it knows it can respond freely with affirmative or negative reply—most often affirmative—and still be regarded as family. As for the people who have honorary status, we feel free to call on them to supervise our children for a fortnight and to share our secrets and problems.

In loyal clans love for each other spills over onto friends of the family. If friends of the clan are living on the other side of the country and need a family for Christmas or a weekend escape from a school dormitory, the good family extends sleeping quarters and Christmas morn to them. The flame of their affection is not dimmed by extending it to others. The worth of the family is best demonstrated by the willingness to share its wealth with those outside.

Great families are above all else loyal. Loyalty comes without asking, and it's a major commodity in ethnic families. "The Italian Connection" or "fierce Irish loyalty" are well known. The passionate loyalty to family stems from an immigrant culture. In an era when blood was more trustworthy in a new country than any government official or local businessman, families survived by depending on each other. Close families worked for each other. In farming communities they lent their machines and muscles to harvest hay, pick berries, or fill a silo. There was no question of exchange of money. It simply wouldn't be necessary, since when it came time to harvest your brother's crop you would be there.

Families were there for any hardship, financial or emotional. In some families money changed hands with scarce recognition of who earned or saved it. It was needed for family affairs, and the one in need or trouble had full access to it.

Loyalty Claims

Loyalty lays claim to family members. Families care very much who is allowed to assume the name. One would not take a wife, for example, in some traditional families without first passing her by the cousins, aunts, and honorary relatives.

The family should, in turn, be vitally caught up in the events of the wedding, if it would come to that. At the wedding ceremony itself, the family enters the church down the center aisle and is led to reserved seats. The bride's family and friends sit on the left side of the church; the groom's sit on the right. If one has befriended both, the decision must be made to sit left or right.

In some clans the loyalty is so strong that we have to be wary of what we speak of in desire. An unguarded sigh over an art deco vase or a ten-speed bicycle can mean the family will work and worry over how to supply it. The storehouse of happy memories becomes furnished with family gifts.

MARILYN:

Uncle Joe loved gift giving. He lavished Christmas and birthday presents on his only daughter. Buying her things she desired seemed to be the major goal of his daily employment. There was only one problem. He could never wait, once the gifts were chosen or laid away, until the appropriate day. He would effervescently tell his daughter of the gifts—ballet shoes, a doll, ice skates, a car—within days of their purchase. Each time he tried again to keep the secret, but it was useless. His joy at giving her things she wanted was just too great to contain.

The blood tie creates a network once we move to a city of strangers. One sister sends word to another that a member of the clan will be arriving in these parts. Whether it is a political event or a brief vacation, duty has it that we meet, even if it is for the first and last time. It is usually understood that family can claim a space in the house of relatives for however long it might be needed.

Political Families

Family loyalty plays out in political affairs. Brothers and sisters work for each other in all manner of campaigns, from high school class office to U.S. senator and president. We all came to a sense of the political family in 1960 when the Kennedys showed how appealing family could be in a presidential campaign. Joseph P. Kennedy watched over it, Robert F. Kennedy ran it, and, except for pregnant Jacqueline, all the other Kennedys marched across America like a small army. Rose, the matriarch, journeyed far and wide and never missed a chance to ask for a vote for Jack. Before the Wisconsin primary, Robert Kennedy arranged for each sister to attend nine house parties a day in every town for more than a fortnight. Edward, a mere twenty-seven, did his share by bearing a striking resemblance to Jack and by visiting campaign headquarters as far as Seattle. The Kennedys gave family and clan glamour. Their loyalty and appeal made us all wish we were from large and great families.

Since then, families have politicked in every presidential campaign. Ethel Kennedy joked with the press; Betty Ford went public with private details of her life and turned them into political assets; Billy Carter drank with the local pols. The Carter family played critical roles at two stages of his candidacy: they helped put him on the map, and once "Carter" became a household word, his family labored to spread the gospel. In these campaigns the family became the microcosm for the nation: Look what we can do when we are united. From Pennsylvania Avenue to Madison Avenue, the family has been a national symbol. If advertising now sells sex and cereal, it once sold family loyalty or at least tapped into it. The famous advertisement for Boys' Town accounts for much of the generosity that built a financial trust. One boy carrying another on his back says: "He ain't heavy, Fatha'. He's my brother."

Family gatherings herald national and private ceremonies, whether the event is a winter Snow Bowl in Minnesota, a campfire when the smelt are running in Lake Michigan, a family tennis tournament in Washington, or a Fourth of July picnic on Long Island; they all contain the urge to show the family colors.

MARILYN:

*The Houser-Elerding clan planned a tribute to family
and its eldest member. He was born in 1889, the year
Washington became a state, and is a vigorous ninety-two at
this writing. It is a great clan for gathering for reunions: to
pitch horseshoes, canoe, or play baseball. Since nearly
everyone in the clan plays tennis and Grandfather Houser
liked the sport very much himself, it was deemed a good
idea to have a picnic and tournament. The family
was nearly broken apart at one point, however, when one
branch came dressed in printed T-shirts.*

*As the T-shirted ones, clearly identifiable, huddled
together to give a homemade chant, tempers flared and
hostility rose. This great family could and has weathered
many a controversy before. That wasn't what disturbed the
others. It was the violation of code. What had been billed as
cooperation (picnic and tennis) was suddenly competition
(uniforms and chants). When the mood is one of getting
family together for fun and food, to have to pit oneself
against another branch violates a sense of fair play. But all
big clans become accustomed to the tug of war between
competition and cooperation, and so this one retired to
potluck supper and presentation of awards. The awards
worked to soothe the sensitive, since they were awarded for
qualities which families prize: driving the Furthest Distance,
Making Most Progress for a Novice, Doing the Most for a
T-shirt.*

Loyalty requires immediate attention and sometimes worry
over the affairs of the clan. One who is ill or unemployed gets
a full share of advice and often a connection for a new job.
For the aging, the family takes on the responsibility of
protection. The family decides what happens to the pair who
are getting too feeble to look after themselves. They bring
'round an apple pie, clean the house to be sold, and dispose of
clothing after a funeral. They rely on no state or charities to

carry out these functions. They believe that charity begins at home.

This kind of loyalty must be learned early. It becomes clear to children from the time they are young that parents take care of them in the beginning, and they will take care of parents in the end. If that obligation cannot be fulfilled, the strong care for the weak.

The sense of being family is a conscious effort. We don't always come from a good family. The point is making the most of family. A good family is the luck of birth; a great family is the effort of life. Great families are no accident. If we don't like what we started with, we can build our own.

Since we have no choice when it comes to the people of our family, we must make the best of it. We do, however, choose our friends. Choice allows us to take up with friends of the road; a family by decision, a circle of friends. Moving from a hometown to a new community offers a sample of new people. We look for common characteristics, the knots of friendship. We sometimes bond merely because to do otherwise seems too painful. The thought of Thanksgiving turkey with trimmings prepared for one or two just doesn't ring true, when every Thanksgiving in memory seated at least sixteen and often as many as twenty-seven. New Year's Eve alone loses its luster, unless it is deliberately chosen as a way to focus on a new year. More often, we gather with a few friends to ring in holidays. What was once a customary gathering of village or clan has become, rather, an observance with friends. Traditions begin in such a manner.

If major difference between friends and family is the choice, even before we acknowledge it, a friend reminds us of our father in stature or supplies us with affection similar to our mother's. More than a few people have found a bond of affection from new friends, co-workers, or a church group, a bond far greater than that known in a dozen years of marriage or a previous seventeen years growing up with the family. At times we recognize that our family simply can't cope with a decision we have made. We have decided to move away in favor of a job or school in another region. We have chosen someone from another race or religion, and our parents can't deal with our choices. But our friends accept us in full knowledge of our decisions. They may be compelled to give us advice on future events, but they have no reservoir of past memories to use against us. Our friends accept us as we are. Some families adopt this pose as well. They decide to treat their children as adults, praising what they like, keeping silent on less-favored outcomes. They let the flow of spontaneous events take over. Perhaps it is the attitude of enjoying the moment with a friend or family that keeps us wanting to spend time together. The best of both worlds is to find a friend in the family and to find family in a friend.

Good friends are buffers against bumps in life. Often, but not always, our spouse becomes best friend, confidant as well as lover. In the beginning of marriage we may think no other person can satisfy us in so many ways. But strains of professional pressures, personal problems, or absence require the bonds of friendship outside marriage. Couples need couple friends, ones whose marriages are stable enough to lend support. We also need friends, perhaps single ones, who stay up late with us, call, write, plan their vacations to include us. No one is paired for life. One day we will all be single. After all, few couples die simultaneously. Whether single by choice or consequence, single friends must be a part of our lives. They are there to get us out of the apartment for a spell, to go to a concert, to come for dinner, to stop in on a surprise visit, or just to let us know they are thinking of us. Some friends are of such merit that we should be willing to "go in the fire for them." A great friend is not chosen by convenience, nor should he be given up because of inconvenience. No matter how far our paths part or how distant the days of our being together or how divergent our tasks become, we should not let go.

Rarely now do we live around the block or even in the same town as our blood families. We see them less than some friends we've acquired. We have moved many times, and

repeatedly we learn to say good-bye to those we care about—
each time relives that first separation from our clan. Parties
sometimes signal the parting of the ways. Graduation, a new
job, a move, all call for a party. Here disappointment and
separation anxiety are met head-on by the celebration. Even if
we might miss them terribly, we celebrate their move. Carole
King declares in song: ". . . .so far away. . . .doesn't anybody
stay in one place anymore?" When we have moved far away
from family, geographically or emotionally, we look for
replacement in the local signs of the family. We look for the
chance to meet halfway down the road.

7

Money: Cheap Is Chic

Somewhere in our past we heard, "Nice people don't talk about money." We do not know where this message comes from—whether it be our parents, the movies, or what. Still, that line, "Nice people don't talk about money," hangs before us, urging us to forget this vulgar subject and move on to another topic . . . anything else. And we are tempted. For one thing, neither one of us knows much about money. For another, we believe there is some truth to the advice not to talk publicly about money. On the rare occasions when people we meet start talking about the intricacies of their finances and probing ours, it is like being rubbed with sandpaper. There is something else, though, that holds us back. Attitudes about money are starkly revealing, and the simple fact is that we are out of step. We, as you will see, are cheap. What gives us the courage to plunge ahead is not that we have anything revolutionary to say. It's a combination, on the one hand, of not wanting to be labeled "nice people" and, on the other, of having seen many people bring themselves to grief over money.

The Future Is in Cheap

It is nearly impossible to grow up in our society and not have one's desire to spend outrunning one's wallet. For most of us, our ability to generate money is several laps behind our wants and our capacity to spend. And that is no accident! Our unfulfilled desires are the engine that keeps American capitalism going. It's not a bad engine, either, if we can somehow keep our dollars and our desires in harmony. But that's harder to do than it sounds.

Our desires get out of control easily. Without knowing it, we build in new desires. We casually thumb through a magazine and come out the other end with a gnawing dissatisfaction with our boxy, slightly dented car. We hardly even looked at those seductive ads for the new sleek (did you hear a sexy purr?) models. We watch television and come away with a new hankering for an instamatic camera that will transform our drab family into a happy, fun-loving group. We go into a department store to get a pillowcase and some jockey shorts for Junior, and we come out convinced that we need an entirely new wardrobe. "Anybody looking at me would know that my husband was an utter failure. Anybody looking at my husband would know that he has a wife who doesn't care if he's ten years out of style." Advertising not only plays on our wants and desires, but it plays strongly on our insecurities. Without really thinking this matter through (which is the genius of advertising), we come to feel that somehow our inadequacies won't show up if we cover them with the creations of this designer and that chemist. Even though we know in the abstract that we are being manipulated, we have found ourselves manipulated right along with everyone else. We have gone for padded shoulders, rejected them, gone for padded shoulders, rejected them, gone for padded shoulders. We have gone from fat neckties, to thin neckties, to medium neckties, to fat neckties, to medium neckties, to thin neckties. We have gone to short hair, long hair, short hair, long hair, short hair. Frailty, thy name is American consumer.

Unconsciously, then, pressure builds to keep up with this style or to satisfy some manufactured need. Historically, this method has made for a strong capitalist economy, selling lots of soap and snow blowers, but it does little to develop or enhance anyone's sense of well-being. For married couples, high-gear consumerism presents special problems.

Ranking high among the many madnesses running loose in the land is our casual attitude toward debt. Currently the average family spends 23 percent of its take-home income on interest, the cost of borrowing money. To express it more sharply, this is the price we pay for having luxuries before we can afford them. One of the causes of this madness is the credit card. Credit cards are great inventions, if they are used correctly. By "correctly" we mean as a substitute for paying cash, rather than a substitute for taking out a loan. Many people kid themselves about their credit cards. They will pay them off at the end of each month and not get caught paying interest. The fact of the matter is that two out of three credit-card holders pay interest on their debt madness monthly.

Living in debt, or at the edge of debt, can sour lots of happy moments. "Let me see now! Am I over the limit on my Visa card?" "Exactly how many car payments do you have to be in arrears before the finance company comes and visits you in the night?"

More dangerous than debt, though, is letting a sense of competition develop between a couple over what economists call "the disposing of discretionary income."

"Are you happy with your new hi-fi deck?"

"Why?"

"Oh, no reason, I just thought because you spent six hundred dollars on it, you ought to be getting a lot of enjoyment out of it."

"Well, it *was* reduced. Anyway, we just spent four hundred dollars on your dishwasher."

"My dishwasher! Aren't those your dirty dishes, too?"

"Ok, but one of the major reasons I got that hi-fi was so you would have good music in your life."

"Oh, come on. The next thing you're going to tell me is that the camel's-hair coat you bought last month was really for me."

"Are you kidding? I bought that coat because you said I go around looking like a bum. Besides, you said I looked good in it."

"I only said that because you were so intent on getting it. I thought if I said no, you would have cried in front of the salesman."

"Cry! Me, cry! Listen, you whined for two months until I borrowed the money for that ski outfit for you . . . and you haven't been on skis yet."

"Well, as long as we're on the subject, when are you going to pay Mother back the money for what you promised was going to be the perfect honeymoon? Ha!"

"Don't start in on that. It was your idea to go to Florida."

"Now, who's kidding? I hate Florida. I have always hated Florida. I knew if I went . . . particularly in the type of bathing suit you forced me to buy, I'd get sunburned. Well, I was right."

And in the words of Kurt Vonnegut, "And so it goes." Add a sense of competition about who is going to spend the extra money from the paycheck to a low bank balance, a drawer full of unpayable bills, and all the other adjustments of marriage, and trouble is programmed in.

KEVIN:

I used to think money wasn't very important. I was wrong. It is very important. Now I work hard, though, so that I won't have to think about it. Let me explain. I spent the first eighteen years of my life in a very snappy suburb of New York City. There were lots of people with bundles of money. My family was quite comfortable, but compared with others, we seemed poor. By any global standards we were extremely comfortable. However, our family felt vaguely poor in that community. We all wore hand-me-downs from neighbors and friends, which were then passed on to other neighbors and friends. I knew in the third grade what I'd be wearing in the fourth grade, in the sixth grade, and in the eighth grade just by looking around the playground at St. Augustine Parochial School to see what Judd Gibbs and the Brennan boys were wearing. We didn't have a car until I was in high school. We did have a once-a-week cleaning lady, but the other kids' moms had "their own maids!" Most troubling of all, we belonged to a yacht club but didn't have a yacht! As a special breed of suburban have-not, I reacted to my condition. I developed the habit of never completely spending my allowance. Not that I ever saved so much, but I always had a little cushion. I just didn't want the trauma of an empty wallet. I did not want to be poor or dependent on my friends with big allowances. The trick was easy once I got the hang of it: never spend all of my allowance; never spend all my paycheck. Instead of worrying about not having enough money for this or that, I tailored what I did to spend less than I actually could afford. The idea of going into debt for a suit, car, hi-fi set (in those days, lo-fi) always struck me as bizarre. My thinking was and is characteristically simple. For me, life is complex and stimulating enough without having to worry about whether or not I can pay for this or that. For me, to go into debt seems as sensible as hitting myself in the head with a mallet. I realize this is a dangerously subversive and un-American point of view. Friends and economic pundits have been telling me for years to "Buy now with borrowed dollars. Pay back later with cheap, inflated dollars." They certainly were accurate for the seventies. And I am sure my approach makes lousy economics. However, to me it makes great psychology.

Luckily, I met a woman who shares the same point of view. I said once I didn't think that money was important, but now I do. Once I left home I realized that places I went, the friends I had, even the things that I put into my head, such as books and plays, were a function of money. In the same way you must make choices about life and about spending time, you must make them about money. One crucial choice is how much money do you want to make? That determines many conditions of life: How hard are you willing to work? What kind of sacrifices are you willing to make? How will you spend your days? What do you really want? As is clear, these are not simply financial questions. They are profoundly personal and religious questions. Maybe that's why I don't like to think about money—because it leads on so directly to the tough questions.

About five years ago when New York City was floundering in a severe economic crisis, a reporter stuck a microphone in front of Mayor Daley's face and asked him how he was able to keep Chicago not only solvent but prosperous, while other cities were experiencing such financial stresses and strains. De Mare, as the Chicago faithful were wont to call him, answered, "I learned budgeting from my mother."

"Well, what did she tell you?" queried the reporter.

"She told me, 'Don't spend it if you don't have it.'" And that is pretty much the way the mayor of Chicago ran the city. He stayed in the black and followed a pay-as-you-go policy. That's not bad advice for a married couple, either.

MARILYN:

Getting and keeping money are two different things. There are people who get it and keep it; there are those who get it and spend it. There are, therefore, two types of people in the world: savers and spenders. I'm a saver. I have always been a saver. Even when as children we had a bottle of nearly forbidden Coke, I would save mine, consuming only sips until I could see that my little sister had finished her bottle. Then with a flourish I would drain my remaining drops. That I scarcely tasted the caramel-colored substance seemed unimportant to me. I wanted to have some left so she would envy me after she had wantonly gulped hers down (in little-sister fashion). "Saver!" she would taunt me angrily. I'm still a saver. As a child, I was given several plastic purses. About ten years of age seemed to be the time to be given purses, the assumption being that by then there was something to store behind those tight zippers. I put a little money in each of the several purses and stashed them away. The money was there not for emergency use, but sheerly for the surprise and good feeling whenever I found one of the purses on the closet floor. (I know, I should have married a banker.)

Whenever we went to town with my mother (the very soul of economy) to do our shopping, my sister brought along her accumulated allowance and bought herself a hamburger and milkshake. Even if she had eaten lunch at home! Even if she didn't have any other money, she would use the last change to get the hamburger and milkshake. No matter how often it happened, "The Saver" was always shocked. Why eat in town on your own money when you could eat at home for nothing! That dictum grew over the years to read: Why eat it and have the sensation in your mouth and tummy for only a few minutes (and on your hips for the rest of your life) when you could wear it on your back for several seasons? And so to this day my sister loves to eat out, and I buy the clothes. Now I always want something in the kitty. I don't even wear my new clothes when they are just home from the store. I save a new blouse for weeks—months—until the right moment comes along.

But even more than saving, I believe in luxury. Life without the treats, without the goodie, without a frill now and then can be dull stuff. Dwayne, the father of my best friend from down the road, was never rich, but he had a great sense of the luxurious. He knew how to make saving and luxury work together. His spirit is best captured in his response to the deprivations of illness. Dwayne had always loved to eat, and he had a faceful of sweet teeth. No weekend breakfast (and several throughout the week) was complete without two or three bear claws, a frosting-coated sweet roll popular in our area. And for Dwayne no bear claw was complete unless lathered with butter, a tablespoon per bite. When he became ill, though, the doctor sharply curtailed his diet. Dwayne had to fight and fudge to get one bear claw and a meager pat of butter. Still, he never lost his sense of luxury. While the rest of us would sparingly spread butter on dry toast, he would gleefully save his day's

*allotment of butter till the very last, then slather the entire
pat on one luxurious bite. He was a saver with style.*

We doubt that money is the root of all evil, but we are sure
the way it is spent can be a source of major irritation in a
marriage. If in a marriage one person buys books and the
other believes in public libraries, if one dry cleans frequently
and the other believes in spot cleaning, if one buys flowers
and the other thinks they are a waste, if one buys clothes and
the other thinks they should be home-sewn, the couple has a
ready source of irritation.

A most burdensome feature of married finances, then, is
reaching accord about what is luxury and what is necessity.
For some, not having a box of tissues within easy reach is
inconvenient. For some, not having a good set of wrenches is
deprivation. For others, not having a supply of perfume is
unthinkable. Having some intimate weekend time together
may be a necessity to the husband and wife who are apart
(psychologically if not physically) for much of the week. But if
going out means being with another couple and spending
more than you both can afford because of where the other
couple wants to dine, then the night out has an unpleasant
edge. While the newly married couple may need to experience some sense of luxury together, it makes little sense to
spend fifty dollars on dinner out when money is short and
when two can eat at home for a week on the same amount.
There are no easy solutions to the expenditure of money for
recreation. The point is that each couple has to work out
(read: much open communication) the sense of luxury and
entertainment for themselves.

What we have observed suggests that in good marriages
either both people have a similar attitude towards money and
spend with similar reasoning, or their attitudes about what is
valuable and what is frivolous have been worked out. Often
this is done through compromise. She quietly puts up with his
burgeoning collection of power tools, and he holds his tongue
about her fetish for handbags. It neither makes sense nor is it

fair for one person to "require" expensive hobbies or diversions, particularly when the other is being deprived. Although we have seen it both ways, many women don't get their share of the luxury-hobby fund because they feel they didn't earn it. Jack is "into cameras," plays indoor tennis, has a season's pass to the Gotham Gorillas' games, and has just made a down payment on a boat. Jill sews, reads (using the public library), and is doing a slow burn.

Often, though, it appears that one person earns all the money and the other spends it. In less traditional marriages, both earn and both spend. The trend recently is for two working people to have their individual savings. Undoubtedly that makes separation and divorce settlements easier! For people who are living together, separate finances may have some logic. But for people who intend to stay married, to go the distance, the money should be banked jointly and spent jointly. Marriage is and always was a financial arrangement. Fortunately, now marriage is a partnership, and the finances should be as well. Practices can vary, though. Some men handle all the money and give their wives an allowance. In other families, the wife does all the bill paying and the taxes. The husband is on an allowance. Regardless of who actually holds the purse strings, both should make the decisions about how money is saved and how money is spent. The fastest way to an extravagant wife (or husband) is to not tell how much is coming in and not allow her a share in the decision making.

There are small ways to save money and preserve the sense of luxury. To us, the picnic is one of Western man's greatest achievements. A private picnic of assorted cheeses and fruits, a loaf of French bread, and a bottle of wine is a feast. Throw in a view of woods or water, and there are few restaurants that can compete.

The tug of war between luxury and economy requires constant balancing. We share a trade-off mentality. We willingly save on the so-called essentials, to have a few good things. For example, we keep our home rather cool in the winter (a friend refers to our living room as the meat locker) in order to save for a good carpet. We will trade a little passing comfort for something of lasting value anytime. We have had bare wood floors and under-furnished rooms, rather than buy cheap furniture that would need replacing as soon as we could afford better. We pack brown-bag lunches every day in order to take more holidays. We even pack lunches for the holidays! On the road in our eight-year-old car we pass by the Howard Johnson's in favor of a roadside picnic. It wasn't until they went to school and their classmates squealed on us that our children discovered that Howard Johnson's is not a gas station and McDonald's is not a chain of boutiques.

We read a column once by Russell Baker in which he explained why the rich are rich: they buy good shoes. Good shoes last longer. They are more comfortable. One does not have to buy shoes so often, and the saved time can be spent making more money and becoming even richer. While we are not sure we could withstand the burdens of being rich, we find the good-shoes approach quite attractive, but for some additional reasons of our own. For one thing, good shoes don't fall apart the way poor shoes do. Also, good shoes, if not always in fashion, stay in fashion longer. Thus, one can lay around in bed more on Saturday morning, instead of wandering around plastic shopping malls being assaulted by Musak and one's fellow shoe shoppers. And to us, one of the most compelling reasons for buying good shoes—or coats, sweaters, hats, rugs, and so on—is that if we buy expensive ones we cannot afford to have many. We are saved from the tyranny of what to do with all the extra pairs: Where to store them? When and how to dust and clean them?

Then there is all the time we save dressing, which we can spend on warm baths and, in general, on wool gathering. Instead of having to sort through all those earth shoes, spiked-heel pumps, Hush Puppies, wing tips, tassled loafers, open-toed flats, wet-look boots, and loafing Adidas and make a decision, we can just slide into those lonely but faithful good shoes.

MARILYN:

The two of us are bothered with the fact that we don't
know what our attitude about money and the goods of this
world should be. Kevin thinks we are moving into an age of
real abundance and that our problem is poverty of spirit,
rather than paucity of goods. He sides with Herman Kahn,
who a few years ago said that people are wrong about the
earth running out of necessities. Kahn claims the job of the
rich nations is not to become poor, but rather to help the
poor nations become rich. I hope he's right, but I'm not so
sure.

I am afraid that our current cultural plenty is exhausting
itself, and we'll be stuck with a high-gear consumerism.
What were our frills a decade ago are now our necessities.
What were unheard of and unimagined luxuries during our
childhood are everday expectations for children. They
"need" three pairs of sneakers (one for gym, one for tennis,
one for coming and going) and lessons to develop their
athletic skills so that the sneakers are not wasted. They not
only need books, but electronic games of wizardry with alien
names like Merlin, Atari, and Data Man.

We have friends and relatives sprinkled around the
country who seem permanently affected by the sixties, and I
continue to admire them. They have dropped out of the
high-tech/high-consumer North American society and try to
live in harmony with the earth. They have learned to find
beauty and entertainment in the natural things around
them. They have gardens and draw much of their own
sustenance from them. They work hard to recycle whatever
they can, and they avoid using nonrenewabe products.
They wear and eat natural fibers. They avoid man-made
fibers which require additional unreplenishable resources in
their production. They eat natural foods both because they
are a part of a natural ecological system and because they
are healthful. They do not need a great deal of money for
survival. They always have products to give away; a jar of

*honey, a loaf of bread, dried fruit, and handmade quilts are
often their gifts. A few of them are self-sustaining systems.
They produce what they eat and wear. And they see
themselves as living out their concern for those who will
trod the earth in the future.*

There is more to this money issue than spending, though.
There is also giving. It is easy to sidestep giving or charity,
especially when newly married. It is odd, but even in our
immensely rich society, most of us feel poor. We feel
deprived. We don't have a really *good* car. We don't live in
the kind of apartment or home we deserve. We don't really
dress the way we want to. We are behind. But things are
designed that way. We are supposed to feel vaguely deprived.
That is not a very good mental position from which to think
about giving. However, a moment's reflection on our lot
compared with that of many in our country and, of course,
vast numbers in the Third World should sober up even the
most self-pitying of us. Without laboring the point, we believe
we lose hold on our humanity to the degree that we lose sight
of our impoverished brothers and sisters. Also, there is no
magic age or income level one reaches before becoming
eligible to give. One rule of thumb is: If you can buy a ticket
to the movies, you can afford to give to charity.

However, we do have one important caution. The Bible
tells us that when we give, do it in secret. Don't let the right
hand know what the left hand is doing. In a moment of folly,
a sad lapse of judgment, we gave some piddling amount to the
Little Sisters of the Hot Cross Buns or Little Brothers of the
Alcoholics, or some such group. Well, the Little Sisters of
whatever cashed our little check. But then sold our name and
address (presumably on some master list of contributors) to
other charitable organizations which solicit through the mail.
Well, first it was the occasional letter, addressed to us
personally, from Common Cause, the American Negro
College Fund, and Save the Whales. But as we ignored their
pleas, they became more desperate. They stepped up the

letters. When this failed, they turned vicious. They sold our name to other, more obscure charitable organizations. Now we get regular appeals (which increasingly sound like threats) for such organizations as Pilot People for Blind Dogs, Society for the Preservation of the Bull Moose Party, Friends of Our Feathered Friends, Hemorrhoid Victims Unite!, and the Leon Flem Institute for the Study of Disco Mania. It has become so bad that these appeals now come more frequently than catalogs! We are thinking of moving away and changing our names. Those busy Little Sisters would probably catch up with us, though.

What we have learned about money can be summarized in a few general principles. First, forget the first-class habit entirely, or until you have been making a first-class income for some time. It's better to start out with macaroni and cheese and slowly build towards steak than to become accustomed to steak too quickly. Much happiness and many of life's quiet pleasures are robbed by over-developed desires.

Second, start economizing with your honeymoon. Most honeymoons are stressful and strained events. Unanticipated difficulties of sexual and emotional adjustments mar many carefully planned holidays. To be spending a hundred dollars a day with some stranger about whom you think you may have made an incredible mistake only compounds an already tense situation. Better a quiet and romantic weekend in the country than two wallet-withering weeks in Wakiki.

Third, make contributions to charities and your church a regular part of your life. Granted, it's the thought that counts, but thoughts plus cash count more!

Fourth, with friends talk about money, but not about your money. Nice people and smart people do talk about money, and they learn valuable things from one another. How do they ever learn to use their money, if they don't talk to their friends! There is a great deal to be learned about disposing of one's income intelligently. And friends can be a tremendous source of information. An occasional conversation about the best way to go about buying a car or interest rates is, however, a far cry from spilling one's financial guts in public. If you talk about your finances with those who are wealthier, they will be bored. If you talk about your finances with those who have less, they will be jealous. Can't win.

Fifth, forget about keeping up with the Joneses. They're probably going to get divorced, anyway. Pick friends whom you can keep up with without putting yourself under a financial strain. It is impossible to hang around big spenders without spending big in return.

Sixth, give everything the forty-eight-hour or can't-it-wait test. Never buy more than a necktie without thinking about it overnight. Do we really need it? Will I be happy about this purchase in six months? Do I really want the task of cleaning, maintaining, and storing this? Is it just something to clutter up my life? How does this square with our financial picture?

Seventh, talk before you leap. Make sure the two of you are in complete agreement before you buy a big item (to us a big item can mean anything from a house to a popcorn maker). Do we really want it? Is this the time? Are you agreeing just because I'm enthusiastic, or do you have some reservations? Are you agreeing with my getting a widgit just because last week I supported your getting a new fandango?

Eighth, don't buy anything big during your first year of marriage (other than a popcorn maker). Millions of people are sitting around today repenting about their silverware, dishes, bedroom set, dining set, and so on. They were so sure they loved the Swedish Baroque style. Better a few years of Salvation Army than thirty years of repenting and being surrounded by Swedish Baroque.

Ninth, do not—repeat, do not—go blithely into debt.

Finally, if you decide to spend your money on some insane extravagance, which will not put you in debt and which you have both talked over and agreed to, *do it right!* Throw yourself into it. Savor it. Remember the bear claw!

8

Moving with the Spirit

We don't know if there is a God. However, we choose to believe there is a God, an all-loving God. Spiritual writers speak both about the leap of faith people must make and about faith being a gift. We believe intellectually and emotionally in His/Her existence, but not without doubt-filled moments and days.* By and large, though, the struggles of faith are behind us. We have taken the jump. In addition, we choose to know God through the Catholic Church. That, too, is an intellectual and emotional choice, and a choice that is behind us. At this point, we think we have signed on for the full trip, through good days and stormy days, sad Popes and smiling Popes, wise decisions and upsetting ones. We may not always like the weather or the things some of our shipmates are doing, but with our own free will we have signed on for the journey. Neither qualified nor disposed, we will not attempt to make a case for religious faith—ours or anyone else's. We want only to share some convictions.

Much more than we did on the day we married each other, we are convinced of the importance of a spiritual perspective in a couple's life together. We need it for both positive and negative reasons. The negative reasons first. Without the spiritual cast or overlay, our earthly lives together can turn to

*Having made a point, we will go back to the conventional He/His form of referring to our nongender God.

mud. Some hypothetical but common examples might help here. Three years into marriage a young man wakes up early one morning and realizes that the woman asleep next to him in bed is no longer special to him. The prospect of spending the rest of his life with this woman as his wife is grim. Her views bore him, many of her attitudes bother him, and her voice is beginning to irritate him. As he lies there, his mind moves to thoughts of leaving her and the green pastures of a fresh start. Yes, it would be good for her, too. They have both made mistakes, and they have probably learned from them. The young baby in the crib in the next room is, of course, a complication. The kid was his idea, too, but better the child be raised by separate and *happy* parents than parents who are at one another's jugular veins every day. And it is easy for the young man to move from these reveries to a divorce, a legal abandonment, since his marriage is planted in a thin soil of self-interest.

If a woman's deepest commitment is to her own self-fulfillment, if she has no religious frame of reference, it is easy for her to look over her coffee cup one evening and come to the cool realization that she has made a ghastly mistake. "I married a slob! What I once saw as his strong, frank virility, I now see as crude and overbearing oafishness." She almost gags watching him chew his food with his mouth slightly ajar. She vows to hurl her cup at him if he picks, licks, or sucks another tooth. She is sure that whatever she felt for him has evaporated. She tells herself that she is still young and has options. It is better to get out now before the two of them really start hating one another. Or worse, before she compromises and settles into a long, dreary marriage.

What these rather commonplace scenarios suggest is that marriage without something more than self-interest is rooted in poor soil. People committed to nothing but themselves find themselves caught in very real and very imperfect situations. For many, their commitment is based on nothing more than a "Have a nice day" morality. When the almost inevitable problems of marriage surface, their only compass in the storm is what's-in-this-for-me. Since self-interest breeds self-interest in marriage, couples can find small problems quickly turning into large problems. The basic problem, though, is that the couple lacks any religious or transcendent view of what they are doing together. There is no common framework in which to put their problems or from which they can work themselves out of trouble. The commitment withers. They make a run for their lawyers.

But that is life and marriage without a religious perspective. What is the view of life *with* such a perspective? We are not familiar enough with other religious perspectives, but being a Christian means looking at the world in a very special way. It means we have, or should have, a set of lenses to view the events around us. In a way, the Christian wears rose-colored glasses, convinced as he is that reality is tinted with rose. While others look out at the world and see a brutish struggle for riches and domination, the Christian sees God's children of many stripes and checks, with great numbers turned towards Him and many struggling to escape from His gentle call.

Religion is not alone in providing us a special lens on what is happening in the world. Our personal politics determine how we view the activities of government and its programs. The same government-sponsored poverty program can be viewed as a generous effort on the part of the haves in the country to reach out to have-nots. It can also be seen as an invidious attempt to keep the poor quiet, irresponsible, and increasingly dependent, while the benefactor, government, gets bigger and more bloated.

Religion gives us a lens to filter the data of our daily lives. We receive varied stimuli that require our attention. Without such a lens, what our eyes see and our ears hear would be literally meaningless. We would be helpless in trying to fathom the flux and flow of the activities that surround us.

Our Christian meaning system is special, though. It assures us that there is more to our existence than meets the eye. We are more than the weight registered on our bathroom scale or the image we see in a mirror. It tells us that we are not merely featherless bipeds struggling in isolation to keep ourselves alive. We have a special place in the universe and in the mind of God. We are connected to one another by unseen but nevertheless real threads. More than that: Our success, our fulfillment in life, is dependent on those around us.

The Christian lens, or meaning system, sees marriage in a very distinctive fashion. It is not merely a social vehicle to sanction sex. It is not simply society's way of assuring a stable unit to bring children into the world and raise them. It is not a mechanism for the orderly transfer of property. It may be all of these, but it is more. Marriage is the means by which most of us fulfill ourselves and live out God's plan for us. That fact sheds a transforming light on the simplest act of the married person. Further, the married person with that light develops a radically different set of purposes for marriage than the person without that light. We marry not to get the "top girl" or "the campus hero"; to capture the one who promises the most pleasure, sexual or otherwise; or to escape our own loneliness. We marry to reach our fullest potential in God's eyes. We marry the person who will help us live Christ's life, to be the best we can. This perspective on marriage does not deny or reject sexual attraction, pleasure, or success. But these other purposes are themselves transformed by the prime purpose.

While all of this sounds very airy-fairy, it has real and practical consequences. The Christian married person both perceives and behaves differently. The man waking up in the morning and discovering he is no longer attracted to the woman asleep next to him knows his feelings are real, but so is his commitment to this woman. He knows, further, that their marriage is in trouble, and he needs to give his mind and his energies to their marriage in a new way. And while the prospect of flight and starting over are attractive, he rejects them as cowardly —nd self-indulgent. Instead, he turns his mind to what can be done to rebuild their life together. And this act of the mind and the will is not cold stoicism, for he knows this is God's plan for him. He is calm because he believes that this is what God has called him to do. He knows that he will find the strength, the inner resources, to deal with the task of revitalizing their lives together. This seemingly negative situation holds the potential for becoming something positive. The Christian, then, has made a bargain with God that in return for his or her commitment to this other individual, God will provide those necessary resources.

So the Christian perception is more than a view through a lens. It is more like a poet's vision that sees below the surface to a deeper meaning. With Joseph, the Christian sees not a pregnant teenager, but the mother of the King of Kings. In Jesus on the cross, the Christian discerns not some self-made untutored rabbi gone afoul of the Jewish Establishment, but the promised Messiah who will in three days overcome death. The committed Christian's vision of the everyday is transformed, too. What he calls success in life is different from that of the uncommitted. He works for the keys of the Kingdom, not the keys to the executive john. Failure is not a lost job, an empty bank account, or, worst of all, children who do not go to college. Failure exists only in our rejections of God's will and in despair. The Christian knows that as long as he has breath, failure is redeemable. He can come back from failure simply by turning his mind to God.

In marriage, the Christian perspective can transform an unanticipated pregnancy into God's surprise. It can help us cope with tragedy, knowing that it is part of a loving God's plan. It can help us deal with worldly success because we have a true measure of our power. The Christian perspective can change a high-voltage marital blowout from the final proof of incapabilities to a chagrined recognition that, "We blew it again, babe; let's cling to one another and begin again."

This sense of Christian commitment can, of course, backfire. And it does. Especially when one is the "committee" rather than the "committer." The security that comes with commitment from another causes some to relax to the point of quietly turning into a slob or a TV freak or a workaholic. On the other hand, we know couples who acknowledge no

God and are deeply devoted to one another. Perhaps they look at each other and say to themselves, "You are all I have. You are the most important part of my life. We're alive on this hostile planet, so let's be gentle and good to one another." It works for them, but it certainly seems like the hard way.

KEVIN: Spirituality

I wanted this person as I never wanted anyone before (or since), and also I was convinced of three things: first, we would live together more happily if we shared the same religious traditions and experiences; second, that this church with which I had grown up was one that I loved and wanted to stay with; and third, I didn't know how any outsider in his/her right mind would find it the least bit understandable, let alone attractive. And as the moment came, when it was now or never . . . when I finally squeezed the world into a moment and spoke, out came this ghastly, awkward question: "Do you think you could become a Catholic?" But amid the barking of a dog, careening out of the driveway, and the meshing of gears, I heard this dear girl say, "I thought you'd never ask." She knew and I knew that I had asked her to marry me, and we were from that moment betrothed. I didn't understand it at the time— indeed, I didn't understand for many years—but she understood perfectly those three thoughts that were careening around in my head.

She took to Catholicism with ease and enthusiasm. And I stood back amazed. The few times we talked about religion, between the proposal and her baptism, I found myself completely at a loss to express what I believe to be the core beliefs of the church. As I have since come to discover, it was primarily a problem of language. I had grown up with the language of the Baltimore Catechism, and I thought about religious experience in the language I had learned: sanctifying, grace, mortal and venal sins, redemption, and the rest. These were not the words of ordinary conversation.

These were not part of the speech of lovers. Marilyn and I had been talking for months about teaching, politics, our own families, what we had done and what we wanted to do. The words just rolled out, but when it came time for me to talk about my deepest-held religious convictions, I lost confidence in the language. Not in the reality behind the words, but in those heavy Latin words like "incarnation" and "sanctification." Since Marilyn had grown up outside organized religion, I feared that she would be repelled by such language. I started to talk about religion a couple of times but became self-conscious and got tangled up quickly. It was not just the words, though; I was also inhibited by the possibility that I was forcing on her something that she didn't want. I didn't like the picture of me using our mutual love as a crowbar to push her into the church. I had forgotten that belief, that faith, is a gift. In the midst of my tongue-tied anguish along came the Holy Spirit in the garb of a witty Irish priest with a soft west country brogue. He had the words and more.

What many married people come to realize is that spirituality—the drive towards God—is not stripped of what is human. On the contrary, spirituality is love and humanness. Now, we grant it takes some unlearning to come to this conception, especially for those who are raised to seek God in hymns and symbolic statues, and to encounter Him on prayerful retreats. What the new spirituality, if we can call it that, teaches is that all of us, especially married people, know divine love through our human love. And human love grows and develops from enhancing and cherishing that which is human. The stuff of spirituality, then, is right around us. The difficult job, though, is to see into the spiritual significance of this everyday stuff.

KEVIN:

Some houses are haunted by things that go bump in the night. Our house is spooked by a spirit that keeps us from

getting to church on time. We like our church, and even
though we know that if we don't get there on time, the pew
pickings are poor, still we just can't seem to make it. Try as
we may, something always happens. One week, we're all in
the car with plenty of time, but the car keys are missing.
There is a mad scramble. Fifteen minutes later we find them
under the front seat or in the vegetable bin of the
refrigerator. The next week we are off and running, actually
out of the driveway, and discover that someone has left my
wallet behind. Back we go in another search. Then there are
the Sunday mornings when someone oversleeps, even
though the rest of us are making enough noise to make the
walls shudder. Every Sunday seems to be something else:
hair that will not curl; an empty gas tank; a telephone call
that has to be taken; and so on. The funny thing, though, is
that it is never anyone's fault. Try as we may . . . and Lord,
do we try . . . we can never find out whose fault it was. "Just
because we found the keys in my briefcase doesn't mean
that I put them there!" "Yes, God does care if you brush
your teeth. But he also cares if we show up at Mass a half-
hour late." "Yes, I know you filled the tank just a few days
ago, but you also drove the car all around town looking for
that stupid basketball hoop!" Probably because it happens
with such frequency, regularity really, we work very hard to
find out just who is the cause this week of our being late.
While we work at it with great intensity, so far no one has
ever admitted to being the cause. No one has pleaded
guilty. No one has been foolish enough to throw himself or
herself on the mercy of our auto court. However, in the
process of trying to determine guilt, tempers rise, and words
and fur fly. By the time we get to church, not only are there
very few seats left, but we are all feeling decidedly
unChristian. Our silence is broken only by mutters about
divorce lawyers and laments about the sad disappearance
of juvenile penal colonies. We march into church sure that
our friends are whispering, "Well, that's twelve Sundays in a
row now!" And, "Have they no shame!" Of course, the only
seats left are those way up in the front. We shuffle stiffly into

the seats and with red cheeks and taut nerves turn to God and pray, "Lord, what did I do to get stuck with this zoo?"

It was on one such Sunday a few years ago . . . I believe it was a lost-wallet Sunday . . . that a bit of religious truth finally pierced my smoldering mind and heart. Just as we approached the door of the church, twelve minutes after the hour, a woman with whom I have been intimate (whose name I am generously withholding from this account) said to me through clenched molars, "I don't know if I believe in divorce, but I know I believe in murder." As we found seats the priest finished the Gospel and began his sermon. It was a familar topic: the meaning of the love of God. "We show our love for God, not by our love for Him as an abstraction, but our love for those around us, those we work with, our children, our spouse." He went on, "Few of us are called by God to do the heroic act, to take on a staggering burden, or to lay down our lives. Instead our way of demonstrating our love and becoming what God wants us to be is by loving and serving those around us." Fresh new idea? No. Complex theological theorem? No. Big impact on me? Yes. It came to me that morning that the martyrdom for which I had been semiconsciously preparing myself was probably not going to come. Nor would I, Paul of Taurus-style, be called dramatically by God to give up my family and go to the other side of the world to convert the heathen (on several Sunday drives to church that thought had had dazzling appeal). What came home to me that Sunday—what finally penetrated after decades and decades of Sundays and dozens of sermons on that very topic—was that my martyrdom would most likely consist of taking seriously my wife's complaints about dirty clothes on the floor and dirty socks under the bed, by giving my attention to a problem that is frustrating her, by getting up from the television set and helping my daughter with spelling lessons, or by giving up some precious weekend time to civic or church work. I saw, not for the first time but certainly in a new and vivid way, that my own road to spirituality was the one right at my front door. It meant that I was to find my relationship with God by developing my relationships with those around me. In particular, it meant that my relationship with this woman next to me had to be more than simply enjoying her mind and her body. I needed to accept and to understand, too! That morning I looked at our marriage through the Christian lens. And it dawned on me that for our marriage to work, we had to be more than legal partners, more than physical partners, more than intellectual partners. This woman—who can fascinate me and who can infuriate me—and I had to become spiritual partners traveling the same road together.

MARILYN:

I was having my gynecology examination. I don't care to share much that is personal with my doctor, because I figure he already knows more than enough of me. This time, though, we fell to chatting about our lives. My doctor said: "You're a very spiritual person, aren't you?" I quickly looked around the room to see whom he was addressing, since he clearly wasn't talking to me. There was no one else there. He was asking me. There was a silence. I couldn't answer any sooner because I never thought of myself as "spiritual." I don't go to church daily, read more than the occasional religious book or newspaper. Apparently he had picked up that I am on the church council at our Newman Center, that I give talks to people preparing for marriage, and do a little teaching in the family religious and instruction program. "You're a very religious person, aren't you?" he said again. A few things clicked into place. I may not have thought of myself as a spiritual person, but I thought enough of the quest that I went to considerable work to participate in the life of the church. I came to the conclusion that if I were to be a religious person, I had to look to the spirit and activate the spiritual in my life. I know well enough from other parts of my life that if I am to have a fit body, I have to exercise it; I have to run or swim or play tennis. If I am to become a good baker, I have to create bread, cakes, biscuits. If I am to have a good ear for music or theater, I have to listen to concerts and watch plays. Therefore, if I am to become a spiritual person, I have to recognize a spiritual flow. The philosopher, René Descartes, said, "I think, therefore, I am." I suppose the spiritual motto of my life is, "I do, therefore, I am."

It is curious that traditional religion has not made the link between living our married and living our spiritual lives more visible to us. It is certainly no secret (except to the newly in love) that marriage is a demanding and difficult way to live. There is a German proverb that says, "Marriage is heaven and hell." On the other hand, Abraham Lincoln claimed that marriage is neither heaven nor hell; it is simply purgatory. Anton Chekhov warns us, "If you are afraid of loneliness, do not marry." Still further, folk wisdom tells us that a marriage is one long conversation checkered by dispute. And men are continually being warned against marriage, with comments like this one attributed to Francis Bacon: "A man finds himself seven years older the day after marriage."

Though people have traditionally thought marriage to be a nuptial bed more of thorns than roses, it has not been seen as the arena for developing a deep spiritual life.

Part of this is undoubtedly due to the fact that our religious superstars, the saints and other holy men and women, were rarely married. One could easily get the message from organized religion that to be married is to be second-class. We are called to do and to be good, but not to spiritual greatness. By omission, it seems that married folk should aim for the bleacher section of heaven. While almost all theologians will claim that view is wrong, it is still widely prevalent.

Recently, the message from theologians is that marriage is a vocation like the vocation of ministers and priests. We are ordained for an intimate union in all dimensions of our lives in a partnership of affection. If religious persons are to set examples by their work and dedication, so we married people must be examples for married life. We are called to be a loving and married people. We need a spirituality of marriage, even of sex. We are called by human love, which has a spiritual dimension. It is biological and human to desire emotional and physical intimacy. The marriage bond is created, then, out of the merger of spirit and body. Furthermore, marriage requires considerable sacrifice. We are required to give up our time, our privacy, and our self-interest; we are even required to curb our sexuality (married people are, after all, still given to sexual attraction and desires which they cannot always cater to). These denials and sacrifices, however, are not just negative and restricting. They are the mortar of the spiritual bonds between two people.

Another part of the problem is with the language of religion. The purpose of language is to facilitate communication among people. And there are many different types of language: There is the everyday language of the street and the marketplace. And there are many specialized languages, such as the language of the medical doctor, the high-energy physicist, and the tax accountant. Although spirituality is an "everyday thing" shared by all of us, it typically has a specialized language. Most of us have a very impoverished vocabulary for religious values and behavior. Words like sanctification, asceticism, resurrection, redemption are foreign words on the lips of most of us. We would feel awkward bringing them up in daily conversation. We do not talk comfortably about "sin" in our lives. Guilt, self-hate, or anger, maybe. But not "sin." For a married person, the language of religion is quite different from the concrete language of the rest of his or her married life: children, diapers, mortgages, breakfast cereals, and, increasingly, gas mileage. Religion, by its very nature, deals largely with the inexplicable, the incomprehensible, the unseen.

The new spiritual writers have acknowledged some of the difficulty our generation has with discussion of spiritual life. The first stage of understanding "spirituality" is to keep the idea present in routine living. Instead of placing the spiritual and religious in a Sunday service and Sunday school category, we match the religious understanding with our human experience. Most of us demand that life make sense. Piecing together the puzzle of our lives takes various shapes. We search for meaning in the events and emotions that confuse or delight us. We sense frustration or anger, joy or despair. We want our relationships to hold up and sustain us. We might express frustration with words like, "Who's in charge here?" or, "I'm not in charge of my life!" "Why can't I find significance in this relationship?" "This is a helluva situation." These events can be given a religious filter. They are real and spiritual everyday expressions of mystery, the search for meaning.

Bruno V. Manno and Michael O'Grady have structured a new translation of religious experience which helps "unpack God" and the spiritual dimension that is often hidden in daily life. Manno and O'Grady set up the new vocabulary parallel to the old, such as:

(NEW WORD)	(OLD WORD)
experience	story
mystery	God-creation
alienation	sin
center	heaven
being at the fringes	hell
dying	crucifixion

Outfitted with a new vocabulary, we can better understand and speak about our daily experience and find spiritual meaning in it. The awkwardness of keeping the religious words for special events can be put aside. Moreover, the godliness within us becomes more apparent. We are the people of God. We are seeking reconciliation in and through marriage. We become numbered among those who seek the significance of daily life. But exactly how we seek this spiritual fulfillment is the question. And it is here that we turn to the answer: prayer.

Prayer is very troubling for many of us. It really seems like something that the religious professionals should be doing for us. After all, we do support them on earth. It seems reasonable that they should do the lobbying for us above. Although this seems like a nice division of labor, it is clear that it is not the way that the Divine Foreman has set things up. We were told quite clearly in the New Testament, "Pray always." Short and to the point! Unfortunately, knowing one should pray is no assurance that one knows how to pray. To exaggerate, it is like getting the heavenly word to overhaul your car when you don't know a spark plug from a cylinder head. On the other hand, we have all recited and heard many prayers, and we are aware in general what the meaning is behind that special language. We know, for instance, that "Now I lay me down to sleep" is religious language for "Good night. I'm going to sleep now." And "Our Father who art in heaven" is something on the order of "My special Father, I recognize and honor you."

It is very easy to get the impression from these formal prayers that the language addressed to the Almighty is a special, elevated language. After all, we are talking to God, and God is, to be sure, the King of Kings, the Supreme Allied Commander in the Sky. God, therefore, must be talked to in a special way! Well, perhaps, but there are other forms of prayer. The "Our Father" and "Lord of Lords" are prayers for the community, often reserved for formal occasions. Then there are prayers, like the psalms, the hymns, and the religious music of the church. The prayer of which we wish to speak, though, is in a different form: mental prayer.

By mental prayer we mean nothing more than thinking in the presence of God. Let us look first at "in the presence of God." If we acknowledge the existence of God, we are stuck with the fact that He is all-knowing. We cannot hide. We cannot simply make contact with Him when it pleases us, when we want His help in getting a job or we feel like thanking Him for a stunning snowfall. We cannot hide our dirty little jealousies, or lust, or vanities, only to turn our minds to Him when it's convenient. It just doesn't work that way. God has full awareness of us: warts and worries, kinks and crevices. Luckily, besides being all-knowing, God is all-forgiving. And for reasons that defy the imagination, He wants our love and attention. That's quite clear. He is a lover with a passionate desire to share our lives and to share Himself with us. He knows, we suspect, that without keeping in contact with Him, we will begin taking ourselves seriously and otherwise run amok. So God is always there, always present to us. It sounds like a boring job, and it is only a small part of His work. But, after all, He chose it.

Being in God's presence—and He in ours—is inevitable. However, what we make of it is a matter of choice. In mental prayer there is both an acknowledgment of God's presence and a free choice to confront it. We consciously recognize His being there and His capacity to be a part of our personal consciousness.

Then there is the thinking part of our definition of mental prayer as thinking in the presence of God. By thinking we mean a whole array of mental activities: planning, mulling over past events, imagining, puzzling something out, worrying, and even woolgathering. Since it is rare for most of us to plan, let alone woolgather, with words like "art in heaven" and "sanctifying grace," we are sure that the language of mental prayer is not this formal, gussied-up language. While it is fine for the special occasions of group worship, one or two thou's and thy's can be a real conversation stopper in what is supposed to be an intimate exchange. We are confident that the God who calls out to us for loving contact, who tells us to pray always, will listen to our unadorned garden-variety language.

In the same way that husband and wife have different types of conversations, from highly focused eyeball-to-eyeball exchanges to the somewhat inattentive, intermittent exchanges of people reading different parts of the evening newspaper, so, too, does our conversation with God vary. Sometimes we need to have the high-attention, sharply focused conversations. "Come on now! I need help, and I need it now!" Or a slightly qualified thank you: "Lord, while I am still smarting over this rather large nose you gave me, you really did make up for it with this great singing voice. We really knocked them dead tonight, didn't we?"

At the other end of the spectrum is the least attentive form of prayer, or thinking aloud in God's presence. You are walking home from work and just going along with the flow of your thoughts from one topic to another, wondering whether the new boss knows what he is doing, thinking that the leaves were a good deal further along this time last spring, thinking about whether or not you really want to get involved with a softball league this year. Or you are preparing dinner and thinking about grammar school and Mrs. Patten, your fifth-grade teacher who understood you like no other teacher before or after. In this type of prayer God is not centerstage. Rather, He is offstage, but supportively watching us from the wings. We may or may not take a quick glance and become conscious of His presence. In any event, as we walk or work along, we are secure in the knowledge that He is with us, watching us with love, forever on our side.

Somewhere in the middle of these extremes is the mental prayer for divine guidance. You have a problem to solve, a personal dilemma to settle, a career decision to make. You are not asking God to pull out all of the stops, part the heavens, and speak to you from on high. You are not asking for another burning bush. You just want Him to help you work something through . . . or at least keep you from making a major mistake.

There are several effects of this intimate, habitual, and sometimes rambling thinking in the presence of God. One is that we see more easily the religious dimension of our lives and of the world in which we live. We put our lives not in the narrow perspective of our own self-interest or of the group with which we feel closest associations, but rather with ourselves as children of God. Another effect of mental prayer is that it breaks down our sense of isolation and loneliness. A friend of ours who at one time was going to her psychoanalyst three times a week expounded the benefits to us. When we suggested that three visits a week has to be immensely time-consuming, she countered with, "But do you know what it's like always to have someone who is completely on your side!" Loneliness is part of the lives of most of us, even of a married life teeming with children. Rightly or wrongly, it is easy to feel cut off, to feel that we are out there fighting the battle alone. The prayerful person has a sense of the continuing presence of a loving God and the belief that Someone with a lot of clout is always on his side.

A final effect. It is difficult, if not impossible, to live in this world and not have what the happiness writers call "negative thoughts." Negative thinking, too, comes in many forms, from mild worrying to hurling curses on an enemy and imploring the Prince of Darkness to do a number on him.

The two of us are worriers. We are not heavy worriers. Rather, worriers second-class. We have little mental tread-mills in our heads which run rather regularly. We worry about World War Three, getting our daily bread, disturbing pains in the lower-back region that we didn't have yesterday, the Greenhouse effect, which of our worst traits our children are inheriting, odd noises coming from the motors of our car or furnace or refrigerator, why we are incapable of growing vegetables, and, alas, why we worry so much.

Big-time negative thoughts can be truly destructive. Few of us go very far in life without coming across small-minded people in high places or people whose greatest gift appears to be to point out our faults to the rest of the world. It is easy to fall into big-time negative thinking when one has been the victim of another's acid tongue. It is here that thinking things through in the presence of God is most needed. Simply from the perspective of self-interest, negative thoughts can hurt us. They destroy peace. They kill karma. They sour the stomach.

And so the knave who originally hurt us has hurt us doubly. Better to turn to God and hand the affair over to Him. If we insist on thinking about it, do it in His presence. It is difficult to plan out carefully how you are going to kneecap your enemy while God is looking over your shoulder.

In spite of all the claptrap about America being a bourgeois reactionary society, ours is, in fact, a very experimental and revolutionary society. And one of the most revolutionary and experimental aspects of American society is that we are trying to be a great society and strong people without publicly acknowledging our spirituality, our relationship with God. Other than a line like "in God we trust" on coins, the spiritual dimension of people's lives and our religious heritage have been taken out of our cultural lives. Take film and television entertainment, for example. If a cultural anthropologist studied only American television and films and from that drew a picture of us, it would be a very distorted picture. One of the major distortions is that we are a godless people for whom church attendance and the spiritual life are all but nonexistent. The religious people in our society who appear on the television news all look vaguely like monkeys and are consumed with the idea that schools are teaching their children that their direct forebears were tree climbers. Or the religious people are crazed maniacs who justify perverse acts because God spoke to them directly from the glove compartment of their pickup truck or a talking dog. The media then present few examples of people with deeply held religious values who make those a part of their regular behavior. Television and film rarely recognize the good works and sacrifices that are made daily in the name of the Spirit. It does not reflect the fact that the great percentage of Americans worship regularly. The media message is one of omission. The message is there, though, hidden but insistent: Religious observance and a quest for spiritual fulfillment are not part of the lives of our society's TV models, such as Marcus Welby, Mary Tyler Moore, Lou Grant, and Hawkeye. In fact, they live their lives quite admirably without God.

The result of all this is that it is increasingly difficult to maintain any sort of religious perspective on what one is doing. We rarely hear people speaking from a religious perspective other than inside our church. In many circles, from university life to business, it is just not correct to speak from or look at the world from a religious view. This is all part of the American experiment. The question that we are confronted with now and will be increasingly confronted with in the future is, "Can we keep our society going without religious values and the benefits that they provide the people? Can we be a great nation if the people are motivated by self-interest, enlightened or otherwise?" But independent of the answer to this heavy problem, each of us has to live out his own life, married or otherwise. We have to decide whether or not we wish to be religious people and develop the spiritual side of our lives. Right now we all get a great deal more social reinforcement for keeping ourselves physically fit and healthy than we do for being spiritually fit.

But in our experience, just choosing to be spiritual is really not enough. We find ourselves easily overcome by the secular. We find it hard to remember where we put the religious lens. It may be an offensive way to say it, but we feel that we have to "program in" the religious and the spiritual, otherwise it gets swallowed up by TV, book club, children, and other demands competing for our attention.

Americans are compulsive list makers. In the format of "how to" books, we even have the chutzpah to make a spiritual list. Somewhere in our past we learned that getting organized required making lists. We couldn't pass the second grade without learning the value of scraps of paper reminding us to bring a note from home, to fetch a cake on Friday, or to make a list of things we were grateful for. So with apologies to the saints of our heritage who prayed from the heart—not from a list—we offer a few suggestions for acquiring a spiritual habit.

Six Suggestions for Keeping the Spirit

First, though we have friends of many stripes and religious views, ranging from highly committed to openly antagonistic, we believe it's important to have a core of religious friends. Quite frankly, we need their example and support. They remind us of how we should be thinking and how we should be living. For most people this can be achieved by being involved with a group of people in one's church.

Second, go to church regularly. It is hard to keep a religious perspective without going to the place where the message is presented. It is difficult to make the necessary connections between where we are in our lives—married and otherwise—and where we are to be going, without being reminded of the message. Churches differ, not just in theology but in personality. Some churches starve us and some nourish us. This means intelligent shopping, until we find the one that best meets our needs.

Third, don't just sit there on Sunday, participate in the liturgy. Listen to the sermons especially, even though it hurts. Once we belonged to a parish that was comfortable spiritually and materially. A young curate came to our parish and for two years tried to rouse us. Finally, one Sunday he had had enough. He scowled through the gospel and when he was finished slammed the book and stared at the people. "Hey, you out there. For God's sake and for your own sake, pay attention to the sermons. It is the only ten minutes out of the ten thousand plus minutes of the week that you hear the word of God. Now, *pay attention.*" And he stalked out of the pulpit.

Fourth, don't just go to church. Become a member of the community. Contribute to the church. Find some work that you can do to make your commitment actual. Whether it is serving coffee and doughnuts after church or visiting the sick is not the essential point. Rather, don't just be a religious consumer. Be a religious producer. Be a religious actor.

Fifth, kick the bunny out of Easter. This is a personal

peeve. A number of years ago there was a campaign to "put Christ back into Christmas." It was an attempt not to lose the meaning of the religious holiday to a reindeer "with a nose so bright." It would appear that the campaign was another failure. Religious holidays like Christmas, Easter, and Thanksgiving have been smothered by cloying commercialism. So, too, with the yearly celebration of Halloween and St. Valentine's Day, the first lost to the candy industry and the second to both candy and greeting card industries. For ourselves and our children we have to rescue our religious tradition and not have it trivialized. We have to wake ourselves up consciously to the fact that amid all of the Christmas madness, the cards, shopping, and assembling of toys, some mystery is going on.

We have to force awareness that the days of Lent are special and that they are leading up to the great event of the church: a celebration of Christ's resurrection and our own. This means using our imagination on how to breathe life into family or religious rituals so that they have meaning for both us and our children. It means making one's own traditions at home, such as making lists of what we are thankful for on Thanksgiving, having special pageants at Christmas, and more thoughtful religious observances and readings during Lent.

These religious holidays and seasons have a purpose. They are old and time-tested methods of keeping us in touch with ourselves. Now, however, we have to force ourselves to get past the jelly beans, cranberries, and tinsel to get to their meanings. Crazy!

Sixth and finally, pray. Prayer is a little word that covers many different kinds of conversation. We need to take advantage of all of those types of prayer. Instead of just going through the empty prayer ritual of Sunday services, we need to speak and sing the prayers with our eyes and our emotions. We must build the habit of serious private and regular conversation with God. And we need to increase our awareness of God as we go about our regular tasks. He must play on the back roads of our mind. In brief, we have to get the conversation going and to keep it going.

What all of these suggestions are getting at is that we must consciously program the spiritual, the transcendent dimension into our lives. This is particularly true today when so much of it has been consciously *programmed out* of our professional and cultural lives. While we are convinced of the ability of most couples to make a good marriage, anyone who looks at marriage statistics knows that isn't happening. It is not just marriages breaking up, but married people living—in Thoreau's words—lives of quiet desperation. Some couples who don't acknowledge the spiritual dimension seem to have forged admirable marriages. They have learned how to forget themselves and attend to the other. We remain convinced, though, that for the great majority of us, marriage without the spiritual dimension is a barren and probably short-term affair.

𝒴 We are not satisfied with survival. Plenty of marriages stick together somehow—though more and more are coming unglued—but we are not going to settle for ordinary marriage. We are high fliers, and when we don't fly, we wonder why. Living together turns out to be different from being in love or having sex with someone. Living together destroys conventional romantic love. Too little mystery and too much grinding reality shatter our false images of ourselves and of each other. Early love, perhaps, carries us through the uncertainties of the partnership. Such love, based on idealistic romance and our own fantasy life, rubs dry with the friction of living arrangements. We prided ourselves on our communication, but the dialogue could become banal or bitter. Both of us violated our expectations for marriage. We were disappointed with ourselves and with the other.

Our dialogue began to focus on the dynamics of marriage, ours and others'. We were watching for others who were more than survivors. Had they, too, passed winters of discontent and summers of hot dispute? Would self-definition whirl us past each other? We learned to detect trouble signs in the marriages we observed, and we learned to decode the tension we saw as simply their style. We began to see patterns develop.

Marriage is not ordinarily recognized as a mental concept, much less treated seriously as a series of learning experiences that evolve in an individual's lifetime. Marriage itself changes radically and sometimes dramatically through life. Ebb tides and high tides roll on in succession. We saw these tides in ourselves and in other couples.

Some scholars place marriage in stages similar to Jean

Piaget's infant and adolescent development theories. One scholar, Roy T. Tamashiro of Ohio State University, considers marriages in four distinct stages. First, a magical falling-in-love stage, like the view of marriage in fairy tales. Second is an idealized conventional sequence in which socially approved ideas of marriage are uncritically accepted by the couple. The couples do all the things "we are supposed to do." Then, third, an individualistic stage requires re-evaluation and criticism. It centers on self-reflection and on an emerging personal definition of marriage. Finally, an affirmational stage arises in which confusion and conflict are accepted as part of all human relationships. In this stage one is able to show concern to affirm oneself and others. Two people do not always arrive at the same stage at the same time. Much conflict flares when one crosses the stage lines out of step with the other. Themes of early stages do not always disappear as one progresses to later stages. Individuals do experience earlier emotions. For example, at the individualistic or affirmational stage a person may still long for the romantic ideal, still want that girl of his dreams he married, still want to be adored as in those early months of the romance. But the longing is qualified by realistic personal goals or other aspects of one's inner life.

With the support of the Reverend Andrew Greeley (at the National Opinion Research Center and the University of Chicago), a group of social scientists and theologians gathered to study marriage. Searching for commonalities in their private lives and in the lives of their friends and colleagues, this group discovered a cycle theory of marriage. Every marriage, they found, goes through cycles of highs and lows. Realizing that these sequences take place in nearly all relationships relieves many people who judge marriages as "one long conversation checkered by dispute." Actually, marriage in which no quarreling at all takes place may well be one that is dead or dying from emotional undernourishment. If you care, you probably fight.

The particular style of passing through the cycles develops in individual marriages, and after a while one recognizes one's own way of getting there. The group labeled the cycles: falling in love (obviously a high); settling down (practical matters); bottoming out ("the pits"); and beginning again.

We had all gone through the cycles of never wanting to be apart, then wanting some private time, to actually needing to get some distance between the two of us. But as with nature and the seasons, the cycles change and we are ready for coming together again. Out of the mirror of broken illusion comes a new reflection. A different love, committed to the other person's growth, maturity, and happiness, grows out of the disillusionment with mystery and romance. We are capable of rejuvenation and renewal. This coming together doesn't just happen. It is not inevitable, like the roll of the seasons. Both our minds and our bodies can help. We can use our minds to fathom what is going on in our married lives. We can consciously learn the craft of living together well. We can adjust, change, learn new skills and patterns. But we are more than minds. Our bodies can draw us together again.

Our love is like a rubber band, sometimes pulling apart, stretching the limits and snapping back at other times. Often sexual passion pulls us back again from the depths of bottoming out, from isolation and loneliness. As Gail Sheehy puts it, "Intimacy is its own reward." We fall in love all over again. Seeing the caring that is behind the quarrel, feeling the attraction once again, the positive energy of being in love makes it easy for us to be generous and helpful once again. Knowing how much has been at stake while the quarrel or period of estrangement was in control, we run back to the haven of our love. The coming together brings back the mood of sensitivity, the generosity of being in love. We not only feel very close to the beloved, but close to others as well. The lure of falling in love is irresistible and once more takes us outside ourselves. We have committed ourselves to this person, allowing her to reach us as no other could. We are excited by him again, being with him, talking about him. We want to hear about her, touch her, be touched by her. We are again "in love." We resolve to conquer the faults in ourselves and in our marriage. We can fly again.

Volume 2

Awakening
the workplace

Achieving Your Connection, Fulfillment and Success at Work

Editors: Adele Alfano and Kathy Glover Scott ■

Published by
Experts Who Speak Books
www.expertswhospeakbooks.com

ISBN 0-9780283-0-9 (v. 1). ISBN 978-0-9780283-2-9 (v. 2)
©2007 Kathy Glover Scott and Adele Alfano

Editors: Kathy Glover Scott and Adele Alfano
Book design and production: Creative Bound International Inc.
www.creativebound.com

Library and Archives Canada Cataloguing in Publication

Awakening the workplace : achieving connection, fullfillment and success at work / editors: Adele Alfano and Kathy Glover Scott.

ISBN 0-9780283-0-9 (v. 1).--ISBN 978-0-9780283-2-9 (v. 2)

     1. Quality of work life. 2. Success. I. Alfano, Adele, 1959-
II. Scott, Kathy Glover, 1958- III. Title.

HD6955.A94 2006   650.1   C2006-901559-7

Printed in Canada

Contents

Introduction

The spark for *Awakening the Workplace* first came to light during our initial planning session for Experts Who Speak Books in 2002. Even at the dawn of our series, as editors we were passionate about communicating the new knowledge and tools needed to address the changes and daily challenges in an ever-evolving workplace. *Awakening the Workplace, Volume 1* is now an international bestseller, also published in Asia. *Awakening the Workplace, Volume 2* is the ninth book in our acclaimed series.

With all of the Experts Who Speak Books, our goal is to provide you with tips, tools, motivation and essential information. In *Awakening the Workplace*, you'll find the collective wisdom, experience and knowledge of 15 top speakers, trainers, facilitators, coaches and consultants from across North America and Australia who specialize in workplace issues and innovation. Where else can you find the proven expertise and essential wisdom of 15 top trainers, coaches and consultants in one book? Each have taken the absolute essence of their work and teaching and condensed it into chapter form. And the information in each chapter is written with a focus on providing you with the new tools, skills and systems you need to excel, all in a format that is easy to read and reference.

What makes *Awakening the Workplace, Volume 2* unique is how it speaks to the reader in a solution-focused way, regardless of their role in any size of business or organization. How we execute our workday has rapidly changed and many of the old rules for how we should work together have been challenged—or thrown out altogether. Yet, there are threads of knowledge and expertise that all people who work require. *Awakening the Workplace* reflects the need for this multi-faceted information.

Experts Who Speak Books is one of the most successful book publishing companies in the world specializing in producing books for professional speakers, trainers, facilitators, coaches and consultants. We create co-authored books that showcase the dynamic, creative and successful people who have chosen these professions. We do it through supporting the writing process and taking care of all the specialized work of design, printing, publishing and distribution. And, we do it from a win-win value base, where cost sharing, cross promotion and mutual support are the keys to our success. You are invited to visit our websites:

www.AwakeningtheWorkplace.com
www.ExpertsWhoSpeakBooks.com
www.SalesGurusSpeakOut.com
www.ExpertWomenSpeakOut.com

Watch for our tenth book, *Leadership Gurus Speak Out*, in late 2007, as well as *Expert Women Speak Out, Volume 7*. Subjects for upcoming books in the series include the Internet, communications and marketing. Let us know if you are in these professions and would like to contribute.

All in all, you are holding in your hands a goldmine of information and expertise, geared to make your work life easier. Our wish is that success flows to you. The choice is yours—to remain where you are or move forward. Not a hard decision to make!

Kathy Glover Scott and Adele Alfano
Editors and Publishers, Experts Who Speak Books

Sarah Cornally

Cornally Enterprises Pty Ltd

Courageous Conversations

Have you ever had the urge to speak out, but held back? Have you ever had a brilliant idea go unexpressed because you felt it wouldn't be accepted? Have you ever realized too late that things would have worked out much better if you had spoken up?

Or have you ever found yourself deciding to speak up, but things turned out really badly? You may have been viewed as superior and arrogant, or critical and demanding, or whining and ineffectual—regardless of whether the other person had completely missed your point or overreacted to what you were saying.

Alternatively, have you been blessed by an experience where you did take a stand and somehow it all came out right? The other person got the message the way you intended and something great happened as a result. You connected with the other person in a way that enhanced you both, coming together to create something better than what you could have created on your own. This is the result of a well-executed courageous conversation.

A courageous conversation takes place anytime you decide to speak up in a situation in order to get a better result. Your intention is to serve the greater good of a situation, whether it is personal or business-related. Your intention may also be to reveal an observation, insight, or response. The situation will call for courage, as these conversations may not be well received.

There are many opportunities every day, in every relationship you have, for a courageous conversation that will move things forward in a constructive way—if only you will engage with the situation skillfully.

A Real Example

One such experience for me happened several years ago. I was referred to a professional services firm to assist with a serious situation with one of the partners. This partner had been accused of harassment and bullying junior professional officers and support staff. The managing director, Fred, briefed me thoroughly—he wanted me to remediate the situation. I met the partner and we developed an intervention plan. The plan was discussed with Fred, who was pleased and positive about the approach. However, it soon became clear that Fred was engaging in his own behaviors, which were reflective of the complaints made of the partner. If Fred did not change his behavior, there was no legitimacy in the intervention. Time for a courageous conversation!

Fortunately, at the beginning of the assignment, I had flagged that Fred would need to be part of the intervention. We met to discuss his role. As we progressed with the discussion, which was amicable, he started to adopt an aggressive posture. His shoulders were expanding, his energy was becoming intense, and his eyes were narrowing—I felt as though I was under attack. I felt intimidated and I wanted to leave the room. I was sure he was not aware of his behavior, nor its effect. I had to decide whether to step up and say what needed to be said right then, or let it go and deal with it later. I chose to practice what I preach.

"Fred," I said, "Could we pause for a moment? I need to ask you something." He stopped in his tracks, confused. "Yes, what is it?"

"I need to check something with you," I continued. "Are you convinced that I am the right person to do this assignment?"

"Yes," Fred replied.

"Do you trust me?"

"Yes," he said again.

"Do you believe I understand the whole situation properly?"

"Yes."

Coming to my point, I said, "Are you aware I am feeling very intimidated by you at the moment?"

"No!" Fred was shocked. "What am I doing?"

"You are becoming very intense in your manner and speech. It is very forceful towards me," I told him. "Are you aware that you do this?"

"No, I'm not," he said.

He turned to the HR director to ask if she perceived the same. Fortunately she confirmed that this was what she observed as well. There was a pause as he took this in, realizing it was true. You could see him visibly open up his mind.

We went on to discuss how this was contributing to the situation and that he needed to adjust his behavior if the other intervention was to deliver the desired outcome. He agreed, and we went on to do some great work together. Excellent results were achieved for this situation—the benefits were expanded to a range of other areas that enhanced his leadership and grew good results in other areas of the business.

Courageous conversations are required if there is something unsaid that would make a constructive difference to the situation. Often we do not know if our comment would make a constructive difference or not, but if we fail to speak then we fail to add our own value to the situation. Let's examine the things you need to be able to have courageous conversations about.

Outcome-Focused

A powerful way to make things flow well in any conversation is to ensure that the people involved are agreed on the outcome they want. You need to be very clear about the outcome you are aiming for:

- If your goal is pure self-interest, things are unlikely to work.
- If your goal is aligned with other people's interests as well as your own, it will have the optimum chance of bringing a constructive outcome.
- The outcome also needs to be focused on the task at hand. What is the best result for the situation as well as the people involved?

Here is another real-life experience:

» On my first day of a clinical placement as a student occupational therapist, I arrived five minutes late. I was in a new country and I had misjudged
the traffic and become lost. However, I was skilled at the art of explaining.
I arrived late and launched into my apologetic performance. The head OT
put her hand up, signaling me to stop. "The only problem with being late
is that it wastes time," she said. "You have just wasted five minutes of our
time; do not waste another five explaining yourself. It is more professional
to simply apologize and get to work. Let's start." She was abrupt but
direct, honest, non-judgmental, and focused on outcomes. I learned
something valuable that day. «

Getting agreement on common objectives and outcomes at the beginning is
extremely useful. If people are heading towards the same goal, there are fewer
opportunities for conflict. People no longer need to worry about whether their ideas
are right or wrong; they only need to work collectively to discover the best way to
reach their goal. This actually opens up space to explore different ideas from the different people involved. You know you will get the outcome you want, and everyone will feel that their contribution is valued. The following are some examples of
actions with desired outcomes:

- The strategic conversation (for example, the top three priorities to work on
in the next quarter);
- The recruitment (for example, the key characteristics for success in the role);
- The performance improvement (for example, what you need to do to achieve
your goals);
- The behavior (for example, agreement on desirable leadership behaviors);
- The upward feedback (for example, that the boss understands how to have
challenging conversations with you in a constructive way).

When thinking about outcomes, most people focus primarily on material ones,
hoping that the relationships involved will look after themselves. Defining your
desired relationship outcomes is, however, equally important. You could include as
outcomes such things as respect, accountability, responsibility, trust, and so on. Your

approach needs to pay as much attention to these relationship factors as it does to the situational factors. If you only focus on one area at the expense of the other, your courageous conversation won't work. Sometimes you need to set different combinations of outcomes for different situations, as this table shows:

SITUATION:	Strategic Conversation
Scenario 1:	
Material Outcome	Top three priorities for next quarter
Relationship Outcome	Accountability
Scenario 2:	
Material Outcome	Top three priorities for next quarter
Relationship Outcome	Trust

Deal With Your Internal Responses

Courage is the ability to act in the presence of fear. It requires the ability to identify a fear and make a choice to act despite its existence. We need to prefer the benefits of acting to what we would gain from being silent.

Courageous conversations need to be free from any excess baggage. Excess baggage includes any unmet emotional needs that you are trying to meet through this interaction, such as a desire for approval or to prove your power. These things change the quality of the conversation so that it is experienced quite differently by the receiver. Often when a courageous conversation backfires it is due to excess baggage.

Any time you feel your emotions rise, pay attention. Emotions are like your other senses—they are trying to get your attention. The challenge is not to let them overwhelm you—that's not helpful. You are not your feelings, you simply experience your feelings, and you can choose what you do with them. Test your emotions to find out how their messages can help you.

What if you asked your emotions what they were seeking to tell you?

If your fear had a voice what would it say?

If your anger had a voice what would it say?

If your excitement had a voice what would it say?

Sometimes we need to find out about other people's emotions. Is the reaction about you or is it about them? What's going on for them? You may need to ask them to clarify. Ask in a non-judgmental way by using an open question (who, what, when, where, why, or how).

When my fear arose with Fred, the managing director, I asked, "Why am I feeling intimidated? It feels as if he is going to attack me! Is it because he doesn't trust me? Is he doubtful about my skill or ability; does he feel I don't understand; is *he* feeling under attack?" I needed to check out his viewpoints.

Emotions will often alert us to important things, letting us know what we need to take care of in a situation. It is important to remember this is true for others as well. Different people have different needs in this regard. To optimize the probability of being heard and understood, we need to ensure that what we choose to say is clean and clear. If we activate fears in others we will complicate the situation unnecessarily.

Position the Conversation Constructively

The conversation needs to be introduced in a way that will lead to a good response. Using desired outcomes as the basis for the conversation is the most constructive way to do this. It will help you to begin well if you are clear on the benefits of the situation and the people involved.

It is critical that you do not proceed until you are convinced you have a common understanding and agreement on your objectives. This will act as the reference point that you may need to return to repeatedly throughout the conversation.

Because most courageous conversations are about getting to the truth of a matter and may have uncomfortable consequences, people will search for ways to avoid dealing with whatever issue you are raising. Sometimes they will attack you, catastrophize, or create a victim story about how they are misunderstood. Use the agreed outcomes and your intentions as reference points. These structures will provide a non-judgmental, gentle way of refocusing the conversation so that it stays on track. For example, if someone blames a whole series of circumstances for their actions, you may say: "That may be true. Right now we are focusing on [the issue]."

As the initiator of the courageous conversation, you need to be well satisfied that you have a sincere commitment to the outcomes by the people concerned, not a superficial one. This requires quality eye contact and speaking directly to the people concerned, ensuring you are answered with a committed "Yes" to the question: "So we are agreed that [x] is the desired outcome?"

If you don't get a committed "Yes," that requires a different courageous conversation. Express what you are observing; for example, "I am not convinced you are committed to this outcome. I sense you are saying "Yes" to comply, but not because you mean it. What is bothering you? What can you be committed to?"

If you are unable to get commitment, there is no point proceeding because the person is not engaged. It is important to understand and deal with their resistance before you try to solve the issue at hand.

Dealing With Resistance or Opposition

When dealing with resistance, the initial task is to understand where it is coming from. You may need to have a conversation with the other person to determine this. Sometimes it will be clear; for example, you will come across people who are clearly mischievous. They are playing a game with you, and enjoy proving that you can't influence them. For them, it's all about the power to refuse to co-operate.

The result of this understanding would determine what your next action might be. Sometimes a conversation is best had about what you are observing. If they are mischievous, tell them that you see their mischievousness and tell them the consequences of pursuing that stance. Ideally, you want to enable someone to see the choices that they are making by their behavior.

If you become convinced that they will not change their point of view, it may be time to change your overall intention. Instead of wondering, "How do I influence this person to change?" you may say, "How do I achieve my objective despite the views of this person?" There might be other ways to reach your goal. It is easy to see the complexity of these sorts of situations—there might need to be a series of courageous conversations before a challenging issue is resolved.

Assess Your Audience

Before you begin your conversation you need to think about the person you are going to have this conversation with. Be mindful that this person will be significantly affected by a range of factors from the situation and context. Thinking about those factors and the way they impact on other factors will enable you to work out an approach that is well-designed, respectful, and likely to get a good response. What you are seeking to do is something worthwhile for both of you, so you need to ensure you know what is worthwhile to them.

Be aware that often people's needs are different than their stated wants. You need to think about what is important to the other person—their objectives and the outcomes they are seeking to achieve. Why are those things important to them? How do these aims fulfill their social and emotional needs? You need to be mindful of relevant aspects of their personality; for example, are they introverted or sensitive, easygoing or volatile?

Ask the questions below and contemplate possible answers. If you have no ideas, you need to find out the answers. Preferably ask the person involved, or if you don't think they have that awareness or insight, ask others who will be constructive in their comments. Ask:

1. What's going on with that person? What are their priorities and why?
2. What's their relationship with the current situation? Do they have the full picture?
3. What's at stake for them professionally? (For example, their reputation.)
4. What's at stake for them personally? (For example, their sense of who they are.)
5. What are the implications for them?

Clive, a client, asked me once for guidance on how to deal with a sensitive matter with his boss, Simon:

> » Simon had recently been recruited to a senior position, reporting directly to the global CEO. The CEO had set some very demanding goals for Simon. Simon had come from a non-corporate role, so he wanted to show his boss that he was a good corporate, can-do man.

Simon then began to direct Clive to achieve a vast range of new initiatives that involved a lot of change. Clive loved this—it was his best suit. Clive had received some feedback about his high degree of innovation but also that he was inconsistent in delivery. People were getting frustrated and starting to doubt his judgment.

In response to this, Clive had requested advice to help him get to the bottom of these issues. He discovered he was not taking the time to make sure other people involved in the projects were clear, capable, and willing to execute. In fact, he realized that the change agenda was way too full and that they would not achieve the expectations the CEO had because they were unrealistic. **«**

Clive needed to get Simon to understand and accept the reality of the situation. Something had to give—the CEO's expectations had to be adjusted, the timelines had to be adjusted, or the resources had to be made more available—in order to have a win for everyone. Clive's courageous conversation needed to be positioned to enable Simon to feel supported in his objective: demonstrating his can-do capability to the CEO in a way that would work effectively for him and his team.

The better you think these ideas through, the better equipped you will be for the situation. Part of preparing is to be aware of what might happen, and think of possible responses to ensure that you stay with your purpose. If you are not prepared, it is quite likely that the other person will say something that taps into your sensitivities. If that happens, you will be hooked by emotional triggers and your responses to those will drive the direction of the conversation. This type of preparation enables you to remain focused, calm, and purposeful.

Creating an Influence Map

When I am working through complex organizational scenarios, I create what I call an *influence map* so I can understand how the whole system interacts and where to intervene with the best effect. When you see these relationships drawn out and mapped you can begin to understand the forces at play. Then you can find the key points of influence for people.

In the following example of an influence map, the different thicknesses of the connecting lines indicate the strength of the relationship between the two people. A real situation would be even more complicated than this, with many more relational and personal factors to consider.

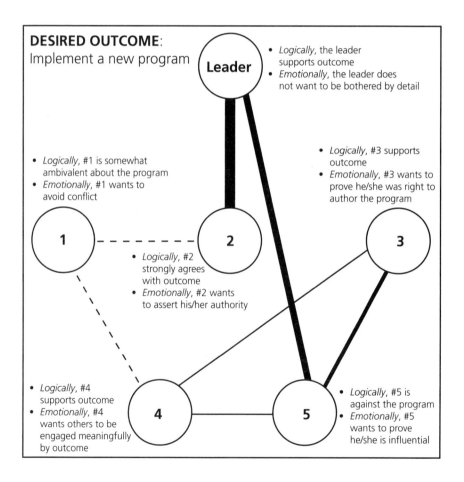

Once you understand the forces at play you can identify which people you need to influence, how to influence them (directly or indirectly), and what messages will have meaning for them. Now you are in a position to craft your message.

Craft Your Message

When we communicate, our words and ideas stimulate thoughts and feelings in other people. We need to have a clear idea of what message we want to construct. How will you build your conversation, given your understanding of the perceptions of the other person and the expectations of each of you?

> » Margaret was a senior director in a professional services firm. She was a very purposeful and committed contributor. She was insightful, highly skilled, and had a great contribution to make. There were a few perceptive people who recognized her skills. However, there were several people, including her boss, who found her frustrating. Her boss thought she always seemed to be resisting him. It seemed that no matter what Margaret did, she couldn't get through to him. Even though she was working very hard to achieve his objectives, he didn't realize how committed she was to those objectives. She was actually so committed that if she began to realize that an initiative wouldn't work, she would resist proceeding and seek to change the approach. «

A new conversation was required. Her boss needed to understand that Margaret was highly committed to what he wanted her to do and that her actions were actually ensuring that his results would be achieved. She needed to craft a message that communicated that to him.

First, Margaret needed to think about opening the conversation, which meant being open and clear about her objective and intent. She let him know she wanted to improve the way they worked together and that her intent was to have a constructive conversation that supported both of them. She then stated her experience and her observations of what had happened in the past. She described how she had thought about it all further and drawn some conclusions about her communication that she wanted to take responsibility for. This was followed by outlining her message—that she was highly committed to what he wanted her to do and that she was ensuring that his results would be achieved. She said this in a clear, precise way, providing evidence for her words, about the reasoning and intentions behind her actions.

This created an open space for Margaret's boss to engage with her and respond. Typically, these crafted conversations unfold in a constructive manner that leads to good outcomes. When Margaret finished her conversation it resulted in her boss's increased realization of her value.

You can use these strategies to craft your own courageous conversations into open, engaging exchanges for everyone involved.

Seeding Thoughts

Sometimes we are in too much of a hurry—we can see an answer and just want everyone else to understand it and get on with it. In our haste, we don't respect what our colleagues will need in order to accept our idea. Other times we think we have an answer, but in fact we are missing part of the whole picture that we may only be able to get from others.

A powerful way to engage others with your outcomes is to seed thoughts and ideas with them. You can stimulate people to think about pertinent issues and factors for themselves, encouraging them to understand what's going on. What's more, if people have developed their own relationship with an idea, they will be much more positive about seeing it come to fruition.

People need to understand the ideas presented to them and why they are worth considering. They need to understand how their work will be worth the investment, and feel capable of carrying it off. Force-feeding people with plans is not helpful because they will not feel committed, but inviting people to think about ideas in a purposeful way helps them to understand. You can seed these thought processes in others by asking them well-designed questions.

>> Elizabeth is a quiet observer. She typically doesn't say much, but listens and thinks about what is going on. She is constantly looking for ways to improve things for everyone. She comes up with some great insights and helpful ideas, yet often people don't hear her or pay attention when she speaks.

Elizabeth was part of a sales team that was frustrated at their management. They could not see that a new process in the call center was not working and that, in fact, it was making things worse. Salespeople were getting very poorly qualified leads and wasting increasing amounts of time. Management was not helping, focusing on fixing everything except the real problem. Elizabeth could see what they needed to understand, but how should she seed these ideas so that the managers would respond constructively? **«**

Elizabeth designed a series of questions to cause people to think about the situation differently. She thought about the end result first, and then worked backwards, determining the questions that would help others think.

As the managers answered her questions, they discovered new insights. By the time they answered them all, they had a new concept of the real situation. Then they embraced Elizabeth's ideas through their own process of discovery. Elizabeth found through this that she could be quite influential without people necessarily noticing what she was doing. The more she did it, the more valuable people found her to be. When people find you to be of value they want more of what you have to offer, which fulfills you personally.

Open and honest communication is often noted as a sign of a healthy culture. People want a culture where courageous conversations are the norm. This requires us to learn the art of courageous conversations. We need to resolve the tension between getting our emotional needs met and creating the results that matter to us and our colleagues.

In my experience, those people who invest in the disciplines required to have successful courageous conversations get a real thrill as they discover they can influence difficult situations. They notice their successes in speaking up, and what they did to make it work. Also, they notice that this starts to extinguish unhealthy behaviors in others. People around them will engage in more open and honest communication because they feel safe—they realize that it is not about being right or wrong, but about searching for the best way forward. This sets people free to express the best of what they have to offer.

People who learn these skills create powerful opportunities for leadership. If these people then facilitate this in others, they create a potent source of influence. The more we all learn to express our concerns in an effective way, the more we are able to make meaningful contributions right where it matters.

There is a vitality, a life force, an energy, a quickening that is translated through you into action, and because there is only one of you in all time, this expression is unique. And if you block it, it will never exist through any other medium and it will be lost. The world will not have it. It is not your business to determine how good it is nor how valuable nor how it compares with other expressions. It is your business to keep it yours clearly and directly, to keep the channel open.

Martha Graham

Sarah Cornally

Sarah Cornally is one of Australia's most sought-after strategic leadership advisors. Her track record at executive and board levels is underpinned by her finely honed ability for spotting maximum leverage points in businesses, people, and organizations. Sarah's qualifications include BAppSc, MSafety Sc, AFAIM, Fellow of AICD.

Sarah has received the prestigious Nevin Award for outstanding service to the National Speakers Association of Australia and the speaking industry. Sarah provides keynote speaking and facilitation services on a wide range of topics including leadership, optimizing performance, strategic thinking, engagement and retention, group dynamics, and managing difficult people and situations. Her clients include PricewaterhouseCoopers, Vodafone, Macquarie Bank, Ernst & Young, and the Department of Prime Minister and Cabinet.

Sarah has co-authored two books: *Lessons in Leadership* (ISBN 0958591857) and *The CCH 2003 OHS&E Guide—On Leadership* (ISBN 186468685 5). Sarah's CD *Ten Top Tips for Leaders* is recognized for its practical insights for leadership effectiveness.

Business Name:	Cornally Enterprises Pty Ltd.
Address:	PO Box 927, St Ives, NSW 2075, Sydney, Australia
Business Phone:	+61-2-9988 3911
Fax Number:	+61-2-9402 7454
Email:	sarah@sarahcornally.com
Web Address:	www.sarahcornally.com
Speaking Affiliations:	Professional Member, National Speakers Association of Australia (Past National President); International Federation for Professional Speakers (Past Representative for Australia)

Favorite Quote:
"Come to the edge," he said. "No, we are afraid."
"Come to the edge," he said. They did. He pushed. They flew.

Apollinaire

That is all business is in the end: communicating experience and vision through a relationship of truth and trust.

John Eitel, *Awakening the Workplace, Volume 1*

Diane King

Group Intersol, Diane King Inc.

Quiet Leaders Among Us

You don't have to be a "person of influence" to be influential. In fact, the most influential people in my life are probably not even aware of the things they've taught me.

Scott Adams

Quiet leaders don't have to move mountains, bring businesses to greatness or rise to lofty political heights. Quiet leaders are content with making a positive difference, whether it's in their family, their community, or their work.

The words "quiet leader" first came to me when I was writing a eulogy for my maternal grandmother in 1990. She was my role model and a light in my life. When I tried to find a word for her, the only thing that kept coming up was "quiet leader." Now, this was a woman who didn't work outside the home, she didn't raise money in her community, she didn't travel in high social circles. No, she was just a rural woman who raised eight children really well. Her legacy is that her children, spread out over Québec and New England, still get together six to eight times a year and talk to each other over the phone frequently.

» At her wake my grandmother's 19 grandchildren remembered her as someone who made each of us feel special. (We all thought we were her favorite!) We remembered her words of wisdom—words that have influenced decisions in my life as well as influenced the things I tell my own children. Her pearls of wisdom include: "soyez toujours fiers" (be proud of who you are), "un éducation n'est jamais perdu" (an education is never lost), and most important, "deux langues c'est deux personnes" (having two languages is like being two people). **«**

All of the grandchildren strive to be the best that we can be, the majority of us are bilingual and all have post-secondary education. And it is extending to our own children. My grandmother may not have thought that she was affecting the world, or even her little community, but her influence on her family is having a far-reaching and positive effect on the world today. She was a quiet leader.

Big "L" Leaders

Society has always valued and emphasized big "L" leadership. Of course we have had great leaders in our times: Martin Luther King Jr., John F. Kennedy, Pierre Trudeau, and Winston Churchill, to name a few. They all shared the same characteristics of great vision, passion, and hard work, and were able to "rally the troops." They led through very difficult times. These big "L" leaders are often used as examples of what to strive for.

We also have examples of great leaders in organizations: people with great vision and the courage to make changes for the good of the organization, for example, Lee Iacocca at Chrysler, Jan Carlzon at Scandinavian Airlines System, and Bill Gates at Microsoft. So, as bottom lines have improved and businesses reap more profits, the characteristics of these leaders have been held up as the Holy Grail of Leadership. But is leadership only about the big "L" leader?

A few years ago an intriguing article, "Level 5 Leadership," written by Jim Collins, appeared in the *Harvard Business Review* (www.hbr.org). Collins sparked my curiosity when he stated that most leaders only make it up to level 4 leadership, which he calls the "effective leader." Of the 1435 companies they researched for this study, 1424 made it to level 4. That left only 11 companies with level 5 leaders! Interestingly, many of the names of the level 4 leaders were recognizable. Not so with the names of the level 5 leaders. The level 4 leaders had the typical traits that we associate with strong leaders: visionary, determined, purposeful. So, what was it that made level 5 leaders so special?

It was actually very simple and very powerful. It was the combination of humility and will: a strong determination to do the right thing, coupled with modesty. And this describes quiet leaders. I'm sure you can think of people you've met within organizations who have these traits. So, who are these quiet leaders?

Quiet Leaders Among Us

Quiet leaders are the lifeline of our families, our communities, and our organizations. They are the ones who ensure that things get done, they take initiative, they live their lives with passion, they care about others, they listen, they take care of themselves. They are genuine. They know their values and they live them…and they do it with little fanfare. This does not mean that they're shy or withdrawn. It's just that they don't call unnecessary attention to themselves.

Quiet leaders are that way simply by being who they are.

You probably recall people in your life who have had a positive impact either on yourself or others around you. These are the people who I consider quiet leaders. Some might be in a position of authority, such as a school teacher, manager, or business owner, but many are just ordinary people doing extraordinary things in their own quiet way. What makes them special is that they aren't trying to be special.

When identifying the characteristics of quiet leaders, the same traits kept coming up time and time again.

The reality is that big "L" leaders are but a tip of the iceberg; they are the *visible* 10 percent. What's beneath the surface are the strong, determined, and modest quiet leaders who are really holding our society together. For without our quiet leaders—in our families, in our community, and in our work—people's brilliance and greatness would not shine through. A colleague, Judith, shared the following with me:

>> The quiet leaders that come to mind are the people that were often called on to oversee a difficult project, or an interdepartmental group whose members might not all be on the same page, because they were known to be able to manage any conflict. But they didn't take charge in an aggressive way, weren't flamboyant, and didn't create or exacerbate crisis attitudes; they quietly and effectively pulled people together and got the job done.

I think a key characteristic of these people is "quiet"—they listen more than talk. And because they listen well, everyone in the group feels heard, and co-operation typically ensues. Maybe people within the group have some conflict, but this person is a common denominator that every-one can rely on to consider his/her points of view.

There's a high level of trust that builds for this type of leader so that even if some within the group don't get their way, they can usually accept the result as being fair because the leader listened, considered, and communicated effectively. «

Judith may be referring to her work environment, but her words also reflect the stories that surfaced about the quiet leaders all around us, in ordinary situations at home and at work. They live, work, and play among us. Sometimes we recognize them. More often we don't because it's easy to take them for granted. But make no mistake, when things are going really well, it's usually because there is a quiet leader nearby who—by virtue of just being who they are and doing what they do naturally—ensures that things go smoothly.

So, the question is, are you a quiet leader who isn't recognizing the positive dif-ference that you make? The following are some of the key qualities and traits of quiet leaders.

#1—Quiet Leaders Are Encouraging

Quiet leaders often focus on the growth of others, whether it's in the family, community or at work. They see the potential in others and help them to develop it. There are countless stories of people taking a young person under their wing and offering him, or her, a chance at education, redemption, a career…it's someone who can see the spark in another and flame the ember so it glows. My friend, Marie, relates the following:

» One of my past dance teachers was a woman who was able to inspire me to pursue my desire to better myself; I think she had the ability to make a quiet difference in many people's lives. She had the uncanny ability to see people's potential and could empower them to translate intention into reality. She would inspire you to take on a new challenge; she would make you feel safe, loved, and self-confident. I'm not quite sure how she did it, but I remember feeling amazed at how she was able to make everyone feel unique and special.

She could focus on me as if no one else was there, and somehow reach in, deep inside of me, to awaken my creative desires. I believe that she nourished herself by helping others progress and I remember how she would ask me to connect with those who had similar passions so that we could exchange value and help each other. Ingrid's life was eventually taken away by incurable cancer, and after her death I remember talking to others about her. It quickly became obvious that she had had the same effect on them. «

Self-Assessment

- Are you more inward focused (on yourself) or more outward focused (on others)?
- Do you take a special interest in what others are interested in?
- Do you give others encouragement that is individualized?
- Do you look for and recognize the potential in others?

#2—Quiet Leaders Are Involved

Quiet leaders are no strangers to jumping in with both feet. They lead through their exuberance, their joy, and their example. Others are swept up in the moment and want to be around the quiet leader. One of my clients, Marc, tells this story:

>> My fondest memory is of my elementary school principal. He was a very friendly man. He always had a smile, no matter where anyone would run into him. Finding warmth from adults in a world that can be so frightening was always a source of security for a child.

Mr. Fraser always partook in all of the activities of the school. If there was a "Jump Rope for Heart" fundraiser, he'd be there in the school brand jogging suit. (It was red and white at the time.) During school liturgies at our church next door, he was often at the front of the gathering with his guitar. He led us all in song with unrestrained enthusiasm. All 600 students from kindergarten to grade six would sing in unison. I have never felt such joy in all my life as I did when that church was full of song. Mr. Fraser was a part of that. «

Self-Assessment

- Do you get involved in activities at work, in your community, or in your family? How do you get involved?
- Are you openly enthusiastic?
- Do people love being in your company?

#3—Quiet Leaders Are Proactive, Passionate, and Purposeful

Quiet leaders see what needs to be done…and take the initiative to get it done. They either do things themselves in a quiet way or they mobilize others because their passion is infectious. They aren't leaders because they're telling others what to do; they're leading by rolling up their sleeves and just doing it. Heather offers the following example of a quiet leader in action:

>> Jim was an Area Commissioner for Scouts a couple of years ago. He

took the job and really made it his own. He organized training sessions for leaders within his area, went to meetings, and took on a personal challenge. His goal was to save the training area nearby from being closed permanently. He researched, wrote to the bigwigs in Toronto, developed a five-year business plan to keep the place functioning, and organized a meeting at the camp for the bigwigs with all the leaders and the Scouts, Cubs, and Beavers in attendance. His quiet determination and leadership saved a valuable commodity for the children to be able to use at no cost for camping, training, and day hiking.

There are many more examples I could give you of other times I've witnessed him in action over the 10 years he was an active Scouting member, as well as at work.

Hope this helps…don't tell Jim, he'd be embarrassed that I told you. He makes me so proud…his influence and example through Scouting, and as a father, have allowed us to enjoy the results in our son; his mannerisms, his pride, his sensitivity and understanding of others…he follows in Jim's footsteps. **«**

Self-Assessment
- Do you feel strongly about things being right in the world?
- Do you take the initiative to get things rolling?
- Are you focused on the goals?
- Are you passionate about it?

#4—Quiet Leaders Have Concern for Others

Quiet leaders are fair and have a genuine concern for others. They want to make a positive difference in other people's lives and will often put others before themselves. This is not about martyrdom, but rather about a true joy in helping others get what they need or want.

In the workplace it might be the manager who unselfishly helps an employee to grow and move beyond their current role, even if it means losing them from their team. There are managers who prefer to stifle a good employee's growth, preventing them from moving ahead, for fear of losing them. That is the antithesis of a quiet leader. A quiet leader revels in the growth and of being able to see someone "spread their wings." Laurie's story exemplifies the quiet leader in a position of authority:

» One of the quiet leaders I am blessed to know is my boss. She has the skills, knowledge, talent, and experience to serve at senior management levels but made the conscious choice to remain as a middle manager (director level) because it positioned her better to influence within the organization.

She has an incredible reputation in our organization for being honest and pushing people to achieve their best. People know that while they may not always like what she has to say, she speaks from the heart and always in their best interests. On a personal level, she has guided me in my development and advised me based on what I needed and what would advance me, rather than only taking organizational needs into consideration. «

Self-Assessment

- Do you help others grow, even if it means them moving beyond you?
- Do you cheer others' successes?
- Do you have others' best interests at heart?

#5—Quiet Leaders Foster Inclusiveness

Quiet leaders see the good in others. They strive to make the world a better place by fostering understanding, acceptance, and love of others. They exemplify their values by how they live and work. Lise shares the following story:

» Frère Artur Gravelle taught social studies at my high school. He could best be described as an avant-garde teacher who was passionate about life, laughter, and learning.

Always in a happy mood and open to human interaction, this man exemplified wisdom and understanding. He valued people from all walks of life and taught us to love one another, regardless of race, religion, or culture differences. He promoted open dialogue on every, and any, subject matter, and taught his students to respect their many differences, even if they did not agree with what was said or put forth. Frère Artur taught us to love our fellow man and to put their needs ahead of our own, even if at times the cost was detrimental to us on a personal level.

The quality that I most cherished in Frère Artur was his ability to make you feel special whenever you came into contact with him. He always had a smile and a kind word and he spread his *joie de vivre* generously. **«**

Self-Assessment

- Do you share your joy openly?
- Do you see the good in people?
- Are you the one who brings people together?

#6—Quiet Leaders Are Pragmatic

Quiet leaders are realistic optimists. They don't see the world through rose-colored glasses, but neither do they focus on the negative. Their motto is, "If the world hands you lemons, make lemonade!"

» About a year ago, my mother-in-law was diagnosed with stage-three lung cancer. A feisty Cornish woman from the Southwest of England, she raised two boys while working shifts as a nurse. How she's handling the disease and her eventual passing is courageous and inspiring.

She's taken a very practical approach to her treatments. She's very straightforward with what's going on. She is her own best advocate and insists on treatments even when doctors have seemed to give up on her. And she talks openly about everything with her family. She jokes about her ashes being put on our mantles, or having them scattered in our gardens. She makes it easy for us to discuss these things openly with her.

She's sold her house of 45 years and, despite living day-to-day, she's moving into a condominium! It's been her dream, since before she got sick, to move into a condo near all her friends. She wasn't about to let a little illness stop her from achieving that. In spite of failing health, she took on this great task. This doesn't mean she's in denial, but rather that she refused the option of putting her dream on hold to lie about the house waiting to die. She decided to *live* with cancer.

Watching someone go through a battle with cancer is very stressful, but the experience has been made less so because of my mother-in-law's attitude toward life. She's helping herself and her family go through this in a practical, realistic, and calm way. I appreciate and admire her for that.

When I think of situations where I might be stuck for a way of handling things, I find myself increasingly thinking, "How would Barb handle this?" and I find myself coming up with just the right answer. She gives me guidance without even knowing it…and I'm sure she will long after she's gone. **«**

Self-Assessment

- Do you see the practical side of things?
- Are you unafraid to deal with difficult subjects?
- Do you take on challenges well?

#7—Quiet Leaders Are Humble

Fail to honor people, They will fail to honor you;
But of a good leader, who talks little,
When his work is done, his aim fulfilled,
They will all say, "We did this ourselves."

Lao-Tzu

Quiet leaders don't seek the attention they sometimes get. They appreciate sincere thanks but are usually surprised and/or embarrassed by public accolades and are often giving credit to others around them. They do what they do because they love it, see a need, and feel that anyone would do the same in their shoes. They usually see themselves as just "normal" people.

» Diane traveled around the world, with her family, for four years, chronicling their adventures in the local newspaper every Saturday. She wrote about the people they met and the situations in which they found themselves. Over time, Diane developed a following of very devoted readers. As the family's travels took them to the world's poorest countries, the tone of the articles changed and it became evident that the poverty, coupled with the immense generosity of the people they met, changed Diane and her family. They became much more aware of the problems in the world and needed to find a way to help.

Through her articles, people were inspired to donate to the various causes that the family came upon. On their return, Diane started a small kitchen-table charity that raises money to send youth to school and to renovate schools in disrepair in Kenya. Through this, she became a reluctant celebrity. This bothered her as people began to treat her differently. She didn't see herself as special; it was the donors who were making a difference.

It was her humility that galvanized people to action and allowed the charity to flourish. Her favorite saying was, "One pebble, plinking down a mountainside, can start an avalanche." She truly believed that one small act could make a big difference in the world and the donors were doing just that. **«**

Self-Assessment
- Do you give credit to others before accepting it for yourself?
- Are you uncomfortable with public recognition focused just on you?
- Do you find yourself often deflecting accolades away from you and towards others who have helped in a project?

Quiet Leaders—Made or Born?

Quiet leaders seem to come into this world with the seeds of these leadership qualities inside of them. For some, these qualities are so strong that their brilliance shines through and they develop into quiet leaders on their own, sometimes without realizing the positive impact that they have on others. These are the quiet, confident leaders who are comfortable being themselves.

Others are the quiet leaders-in-waiting. They're the ones who have the seed in them but have been socialized or persuaded by society, school, or work to be someone they aren't. They have bought into the paradigms of the big "L" leaders and either work hard at being like that (and are usually uncomfortable doing it) or they give up ever thinking they can make a difference.

For quiet leaders-in-waiting, the right conditions can lead to a shift in perspective, allowing their brilliance to shine through. Self-reflection, or a profoundly transformative life event, can also lead to someone becoming more comfortable with who they really are. Anne-Marie shared the following story:

» When I was 16, I attended a youth leadership camp. It was a very intense experience for me as I seemed to be quieter than the others and wondered what I was doing there. The others were all striving to show off their leadership abilities and I was more than happy to stay in the background and let them take their place.

One day we did an activity in silence, or at least as much silence as some of these people could muster. We had to figure out a solution to a maze and get people in the right places. There was much confusion and commotion: arms flailing, grimaces, and grunts as people tried to tell each other what to do—in silence! I saw the solution fairly quickly and was amazed that no one seemed to be getting it. There was lots of action, but no results.

I waited and waited for someone to come up with the answer, sure that one of these strong leaders would see it soon enough. Finally, I couldn't stand it anymore and I raised both my arms and made signals for people to look at me. I outlined the solution and got people moving in the right direction. I got them out of the chaos!

In the debriefing afterwards, the facilitator confirmed that I had had the solution fairly early and asked why I hadn't said anything. That's when I realized that I wasn't comfortable taking the lead on things and usually stayed in the background. That exercise made me realize that just because there are people who are busy being leaders, it doesn't mean they actually know what they're doing. It made me value my own intelligence, intuition, and abilities. It was a turning point for me—in my confidence level—for I realized that leadership was not simply about doing a lot of things. It was about being there, quietly observing, trusting myself, and having the confidence to step in when needed. I've since been very comfortable with my leadership abilities, knowing that I can just be a leader by trusting myself and being me. I'm lucky, I learned that at 16. **

Are You a Quiet Leader?

Society seems to put such an emphasis on the big "L" leaders, and the things that they accomplish, that it's easy to overlook the value and importance of the quiet leaders. People who go about their lives making a difference often have an attitude of "that's just me." They think they are not doing anything "special"; they're not even necessarily aware of the ripple effect of their actions. I'm sure that the quiet leaders in the preceding stories were aware of the results of the things they did, but were they aware of the unseen differences they made in people's lives? The feelings of hope, confidence, and joy that they engendered just by being who they are—the role models that they are to others. Quiet leaders, ironically, aren't often privy to the real difference that they make. It's about touching someone—in their heart and in their soul.

So, are you a quiet leader or a quiet leader-in-waiting? How do you choose to live your life? A good friend once said, "To the world, you might be one person but to one person, you might be the world."

Being a quiet leader is being that one person.

Diane King

Diane King is a bilingual facilitator, coach, and consultant, whose main passion is working with intact teams, helping people work better together through more effective interpersonal relations. Her approach is practical, collaborative, and is inspired by an unquenchable desire to bring out the best in her clients. Diane is a playful inspirer of teams, whose insatiable curiosity helps members and their leaders discover their own brilliance.

In addition to numerous professional development courses, Diane holds her Masters in Human Systems Intervention (Organization Development) from Concordia University and her BA (Social Communications) from the University of Ottawa. She is a neuro-linguistic programming (NLP) practitioner and has her Advanced Mediation Certificate (University of Windsor).

Diane has also co-authored two books: *Achieve It! A Personal Success Journal* (ISBN 0-9699941-0-9) and *The Standard Clause Handbook* for the real estate industry in Halifax.

Business Name: Group Intersol, Diane King Inc.

Address: 211 des Fondateurs, Gatineau, QC J9J 1M4

Telephone: 819-682-6021 or 613-230-6424

Email: dking@intersol.ca

Web Address: www.intersol.ca

Professional Affiliations: International Association of Facilitators; Organization Development Network of Ottawa/Outaouais

Favorite Quote:

Heaven's not a place that you go when you die. It's that moment in life when you actually feel alive!

From the song "The Tide" by Spill Canvas

Laurinda Dovey

Horizons Unlimited

Communicate for Success

> *Real communication occurs when we listen with understanding. It*
> *means to see the expressed idea and attitude from the other per-*
> *son's point of view, to sense how it feels to be him, to achieve his*
> *frame of reference in regard to the thing he is talking about.*
>
> Carl Rogers, Psychologist

From that first momentous breath of life, humans communicate both verbally and non-verbally. A baby communicates its hunger by crying and its happiness by laughing. A toddler shows its displeasure by stomping its feet, crying, or shouting. As we grow into adulthood, our communication skills become more refined, and it is these skills that we carry into the workplace.

Excellent communication and interpersonal skills are vital for the success of organizations. True communicators quickly separate themselves from others in terms of their success in leadership and management roles. Listening, speaking, and being seen as a polished professional are key components of the communication process and essential for a thriving workplace.

Wikipedia, an online encyclopedia, defines communication in part as a "social interaction or sharing of information for the purpose of understanding." What happens between the sending and the receiving determines whether the message is understood in the way in which it is intended.

Your non-verbal cues, such as tone, facial expression, posture, and grooming, can either detract from or enhance your message. When you are the receiver of information, observe the body language of the sender. Is it congruent with the message you are hearing? (More will be discussed later in this chapter on the impact of non-verbal communication.)

Effective communication is fundamental to all relationships and is a key part of business success. How you communicate will be a predictor of the quality of your relationships and your achievements in the workplace.

A lack of honest communication was cited as the top morale buster at work, according to surveys developed by a Menlo Park, California-based office team. In a study published by the Society for Human Resource Management, entitled "The 50 Best Small and Medium Places to Work," the common attribute among the winning organizations was "good communication." These organizations not only kept communication flowing from the top down, they listened actively to the feedback from staff.

We assume that because we can listen and speak, we can communicate well. The real questions are:

- Do you listen with understanding?
- Do you communicate assertively and honestly without aggression?
- Do you communicate with respect while upholding your beliefs and values?
- Do you present yourself as a polished professional?

Children in school are taught from a very young age to read and write, yet there are no courses offered on effective communication. Some of these concepts are presented in college and university, well after we have learned all of our basic communication skills. The result is that many well-educated professionals do not have the communication skills to be effective in today's workplace.

Having superior communication skills will help you gain credibility with your colleagues and advance in the workplace. Most importantly, they will have a positive impact on your day-to-day relationships with your co-workers. Establishing collegial relationships in the workplace contributes to improved morale, higher productivity, and lower turnover.

Listening, speaking, and your physical presentation are the foundation for successful communication in the workplace. Communication is circular and involves information traveling from the sender, through filters and non-verbal cues to the receiver, who then starts the process over again. The following diagram illustrates this concept.

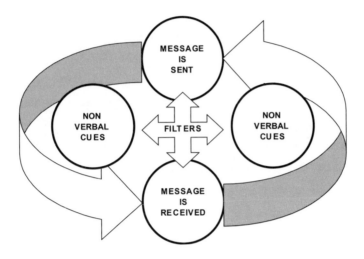

This chapter will give you tips on listening actively, speaking assertively without being aggressive, and presenting yourself as a polished professional. If you practice the tips outlined, you will be off to a good start in awakening and polishing your communication skills.

Listen Actively With Understanding

Seek first to understand, then to be understood. When we listen with the intent to understand others, rather than with the intent to reply, we begin true communication and relationship building. When others feel understood first, they feel affirmed and valued, defenses are lowered and opportunities to speak openly and to be understood come much more naturally and easily. Seeking to understand takes kindness; seeking to be understood takes courage. Effectiveness lies in balancing the two.

Stephen R. Covey
The 7 Habits of Highly Effective People

While reading this, you could be thinking: "I don't need any tips on listening" or "I listen all day long at work—to my co-workers, to my boss, and to my clients!" But do you really listen actively with understanding? Your brain has the capacity to listen at about four times the speed of speech. That leaves a lot of time for you to think about other things while people are speaking to you. So what steps do you need to take to improve your listening skills?

Barriers to Active Listening

Before we consider the tools for active listening, let's reflect on some of the barriers and filters that hinder this:

1. **Message overload:** There is too much information to take in. It is physically impossible to listen to everything you hear.
2. **Physical noise:** A photocopier is running in the background or staff are congregated around the water cooler.
3. **Psychological noise:** You are thinking of the assignment sitting on your desk or the next meeting that you have to attend.
4. **Thinking of your response instead of listening:** You know so much about what the speaker is saying that you can't wait to interrupt with your response.
5. **Time constraints:** You are in a rush to get somewhere or you have a project deadline to meet.
6. **Filters:** You are not open to what the speaker is saying because of personal biases, values, and differences in culture, socio-economic status, life experiences, or gender.

Keys to Active Listening

The following active tools will help you to overcome these barriers. As you apply them, you will notice a positive improvement in how others respond to you.

1. Pay attention and don't interrupt. We have all been taught that to interrupt is rude. Part of "hearing" involves clearing your mind of your own thoughts and focusing on what is being said. This takes much effort and practice but you will improve. Instead of planning your response, pay attention to what you are being told.

2. Put the speaker at ease and show that you want to listen. Make eye contact and face the speaker, or lean slightly towards them. A friendly expression on your face will tell them that you are interested and willing to listen. Jot down the important points if you will need to refer back to them. Nodding your head and using short phrases such as "I see" or "Oh, really?" will encourage the speaker and let them know that you are listening and understanding them.

3. Remove distractions. If there is physical noise, suggest moving to a quieter spot. If you are in your office, let your phone go to voice mail while the person is speaking and close your office door to discourage drop-ins.

4. Show patience even when you are busy. If someone approaches as you are heading into a meeting, suggest that you spend some time with them a little later in the day when you can give them your full attention. In a busy workplace, this is appropriate and people will recognize this as your desire to give them your undivided attention.

5. Observe non-verbal cues. Be aware of the speaker's body language. Do they appear to be nervous or uncomfortable? Are they avoiding eye contact? Is their facial expression congruent with the message or information that they are delivering? Non-verbal cues say more than the words that are being spoken. If these are not in sync with what the speaker is saying, the message will be unclear.

6. Ask questions and paraphrase. When the speaker is finished, paraphrase back to them what you think you have heard. Using phrases such as, "So I think what you are saying is…" or "I just want to summarize what you have said, to ensure that I understand," are ways of solidifying the information in your own mind while allowing for clarification if necessary.

7. Be aware of filters. You need to be aware of your own filters if you are the listener. In turn, when you are speaking, be aware of filters that may be present in the person to whom you are speaking. These filters can prevent effective communication between the sender and the receiver. Here is an example:

>> You are supervising someone who has a number of performance issues that you have had to address. Typically, these meetings have not ended on a positive note. You now need to discuss with him a special project on which he is going to be working (totally unrelated to performance). Upon entering your office he appears to be suspicious and uncomfortable. As you excitedly communicate the information about the special project, you sense a resistance or perhaps even a lack of co-operation. Why? This person is probably thinking about the previous negative meetings over performance and this past experience with you is acting as a "filter" to the information that you are trying to share. <<

Other filters present themselves because of culture and ethnicity. It is important in today's culturally diverse workplace to be proactive in educating yourself and your employees on the differences in how staff may send or receive communication based on their culture. No two individuals have accumulated the same filters throughout their life.

Listen to others in the way that you would like to be listened to when you speak. Be aware of filters and other barriers that can break down effective listening. Active listening shows respect for others and their ideas, and can do much towards building a strong foundation for positive relationships and problem solving in the workplace.

Speak Assertively With Respect

Our words are often hidden containers of hidden hopes and cloudy expectations. Our silence assumes a power to communicate it does not have. Our timing tires and offends. Whenever we have expectations of others that we do not say directly, we set ourselves up for disappointment.

Fran Ferder, Author

Do you have difficulty respectfully stating your needs and feelings when they are at odds with what others want? Do you find yourself getting angry or responding inappropriately and then regretting it later? Perhaps you don't speak up at all and then become frustrated with yourself because you have not done so.

Just as active listening improves communication between people, using assertive speech skillfully and tactfully can also enhance your relationships and build mutual respect. The word "assertiveness" sometimes conjures up visions of anger, aggression, and conflict. Many people shy away from being assertive for fear of upsetting others or being viewed as aggressive. Contrary to this belief, being skilled at assertiveness often saves misunderstandings in the first place. There are four basic styles of communication—passive, aggressive, passive-aggressive, and assertive. Let's take a look at them:

1. Passive: Passive is defined as, "not actively taking part, usually letting others make decisions, tending to submit or obey." If you are passive, you do not confidently express your thoughts and feelings and you may give the appearance of being indifferent. You do not want to deal with conflict but often end up angry with yourself for not stating your opinion. You may appear to be timid and unsure of yourself.

2. Aggressive: One definition of aggressive is, "attacking or taking action without provocation." You do not take the other person's goals or feelings into account and you may exhibit confrontational or even abusive behavior. Workplace bullying falls into this category and is degrading to all parties involved. Aggressive behavior will quickly tear down relationships and have a negative impact on the workplace. Sometimes the damage is irreversible.

3. Passive-Aggressive: This style of communication initially avoids conflict but later behaves aggressively and often sarcastically. It is passive in expression but the intent is malicious. If you are passive-aggressive you may appear to be well-meaning on the surface but you then express anger or discontent behind the scenes, sometimes going so far as to sabotage the efforts of others.

4. Assertive: Assertive communication is characterized by determination, energy, and initiative and the ability to confidently express your feelings appropriately with *sincerity and respect for yourself and others.* Think about those two attributes—

sincerity and respect. These can form a strong foundation for solid communication and they can help to build solid relationships within the organization. An assertive person is usually respected for their honesty and their ability to express their opinions without demeaning others.

While being assertive is usually the most effective form of communication, there are times when you choose a more passive or a seemingly aggressive approach. For example, if you are involved in a discussion with a colleague regarding a policy change that does not impact on your department, you may choose to be passive and simply not express an opinion. If a situation requires someone to take charge quickly, being strategically more forceful and direct by using more emphasis and emotion is your choice. The key is not to move into aggressive behavior.

Do not assume that being assertive is only to be used in conflict situations. It is quite the contrary. Some people are naturally assertive and they are the ones who often avoid getting into conflict situations. This is because their way of communicating is honest and straightforward and people are not usually left guessing what this person is feeling or thinking. People who communicate assertively clearly state their position while respecting the views of others. Conflict frequently arises because people are not honest about their feelings and they do not have enough trust in themselves, or the other person, to openly state how they feel. Being assertive requires a lot of practice, and care needs to be taken so that you do not appear to have a chip on your shoulder.

Assertive speech involves using "I" statements rather than "you" statements. By using "I" statements, you are placing no blame on the other person but simply taking responsibility for your own feelings and stating them honestly. Let me illustrate:

One of your colleagues is continually late for meetings. Your response could be:
"Why are you always late for our meetings? Can't you ever be on time?" *(aggressive)*

Or: **"I need our meetings to start on schedule so that the rest of my day does not fall behind."** *(assertive)*

A committee member puts forward a proposal with which you strongly disagree. Your response could be:
"That doesn't make any sense at all. How did you come up with that?" *(aggressive)*

Or: ***"I can see you have put a lot of work into your proposal John. I think we should give some consideration to…(state your own ideas)."*** *(assertive)*

You are chairing a staff meeting and introducing a new procedure for staff attendance phone calls. At the end of your presentation, you ask if anyone needs clarification. One person who looks quite annoyed says sarcastically:

"No, I have no questions." *(passive-aggressive)*

The more honest response to you would have been: ***"Yes, I have some questions and I would like clarification on why the company feels a need to change the existing procedure."*** *(assertive)*

A colleague drops by your office regularly to have lengthy, personal conversations. You are irritated and have work to do. Your response could be:

"Don't you have enough work to do? You are constantly interrupting me!" *(aggressive)*

Or: ***"I have a lot of work to do and I don't have time to chat right now. Perhaps you could catch up with me at break time?"*** *(assertive)*

Notice in the aggressive examples, the use of "you," while the assertive examples make use of "I" statements. The assertive statements are respectful yet honest. People may not always like your assertive response, but generally you are happier with yourself if you speak up and state your feelings honestly. It is important to remember to use tact and courtesy with your assertive statements. Commend someone or state the positive first, and then follow up with what you need to say. When you are using assertive communication use the following guidelines:

- Be specific about the behavior or issue that concerns you and stick to the facts;
- Do not demean the other person's character or use innuendos;
- Be objective and try to see your colleague's side of the issue;
- Be honest and sincere in your statements. Others quickly see through someone who is not genuine;
- Deal with emotions first. If they are running high, put off speaking until later.

When you are communicating in the workplace, everyone deserves to be treated with respect and courtesy and you need to be sincere in stating your feelings. The way you communicate can be the primary determinant of whether the person you are speaking to will listen and consider what you have said, be indifferent to it, or completely oppose it.

Doing anything well requires effort. Begin practicing using your assertive "I" statements when appropriate and express your feelings openly and honestly, even when they are at odds with those around you. Be aware of what you are saying and the effect it has on others, and keep in mind that your goal in communicating for success is to elicit co-operation in the workplace, rather than argument or confrontation.

Polish the Package

Now that you have learned some tips on active listening and speaking assertively using sincerity and respect, let's polish the package. If your non-verbal communication is not congruent with your message, people will tend to believe what they see as opposed to what they hear. Your appearance and body language have an enormous impact on how your message is received, and on how you are perceived as a professional. There are four main areas of non-verbal communication:

1. Personal appearance;
2. Eye contact and facial expression;
3. Vocal tone;
4. Posture.

Let's review some guidelines for each one, knowing that often the rules of non-verbal communication are based on your role within the organization and on your relationship with the person with whom you are communicating. Albert Mehrabian, psychologist, researcher, and author on communication, found that when communicating, your actual words count for seven percent and your body language, tone, and appearance count for the other 93 percent. This should awaken in us the need to enhance our non-verbal communication skills, and to be seen by others as polished, professional, and credible. Because we are seen before we are heard, let's look first at personal appearance.

1. Personal Appearance

People will make assumptions about your professional credibility and potential performance based upon your appearance. No matter what your knowledge or expertise may be, it is difficult to overcome a negative first impression. If you are unsure about the dress code and culture of an organization that you are entering for the first time, it is better to err on the side of being overdressed rather than being dressed too casually. The following example illustrates how important it is to be appropriately groomed.

> **»** My colleagues and I were interviewing candidates for a clerical position within the company. One applicant came into the interview dressed sloppily, with a stain on her clothing and smelling of tobacco. My mind was made up before she even sat down. Her non-verbal cues had told me that she was careless and sloppy and would probably take that same approach with her work. At this point her skills were irrelevant because of the first impression she had created. **«**

This example emphasizes just how much appearance can affect how others perceive you and how successful you will be professionally. The following guidelines would have helped that job applicant:

- Clothing should be clean, pressed, and fit properly;
- Shoes should to be polished;
- Keep your accessories simple so they do not detract from you;
- Ensure that your hair is clean, neat, and tidy;
- Avoid heavy scents—if in doubt, wear none;
- If you smoke, be aware that the smell of tobacco may be offensive to others;
- Make sure that your purse/portfolio/briefcase is neat and clean;
- If you are female, short skirts or revealing clothing will only detract from your credibility;
- Always give yourself a last check in the mirror (front and back) before you leave the house.

Following these suggestions, no matter what your role is in the organization, will "dress up" your communication skills. Remember, you are seen before you are heard.

Having a polished professional appearance will boost your image and your self-esteem. Be the one who sets an example for others, and if you are hoping to move up in an organization, dress as if you are already there. Appearance does matter!

2. Eye Contact and Facial Expression

When you are speaking, people want to see your eyes. So make eye contact! If you are speaking to one of your colleagues, make frequent eye contact without staring or making them uncomfortable. If you are presenting to a group of staff, break the room into thirds and direct your comments back and forth to one person in each area. The others around that person will feel as though you are speaking directly to them. Ensure that your facial expression is congruent with your message. When discussing company layoffs your expression should be serious and empathetic. If you are commending staff for increased productivity, your face should reflect happiness and enthusiasm. Think about the message you are delivering and be cognizant that your facial expression matches.

3. Vocal Tone

Vocal tone can change the meaning of spoken words. Anger, irritation, happiness, and enthusiasm can all be detected in your tone of voice. Speaking very softly could indicate nervousness or indecisiveness. It is important in the workplace not to let your tone change the message you are sending. Asking a colleague to come and speak with you in an angry, raised voice would indicate to her that there is a problem of some sort. That same request uttered in a friendly, pleasant voice conveys something quite different. Be sure that your tone matches the message you are delivering. In most cases a raised voice in the workplace is inappropriate and will only contribute to poor communication and conflict.

4. Posture

Your posture depends on the situation and your relationship with the person with whom you are communicating. If you are listening to instructions from your supervisor you should present an alert and open stance, one that shows you are open to receiving the information being conveyed. If you are speaking, a relaxed stance with your arms at your sides is recommended. A slouched posture could indicate a lack of interest or indifference. Ensure that your posture is appropriate for the situation and that it enhances your other non-verbal modes of communication.

Your body language and appearance are like accents or accessories to your verbal communication. They can add emphasis, interest, enthusiasm, and more importantly, credibility to what you are saying. Use them effectively to enhance your message in a genuine and sincere manner, and observe the difference it makes in how you and your message are received.

Excellent communication is fundamental to success in your workplace relationships. Listening with understanding and speaking to others with sincerity and respect will build trust with your colleagues, and your messages will be received positively. Being assertive and honest will help to avoid misunderstandings and the conflict that can follow.

Your grooming and appearance do matter. Dress and carry yourself professionally no matter what your role is within the organization. This will not only enhance your credibility and promotability, but will increase your self-esteem.

Communicating for success will enhance the atmosphere in your workplace, will build trust and rapport among co-workers, and will facilitate your professional growth and development. Start today and see the results!

> *Courage is what it takes to stand up and speak.*
> *Courage is also what it takes to sit down and listen.*
> Winston Churchill

Laurinda Dovey

Laurinda Dovey's 15 years of experience working in the public sector, in business administration and management, provides her with extensive knowledge in leadership, supervision, and effective communication skills. Throughout her career, she has been a leader in staff training and development.

She motivates people with her unique blend of business management and fitness experience, and provides audiences with strategies for success in both business and other areas of life. She stresses the importance of health and wellness in order to maintain balance in life. Clients include both business and not-for-profit organizations, including Toronto Rehabilitation, Children's Aid Societies, Niagara College, and chambers of commerce.

Laurinda is a Can-Fit-Pro™ certified Fitness Instructor and Personal Trainer. She has worked in the fitness industry for 10 years and enjoys motivating people to take care of themselves and to achieve their fitness goals.

Business name:	Horizons Unlimited
Address:	7 Prince Henry Court, St. Catharines, ON L2N 2X8
Telephone:	905-937-4445
Email:	horizonsunlimited@cogeco.ca
Web Address:	www.horizonsunlimited.ca
Professional Affiliations:	Canadian Association of Professional Speakers; Canadian Association of Fitness Professionals

Val Carter

The Success Centre

How to Win a Goat

Would you like to achieve more in life? Are you full of good intentions but find it hard to get started, to visualize your success, and to find the time you need to dedicate to your objectives? Let's look at how to transform your intentions into achievements, and your frustration into satisfaction. It is easy to be discouraged from achieving your goals, yet through tackling them, in an intentional and systematic way, you will have success. They will no longer be wishes and regrets, but achievements you're proud of.

The Way It Used to Be

> » I used to find it hard to get motivated. If there was a deadline, I would put off the task until the last possible minute; if there wasn't, I would often not get around to doing it at all. I justified this behavior to myself, saying "I'm too busy right now," or "I'm thinking about it," or my favourite, "I'll do it next." Somehow "next" never came. I was constantly stressed, always playing catch-up, sometimes missing deadlines, and just not making time for many goals that I knew were important. «

That was my life—until the day I won a goat! That day changed my approach to life. From that day onwards, not only did I add "goat winner" to my list of achievements, but I also learned how to get the traction to achieve my goals. Let me share with you this success approach that can change *your* life for the better as well.

The Goat Contest

» Imagine driving across the Canadian prairies on a dreary winter day. If you haven't experienced the prairies, they're flat. We're not talking fairly flat—they are tabletop flat. You can sometimes see a train on the horizon, maybe one hundred cars long, from the engine right to the caboose. It's the kind of place where it's hard to believe that the world is actually round.

Most of the time there is a certain beauty in the open landscape with its vast fields stretching to the horizons, giving a feeling of infinite space. Today however, there's a chilly mist, heralding snow, that's masking the view. The fields on either side of the road are no more interesting than a tabletop in a fast food outlet.

As I surf through the radio stations, I hear, "…and the prize will be a real, live goat; the only live goat ever given away on national radio. Now to our afternoon feature…" I'm hooked. I have to find out what they're talking about. I listen for an hour before the goat is mentioned again. "To return to our goat contest…" I turn up the radio. "A real live goat will be awarded to the person with the best story about a homemade gift."

I can't believe what I'm hearing! After all, this is CBC Radio, the normally sedate national radio of Canada. The absurdity of this challenge captures my imagination. Something takes a hold of me. I'm not sure if it's the monotony of the drive or if I've finally flipped. All I know is…I just have to win that goat! «

It started out as a strong desire to win. But a strong desire for all kinds of things hadn't necessarily helped before. What was different about this goal? What was so special about this contest and its zany prize? Aha! Thinking beyond the goal of simply winning the contest to visualizing the end result was something new. I could see myself using the story of winning a goat in my work. People would laugh at "the goat lady" story. I could visualize myself having my photo taken with the goat! It felt good!

It wasn't a particularly good time for me—I was very busy trying to start my own business as well as being a wife and mother. It was easy to think of all the perfectly valid reasons why it wasn't worth entering the contest: I'd never entered a radio contest before; couldn't listen to the show to hear other entries; there wasn't time to work on this—you name it, and there was an excuse that covered it. To get around to even entering the contest, let alone winning, the story would need to be prepared in small time slots carved out between my other commitments. Preparing my submission for the contest would need to be done in tiny steps. There wouldn't be the luxury of dedicating hours to work on the entry—and yet the contest was closing in nine days.

For those nine days, I managed to squeeze the tiniest little actions into the small amounts of spare time available. There seemed so much to do in order to achieve success and win that goat. First, it was important to understand what type of story appealed to the radio station. I had a great story about a homemade gift, but how should it be presented so that it caught their attention?

The next morning, I just opened my diary for the week and left it prominently on my desk before heading to a meeting. Returning to my desk, the first thing in front of me was the open diary so it was easy to look at the week's schedule. Blocking off the only remaining free time in the afternoons, and rearranging a couple of commitments, meant that I could be in my car on a couple of afternoons to listen to the CBC show.

The next step was to put a notepad and pen in my car. When the radio show was on, I pulled over as soon as the presenter began to read examples of the contest entries. I took notes on the types of stories that were being aired; counted the number of paragraphs; noticed that most of the stories had a little twist at the end; checked the type of language used; in fact, anything that might be useful for matching the style of my story to the way the CBC wanted to hear it.

Over the next few days, I wrote my opening line while waiting at the checkout in the grocery store. The first paragraph was finished at the gas station. While waiting for a meeting, I finalized the ending. Little by little, piece by piece, I managed to keep myself motivated and on track. At last it all came together. A few hours before the deadline, I called the CBC voice mail number and read out my homemade gift story.

The feeling of elation was huge. Usually, I would have found all sorts of excuses why it was too difficult to complete the steps needed to enter the contest. It felt so good to achieve my goals of submitting my entry, matching the style of my story to the examples the CBC had aired, and delivering it all before the deadline.

Success! Andy Warhol said that we will all be famous for fifteen minutes. My fifteen minutes came when it was announced on national radio right across Canada that I'd actually won the goat. This set me wondering what exactly had been done differently. What had changed from my previous approach to goals? How had I achieved success in this contest?

Lessons Learned

I realized that this experience had made me stumble across a successful strategy that took me from that drive across the prairies to being a goat-winner. I'd built a set of specific, manageable steps to achieve success with the resources and time available. If this technique worked for winning a goat, it could also be used to achieve success in other goals in life. I tried it on other goals and it worked! It worked so well that I started to achieve more than I'd ever thought possible—and I was enjoying the ride! I'd like to share the strategy with you so you can use to achieve success too.

The five key points of this strategy are:
- *Affirmation*—Owning your success;
- *Goals*—Clarity is the key;
- *Outcome*—What does success mean to you?
- *Action*—Moving forward;
- *Timing*—The catalyst for success.

1. Affirmation—Owning Your Success

You may be having a bug day, not a windshield day. Maybe you're enjoying one of those days when life is wonderful; or it could be you're so busy on your daily treadmill that there isn't even time to analyze your feelings. Whatever sort of day you're having, what will you say at the end of it? It's probably, "I've still got so many things I want to do!"

Another way of looking at this is to see success as a series of small steps. Although you may not feel you've made enough progress, you've almost certainly been working towards achieving a few things today. In fact, you achieve success in many things each day. Taken individually, they may not be grand, life-altering successes. You're not going to rush to the nearest hilltop with a bullhorn and announce these successes to the world. Nevertheless, each of these small steps can move you towards your bigger goals.

Take the time to recognize that you've achieved plenty of successes in your life so far. This is really important for good self-esteem, and yet so few people do it. When you make progress towards your goals—especially when you take tiny steps towards success—it's easy to forget to pat yourself on the back. It's the celebration of each small step in the journey, and the rewards at every turn that will keep you motivated, eager, and ultimately, will make you successful.

Starting today, give yourself credit for a job accomplished or a goal achieved—no matter how large or small. This builds a foundation of strength and esteem within you that will be the catalyst for more achievement. By doing this, you prove to yourself that you can achieve your goals.

Exercise: Own Your Successes

Find a pen and notepad (or an old envelope, or a cocktail napkin) to work through this exercise. Please, if you're driving, flying a plane, or operating machinery, just do the exercise in your head!

- Write down at least three successes you've achieved in your life (there's no upper limit). Try to include at least one success you have had this week. These can be big successes: succeeding in a job interview, passing an exam, or rowing single-handed across the Atlantic. Or they can be tiny: making it to work on time despite a problem, changing the oil in the car, or simply taking some quiet time to do this exercise. Any type of success in between big and tiny is okay too.

Think about the successes on your list. Were some of those hard to achieve? Well, you got there, didn't you? Good job! Did you worry about completing some of them? That's definite proof that you can beat procrastination. Celebrate your achievements! Reward yourself for a job well done.

Starting today, give yourself credit for the jobs you have completed or the goals you have achieved—no matter how large or small. This will build a foundation of strength and esteem within you that will be the catalyst for greater achievement.

2. Goals—Clarity Is the Key

It's essential to know what you want. This sounds obvious, but I'm sure you often spend more time thinking about what you're going to eat for lunch, or where you're going for your next vacation, than you do planning the important things in your life.

When it comes to setting goals, it is essential to make them specific and detailed. Rather than "finish the report by the deadline," your specific goal must include all the information you need to make sure you know exactly what you're aiming for. To make it really clear what you need to do, it's better to phrase it as "Work on the report for two hours each day this week so that it's ready by 4 p.m. on Friday afternoon."

Specific Goals Give You the "What"

You need a firm vision of what you want to achieve. It takes away the wooliness that surrounds your thinking so that you know exactly where you're headed. It also removes the fuel that you use for justifying procrastination. You can't pretend to yourself that it will be okay to miss the deadline and work on the report over the weekend instead. You *know* it has to be finished by 4 p.m. on Friday! Here are some tips for setting your goals:

- Write down as many goals as you want, large or small. Anything works! Don't start to think of the potential obstacles—just get the ideas down on paper.
- Keep an ideas list of possible goals—some may come to as you read this chapter. Prioritize them.

- Make your goals specific. Specific, detailed goals will focus your energy on what you're trying to achieve.
- Do you know exactly what you need in order to achieve success? If not, add details until your goal is definite and concrete.

3. Outcome—What Does Success Mean to You?

When you lose sight of why you want to reach your particular goals, movement towards them becomes difficult. The outcome gives you the "why." It answers the questions, "Why am I bothering?" and "What's in it for me?" The outcome is the *consequence* of achieving your goal. "What will it be like once you've succeeded? What will have changed? How will your life be better?"

To describe the outcome, imagine how it will feel to have achieved your goal. Close your eyes if it helps. What will be different? Will you feel relief or a sense of achievement? And, most importantly, how will you reward yourself for your success?

What's in It for You?

Let's go back to that report that needs writing by 4 p.m. on Friday. Visualize the weekend free of stress because you completed it by the deadline. Anticipate your satisfaction when the report is acknowledged in your next staff meeting. When the plans outlined in your report are implemented, think of the benefits to your colleagues and the organization as a whole. And what are you going to do to celebrate?

By concentrating on the good feelings you'll experience at the end of the project, you're giving yourself something worthwhile to aim for. No longer do you have the feeling that you're scrambling to finish a report by the deadline. Now you'll see the benefits of completing the task and can look forward to that moment of success.

Your Feelings of Success
- Go back to the goal you've decided to work on. Jot down all the ideas that pop into your head about how you'll feel when your goal is finally achieved. Nobody else is going to read your notes, so be as honest as you like!
- Make sure to include your reward. It may be something small, like having a

cup of coffee or a cookie. It may be large—taking the weekend off, buying a treat or booking a trip. Make it achievable and meaningful for you.

Visualizing how success will feel will give you the energy to move forward. Rewarding yourself for each achievement along the way will motivate you to more successes.

4. Action—Moving Forward

Knowing goals and imagining outcomes are great first steps. However, they won't get you to success without action. There are plenty of motivational strategies out there telling you simply to visualize success and it will come. But they're like a gym membership you buy on January 2nd. Paying for the membership card won't get you fit—you actually have to work out, too!

You know what you have to do. You know how great it will be once you've done it. So why is it that you get stuck? Why don't you move forward towards your goals? You make excuses. You'll tell yourself that once you've cleared all those little tasks on your to-do list, you'll get to your main goals; then you find several other things to do that you convince yourself are more urgent than your bigger goals.

A journey of a thousand miles begins with a single step.

Chinese proverb

The secret to success is that small steps are often more effective than big ones. When you make those steps *so* small and *so* manageable that you can't help yourself—you find you're actually moving forward, one tiny step at a time.

Now practice with another goal here—how about losing weight? The key secret is to think of the tiniest step that will be the start of losing weight. The first step may seem ridiculously small and insignificant—but it will, nevertheless, be a start. Just try it.

Maybe you have been thinking of changing your eating habits? That's a daunting task in itself! You'll need to plan menus, count calories, check nutrition, write a shopping list, and choose healthier food options. If you start with planning menus,

Awakening the Workplace

you'll need to make a schedule for the coming week so that you can plan your meals. But…that's quite a large task.

Make the task easier by breaking it down further. Pick up a blank sheet of paper and keep hold of it. Fetch that paper, and you've achieved something—you've taken action and you're on your way. Now that you're holding that piece of paper, do you think it's going to be easier to make a menu plan for the upcoming days this week? You bet! You're going to feel pretty silly walking around with a blank piece of paper in your hand. So go ahead and make the menu plan before you put down the sheet. You've taken the first step—celebrate! Pat yourself on the back, watch your favourite TV show, or enjoy whatever reward you've promised yourself. You need to celebrate that achievement.

The Key

You have to reduce your actions down to the tiniest level possible. If the step's too large, you won't take it. The simplest and often the silliest-sounding little action is the one that gives you the nudge to get moving.

Decide Your Action Steps

- What will your first steps be for your goal? Remember, the simplest and smallest ideas will get you started best.
- Write down five or six more actions that will take you beyond the first step. Continuing the weight loss example, these could be: drive to the supermarket parking lot and sit there (buy healthy food); or put the phone directory on your desk (call the gym to enquire about membership). This is the part of the process that will have the most impact. It can be tough at first to break goals down into the world of nanotechnology!
- When you've made your list of actions, dig deeper, go smaller if you need to. It's often helpful to brainstorm with someone else. Others can sometimes see a simpler step. When presented with the exercise about losing weight, most people start with "eat healthily" or "go to the gym." That's so huge that you never quite get round to it. You mean to, oh yes! But without action, intentions are just dreams.

5. Timing—The Catalyst for Success

Now you know what to do, why you're doing it, and you have your actions lined up. The final piece in the puzzle is deciding when you'll take action and when you'll complete each step towards your goal.

If you are an organized person, it may be enough to post timelines in your calendar or on a sticky note on your computer screen or on the refrigerator—especially when you make a point of celebrating each action as it's crossed off your list. However, if you are one of the vast majority of people who have difficulty keeping themselves accountable, this is where it's really helpful to have a buddy. By telling someone what you are going to achieve and when you will achieve it, you are now accountable to that other person as well as yourself. It'll help to keep you more honest. Be sure to involve your buddy in the celebrations!

Timing Is Everything

- Write timelines for completion of each of your actions. Make them achievable. Don't aim to start your healthy eating and exercise plan just when you are heading away for a vacation. However, is there a tiny action you can achieve after the vacation? Set a time when you will pick up that blank sheet of paper as the first step to writing your menu plan. Set a timeline for achieving each tiny step…and stick to it.

From Dreams to Actions

Following this process has made a powerful difference in my life. You too can achieve the personal goals you've been putting off. I know it works. I used to be the best procrastinator in the business, so if I can do it, so can you!

If you follow the steps—know where you're heading; recognize what success will mean to you; break the goals into tiny, manageable steps; set timelines; and celebrate each step along the way—you will accomplish more than you thought possible.

» So are you wondering what happened with the goat? When I won the contest, CBC radio donated money to an overseas aid agency who bought a goat on my behalf for a family in a Third World country. Rest assured that I don't have a goat in my garage! **«**

Have fun achieving your goals. I know you can win your own goat. Make it a whole herd!

The secret of getting ahead is getting started. The secret of getting started is breaking your complex, overwhelming tasks into small manageable tasks, and then starting on the first one.

Mark Twain

Val Carter

When **Val Carter** speaks, people connect. You hear them saying, "I can do that!" They're engaged by Val's humor and infectious enthusiasm, challenged by her thought-provoking concepts, and inspired by her down-to-earth strategies for change. Whether attending a training program or a keynote, they leave with new perspectives and renewed vitality, eager to take action right away.

She's walked the talk. She knows the issues. As a Certified Human Resources Professional (CHRP) with over 20 years of experience in the corporate, entrepreneurial, public, and non-profit sectors around the world, Val has gained a wealth of knowledge—plus some excellent stories.

A sought-after speaker, Val is also founder of The Success Centre, committed to providing enjoyable, results-oriented personal and professional development programs for those in today's busy world.

Val is passionate about her work—and it shows. **"I've found what I want to be when I grow up," she laughs. After all, we learn more when we're having fun!**

Business Name: The Success Centre (A division of Calgary Training Inc)
Address: #268, 440–10816 Macleod Trail S., Calgary, AB T2J 5N8
Telephone: 403-281-8841
Email: val@successcentre.com
Web Address: www.successcentre.com
Professional Affiliations: Canadian Association of Professional Speakers; International Federation of Professional Speakers; Canadian Society for Training and Development; American Society for Training and Development; Human Resources Association of Alberta

Patricia A. Muir

Maestro Quality Inc.

Develop Your Own Personal Quality System

Quality is more than an attribute; quality is an attitude.

Narrator, *The Human Nature of Quality* (Dartnell)

Business organizations of all sizes have management systems. Effective management systems are developed, implemented, and maintained based on a recognized
standard or a set of universal principles that drive best practices.

The overall management system of any business organization includes several
intricate systems: sales, human resources, accounting and finance, manufacturing
or service delivery, and quality assurance. When each one of these systems is based
on a recognized standard or a set of universal principles that drive best practices and
is fully integrated with the other interdependent systems, the business organization
has a strong foundation and is robust.

Robust: strong in constitution; hardy; vigorous. Sturdily
built; straight forward and imbued with common sense.

Collins English Dictionary, 2nd Edition

This chapter focuses on providing you with a personal management system that
promotes quality assurance in your work and home life. You will be introduced to
the key points of how to develop and implement your own personal quality system

so that you can carve out your optimal workplace experience and enhance your quality of life.

Two Powerful Concepts Meet

Over the past several years, various models have evolved using professional coaching concepts and principles to serve individuals, management teams, and corporations. At the individual level these models enhance the effectiveness of those who are committed to quality of life personally and professionally. At the same time, business system models have evolved rapidly. These systems now include quality assurance concepts and principles that are specifically designed for organizations committed to providing quality products and services. This is my inspiration for developing the Personal Quality System (PQS):

The real power for implementing quality on a personal level lies in the successful integration of these two universal and complementary sets of standards, principles, and concepts: professional coaching and quality assurance.

The What, Who, and How of You

In making the conscious decision to develop and maintain your own personal quality system, where would you begin? What concepts, principles, and standards would provide structure for you in developing and maintaining your unique personal quality system?

Your personal foundation consists of *what, who*, and *how*. The "what" is the "package" that you present to the world, your public self, your behavior. The "who" is the real you, the core of who you are, your values and your spirit. The "how" is the set of processes that drive your behavior to ensure that your actions reflect the real you and that you are consistent in word and deed. By integrating quality assurance in the "how," you will boost your personal foundation to a state of personal quality. You will create and experience a robust quality of life. The reality that you carve out for yourself will boost your personal and professional power with a radiating effect on the lives of people in your workplace, family, community, and the world.

> *Life isn't about finding yourself…life is about creating yourself.*
>
> E. W. Wilcox

A New Route to Creating Yourself

A roadmap is always helpful when taking a new route in life. The Personal Quality System—or PQS—that you will learn grew out of discovering the power of having 1) a strong personal foundation in life, and 2) quality assurance evident both at work and at home. This approach not only provides you with the roadmap, it provides an energy source and resources to propel you in creating the optimal "you."

The PQS consists of seven elements that will direct you on your journey:

1. Take a leadership role in your life;
2. Create your personal quality statement;
3. Develop your personal/professional management team;
4. Understand the expectations of others;
5. Design and implement personal best practices;
6. Create a problem-free environment;
7. Create your personal quality development plan.

Before You Begin

You are both the Chief Executive Officer for Operations (CEO) and Quality Manager of your life. You have been given management responsibility for leading and driving this initiative. Before you begin, you will need to take the following steps:

1. Create your intention and declare your commitment to your personal quality system. Write your intention statement as though you are already living and radiating your robust quality of life. As you proceed, describe how you feel, and how you are affecting others at work. Visualize the radiating effects beyond your own workspace and backyard.

Act as if everything you desire is already here.

Wayne Dyer, *The Power of Intention*

2. Assess your readiness. The process you are about to embark upon involves a *deliberate investment in yourself that requires time and energy.* Your energy in particular needs to be focused on who, what, and how you truly want to be. Reflect upon and write your answers to the following questions:

    - Are you prepared to give priority to this initiative?
    - What needs to shift in your life to free up the time and energy required to develop and implement your personal quality system?

Now that you have declared your intention and readiness in writing, you are ready to start your journey using the seven PQS elements.

Element #1—Take a Leadership Role in Your Life

Organizational leaders are selected based on their ability to provide an environment that inspires and motivates individuals, teams, and the organization to greatness. Organizations set standards for a variety of business activities: customer service, product performance, employee performance, and workplace behavior, to name a few. Standards provide an even playing field in the workplace to address differing perceptions. Standards and consistent adherence with those standards creates the workplace culture. Have you ever worked in a culture of very high standards, or a culture that lacks standards, or a culture that has standards but lacks consistent adherence?

There is no one better qualified than you to take this leadership role in your life. Your leadership role includes responsibility and accountability for setting and respecting standards that serve you in achieving the quality of life that inspires and motivates you to greatness.

Your standards are how you have decided to be and how you act in the world. Your standards differ from those of your colleagues. Your standards may differ drastically from others because everyone has their own perception of reality.

People Live from their Perception: Recognizing that people perceive reality through their own filters leads to effective communication and creates a platform for positive action. An inclusive, present-based perception of reality is the platform for effective action.

Coach U, *Guiding Principles for Organizations and Individuals*

The micro-culture that you create for yourself in your workplace is based on your perception of reality. The standards that you create for yourself shape your micro-culture. Your standards are qualities and behaviors that you hold yourself to willingly. Your standards are not expectations that you impose on others. Others create their own standards based on their own perception.

Setting standards that are healthy and easy for you to honor is the first step towards enjoying a higher quality of life at work. The next step is raising your standards.

Raising Your Standards

The benefits of raising your standards will be that you grow into the person you want to be. You attract more of who and what you want to support you in being the person you want to be, and you are comfortable in reinforcing your boundaries. You will be known and respected for your standards. To begin raising your personal standards in the workplace, identify people in your workplace who you admire for their qualities, behavior, and how they relate to people and their work. Then identify what personal standards you would like to raise to reflect what you admire. Be attentive to the following points to remain true to yourself and to others:

- Focus on what fits for you to remain authentic and avoid becoming a carbon copy of someone else.
- Put your integrity first. Ensure that your actions are aligned with your intentions and values.
- Respect and honor the standards of others.
- Take responsibility and be accountable for your standards.

Element #2—Create Your Personal Quality Statement

An effective quality statement is one that is developed in alignment with the organization's vision and mission, and includes *measurable* quality objectives. Adding a statement that describes what will be done consistently to enhance quality and add value boosts the power of the organization's vision and mission statements. Measurable quality objectives drive continuous improvement.

The following are simple steps for creating your personal quality statement. To reap the life- and work-altering benefits, select an inspiring location and occasion: a retreat, your birthday. An inspiring environment and occasion will help to cultivate a joyful and creative experience. Quiet solitude or meditation will enhance your experience. A journal will preserve your experience.

1. To begin, explore and journal your responses to the following questions:
   - What does your quality of life look like in the future? This is your vision.
   - What do you do best each day to contribute to your personal and professional quality of life? This is your mission.
   - What quality objectives align with your mission and vision to add value and sustain your desired quality of life? How will you measure your quality objectives to ensure that you continuously improve the quality of your life?

2. Create an action-oriented theme to brand your personal quality statement and make it come alive. Your theme will become imbedded in your spirit and act as a quick reference guide linking you to your vision and mission. Before investing your energy in any action personally or professionally, you will naturally check for alignment with your theme.

3. Write simple statements that articulate your vision, mission, and quality objectives. Include how you will measure your quality objectives.

4. Print your personal quality statement on special stationery, then frame it and display it to create a visual reminder. Create other visual reminders on your bulletin board, in a special page in your appointment book, or a memo item on your PDA.

The following is an example of a personal quality statement:

Theme: *Owning My Power*

Vision: *I lead with inspiration, courage, and commitment to make the workplace and the world a better place for everyone.*

Mission: *I model leadership by stepping into my personal power to contribute to my workplace, family, community, and the world. I communicate and demonstrate my commitment to personal and professional quality through interactions with my family, co-workers, colleagues, friends, and associates.*

I am committed to maintaining my personal quality system that is aligned with my vision, mission, and the following quality objectives:

- *Consistently and reliably respond to the needs of others while honoring my own self-care.*
- *Conduct my personal and professional life with integrity, professionalism, and a spirit of excellence.*
- *Attract opportunities to continuously improve my personal and professional effectiveness.*

Measurables: *Each quality objective above is measured using various tools, such as annual surveys and other appropriate tracking systems. The true measurable is the enhanced quality of life that I experience as a quality person, and the effect that I have in the workplace and the world.*

Element #3—Develop Your Personal/Professional Management Team

An effective management team works together to achieve the organization's objectives. Alignment of objectives within the management team and within the organization creates a powerful force for effectiveness in achieving objectives and supporting success. If you embraced this concept and developed your own personal/professional management team, how much more effective would you be in achieving your objectives and supporting your success?

Step into your power as CEO and Quality Manager by developing your team and creating your own personal organization chart. An effective personal organization chart visually clarifies who contributes to and influences achievement of your objectives and the success. The personal organization chart below can be used as a model. You can sketch your chart with pen and paper or use a software application to illustrate your organization. Create a visual reminder of your personal organization chart on your bulletin board, a special page in your appointment book, or on your PDA.

The following steps will help you develop and illustrate the interdependence and the power of your team:

1. Identify the people who contribute to or influence your ability and effectiveness in achieving your objectives. These people are part of your interdependent supportive network.

2. Identify how these people can support you. Some support you with their knowledge, experience, skills, products, and services. Others support you by providing encouragement and guidance. Explore how they may work together to enhance your effectiveness.

3. Inform the people on your team about your objectives and how you would like them to support you. Confirm that they are willing, able, and capable of providing the support that you need.

Element #4—Understand the Expectations of Others

A business organization that takes the time to understand client expectations and assess its capability to meet those expectations enhances its success. Its resources are deployed to deliver exactly what its clients expect on a consistent basis. The benefits lead to increased business and increased profits. The benefits include:

- Increased client satisfaction;
- Reduced financial and human-energy costs;
- Availability of financial and human resources to be deployed to add value;
- Increased employee satisfaction.

Taking the time to understand the expectations of people with whom you work and other key influences that affect your success will attract similar results. When you understand the expectations of others, you are better able to assess and communicate your ability and capability to meet their expectations. You are better able to communicate confidently and assert your standards and boundaries. Your personal benefits include:

- Increased satisfaction in your relationships—mutual understanding and appreciation;
- Reduced drain on your energy and resources—stronger boundaries;
- Increased opportunities to add value—ability to exceed expectations when appropriate;
- Ability to enhance quality of life in your workplace and beyond—rewarding contribution.

When you understand and respond appropriately to the expectations of others, you become a source of value to them and they become a source of value to you. In addition, you honor yourself by making well-informed and trusted decisions based on your assessment of your ability and your capability to meet those expectations. Quality and added-value become an important part of "who" and "what" you are in your relationships, including your relationship with yourself.

Element #5—Design and Implement Personal Best Practices

Well-designed and well-implemented best practices serve a business organization and its key influences by instilling consistency. Consistency increases quality and reduces waste. Consistency in your personal and professional life enhances the quality of your life and reduces wasted resources, such as money, time, and energy. Personal best practices consist of a series of actions that you have designed and implemented to *consistently* produce desirable and effective change or development. There are two key benefits:

1. Your energy is freed up to observe and appreciate your quality of life with ease, joy, and grace.
2. Your actions are aligned with your intention and your values. Your integrity is strong and you can trust yourself to behave consistently.

What are your personal best practices? Are you consistent? Does each practice add value and improve your quality of life at work?

Personal Best Practice: Create and Practice 10 Daily Work Habits

The following steps will help you become more aware of best practices in your daily life and help you to assess how well you follow what really matters to you:

1. To begin, ask yourself:
   - What work habits do I want to develop that will enrich and add quality to my life at work each day?
   - What work habits can be easily implemented to ensure consistency and success?
2. Write your answers in a journal or in a document or file dedicated to this exercise.
3. Take your findings and make a list of at least 20 of your best daily work habits.
4. Choose 10 of these habits and create a visual reminder or a tracking system to support you in consciously implementing these habits. Your visual

reminder can be an index card placed on your bulletin board or in your top desk drawer, a special page in your appointment book, or a memo item on your PDA. The following is an example of a visual reminder.

My 10 Daily Work Habits	
1.	Arrive at my desk with time to relax into my day.
2.	Review my priorities at the beginning of my day.
3.	Greet clients, colleagues, and visitors with eye contact and a smile.
4.	Take mini-breaks to stretch and refocus.
5.	Eat a healthy lunch.
6.	Network with co-workers and colleagues. Abstain from gossip.
7.	Acknowledge and endorse the efforts of others—often.
8.	Review voice mail and email only at specific times.
9.	Review my progress for the day with a focus on my effectiveness and satisfaction.
10.	Clear and organize my workspace before I leave. Turn off computer and lights.

Element #6—Create a Problem-Free Environment

The Collins English Dictionary, 2nd Edition, defines a problem as any thing, matter, person, etc., that is difficult to deal with, solve, or overcome. At times, people and organizations substitute "problem" with other words or phrases, such as "challenge," "obstacle," "annoyance," "non-conformance" and "deviation." The word "problem" is substituted to diminish the impact and the need to find an effective long-term solution that prevents recurrence.

Fortunately, enlightened organizations are making the shift to valuing workers who create and support a problem-free environment. Enlightened workers are making the shift to valuing creativity and innovation as sources of job satisfaction. Enlightened organizations, wishing to raise standards, will implement a five-step process that expands awareness and instills the intent to eliminate the cause(s) and recurrence of problems. Organizations that excel in this process choose to focus on preventing problems, thereby creating a problem-free environment that advocates creativity and innovation over problem solving and firefighting.

Are you ready to examine your perception about problems at work? Do you enjoy problems? Is problem solving a source of satisfaction or an energy diversion for you? If you value problem solving over creativity and innovation, are you willing to make a shift in your perception?

Are you ready to create a problem-free environment? Create your Problem-Free Action Plan as per the template below. List three current problems that you believe hold you back at work. Follow the sequential five-step process illustrated in the action plan to:

- Expand your awareness about the underlying causes of each problem;
- Identify appropriate action that will resolve each problem permanently;
- Monitor implementation of action to completion;
- Follow up and verify that the action taken was effective in eliminating the cause(s) of each problem.

Make a commitment to take action on each problem within 30 days.

Problem-Free Action Plan				
Step 1: Problem	Step 2: Cause(s)	Step 3: Appropriate Action	Step 4: Completion Date	Step 5: Follow-up Date
1.				
2.				
3.				

You can use this action plan template and the five-step process to prevent problems and maintain a problem-free environment by identifying *potential* problems and eliminating causes before problems can occur.

The act of acknowledging personal responsibility for problems and using this five-step process will help you move towards creating and maintaining a problem-free environment. Your problem-free environment will enhance the quality of life for you and others inside and outside your organization. You will be revered for the increased energy that you contribute to the creative and innovative processes in your organization.

Element #7—Create Your Personal Quality Development Plan

Enlightened organizations invest in the appropriate facilities, technology, equipment, and human talent in order to improve productivity and maintain a competitive advantage. These organizations budget for investment in these areas so that growth is predictable and sustainable. Wise investment in these areas provides spillover advantages that contribute to the quality of life in the workplace. One of these key areas for investment is in human talent.

Enlightened companies provide opportunities for job-specific training and professional development, which contribute to a worker's ability to perform their work well with less wasted energy and frustration. Working with other educated, well-trained co-workers, and sharing in individual and organizational successes will further enhance job satisfaction.

In addition, the organization sends two powerful messages:

1. The organization understands that workers excel when they are able to perform their work well, with pride, well-channeled energy, and joy.
2. The organization values its workforce and the individuals within it as one of its greatest investments.

You are your greatest investment. You are worth every investment you choose to make in yourself whether it is time, energy, or money. Most people can justify investing financially in education and skill development. By expanding your focus to include both personal and professional self-investment, you will experience benefits that will impact the quality of life for you and others both inside and outside your organization. These include:

- Greater self-worth;
- Consistent return on your investment;
- Confidence in your ability to invest in areas that will produce the greatest return;

- Greater appreciation for your power and ability to influence your present and future.

Create your personal quality development plan and begin investing in your personal and professional quality of life. Make your self-investment a lifetime habit.

Steps for Creating Your Personal Quality Development Plan

1. Identify the areas of your life that would give you a return on your investment. Investment can include money, time, energy, emotion, passion, or simply extra consideration or thought.
2. Sort these areas into categories. Categories can include physical, emotional, intellectual, and academic. Categories can be job-related, relational, or spiritual in nature.
3. Prioritize your list. Determine the approach that will best contribute to your well-being and quality of life. You may choose one item in each category and take action on each of those items, right now. You may take one category and make a major investment to complete that category. The approaches are limitless.

Tips for Investing in Your Life

1. Determine what you can invest and what you are willing to invest. For example, can you invest money? How much money can you and are you willing to invest?

2. Monitor and maintain a balance in your investments. Be aware, for example, that investing time and energy in one area, or category, will reduce resources in another. Avoid spreading your resources too thin.

3. Invest with the expectation of return. This will encourage you to do your homework and invest wisely.

4. Focus on those investments that will provide a greater and more desirable return. This will also help you to avoid spreading your resources too thin.

5. Work with your coach to keep you focused on what is best for you as you invest to enhance your personal and professional quality of life.

You Are the CEO and Quality Manager of Your Life

Always remember that you are the CEO and Quality Manager of your life as you continue to develop and maintain your personal quality system. You are leading and driving this initiative. You are carving out your own workplace reality.

Your choice to develop your personal quality system using the PQS model will have profound effects in your workplace, family, community, and the world. Your personal quality system will lead you to enhanced visibility and respect and will help awaken your workplace for you, your co-workers and colleagues and everyone in every organization you touch.

My dear, late father, Stanley Wicketts, was a Master Tradesman and he has inspired me to help make the workplace a better place for everyone. His profound wisdom is captured in the following quote:

Take care of yourself;
Do what's BEST for you; and
Don't jeopardize what you have built for yourself.

Patricia A. Muir

Patricia A. Muir is president of Maestro Quality Inc., a professional consulting and coaching firm that assists organizational leaders to lead business transformation with a focus on integrating quality in all aspects of their lives and their workplace.

Best known for modeling "professional composure," Patricia's leadership abilities are recognized by over 100 organizations, including IBM, Business Development Bank of Canada, and DaimlerChrysler Canada.

Patricia developed the Personal Quality System (PQS) model for incorporating personal and professional authenticity and quality that delivers positive results affecting quality of life in the workplace. She delivers presentations and workshops on topics related to personal and professional quality of life.

Patricia is a CoachU graduate, a certified Retirement Options Coach, and is working toward accreditation with International Coach Federation (ICF). Patricia is a dynamic leader in Meadowvale Toastmasters. In her youth and throughout her professional life, she has received awards for leadership, writing, and speaking.

Business Name: Maestro Quality Inc.
Address: 7207 Joliette Cr., Mississauga, ON L5N 1Z2
Telephone: 905-858-7566
Email: patricia@maestroquality.com
Web Address: www.maestroquality.com
Professional Affiliations: International Coach Federation; Meadowvale Toastmasters

Doon Wilkins

Doon Inc.

From Here to Heaven

Awakening the workplace is a matter of unleashing and revitalizing the positive energy, intelligence, and spirit that already exists within each member of your organization. Can you recall yourself as a new hire? You arrived at the workplace filled with optimism and energy. You came to work ready to offer your best. There was an excitement about being part of a team and in participating in a meaningful enterprise. You may have been naive but you were eager to learn and ready to laugh. Nobody needed to motivate you. You were motivated from within. That optimism and energy is still there inside you and within each member of your work team. The following are three principles for rekindling that youthful can-do spirit and energy:

1. **Accelerate learning and growth.** If you can get people learning and growing faster than they thought possible, you have tapped into one secret of empowerment and awakening.

2. **Build on strengths and passions.** Help people find ways to develop the strengths and passions they arrive with in the first place. Get them into work roles that are congruent with inherent strengths and interests.

3. **Create a practice for development.** Create a simple practice for staying focused, keeping track of progress and avoiding distractions. It's the key to getting the best you possibly can out of yourself.

Whether you are in management or on the front line, these three principles will help you and your colleagues awaken the workplace. They will help you and your team move up the scale from where you are (here) toward heaven in the workplace.

#1—Accelerate Learning and Growth

Reflection and self-assessment are two keys to helping adult learners get excited about learning, growth, and moving forward faster. Get people thinking about where they are, what could be, and what would help them and the organization to grow. Help them determine growth initiatives that fit within the context of existing priorities.

From Here to Heaven

How would you reply if someone were to ask you how awakened and healthy your organization is today? Where would you place your organization on a nine-point, heaven (9) to hell (1) continuum? Just by asking yourself this question and taking a little time to reflect on it, you are beginning the journey from here to heaven. Before you select a rating, let's think about the two ends of the spectrum.

The Workplace From Hell

If a 9 represents heaven in the workplace, a score of 1 would describe the extreme opposite (hell). No one in his or her right mind would consciously try to create a workplace from hell, but let's face it, we seem to be able to make it happen. Most of us have been part of an organization that was toxic in spite of best intentions. If people generally have good intentions, how do organizations become toxic? We must do it unconsciously—yes? Let's bring some consciousness to what seems to happen unconsciously.

What would you write if you were charged with creating a mission statement for the workplace from hell? If we wanted to deliberately create a set of guide-lines for failure, distrust, discomfort, and discouragement, it might look something like this:

"Deteriorata"

» Chaos is not just a concept. It is a commitment. Reorganize as often as possible and change priorities monthly. Strive always for inconsistency. Word your goals indistinctly so as to make them seem lofty, ethereal, and unachievable. Communicate minimally so as to maximize confusion and misdirection. Avoid commitments—people will hold you to your promises. Focus relentlessly on weakness and discouragement. Who needs a strong, confident staff? Avoid recognition of significant contributions. This is what people get paid for. Reward the inconsequential. It keeps people guessing. In the face of problems, overreact and know that what is absolutely essential is finding someone to blame. Discourage laughter. Employees can laugh on their own time. Criticize in public. That way everyone learns from the example. Avoid training. It's expensive and just gives people ideas. Besides, someone may prove to be smarter than you are. Strive always to place people in roles they hate. This builds character. Never consult an employee regarding what is best for him/her. Avoid equipping people with the tools to do the job. This only encourages accomplishment. Tell rather than listen. It's so much faster. Know that in every organization there is always one person who really knows what is going on. This person must be fired! «

You can likely add a few more gems to this list, but if you found yourself smiling or perhaps flashing back to a toxic work experience, you've tapped into the usefulness of this mission statement for hell. In spite of inherent intelligence, positive intention, and goodwill, we really can unwittingly create workplace disasters. In my years of working with organizations, I have yet to meet even one person who deliberately sets out each day to cheese off as many people as possible and consciously sabotage success. But given enough stress, pressure, deadlines, and confusion, we do some of the things on this list. If we simply operate according to our best instincts, our best instincts can lead us into trouble when times are tough, stress is high, and deadlines are looming. We need some sort of anchor to help keep us sane when thing get insane.

In working with people in discouraging work environments, here is what I have observed. Struggling organizations are filled with caring people, who are usually just as bright, try just as hard, and are just as talented and success-oriented as people in positive work environments. While they are often discouraged, disillusioned, and disheartened, they want desperately to be part of a successful organization.

> **One key difference between the awakened positive workplace and the discouraged workplace is consciousness. People in awakened workplaces make conscious, positive, pro-people choices under pressure.**

They create a culture built around pro-people choices. They choose to support rather than criticize, to laugh with rather than belittle, to forgive rather than blame. They help others learn to think rather than simply offering solutions. One way to help people create such a culture is to create a plan collectively specifying how we wish to be treated and how we will treat others.

The Workplace From Heaven

Let's apply all of this to the creation of the workplace from heaven. If we, who work together each day, can create a short, simple vision of how we want to treat each other and be treated in return, we have something that can help us act in accordance with higher values through storms and setbacks. This statement can serve as our anchor or bill of rights. What does your vision of a heavenly workplace look like? Here's a starter:

» There is positive can-do energy here. We take ourselves lightly and our work seriously. We focus on learning and solutions rather than shame and blame. We forgive mistakes and treat them as learning experiences. We care enough to dispute, but we fight fair and don't hold grudges. We have a positive passion for the success of the organization and for each other. We go the extra mile. We believe we are doing something worthy, special, and important together. We set our sights high. There's a sense of adventure, a feeling that if we all give it our best, we might just be able to pull this off. We know where we fit in the big picture and have the tools to do the job. We get to do what we do best. We're a family. «

Awakening the Workplace

Now it is your turn. Create ten or so anchor statements that describe the kind of workplace that characterizes your vision of a workplace from heaven. Feel free to use a few mentioned above. There's no need for flowery or elaborate statements. Generate thoughts that get to the heart of what "the workplace from heaven" would look like for you. Use "we" words rather than words like "people" and "the organization" so that you can tap into what it looks and feels like at the gut level for you and your colleagues.

The Workplace From Heaven

1. _____
2. _____
3. _____
4. _____
5. _____
6. _____
7. _____
8. _____
9. _____
10. _____

Now let's assess your current workplace according to these statements. Take each point you listed for your vision of a heavenly workplace and rate the current status of your organization from 9 (heaven) through to 1 (hell).

9. Heaven on earth—an enlightened, awakened workplace!
7. A supportive workplace
5. Okay
3. An unsupportive workplace
1. Hell—a dark pit of despair

Using This Exercise in the Workplace

Average your totals and you have a current rating for your organization. When you look at higher scores, you can see places where work may already be in progress. You will also likely see starting points for growth. You don't have to be in management to begin to act on creating a better workplace. You may wish to begin with a small initiative in one little area. For example, if you decide to bring more laughter to your organization, where does it start? It starts with one person (you) lightening up the workplace in some small way—today. Begin by simply brightening your own little corner.

If you are in management you may wish to have your team do this exercise. Have them create such a statement collectively. When people create a statement together, they take ownership. Get the team to identify challenges, cite practical examples, and discuss solutions. The primary gift that comes through this process of reflection and self-assessment is engagement. People take a greater stake in issues when they are consulted and feel they are part of designing solutions.

Solution-Based Thinking

Solution-based thinking involves asking questions that are designed to engage people and help them focus on solutions. Ask people questions that will result in thinking about solutions and moving forward rather than sinking into the abyss of who's to blame, what terrible things happened in the past, and how badly off we are.

There are six essential questions: *who, what, when, where, how,* and *why.* One of these questions keeps people emotional and stuck in the past. If you want to keep people stuck and emotional, ask **why** questions. For example, ask your spouse **why** he didn't take the garbage out before leaving for work. Ask your child **why** she didn't do her homework. Ask an employee or co-worker **why** he was late. Watch for the response. Here's a typical script:

You: "Why are you late?"

Other: "There are 12 people in this department! Why are you singling me out? Do you know how much overtime I put in last week?" (emotional reaction that moves to past justification).

Why questions tend to move people first into emotional defense and secondly into the past (as above). Neither of these places encourages solutions. Change occurs now. Solutions are designed with the future in mind and are enacted in the present. Solution-based thinking is designed to get people engaged, thinking, and directing energy toward solutions and away from blame.

The game plan for solution-based thinking is simple. Ask any of the other five questions. Just stay away from *why* questions! Ask your spouse *how* he might find time to take out the garbage? Ask your child *what* ideas she can think of that would help complete homework at night. Ask the colleague *how* he could plan his responsibilities so that each day, he arrived at work on time.

Try this for yourself—don't just accept my script. Take on the personal experiment of asking *who, what, when, where* and *how* questions, both at home and at work—especially around emotionally loaded issues. Observe the results.

Solution-based questioning takes practice. We tend to be very conditioned to asking *why* questions. Initially it may feel a bit clumsy, but if you stick with it, you will find yourself enabling people and encouraging them to think through problems rather than getting caught up in emotions.

Now look back at the exercise you just completed. Think of a number of questions you can ask to get people engaged in thinking about practical initiatives for moving a few notches up the scale toward the workplace from heaven. Notice what happens when you ask *who, what, when, where* and *how* questions. People naturally move toward solutions.

#2—Build on Strengths and Passions

For better or worse, people don't change much in terms of the passions, strengths, and aversions they bring to the workplace. Within this insight lies a gift for those of us who wish to help people move forward faster and awaken the workplace. The gift is this: if people don't change much, stop trying to mold them to fit what they don't do well. Stop focusing on weakness and deficiencies. Start focusing on strengths and passions. Find ways for people to swim with the current—following natural strengths and doing what they already like doing. Work at aligning the natural strengths and passions of people with organizational goals.

**Organizations can't be all things to all people. They are
designed to accomplish business goals. There isn't
always a perfect match between each individual's passions and the limited array of organizational roles that**

are available. But even if people can spend just a little bit of time each week doing what they are passionate about, the payoff is immense. The payoff comes through employee buy-in, increased morale, and increased productivity—an awakened workplace.

The following is an exercise that will help you focus on strengths and passions, while taking into account that we live in a real-life workplace. In the spaces below, list the various areas of your job description. Then follow the instructions below to complete the exercise.

Area	Competency/Strengths	Passion
a) _____	_____	_____
b) _____	_____	_____
c) _____	_____	_____
d) _____	_____	_____
e) _____	_____	_____
f) _____	_____	_____
g) _____	_____	_____

In the spaces under the heading *Competency/Strengths*, write the number that best describes your current level of competence in each area:

9. Absolute mastery: You are the best in the business
7. Highly skilled: You know this part of your job inside and out
5. Adequate: You know the basics and are adequately skilled
3. You are just learning or need help in this area
1. Low skill

In the spaces under the heading of *Passion*, write a number that corresponds to your current level of passion for each area. How excited are you about doing this work role?

9. I love doing this
7. I like doing this
5. It's okay; part of the job

3. Little passion for this

1. No joy here

In the spaces below, list any areas or pursuits that are possible within your workplace but that are not currently a part of your job description. Complete this list in the same way as above:

	Area	Competency/Strengths	Passion
h)	_____	_____	_____
i)	_____	_____	_____
j)	_____	_____	_____

The Employee Named Doon

In completing a similar exercise several years ago, I looked at my own patterns. There were some huge variances. These pointed toward several options for my professional and personal development. As a professional speaker, my highest/lowest job descriptors looked like this:

Area	Competency/Strengths	Passion
Music	7	9
Presenting	8	9
Accounting	2	0
Marketing	3	2
Coaching	5	9

When you think about developing an employee, there's a natural inclination toward the remediation of deficits. Surveying the above pattern, one might very likely say, "Help this man get some accounting and marketing courses A.S.A.P.! He's a liability here!" Mistakenly, I spent much of my life with this focus. There is merit in addressing weaknesses, but if our primary focus is helping people get better at what they hate, it's a recipe for helping someone grow to hate his job. Focus on weakness results in compliance at best, and despair and discouragement at worst.

Focus on strength taps into inspiration and energy. A key to creating an awakened, inspired workplace is to bet on strength and passion.

Building on Strengths and Passions

Rather than having me study accounting and marketing, the company hired someone with accounting and marketing strength so that I could spend time and energy on speaking and singing. This move made a critical positive difference. It created the fundamental shift to strength-based living. Not only did quality of life improve dramatically but the fortunes of the organization also improved. Currently, I travel around the world speaking, singing, writing books, and playing music. I live where I love and work from home—the workplace from heaven. Plus the profits of the organization have increased.

There is more to the story. The person who was hired to do the accounting and marketing also flourished—so much so that she has moved to her dream home on a coastal island, works from her home, and has created her version of the workplace from heaven.

There is one last piece to the story. The company hired another employee who is highly competent and passionate about coaching. Her excitement and insights about the power of coaching have spread to the rest of the organization. At 59 years of age, she reports that she has never been so excited and motivated about her work. There's a new focus on results, follow-up, and helping clients to integrate skills. This, in turn, has led to some reframing and redefinition of the focus of the entire organization.

If you are managing others, the passion/competence exercise is a nice first step toward helping people align work roles with strengths. We live in the real world where the organization cannot be all things to all people. However, it is remarkable how often this type of exercise serves as a launch pad for juggling work positions and job definitions slightly so that people can spend at least some of their workweek doing more of what they love.

As you learn people's strengths, you find interesting variations between people. You can often find creative ways to alter responsibilities so that the person who loves sales and hates accounting is allowed to trade off some duties with the person who loves accounting and detests sales. There isn't always a perfect fit, but if you can succeed in helping a person move into a realm of strength, even for a small part of the workweek, there is an immediate payoff in terms of workplace satisfaction, even when people know you are simply looking out for opportunities for them to buy in. It also encourages the creative instincts of the employee. You find people coming back to you saying, "Hey, I've got an idea I want to run by you!"

It isn't this specific exercise that is magic. It's adopting the mindset of helping people develop strengths and passions. As people focus on learning and solutions and as they find a best fit for strength development, the reward is a happier workplace. Begin to see yourself as a developer of people and you will see people giving more back to the organization.

Now how can you help people move forward in a determined, realistic way that creates tangible results for them and for the organization? Encourage a practice for development.

3—Create a Practice for Development

Many of us live life with a vague sense of dissatisfaction. It isn't that we're failing. It's just that we aren't spending our precious time and energy doing what we feel called to do. If you wish to awaken yourself and your workplace, build a boat with struts constructed from strengths. Help others to do the same. Your practice is simply your daily plan for staying focused, planning actions, and assessing what worked and what didn't. Your practice is a way to chart your course intelligently through the circumstances and obstacles you will encounter. A daily practice is what makes the difference between focus and diversion, between dreams and reality.

Here is a practice that is so simple that you may say—that's it? That's all I do? The answer is yes! *Simply write a daily journal of your intentions, actions, and results.* There are 16 years of journals sitting on my mantle—16 years of daily echoes of this simple practice. Tallied up, these 16 years are becoming a life story. They are certainly the story of a journey from a satisfactory workplace to a heavenly workplace. What began as a casual relationship with journaling has blossomed into a love affair. The few minutes taken each morning to think, plan, and reflect have become some of the most precious moments of each day. They are the difference between living consciously and unconsciously. And they will move you out of fantasizing where you want to be in your life and into the daily actions that create the reality.

Your Daily Practice

1. Find a journal that has one full page dedicated to each day of the year. Begin recording your story at today's date.
2. Set a strength-based developmental goal: for example, awakening my workplace.
3. Make a plan of action for the day.
4. On waking tomorrow, record what you did and what you learned.
5. Make another plan for the day ahead. Remember what is important. Write about what you learned yesterday. Do it again tomorrow, through the year and through the next year. As you repeatedly follow this practice, you will learn to ask one essential question again and again, which is: "What did you learn?"

Results

Your workplace is where you will spend much of your lifetime and will do much of your life's work. It is a perfect place to begin a practice for moving yourself and others from here toward heaven. These are the people who you hang out with every day. Why not start here?

As people take pride in learning and accomplishment, the results overflow into the workplace. I receive emails from teachers, nurses, bankers, forestry workers, musicians, farmers, business people, and oil workers. Each of these people has started right where they are and is creating a strength-based development practice. How far they will go, nobody knows. Each is a work in progress. Each is doing what he or she can to move just one notch higher on the journey from here toward heaven. Here is one such story:

>> Brigid is a nurse who has worked extensively in the area of geriatrics. She's a long-time, highly committed nurse, but she has another undeveloped passion that calls out for expression. She's a natural-born storyteller.

Patients and staff respond to the inspirational power of her stories. She sought to find a place to speak to people about the importance of her work and to share the humor, hope, and compassion she's learned in working with the elderly.

Clarifying her passion through writing and journaling caused her to garner the momentum to take some calculated risks. She took the risk of flying a few trial balloons by offering presentations to hospital staff and helping professionals. The responses validated to her that she indeed has a talent for presentation.

Brigid proposed a shift in work responsibilities that entailed moving out of full-time and into a two-thirds work assignment, offering her time and energy to work on a book of her stories, and to speak more frequently. The organization approved. She took action. Doors began to open. The new reality ensued. **«**

Brigid recently came to a deep realization. She always liked her work. But now she loves her work. Her spirit, energy, optimism, excitement, and passion are renewed. Plus she broadcasts this positive energy out to others who need to hear the message. It wasn't that big a change, but it has made all the difference. Brigid's workplace from heaven is the same place she's always worked.

Remember these three principles:
Accelerate learning and growth;
Build on strengths and passions;
Create a practice for development.

Doon Wilkins

When organizations want to make the best use of employee intelligence by creating a more inspiring, engaging workplace, they call **Doon Wilkins**. Over 100,000 people across the globe have heard Doon speak on how to live with intention. Doon coaches people beyond "change" toward productivity, progress, and unity. Together with management teams, Doon creates environments where people feel supported while they learn and integrate the skills needed to make progress together. Hiring the brightest and best is just the start of taking good to great. Organizations and individuals thrive when managers know how to develop and position people where they can contribute their best. Doon leads teams in defining strengths and harnessing talents in the service of the organization. Good people thrive and stay in organizations where they are challenged, delighted, engaged, and understood.

Doon is the author of the popular *Stumbling Toward Enlightenment—A Pathway to Better*. Individuals wishing to live an inspired life, embrace the process outlined in this guidebook. They learn how to take charge of their own growth and maintain a commitment to learning and continuous self-improvement.

Winner of the Bronze Trophy in the World Championship of Public Speaking, Doon possesses a Bachelor of Education Degree and a Graduate Diploma in Psychology.

Business Name: Doon Inc.
Address: 638-7 Street, Canmore, AB T1W 2C6
Telephone: 403-678-9838
Email: Dooninc@shaw.ca
Web Address: www.doon.bz

Sue Edwards

Development by Design

You've Gotta Flip It on Its Head!
Four Key Strategies for Leadership Success

» Lorna sits facing me in her tailored pantsuit, hands tightly clasped, her jaw firmly clenched and says, "I've finally been promoted to the executive team. All the others on the team are men. What tips can you give me to fit in? I've also been getting some feedback that I'm too angry-sounding and edgy with people, which is intimidating others. What can you do to help me fix this?" «

What career moments have you experienced that remind you of this scenario? Have you ever found yourself longing for a cookbook on how to fit in, or wished you could be granted a quick-fix solution to change how others see you? If so, you are not alone.

Now, step back from this and consider another perspective. Can you recall a time when you've been frustrated by the seemingly false behaviors of others at work? Can you relate to the feeling of wanting to take a colleague by the shoulders, look her straight in the eye and say, "Just be yourself!" Oddly enough, the behaviors that get in the way of people having a positive impact on others are often the *very behaviors* they've been trying hard to demonstrate. How ironic is that?

In my coaching with leaders, I find they frequently discover that their long-held beliefs about what makes leaders successful flies directly in the face of what happens in real life. They demonstrate leadership characteristics based on commonly held beliefs, such as:

- **Belief #1:** All leaders must communicate verbally with power and charisma.
- **Belief #2:** Leaders must convey a steely strength.
- **Belief #3:** Leaders must compromise themselves for the good of the organization.
- **Belief #4:** Previously gained skills are the foundation for success at the next level.

Down the road, they get the startling wake-up call that these purposeful behaviors have not resulted in the successes they had hoped for, after all. Frankly, they would do better to flip these beliefs on their head!

> **True leadership success and your greatest impact comes from the flip side of behaviors that you may have been socialized to exhibit as a strong leader. Your real power lies in awakening to the leader already inside you rather than layering on externally driven leadership qualities like a corporate cloak.**

I invite you to consider how four leadership success strategies may apply to you. You've gotta…

1. Listen to be heard;
2. Be vulnerable to be strong;
3. Be selfish to serve;
4. Let go of what got you here.

Success Strategy #1—You've Gotta Listen to Be Heard

Seek first to understand, then to be understood.

Stephen R. Covey

Great leaders are known for articulating powerful visions and then galvanizing people towards this vision. For the rallying cry to echo throughout the organization, the leader's voice must be heard.

Yet, when I work with leaders moving into new organizations, and using my Clearing the 90-Day Hurdle™ process, I point to research showing that the most critical behavior in the first 90 days is to "listen, observe, and ask questions." The new leader who rides in on a white charger with a predetermined vision and strategy can find the organization quickly turning its back. He or she has not yet earned the right to be heard about ways the company needs to profoundly change course. A receptive audience for a new vision is nurtured through a leader who demonstrates intentional listening, observation, and reflection prior to creating a vision. Yes, the critical step that comes first is listening.

>> Mike is a charismatic leader and an exceptional presenter. He has a particular gift for inspiring a large room full of people. His speeches paint a picture of an exciting future. His stories are engaging and spoken with a confidence that conveys his opinions as THE truth.

This gift helped Mike to stand out as a leader early in his career. However, as Mike progressed through higher levels of leadership, his direct reports and peers began to express concerns. They grew tired of the storytelling and wanted more interactive, reciprocal discussion. Frankly, they started to see Mike as being so focused on what *he* had to say that they felt they weren't being heard.

Mike would describe his relationships with his direct reports by saying, "We have great conversations!" As his coach, I pointed out that, in fact, he likely was having a great conversation—with himself—in front of an audience of direct reports. (I call it "speechifying.") There was no room for Mike's direct reports to process, question, and give their own reactions and ideas.

I challenged Mike to consider, "What would it be like to set aside the speech and simply listen, ask questions, and explore ideas with one another?"

Over time, as Mike has learned to incorporate powerful listening into his conversations with others, his relationships have strengthened. The accountability displayed by his staff has soared. Most interesting of all is that others in the organization are now more eager to truly listen to, rather than simply applaud for Mike's speeches. **«**

This is how it works with *being heard*. It seems that it's not the person with the loudest voice that is heard but, rather, the leader who exhibits the most powerful listening.

Women in particular are often coached to "speak up" to ensure they are heard. The traditional advice to women in a male-dominated sector is to assert themselves like the men and to communicate in a strong, powerful voice. My response is…a resounding *maybe*!

For some women, demonstrating more assertiveness in a group—particularly a group of men—is a critical developmental step. There is also strong merit in training one's voice, learning about the use of breath and knowing how to speak from the diaphragm. This is all great advice.

At the same time, those of you who are proponents of a strengths-based leadership philosophy will likely relate to an alternative strategy. How about a flip? Rather than simply focusing on strong verbal assertions, what about the value of leveraging innate *listening* skills by:

- Listening intently to what's really being said;
- Being the bridge that helps people hear what each other is saying;
- Listening for the "elephants in the room"—those unspoken assumptions that stall effective communication.

These are the strengths that good listeners bring, and they apply equally to effective listeners of either gender. Some of you can readily "hear" the dynamics in a room. Once others identify you as someone who listens so attentively that you can even hear what's NOT being said…they will relish learning what you hear and invite your insight. Your listening strength is, ironically, your ticket to be heard.

Being right too soon is socially unacceptable.

Robert A. Heinlein,
American science-fiction writer

Coaching Questions

- If you have a tendency to "give speeches," even in one-on-one conversations, when could you replace this with true reciprocal dialogue?
- If you are a strong listener, how could you leverage this power and ensure that your observations are made available to the group?
- If you are not a naturally strong listener, how might you develop this muscle?

Exercise

Here's a simple, yet revealing exercise to raise your awareness of the impact of "feeling heard."

- During the next two weeks, notice what happens when you don't feel heard. How does this impact YOUR ability to fully listen?
- Observe yourself in various situations—both at work and home.
- If you can, ask others what they notice about you at these times.

Success Strategy #2—You've Gotta Be Vulnerable to Be Strong

> *Water is fluid, soft, and yielding. But water will wear away rock, which is rigid and cannot yield. As a rule, whatever is fluid, soft, and yielding will overcome whatever is rigid and hard. This is another paradox: what is soft is strong.*
>
> Lao-Tzu (600 B.C.)

Think of times when you've felt vulnerable at work. Asking for help may have left you feeling vulnerable with the person you asked. Or, you may have experienced regret after admitting a weakness or disclosing a need for personal development to others. This is very natural in a society that teaches that vulnerability represents weakness. In fact, definitions of vulnerability refer to susceptibility to physical or emotional injury, criticism, or attack.

Yet, time and again, I've seen employees walk over hot coals for leaders who express vulnerability versus those who convey omnipotence. It is difficult to hook in at an emotional level with a leader who wears an armor of perfection. Much of my coaching work with both male and female executives involves supporting them in removing the Teflon® layer of self-protection that gets in the way of their ability to lead from a place of true power. They are inevitably seen to be stronger leaders as they mature in their willingness to demonstrate vulnerability.

Leaders who are able to deliver effectively stated requests for help are seen as resourceful and strong individuals. When they demonstrate the humility to ask for help, they earn the respect of others. In turn, the leader who asks for help is strengthened by the very support that is provided.

» Kira recently made a shift in how she was interacting with her boss. When he asked her to prepare presentations, she assumed that she was expected to go away, develop the content, deliver it at the required meeting, and then wait for feedback from her boss. Her boss was highly regarded for the impact of his presentations and his openness in asking others for assistance. Kira, on the other hand, was well aware that presentations were not her strong suit. When she took a hard look at how this approach was working for her, Kira was able to see that she was not fully leveraging her boss's support. She could learn far more about creating presentations that have "oomph" by walking through a draft with her boss—focusing on the content plus her delivery—and obtaining feedback earlier in the process. So, she made the request for his upfront support.

The outcome? Her boss was delighted to coach Kira and was enthused about the opportunity to leverage his own strength and impart skills to her. By taking the time to work together preparing for a number of Kira's key presentations, she benefited from her boss's thought process. Kira's presentations now have punch! She delivers with the confidence of someone who has great material and is well-prepared. She now rarely needs corrective feedback after the fact. Equally important is that in the very act of asking for help, Kira has demonstrated to her boss that she is effectively leveraging resources around her. «

Leaders also demonstrate strength in vulnerability through their response to receiving tough feedback. Many leaders have experienced 360-degree feedback assessments (surveys that provide feedback from the boss, peers, and direct reports). In observing the reactions to feedback for more than 100 leaders, it is clear to me that those who benefit most from a 360-degree process are those who disclose the results and build collaborative development plans in response. Recently, one of my coaching clients was told by her peers that it was extremely brave of her to reveal the themes in her feedback. They admired this disclosure and even asked how they could support her. Of course, the more support she receives, the stronger she becomes. The reinforcing cycle of strength through vulnerability continues to spiral upwards.

Coaching Questions

- How are your assumptions about vulnerability preventing you from building strong connections with others?
- If you had no concerns about being personally criticized, what might you disclose more openly?

Exercise

Consider an important goal that you are stuck on right now and can't seem to get any traction on.

- Think of someone you could ask for support to get you jump-started with respect to this goal. What specifically do you want to ask of them?
- How can you establish accountability to yourself to ask for help in achieving this goal?

Success Strategy #3—You've Gotta Be Selfish to Serve Others

[Spoken to a mother] *"How are you looking after your children's mother?"*

Dr. Phil (McGraw), television personality and psychologist

If we were to take Dr. Phil's philosophy about the importance of self-care as a way to serve others and apply it to you and your team, you might ask yourself questions such as: "How are you looking after your team's leader? (a.k.a. You)" and "Who is ensuring that your direct reports have a resilient leader who is clear-headed and who is modeling self-care?"

What may seem to be a very selfish approach to managing your role and your time is often the very approach that will best serve those around you over the long run. Consider that...

- In "selfishly" saying "No" to tasks that you are unable to complete within the required deadline, you are more honestly serving your customers.
- In "selfishly" asking your manager for exactly what you need from her, based on your own particular communication style, you create clarity and serve your manager and team well.
- In "selfishly" managing your work time so that you create space for your family life, you are serving your workplace by bringing a positive attitude and reduced resentment of your work.

When my coaching clients set clear parameters at work to achieve what they perceive to be their "selfish" *personal goals*, it has a profound positive impact on their productivity and satisfaction *at work*.

» Brian, a vice-president of operations whom I coach, has recently achieved fantastic improvements in his clarity and effectiveness at work. He started with one small personal commitment. Brian decided that every Thursday he would commit to taking his daughter to her after-school activity. He started structuring every Thursday so that he could successfully meet this commitment. This led to Brian finishing initiatives at work in time to leave the office. He was energized by *knowing* that he would be meeting a commitment to his family, instead of wasting energy worrying about whether he should stay at work or attend the after-school activity. For one day each week, the decision was already made. This became the parameter and work simply had to fit into the time allotted each Thursday.

The effect of this one small personal commitment rapidly began to spread. In no time, Brian could see that in meeting his commitment to his family and keeping his workday *defined* instead of open-ended, he became more efficient. His employer benefited, not just his family. His confidence strengthened as he began to redefine himself as someone who makes and keeps commitments to himself and others, instead of as someone who stretches to accommodate others' requests and compromises what is important to him. **«**

In our minds, we know that work always expands to fill the time allotted. Yet, as a society, we are uncomfortable setting limits. The bottom line is that it is often not until we "get selfish" and set limits that we become truly LIMITLESS in our impact.

One strategy to achieving greater productivity at work is blocking off certain times as "no meeting hours," or "email time," or "focused time for strategic projects." When it fits for their work, some people even schedule time to work at home or in another environment where there are no distractions or interruptions. Others schedule their fitness sessions into their calendar, to ensure that they respect these commitments to themselves. In "being selfish," they create a great return to those around them.

Coaching Questions

- What parameters do you need to set to ensure that you are meeting personal commitments, honoring your personal values, and remaining effective at work?
- If you were fully modeling the way you want your direct reports to look after themselves, what would you be doing differently?

Exercise

- What one small, "selfish" commitment can you make to yourself this week?
- What self-care habit or ritual will you establish regularly on an ongoing basis?
- How will you maintain accountability for this new habit?
- How will you celebrate when it becomes an established habit?

Success Strategy #4—You've Gotta Let Go of What Got You Here

If you only do what you know you can do, you never do very much.

Tom Krause, motivational speaker, teacher and coach

Sooner or later after a significant promotion, this challenge seems to hit all leaders between the eyes. Letting go of previously successful approaches is one of the most frequent coaching topics for my executive coaching clients. It's especially a challenge when the approaches that are no longer appropriate to rely on are the very behaviors that led to the promotion.

Why this sudden about-face? Why would certain behaviors be considered strengths one day and weaknesses the next? Are organizations this erratic?

Think of situations where you've been recognized for a particular strength—let's take "rolling up your sleeves and getting things done" as an example. For much of your career you may have been rewarded for showing initiative and accomplishing things yourself. Then suddenly as you are promoted to the director level, this strength doesn't seem to earn you the respect it once did. Your boss starts telling you to stand back and get things done through others instead. You are told to get your nose out of the day-to-day issues and address longer-term strategic concerns. You are encouraged to hold back your own answers and coach others to figure out their own best solutions instead.

» Valerie was recently promoted to Controller from the position of Manager, Strategic Alliances. In her previous role, she operated as an individual contributor. Her analyses of potential alliance opportunities required her to be very hands-on and focused on detailed information. She was recognized as being one of the strongest individuals in the company for knowing specific facts and being able to answer any question at all about the smallest piece of data.

In her new role, Valerie gained a team of managerial-level direct reports. In no time Valerie's team told her that she was micro-managing them. When she asked detailed questions about specific budget lines, they felt that Valerie didn't trust them. Her highest potential direct report resigned within one month, expressing that Valerie was too involved in the day-to-day details and required too much detailed information. Clearly, Valerie needed to let go of her detailed analytical strength and her desire to keep all of the details in her head. She needed to step up from individual contributor to a leader who "gets things done through others." Continuing to rely heavily on the skills she was recognized for in her previous job would sooner or later derail her at this new level. **«**

Interestingly enough, I've noticed that the challenge of making these shifts seems to be most difficult for people who have had the most previous success. The louder the applause, the more the individual wants to repeat the same behaviors. It can be frightening to move from a place of high achievement and strong recognition to a place of "not knowing" and uncertainty. It can be uncomfortable to move from expert mode to learner mode. It's very natural for this discomfort to result in resistance to pursuing new skills and a desire to continue relying on proven success strategies from past roles.

Accountability partners, such as your manager or a mentor, can be of great support in helping hold your feet to the flame and try out new behaviors. The services of a professionally trained leadership coach are particularly valuable to support you with these challenging skill transitions.

> It is necessary to any originality to have the courage to be an amateur.
>
> Wallace Stevens, poet

Coaching Questions

- What past skills or strengths are at risk of becoming (or may already be) liabilities for you at your current level in the organization?
- How can you shift your attention to the necessary new skills that are important for success in this role?

Exercise

- Consider the next significant developmental step ahead for you. Arrange a conversation with your manager, human resources, internal mentor, or external leadership coach to talk about what skill transitions are most important for success at the next level.
- How can you establish a plan for being deliberate about these skill transitions ahead?

So, Get Flipping!

Let's revisit Lorna, whom we met at the beginning of this chapter. Was she able to move from wanting a quick-fix approach to being coached? Did she learn to flip her leadership beliefs on their head?

» "Tell me about a leader you've worked with and truly admired," I asked Lorna in our coaching sessions. Her eyes softened and her shoulders relaxed. "Our previous CEO was revered by everyone. You knew where you stood with him and yet always felt cared for and as if you really mattered. He really looked after this company and he took time with people."

"Interesting," I smile. "Tell me again what you'd said about leaders who are warm never making it to the top in real organizations?" Lorna smiled too, "Point taken...but he could get away with it because he's a man." I held Lorna's gaze and asked, "What if your efforts to demonstrate such a tough exterior and operate in the way you perceive men to behave is actually getting in the way of you creating a positive impact? What if it was, in fact, undermining your strength? How might your 'edge' and 'anger' be a result of working so hard to portray an image that's not fully you?"

In a few short weeks after this "aha" moment, Lorna noticed the impact of "lightening up," listening more, and not charging in to make a point and demonstrate her expertise. In doing so, her peers were able to hear her advice and not see her as being on the attack or acting out of defensiveness. She started asking her colleagues for support in areas outside of her expertise and began sharing with them what she was trying to improve in her own leadership. She enrolled her boss in supporting her by providing feedback when he observed her trying out these new behaviors. Lorna started taking walks with a colleague at lunch and eating in the cafeteria instead of at her desk. She began trusting her direct reports to take on more ownership for initiatives themselves. This lightened her load, helped her feel better about their development, and caused others to see her operating at a much higher level. She was less uptight at work, worried less, and slept better. In working with all four strategies for leadership success, Lorna has begun to create a powerful platform from which to lead. She's become more herself and much more likeable to boot! **«**

To sum up, for me what's "hardest" about leadership has little to do with learning tips and tricks to fit in or to portray qualities that are not our own. The real work of discovering your leadership strength and optimizing your impact is figuring out how to stop trying so darn hard to be something that you're not and to lead from a more authentic place. I encourage you to challenge what you've long THOUGHT to be true about great leaders and listen instead to what you KNOW in your heart and in your gut to be true about who you are as your own best leader.

So I'm curious…what will you flip on its head to step into your full potential as leader?

> *Your time is limited, so don't waste it living someone else's life. Don't be trapped by dogma—which is living with the results of other people's thinking. Don't let the noise of others' opinions drown out your own inner voice. And most important, have the courage to follow your heart and intuition. They somehow already know what you truly want to become. Everything else is secondary.*
>
> Steve Jobs, Apple co-founder

Sue Edwards

Sue Edwards brings a powerful blend of passion and professionalism to her coaching with executives and leadership teams and is an international conference speaker. She founded Development by Design in 1996 and she works globally with clients in various industries, including technology, manufacturing, consumer-packaged goods, as well as universities. She specializes in working with successful leaders transitioning into a new organization or upward into significantly more challenging levels of leadership. Sue previously held senior HR roles with Campbell Soup, Bayer, and Imperial Oil.

She is a graduate of Corporate Coach U and is an accredited coach at the ACC level with the International Coach Federation. Sue is an Industrial Psychology graduate from the University of Waterloo, with MBA courses from Dalhousie. She has achieved her Certified Human Resources Professional (CHRP) designation. Sue is qualified to administer MBTI®, Thomas International (DISC) Personal Profile™, and Benchmarks®.

Sue is the author of *Congratulations, You're Hired! A Coach's Guide to Ensuring a Successful Transition*. She is developing a workbook entitled, "Wow Them in Your New Job! (and Reduce Your Overwhelm)…It's Easier Than You'd Expect." She has been interviewed on CTV's "Canada AM" and profiled in the *National Post*. She writes regular columns on leadership issues.

Business Name:	Development by Design
Address:	2218 Vista Drive, Burlington, ON L7M 3N5
Telephone:	905-336-6129
Email:	sue@development-by-design.com
Web Addresses:	www.development-by-design.com and www.clearingthe90dayhurdle.com
Professional Affiliations:	Human Resources Professional Association of Ontario; International Coach Federation; CoachesCanada.com; Company of Women; Career Professionals of Canada

Favorite Provocative Question:
If everything was possible and you had all the courage in the world, what is the bravest thing you could do?

Donna Devlin

Donna Devlin Consulting "Reflections of Light"

Decoding Grief in the Workplace: The Ultimate Awakening

> *When a colleague dies or one is grieving a death or a loss, the impact on his/her co-workers can be tremendous and can influence the workplace in a variety of ways.*
>
> Kirsti A. Dyer, MD, MS

Decoding grief in the workplace is not your usual welcome subject. It is one we may go to great lengths to avoid. It is not that we are unfamiliar with the territory of grief. Some of us will be very familiar with this journey and I would suggest that most of us have experienced grief in some form. It is a subject that is difficult to address on our own turf, never mind the workplace. We are a death-denying, change- and pain-avoidant culture.

> *When a person is born, we rejoice, and when they're married, we jubilate, but when they die, we try to pretend that nothing happened.*
>
> Margaret Mead, anthropologist

Todd Van Beck, a popular speaker about death and dying, asked an audience what they believed to be the death rate in their city. Everyone threw out stats and then Todd replied, "It is 100 percent." We usually associate the term grief in relation to death. However, we grieve for many losses and change experiences, such as divorce, illness, change of position, loss of hopes, dreams, and self-esteem, to name a few. Decoding change, loss and grief provides unparalleled opportunity to bring consciousness and perspective into our life and work.

> **The journey of decoding grief at work opens the possibility of our ultimate awakening. Know that grief is the vital sign of life and it is not going away.**

Recently, I was telling a client about this project of writing on decoding grief at work and she could hardly wait to tell me, "Grief is everywhere." She went on to explain that in her office of twenty people she could identify many people that she believed were grieving in some form. "No one talks about this and calls it what it is. We don't pay attention. There is this "buck up" attitude; get on with it. We are "just too busy," my friend says. The following is a story from her workplace:

» My client explained that her company's motto is to be an employer of choice. She believes that her company's actions when dealing with people who are grieving is incongruent with its declared motto. An administrative assistant, for example, had recently separated from her partner and needed to move out of her apartment immediately. She asked her employer for a couple of hours off. Her request was declined because they were too busy. She was told that she should do this on her own time. To further complicate the situation, the recently separated woman was accused of having a bad attitude.

In the same company, down the hallway, an individual sat at his desk holding his head, and looking at a massive stack of papers. During the last few days he has been getting the reputation of being a "slacker." Another colleague finds out that his wife of forty years has just filed for divorce. Down another hallway, a man rushes off to catch a flight out of the province to visit his dad who is in palliative care and close to death. Without knowing the situation, a co-worker comments that he is always out of the office and not available. «

We Are the Workplace

Kind words can be short and easy to speak, but their
echoes are truly endless.

Mother Theresa

The understanding that "we" are the workplace needs to be reached. What we bring into the workplace is the gift of ourselves. That includes personalities, character, skills, knowledge, experience, and compassion. That full package deal is the essence of what it means to be human. These are the aspects that make us unique. Grief breaks down that separation and reveals the humanness in all of us. We all share in the collective coding of grief, and with that comes the responsibility of decoding and shedding light on a taboo subject. The value has to be seen in that "our people," "our collective losses," and "our avoidance" of these losses interferes with "our ability" to transform our grief.

Death, loss, and grief are some of life's great mysteries. It is in honoring these mysteries—not avoiding them and pretending they don't exist—that the true personal and workplace awakening can emerge. Grief knows no boundaries and has no preference for gender, ethnicity, title, or income. Loss is a side effect of being alive. We spend one-third to one-half of our waking hours at work. Since we are the workplace, where people come together for a common purpose to create and produce, a side benefit would be in the ability to identify and transform our grief. We can deal better with loss and the resulting loss of productivity in our workplace with understanding and an open, compassionate approach.

Behold, I show you a mystery; we shall not all sleep, but we
shall all be changed, in a moment, in the twinkling of an eye...

Corinthians 15:51

Change and loss equation:
Change = loss = grief

A change of any type will often produce a loss and will eventually produce a grief reaction. William Bridges, an authority on change, believes that change is not the same as transition. Change is the outside response—the situation you find yourself in—the new role, boss, protocols, and location. Transition has to do with the psychological, inside response to change. All the behavioral, emotional, physical, social, and spiritual reactions are all part of transition.

The amount of change experienced by organizations and individuals is enormous. It is overwhelming for all involved. We either "bulldoze" through—hard, fast, unfeeling—or we "doze" through—sleeping, just going through the motions. Finding a middle ground and acknowledging our fears and concerns are paramount to decoding our grief. We don't often think of grief as coming to work, yet if one is at work, grief is there too. The workplace itself can be the cause of the grief or the cause may connect to events outside work.

> *We don't use the word grieving…instead we speak in code and say that morale is down. We wouldn't go into a house where someone has died and say, "Hey the morale really sucks here." But we do that in organizations. Morale is not down. People are grieving.*
>
> William Bridges, speaker and author

The obvious losses are usually associated with death. Dealing with the death of a colleague, a family member, or friend has many rippling effects. Let me share a short story of a company reeling from the suicide of a colleague:

>> When I received a call to assist with a debriefing after a completed suicide, I was faced with a range of people with different styles of coping with traumatic situations. Some wanted to avoid any discussion and go on with "business as usual"; others needed to talk and process the situation they found themselves in.

Some believed it was better to keep themselves busy and clean out the cubicle of the deceased colleague as soon as possible. Others wanted to keep his desk the way it was for a while and create a memorial. <<

There is value in open, compassionate, non-judgmental discussions. This situation was a microcosm of some very polarizing grief reactions. Acknowledging the suicide and accepting that it did occur becomes extremely important. Identifying that it was the fear, pain, and sadness that were limiting those who wanted to get on with things—and not the loss itself—is vital. We cannot get on with things unless we identify what has happened and greet the grief. Creating rituals and memorials are some of the ways we can express our grief.

Defining Grief and Mourning

Beginning of wisdom is to call things by their right names.

Chinese proverb

Grief and mourning are different processes that occur after a change and loss situation. It is helpful to define these terms:

Grief is our personal, internal reaction to a loss situation. It assaults our entire being, mentally, emotionally, physically, socially, and spiritually. We have "grief gusts" as a natural course of grieving in which we feel sudden, intense, raw, painful gut-wrenching reactions. This usually takes us by surprise when we think or experience something or someone that reminds us of our loss. Once again we are reminded of the volatile, unpredictable nature of grief.

Mourning is the external expression of our grief. Mourning usually involves the use of rituals as a way to express our internal grief. There is a behavioral component associated with mourning that is strongly influenced by cultures and rituals. Memorials, funerals, writing, and journaling are some examples of rituals that offer a way to honor, move and express our grief. It has often been said that when there are no words for grief, use a ritual.

Grief and mourning are two different, necessary processes that aid in our grief transformation. We see ourselves in others' pain, suffering, and loss, yet we are paralyzed by our fears of death, change, and loss. As a result we rarely bring light to the grief of others. There is nothing like looking into the face of another who is suffering to see ourselves. Consequently, we often don't look. It is too painful. We think of other ways to address the workplace difficulties associated with change, grief, and loss.

What Are We Afraid Of?

To understand our own grief—or the grief of others in the workplace—it is helpful to look at four aspects of grief that keep us immobilized:

1. Not knowing what to say: The bottom line is that people often fear grief, especially at work, because they simply do not know what to say. Connected to this is the belief that the workplace is not the place to address it. Fear of inadequacy and fear of rejection are the central themes surrounding a person's response to loss situations. Can you think of a change, grief, and loss situation where fear may have influenced you? What were you afraid of?

> I choose to rise up out of that storm and see that in moments of
> desperation, fear, and helplessness, each of us can be a rainbow
> of hope, doing what we can to extend ourselves in kindness and
> grace to one another. And I know for sure that there is no
> them, there's only us.
>
> Oprah Winfrey

2. Perception of grief: The intensity of the grief reaction has to do with how the loss is perceived. We often view our grief reactions as abnormal when, in fact, the whirling, messy, intense reactions are natural and necessary. The sleeplessness, confusion, depression, lethargy, anger, irritability, difficulty in concentrating, and weepiness are some of our common grief responses as we navigate through change.

We can never underestimate how someone will perceive a loss situation. You don't know what the change means to you or someone else until you ask. Think of a change situation. What changed? What does this loss mean to you? What are you losing? What will you miss? How did you react and cope?

What you see and hear depends a good deal on where you are
standing; it also depends on what sort of person you are.

C. S. Lewis, spiritual philosopher and author

3. Believing grief is a morale issue: We may address grief as poor morale. We may avoid it and pretend it is not happening. Morale is defined by www.worldreference.com as the spirit of the group; an individual psychological well-being, based upon a sense of confidence, usefulness, and purpose. Grief will undeniably affect our emotional well-being, our sense of confidence, and our purpose, and will occur in reaction to a change and perceived loss experience. Labeling it morale negates the reality that most companies are experiencing enormous ongoing change and grieving.

4. Obvious and hidden losses: We can identify the obvious losses associated with grief, such as death, divorce, failing health, separation; however, can we take a step further and actually acknowledge and respond to these losses? The hidden losses may involve such change as loss of advancement, position, relocation, responsibilities, change in managers, roles, technology, death of a pet, miscarriage, Alzheimer's, AIDS, loss of confidence, financial loss, loss of self-worth, and loss of control. Kenneth Doka, author of *Disenfranchised Grief: New Directions, Challenges, and Strategies for Practice*, talks about these hidden losses resulting in disenfranchised grief. This means that these types of situations and the grief associated with them may not be socially recognized or supported.

Awakening Through Alchemy

The Divine Alchemist can miraculously change a sorrow-
ing heart of lead into a golden mellowness that sings
praises through tears.

S. L. McMillen, physician and author

Alchemy has been defined by the *Oxford Dictionary* as the science and art of transformation-energy involving emotions, behaviors, material, feeling experiences, and thoughts. The use of the term "alchemy" serves as a metaphor and a tool to highlight the salient features of navigating and transforming grief. Alchemy, like grief, involves certain elements that will aid us in transforming raw material/raw emotions into gold (your outcomes). A raw material such as lead is cold, dark, heavy, and bleak, not unlike the painful, raw emotions of grief. Gold is light, bright with quality, brilliance, and depth. Alchemy of grief is not a problem to be solved but a process to be experienced, and the elements below are central to a positive "gold/growth" outcome.

Alchemy's Grieving Elements

A—Acknowledging

L—Lamenting

C—Choice

H—Holy

E—Endogenous

M—Moving

Y—Yielding

Acknowledging

The alchemy process involves *acknowledging* grief and being aware of grief as a natural and necessary reaction to change/loss experiences in the workplace. Allowing for the creation of sacred space in our work environment where we can go for support and understanding without judgment becomes essential in our transformation of grief. The following story from a client illustrates the central element of acknowledging a grieving worker with an open, compassionate, supportive, and understanding attitude. This is easier said than done. Whether we are grieving ourselves or a colleague is grieving, we spend a lot of energy and time avoiding and pretending nothing has changed—when everything has changed.

>> Martha had always been described as a super employee and now she is grieving the death of her 17-year-old son. On her first day back from bereavement leave, her well-intentioned manager said, "I've got something to keep you extra busy, a new assignment that I know you will love."

"How is your husband doing? How are things?" colleagues asked

Martha. Some people in her workplace acted as if nothing had happened. Her going to the water fountain was like the parting of the Red Sea. Her colleagues were talking and acting in code.

What Martha found to be helpful was for people to acknowledge her loss directly, saying, "I am sorry about your loss. You're in my thoughts and prayers. How are you really doing?" and taking the time to listen, without judgment and advice. Sometimes a hug was even more bearable than words. Every grief situation is so unique, and should be treated as such. **«**

Openly discussing with the bereaved employee how they would like to handle their return to work can be helpful. Do they need flexible time, different work assignments, maybe time away from the public? Do they feel uncomfortable with many colleagues asking them how they are doing? Would they prefer only one person to approach them? Is there a quiet place to go at work where they can regroup when they are overcome with grief?

Lamenting

Lamenting is honoring and expressing all the facets of grief. Grief assaults our entire being: physically, mentally, emotionally, behaviorally, and spiritually. It is hard work that can leave us exhausted, unable to concentrate, sad, angry, and questioning the meaning of life and God. This is an intense element, filled with pressure, pain, and unpredictability.

> **»** A client relates that a side effect of his grief is that he is an embarrassment to himself and others. He further explains that when someone says they are sorry to hear about the death of his wife, he starts to cry and there is a mass exodus from the staff room. "When I cry in front of others they do not want to be around me," he says. **«**

Lamenting is leaning into grief and is a way through. For what we resist persists. It is leaning on others for support. Let it be—our grief, without shame and judgment. Can you be with someone in moments of pain and distress? Can you tolerate not knowing, curing, and solving the problem? Can you listen and be available? What do you do when you find someone in distress? What have you found helpful when you have felt vulnerable, sad, and in distress? Is there someone you can reach out to right now? Is there a human resources or support department in your workplace that someone can go to for further support? Hallmark, the card company, has a volunteer employee support network called Compassionate Connections. Is there a support system you could help set up in your company?

Choice

There are places in between our loss and grief where we have the ability to choose. As one daughter said after her father died tragically, "Choice is an affirmation to live. I chose to embrace my pain and grief and I also chose to go forward." Chaos and courage are part of this element of choice. Dr. Elisabeth Kübler-Ross, pioneer researcher and educator on death and dying, says, "I am not okay, you're not okay, and that is okay." Courage helps us in our transition; to leave what was—not forget—for what is. One person told me in a grief group that the only courage that mattered was the one that got you from one moment to the next.

What choices do we have in our own grief? What choices do we have in responding to someone who is grieving? Can we choose to be compassionate, sensitive, and patient? Can we listen to the griever's story when it is told again and again? What courage do we need to have to help a grieving colleague in the workplace? What courage do we need to have to help them mourn in the workplace?

Holy

There is a *holy*, sacred, mysterious element to this alchemy process. The holy helps us search for something that takes us beyond our self and put us in touch with something larger than ourselves. This essentially is our spirit. This is where our relationship with our God, source, and creator can serve us with rootedness and comfort. Some people find this experience when they are out in nature. What grounds and anchors you in times of distress? What provides you with comfort and hope? Is the workplace accepting of the various spiritual traditions? Is there a place at work that has plants, trees, water, and soothing music? Can you get out and are you encouraged to get out in the fresh air during the day? This is where we may ask questions about the meaning of life. We may even question the meaning of our work. What makes work meaningful?

Endogenous

Endogenous means a growing from within. It comes through the persistence of putting one foot in front of the other and enlightenment occurs. You keep going and see things differently. You are different. You have an understanding. There is no set timeline to the alchemy process of grieving. It is not a linear process and you may experience many of these elements many times. The following is a story of a client coping with change and loss at work.

>> The client's company had mandated a uniform policy. She claimed to have been labeled as "difficult" and "inflexible." Other staff couldn't understand why she was having so much difficulty with this company change and encouraged her to see it as "cost effective," in that she would no longer have to buy her "expensive" clothes. There was a shifting and growing from within when she started to understand what having to wear a uniform meant to her: loss of self, confidence, choice, identity, and power.

We all have stories. Hers was one of being raised in a very poor family in which she wore used and tattered clothing. Clothes were much more to her than something that covered her body. <<

This is a good reminder to search for the personal uniqueness behind every change and loss experience. It also serves as another great reminder of how quick we are to judge ourselves and others' loss experiences as an "overreaction."

How have you changed after a grief and loss situation? What do you know now about yourself that you couldn't have known without this experience?

Moving

This element involves *moving* through the alchemy process. This is where rituals and mourning become integral to converting our raw material to gold. This is a unique process; no one will or could have the same process as another. There will be common features, yet each person alone knows what he or she has lost and what he or she will miss, and no two people will react and navigate the same way.

As a person attending a grief group once stated, "We all miss Dad, but we all miss him for different reasons." We move and we release; we convert relationships from those in the present to those of memories. It means making room for memories and the shifting and releasing of the relationship as we knew it.

» At one place of work, colleagues left a book in the front lobby where they could write about what their deceased colleague meant to them and what were their fondest memories. Eventually this book was sent to the surviving family members.

Another company was changing its name and service focus and had a name-changing party. The company gave out items with the old company logo to the staff. They used this opportunity to discuss their fears of the new program and what they would miss from the old one. After the merger the company held a competition where each team built towers from out-dated business cards. «

Rituals such as these are essential to moving and growing through change, loss, and grief. Can you think of how a ritual can be used with a change you are currently experiencing?

Yielding

Blessed are they that mourn; for they shall be comforted.

Matthew 5:4

The alchemy process starts and ends with a yielding element. *Yielding* as defined by the *Oxford Dictionary* is a surrendering, producing, generating, and proceeding. We are giving rise to our new selves or new workplace in this process, and it is a sacred, life-affirming, and honoring process. As one client commented, "When I surrendered to my grief, a new me began to emerge." Is there a workplace change/loss situation that you need to yield to in order to allow a new opportunity or growth to occur?

Water is fluid, soft, and yielding. But water will wear away rock, which is rigid and cannot yield. As a rule, whatever is fluid, soft, and yielding will overcome whatever is rigid and hard. This is another paradox: what is soft is strong.

Lao-Tzu, philosopher, 600 BC

Ultimately Awake

Life teaches us about surviving; death and grief can teach us about living. We can learn so much about ourselves in how we approach grief and death. Do we fear death? What does it mean to be alive? What does it mean to be awake?

...I would claim that grief, if it is endured, can restore to us a sense of the sacred and the holy which our technological consciousness lacks and desires. Perhaps at the core of our grief, just beneath the skin of depression, is a deep hunger for an epiphany of the divine.

Robert Romanyshyn, author

Having the privilege of journeying with others during the most traumatic times in their lives, I have received many grace-filled moments. Grace is a gift of consciousness, unexplainable divinity, sacredness, and touching of the core of your being. Grief, like no other experience, offers the possibility of transformation. If allowed, our workplace grief becomes decoded, and in its wake is our humanness, a consciousness that ripples into all facets of our lives. We emerge through this process ultimately awoken; we will no longer sleep.

The most minute transformation is like a pebble dropped into a still lake. The ripples spread out endlessly.

Emmanuel

Donna Devlin

Donna Devlin is well known in health care as an inspirational, knowledgeable, and gifted speaker. Donna's message is clear in any of her presentations: "Bring light into all facets of your life and work." Her audiences and topics are as varied as life itself, from death and grief (the ultimate awakening), to humor and play (the principles of perspective).

Donna has spent 23 years working in the mental health field. Donna has trained as a Registered Psychiatric Nurse, Mental Health Therapist, Critical Incident Stress Debriefer, and she worked with survivors after the 1987 Edmonton tornado. All of this set the stage for her educating and speaking career.

She holds a Bachelors degree in General Studies, with emphasis on sociology and communications, from the University of Calgary. She is an educator and consultant to the Calgary Health Region and McInnis and Holloway Funeral Homes.

Donna has been interviewed on national television and radio and in newspapers. She has been nominated for an international Human Interaction Best Practice—Spirit of Caring—Award. She is presently working on her upcoming book, *Magic Moments in Health Care—Making a Difference One Moment at a Time.*

Business Name: Donna Devlin Consulting "Reflections of Light"
Address: Box 2, Site, 2, R.R. 2, Cochrane, AB T4C 1A2
Telephone: 403-932-2645
Email: donna@donnadevlin.com
Web Address: www.donnadevlin.com

Carol Ring

Carol Ring Enterprises

Boomerang Your Way to Best Possible Solutions at Work!

Are you sitting in yet another meeting? Are you facing another cost-cutting exercise? Does your team look at you with blank faces when you ask for solutions to today's issue? Is your best resolution just a tweak on an old process? Are you struggling with new ways to do business?

None of this is really surprising. The way we think today rarely allows us to unlock the limitless potential of our mind. Too often, we seem to be on autopilot, just providing a knee-jerk response to any problem that may arise. The reason for that isn't so much because of *what* we think as it is because of *how* we think.

Most of us don't use the full capabilities of our minds to find better answers to today's tough problems, even though that's possible. Instead, we've trained our way of thinking to follow a straight line, rarely veering off a predictable path. We'll do it this way because we've always done it that way. Or we'll choose this solution because it's the easiest one.

But that way of thinking limits us in our professional and personal careers. Often, the best answer is not the first one or the obvious one. It's the one that comes to us after some clear and original thinking.

To do this, we need to release the talents and experiences we all have inside of us, and one way to accomplish this is through a method I've developed called

Boomerang Think™. To fully understanding this method, it helps to look at the way we've been taught to think. In today's world that's drastically different from how we thought in the Industrial Age, where workers were expected to man the assembly lines and work *without* thinking. Understanding how we think, learn and make decisions in today's world is imperative.

**Removing the barriers to creative idea generation
is a must in order to be a truly successful manager
of life and at work.**

How Our Minds Work

The brain consists of three main sectors: the forebrain, the midbrain and the hindbrain. The forebrain makes up 80 percent of the brain and is the most advanced portion of that organ. It includes the cerebral cortex and wants to be in control but has very little power. The cerebral cortex contains 10 to 20 billion neurons, compared to the 100 billion neurons contained in the entire brain.

The midbrain houses important centers for regulating body movement in response to visual and auditory stimuli. All sensory and motor information that transfers back and forth from the forebrain to the spinal cord must go through the midbrain. Midbrains vary by species. A hawk, for example, will have a prominent and bulging visual region, while a bat has a small visual center and a large auditory center.

The hindbrain is the oldest part of the brain. It is often referred to as the reptilian brain, or even the "gator" brain. It contains structures that carry out such basic survival functions as sleeping, waking, and breathing. It includes the cerebellum that maintains our balance and equilibrium. It is also involved in learning and remembering. As cave dwellers, our hindbrain focused on the fight-or-flight response in order to survive. Today, it's not physical survival that guides us, but nonetheless, we still filter information through the flight-or-fight reponse. Our hindbrain is the part in control!

Learning and Behavior

Many of the decisions we make at home and at work come from previous learnings that are stored in our hindbrain. These learnings can become so conditioned or automatic that we lose that "creative" ability.

The *Merriam Webster Dictionary* describes learning as the "modification of a behavioral tendency by experience." Many of us remember the story of Pavlov's experiments with dogs. Pavlov would ring a bell and then produce food for the dog. After numerous repetitions, the ringing of the bell would result in involuntary salivation by the dog. This type of learning is known as classical conditioning. It happens when a previously neutral stimuli (the bell) ends up causing a feeling of anticipation, or fear or anxiety, or an involuntary action. Think about those first visits to the doctor for vaccinations. The doctor would swab your arm with rubbing alcohol before inserting the needle. The needle would normally elicit a feeling of pain. Now after a series of these experiences, every time you smell rubbing alcohol, especially in a medical environment, you will start to experience anxiety associated with the expectation of pain.

Another form of learning is operant conditioning. With this type of learning we change our behavior because of the consequences that follow. Thorndike's Law of Effect states that responses that lead to positive outcomes are more likely to be repeated. Responses leading to negative outcomes are less likely to be repeated. Harvard psychologist B. F. Skinner describes our environment as being filled with positive and negative consequences. We can see this occurring with friends and family who "control us" with their approvals and disapprovals. Affection and respect can be withheld until we conform to their expectations. At work, we are rewarded for behaviors that are valued by the company. Modeling shapes behavior on the basis of what others do. We are most likely to imitate behaviors that get rewarded versus those that are punished. Paraphrasing from Glenn Clark, businessman and author, "If you wish to travel far and fast, travel light. Take off all of your envies, jealousies, lack of forgiveness, selfishness, and fear."

Memory

Just as learnings can shape our creativity, so too can our memories. Memories with great personal emotion and meaning can override attempts to be creative. There are three types of memories: sensory, short-term, and long-term. We have a large capacity for sensory memory, up to twenty items, but the duration is very brief, no more than half a second. We process and discard information all the time.

In the short-term memory stage, we "encode" the learning. This encoding can be based on the rehearsal of the information (for instance, repeating a telephone number three times), the association with an existing long-term memory, motivation to remember, emotion, or novelty. Without these encoding tools, we simply lose the information. We have a much smaller capacity for short-term memory, approximately seven items, and retention is brief, about 15 to 20 seconds.

Long-term memory encodes learning, but it also stores and retrieves memories. As children we are engaged in effortful encoding, where we work hard to encode written words. As adults we can read effortlessly due to automatic encoding. When memories are formed, the context surrounding the memory is also encoded.

According to Tulving's theory of multiple memory systems, our memory is a collection of three memory systems:

1. **Procedural memories** do not require conscious awareness and are learned associations between stimuli and response. Touching a hot stove, which elicited feelings of pain, causes an immediate learned memory.

2. **Semantic memories** contain information about the world around us. That's where we store all the basic facts of life: Ottawa is the capital of Canada. My cat has four legs.

3. **Episodic memories** have greater personal meaning and emotion. They are unique to each person. Memories of our family vacations are episodic memories. You remember the cottage where you spent your summer vacation when you were 13. You remember when your father took you fishing and you caught that large bass.

Tulving describes explicit memories as being those that require conscious awareness and reside in the forebrain. Implicit memories are memories without awareness and reside in the hindbrain.

The state of your life is nothing more than a reflection of your state of mind.

Dr. Wayne Dyer

Decision Making

We have looked at learning and memories because of the impact they can have on our decision making at work. The mechanisms that our brains use to make a decision can also impact our creativity. Decision making is influenced by the value that we place on outcomes and the probability that we place on varying alternatives.

There are three types of decision making. The first, classical decision making, occurs when we are fully informed about all possible options, outcomes, and consequences. The decisions are fully rational. With the second, subjective decision making, there is a more subjective value placed on the outcomes and the various alternatives. But most of our decisions are based on the third type of decision making, *bounded rationality.*

As humans, we are limited in our processing capacity, speed, information gathering, and overall knowledge. According to Edward Hallowell, in his article titled "Overloaded Circuits," (*HBR OnPoint* article, January 2005) when we are faced with ongoing decisions after multiple interruptions as we search for missing information, while the twelfth impossible request arrives in our inbox, our brain begins to panic. As a result, we often choose the very first alternative that meets the immediate need. This optimizes our time, our energy, and our cognitive load, but potentially we have selected a less than optimal solution.

Tradition is a way of solving problems. These inherited decisions work as long as you have inherited the same problems.

Larry Wilson, *The Fine Art of Doing Better*

Conditioned Creativity

We have learned through many experiences in our lifetime. We have stored memories with context about positive and negative outcomes. Many of them lie in our unconscious and we are not even aware that we are processing them as we interpret new situations in our lives, every day. In an environment of criticism and fear, our reptilian brain takes over, and creativity is stifled. According to Tim Hurson, professional speaker, "Our brains are hard-wired to judge ideas at the same time as we generate them. As fast as the mind generates possibilities, an inner judge is ruling on them" (*Globe and Mail* posted online 12/08/05). These rulings take place based on our previous experiences with outcomes. If we present ideas that consistently get quashed because there is no budget, after a while we stop presenting new ideas because we become conditioned to the negative response. The inner ruling becomes almost unconscious and we find ourselves unable to innovate. We have problems seeing alternatives.

The Ladder Climb

» The carnival area of the amusement park is full of games. The "carnies" call out to with your chance to win large stuffed animals by simply tossing a ring over the neck of a glass bottle, tossing a basketball into a wooden basket, or knocking down a stack of bowling pins with a softball. One of the most challenging games is the ladder climb. A rope ladder is strung across a large inflatable bed, just like those used in the movies to break a stuntman's fall as he jumps off a small building or platform. The idea is to climb the ladder and ring a bell at the top. At first glance, it appears simple.

However, if you choose to play this game you will quickly see that the journey is much more treacherous and precarious than you had imagined, because the ladder rotates freely. You attempt to climb up the rungs, but unless you have perfect balance, the ladder flips over and you fall off. You may try to do it quickly, slowly, or on your knees, but you will still fall off. «

The reason we fall is because of learned assumptions. We learn to climb a ladder by putting our feet on the rungs and moving up a step at a time. That's the way we've been taught and that is what's in our brain. When we see a ladder, that learning kicks in and that's what we put into practice. But the trick to this game is to engage your conscious mind, your forebrain. If you stop focusing on the negative outcome and high probability of falling, and the idea that the structure you are climbing is a ladder, you have a better chance. The game operator knows how to scamper up the ladder by placing his feet on the sides of the unit between the rungs. He moves the opposite hand and leg in unison to maintain his balance on the ladder. By keeping the pressure on the outsides of the ladder and not the rungs, he can keep himself from being tipped once again onto the mat. According to mathematician Robert Kaplan, "If you look at zero you see nothing, but look through it and you will see the world."

So how do we find the alternatives? How do we keep conditioned learnings, memories and decisions from locking up the limitless potential of our mind? We have to use a technique that allows us to reach for best possible solutions to our issues at work rather than settling on the first idea that our brain judges as good enough. Unless you have a strong vision for where you want to go, you will invariably settle for less than the best. You have to stretch your mind to define that best possible solution.

And this is how Boomerang Think™ came to be. It is a technique that encourages people to think positively and to stretch for best possible solutions. Too often we start our so-called creative thinking by listing all the barriers or limitations. People are quick to rattle off the limited number of resources or unbudgeted dollars before they even think about possible solutions.

Plane Rides From Hell

» The genesis of Boomerang Think™ came about when I was speaking at a corporate human resources function. There were about 70 people in the room sitting at a number of round tables. The ages, careers, positions, and life experiences of everyone in the room were as varied as you could get. I was asked to speak on the upcoming challenges in the organization, highlighting, in particular, where human resources could play a role in overcoming those challenges.

After about 20 minutes of reviewing some of the challenges, I paused at the front of the stage. I asked audience members to indulge me in a little exercise before I continued, and I left the stage and walked down among the tables. I asked people to describe their worst possible plane trip. Almost instantaneously, the room came alive: "long line ups," "lost baggage," "lousy food," "late departures," "turbulence," "aggravating person in the next seat." The list went on and then finally someone shouted—"a plane crash!" The finality and mutual agreement that this would most certainly be the worst possible plane trip brought the conversation to an immediate halt. It was interesting to observe how quickly the group was able to define these worst possible experiences. The barriers and limitations to a good plane ride came fast and furious.

After a pause, I asked the same group of people to describe the best possible plane trip. Slowly they started to answer, mostly with example-sopposite to those on the first list: "no line ups," "good food," "on time departure," "smooth flight," "no aggravating person in the next seat." But this time the answers were slower, and people often seemed confused by the question. Is it because they had only experienced bad trips? How had their thinking been influenced and conditioned by previous encounters on flights? I made my way to the center of the room. "People," I exclaimed with my arms flung wide open to embrace them. "I am talking about the *best possible* plane ride and this is what you come up with?"

Silence continued, and in that silence I turned to a gentleman named Max who had made the initial comment about "lousy food" and had followed it up this time with "good food." "Max," I said, "you mentioned good food, but if this was the BEST possible plane ride, what kind of food would it be?" With a grin on his face, Max responded, "It would be a steak!" Someone else added in, "With champagne!"

"Folks, this is the *best possible* plane ride—where would you be going?" I asked. They took a minute to think about that and then they shared destinations like Hawaii, Europe, or to visit their grandparents in Vancouver. When they had finally been encouraged that anything goes, they refrained from letting conditioned learnings, unconscious prejudgments, and first possible solutions cloud their responses. **«**

Take a minute to think about your best possible plane trip. Where would you be going? Who would you be going with? What would that whole trip—from the time you left your front door to the time you reached your final destination—look like? Most likely you will have to work hard to repress those emotional negative memories. You will have to leave the conditioned barriers aside.

Boomerang Think™

A boomerang is a tool and weapon of Australian aboriginal origin that comes back to you if you throw it properly. It is usually carved out of wood and consists of two wings connected at an angle. One side of the boomerang will be slightly curved, and this is usually decorated. The other side will be flat. Of importance is the smoothness of the boomerang, as the wings act as an airfoil. As the air travels faster over the surface of one wing than the other, lift is created. The angle of the two wings causes the boomerang to fly out straight for a distance and then begin to turn to the left, returning to the thrower. One of the secrets to a successful boomerang throw is the smoothness, the lack of burrs, or extra weight along the wings.

Just like the successful flight of the boomerang, Boomerang Think™ has special features and steps:

Step #1—Boomerang Think™ requires having minimal barriers against the flight of ideas. Don't think about the cost, that the boss will never agree, that it's never been done before. Just throw it out there.

Step #2—With Boomerang Think™, once you open your mind and toss the boomerang, you are now into the second step, or the straight part of the flying pattern. This is the opportunity to stretch your thinking and come up with that best possible solution.

Step #3—The third step of the process is achieved at the apex of the flight. Here you list all the elements of the best possible solution.

Step #4—Then, just like a real boomerang comes back to your hand, you have to bring your best possible solution back to the current business situation. As you try to implement that solution, the ideas turn and start to come back to what can realistically be done. The following is an example of how to use Boomerang Think™:

> » I had just joined my new management team in Toronto after spending 12 years in the Ottawa division of our company. We had a large workforce of about 400 in-house and contracted technicians. Our internal training group had developed a wonderful technical certification program, and our business unit was the last to get engaged in certifying our workforce. I knew that the discussion was going to be fraught with barriers as to why the Toronto workforce wasn't yet certified. Instead, I focused the discussion on one question: "What would be the best possible implementation for certifying the Toronto workforce?"
>
> One of the solution gems that came out of that conversation was to create five or six training locations across the GTA instead of just the two at our regional office. This would increase the amount of training we could do at one time, address the parking restrictions we had at the regional office, and reduce the technicians' travel time, allowing them to arrive in a better frame of mind. With that in mind, we asked our contractors if they had any in-house training facilities. Lo and behold, a couple of them were just in the process of moving their offices and were more than happy to include our training requirements along with theirs. «

Instead of starting with the *worst possible* solution (such as it's too costly to build more training facilities and ending the discussion there), we started by thinking about the *best possible* solution. This created the foundation to allow us to look for optimal solutions to our needs. We threw it out there to get the best possible solution and its elements at the apex of the boomerang throw. As the boomerang came back in, we thought about the various paths that we could follow to achieve the best possible solution.

In reality, you don't often get 100 percent of the best solution, but 80 percent of the best is always better than 100 percent of some mediocre first idea.

Throwing Your Own Boomerang

Remember the first time you went ice-skating or tried to ride a bike? Just trying to balance on two blades or two wheels was challenging enough without the added complexity of moving across a hard, unforgiving surface. Acquiring a new skill requires conscious effort. On the next page is a worksheet to help you with your first Boomerang Think™. Use the following five steps to complete the worksheet and learn how to throw your boomerang:

1. The first step requires you to hold the boomerang in your hand. Identify a challenge or an upcoming event that you're facing. Briefly describe the situation and write it down in the space provided.

2. Next, you must relax, close your eyes, and stretch your mind to think only of the best possible solution. Keep the reptilian instant solutions and judgments at bay. Be the most optimistic person you can be. Now bend your arm and strongly toss the boomerang way out there. As it spins farther and farther from you, it is flying closer and closer to the best possible solution. Once you have that vision in mind, write down as much detail as you can about this best possible solution.

3. Looking at this best possible solution, how many elements of it can you easily achieve? Allow the boomerang to start bending its trajectory back towards you. Perhaps there is minimal cost associated with a couple of the activities; perhaps some elements are already in place. List these under Step 3.

4. In the table towards the bottom of the worksheet, list the remaining elements in the left-hand column. This is where you have to start lining up the return of the boomerang. Don't let it run out of steam and fall short. Brainstorm. Engage others in a discussion. Do some research to find some alternatives to achieving these challenging elements. List these alternatives in the right-hand column.

5. Finally, reflect back over the worksheet. How much of your ideal state were you able to create?

Boomerang Think™ Worksheet

Step 1:

Briefly describe your current challenge:

_____

_____

_____

Step 2:

What is the *best possible* end state?

_____

_____

_____

Step 3:

List those elements that are easily achieved:

_____

_____

_____

Step 4:

Complete the Challenge Table:

Challenging elements of ideal state	*Alternative options to achieve this*
_____	_____
_____	_____
_____	_____
_____	_____
_____	_____

Step 5:

How much of your ideal state were you able to achieve? _____

Leave the Reptiles Behind

In our frenetic lives, it's difficult to wrench control from our reptilian brain. It's just easier to let it make all the decisions. Time and energy seem to be commodities that are harder and harder to harness. However, we're no longer cave dwellers; the Industrial Age has long since passed and we are now in the Information Age. Providing positive feedback, such as praise and security, and rewarding creative thinking, will condition your employees to continue to do this. Unlock the judgments that have been filed away in their long-term memory by implementing Boomerang Think™!

> *If you can dream it, you can do it.*
> Walt Disney

Carol Ring

Carol Ring has more than two decades of experience in retail, manufacturing, and telecommunications. Over the course of her career, Carol has become passionate about bringing more creativity into the workplace. Carol is the creator of Boomerang Think™, a program to quickly shift how people think and problem solve.

Carol is also an expert on Integrated Life™. Integrated Life™ is experiencing a unified physical, mental, and spiritual life by braiding personal talent and creative thinking, such as Boomerang Think™, around core values. It creates a life that matters. Through her presentations and seminars, Carol empowers audiences, including those at business, entrepreneur, and leadership conferences, to integrate their values with their personal and professional lives.

She is the regional president for Rogers Cable Communications in the Greater Toronto Area. In her climb through the organization, Carol has maintained a successful and busy community and family life. Carol has walked in the shoes that others are currently walking in and uses that experience in a fun, daring, and holistic manner. Those who come to know her, continually ask, "How do you do it all?"

Business Name:	Carol Ring Enterprises
Address:	43 Gould Lane, Thornhill, ON L4J 9B5
Telephone:	905-326-3251
Email:	dcring@rogers.com
Web Address:	www.carolring.ca
Professional Affiliations:	Canadian Association of Professional Speakers; Canadian Women in Communication; Certified Management Accountants (Fellow)

Victoria M. Schlosser

Victoria M. Schlosser International

Life Is Like a Marathon...
We Are Always in Training for Something!

Training and running the Honolulu Marathon was a life-changing experience for me in so many ways. It assisted me in discovering who I was, allowed me to cross many finish lines, and to give back to society by fundraising for a great cause. I experienced many monumental and pivotal moments. It reinforced my belief system that you should never take anything for granted, whether it's your health, family, friends, career, or the fond memories you have acquired over the years.

» During my marathon training, on October 31, 2004, I had to complete what we referred to as the "Train Run" of 18 miles. Being overwhelmed with emotions—excitement, anticipation, nervousness—I hardly slept and actually woke up at 3 a.m. thinking I would sleep right through my alarm. All 300 runners, myself included, boarded a train that dropped us off in Oceanside, California. The view on the way up to our destination was beautiful, overlooking the ocean, with clear blue skies and bright, hot sun.

How amazing to set off on an 18-mile odyssey of self-discovery with nothing more than my body and mind. My learning that day came not from a coach or mentor but my own feet. Each step revealed new insights and feelings. Success was measured by how hard I pushed myself during the group run. I was challenged mentally and physically, as well as emotionally, to excel past my personal limitations. Being determined not to quit and to cross that finish line taught me that I can mentally overcome any obstacle that crosses my path and have the strength to accomplish any goals set forth. The words "winning" and "losing" were soon replaced by the words "doing" and "being." I completed this challenging 18-mile run in 3 hours and 10 minutes and in the top 10 percent. **«**

Rising to the occasion is sometimes painful. Since starting to train for the marathon, I've redefined the pain of growth and it is my new friend. In the workplace and in business we are also running a marathon; we are also training and taking risks. New projects are opportunities to excel outside our current personal limitations. We must allow ourselves to go beyond our comfort zones into the world of the unknown.

People are now beginning to understand that their work is not simply a job but a "calling." The benefit of looking at it this way is twofold—both personal and societal. Personally it can mean your greatest possible growth, success, and happiness. In a broader context it is also the avenue through which you can make a great contribution to the world. Everyday you are presented with opportunities to define who you are and who you will become; and to determine how effective you will be at work and the quality of the impact that you make on society. And by being part of this training program called life, you are placed daily into opportunities to engage in new forms of thought, behavior, commitment, and focus, with the ultimate goal of reaching a new personal level of excellence in all areas. And for optimal learning in this training program, you need to be ready and willing to do doing something different than you're already doing today, to produce new results for tomorrow.

**Life is like a marathon...we cross several finish lines
throughout our lives, and most of our time
on this earth is spent in training. And this process
of training is not always easy—you will encounter
many highs and lows, but the satisfaction of crossing
these finish lines makes it all worth it.**

Know that every time you walk out your door each morning and step into any business situation or workplace, *you win*! Every time you finish a goal you have set for yourself, you win because you have inspired your own success and unleashed your uncharted possibilities.

The following nine-point model will assist you in recreating and transforming yourself from where you are now to becoming an exemplary individual, both personally and professionally. It includes the principles for in-the-moment focus, as well as processes designed to enhance your experience of life:

1. Self-discovery
2. Commitment
3. Preparation
4. Setting your goals
5. Embracing personal growth
6. Execution
7. The journey
8. Contributing to society
9. Your legacy

#1—Self-Discovery

*The longer you wait to decide what you want to do, the
more time you're wasting. It's up to you to want something
so badly that your passion shows through in your actions.
Your actions, not your words, will do the shouting for you.*

Derek Jeter, baseball player

Once you choose to stop denying what makes you happy, your life naturally evolves. All the signs are there, so don't ignore the obvious. When you decide to let yourself be directed by your natural enthusiasm it gives you clarity. When you do what you love it isn't work anymore but a lifestyle. If you are still unsure of your talents, the following questions will assist you in determining what's important to you:

Three Key Questions for Awareness

1. Do you understand the commitment, dedication, and discipline necessary in becoming successful?
2. Did you know you would have to accept nothing less than your personal best in all aspects of your life, both personally and professionally?
3. Do you allow yourself to daydream, zone out, or experience reverie?

Do you understand that it will take continuous growth and personal development to exceed your expectations and step outside your personal limitations and boundaries? Do you know that you set your boundaries based on your internal beliefs?

Now Ask Yourself the Following Questions

- What are the fears you have that you know are holding you back?
- How do they appear in the workplace or in business?
- If you took all of the time and energy you waste thinking about those fears, and spent it all following your passion and your dreams instead, how would you see your life now?
- What would it be possible for you to accomplish if you had no obstacles or limits?
- What is it you want that you have not already achieved?

#2—Commitment

Training for personal greatness must become a commitment to discipline. It's an opportunity to break out of stagnant, automatic living. Promotions in the workplace and in business are not given to you...they are earned as a result of following the path of your commitment to excellence, personal development, and perseverance, as well as stepping outside your comfort zone. In athletics, the same process applies. Placing in the top of your event, or even crossing the finish line at all, requires all of these disciplines.

Currently, I'm training for my first Ironman event. During one of our recent group training bicycle rides, we completed Palomar Mountain, which is a 13-mile, uphill climb to an elevation of six thousand feet. I could have stayed in bed, since it was cold, or stopped partway and turned around, but I would have been letting myself down by not crossing that finish line. Our training is a huge commitment and during the first three months it is considered a part-time job. It takes discipline, commitment to excel outside of your usual comfort zone, mentally pushing yourself beyond your personal limitations, and digging deeper than you ever have previously to find the strength to persevere. The goal may seem impossible, but imagine the feeling of jubilation as you cross that finish line and hear those three words you so long for…YOU'RE AN IRONMAN.

The willingness to change and embrace commitment requires the recognition that whatever you have achieved and whoever you are is not yet enough. Otherwise, you would be utterly content. Continuous work on your "master plan" is required in order to continue to reach for higher goals.

Remember that your ultimate evolution is up to you. Don't be satisfied by superficial representations of success, fulfillment, and joy. Don't give up striving to be better, wiser, nobler, or kinder just because you have received validation from the world for some level of success. Let your enthusiasm for personal change motivate your decisions in all aspects of your life. Regardless of how your world reflects back to your achievements—whether you are glorified or ignored—keep striving! Celebrate your commitment. Go all the way…this is your time!

#3—Preparation

When you are in training, as you complete your rides of up to six hours in the heat, you have to keep a log of how you feel physically and emotionally, how much fuel you consume, and if you were hungry or dehydrated during or immediately after. You consistently monitor your progress.

In sports, as in life, you have to be prepared for the unknown. We practice changing flat tires and checking air pressure because, after all, it's just you and you alone out there on the course. Don't assume you will have any assistance; you have to assume you will be changing the flat or fixing your bike chain on your own.

In business you should follow the same preparation plan. You don't go into an important client presentation without rehearsing your communication skills or reconfirming you have obtained all the statistical data or appropriate information. Ask a colleague you can trust to provide you with constructive criticism.

As you go through life, revisit your training program daily because, after all, it's a never-ending process of mental and physical preparation. Don't skip a day. Even tri-athletes have days when they don't want to get out of bed to swim, cycle, or run. But discipline and commitment keep them going. How would they feel about the end result if they didn't give it their personal best? Athletes can't settle for mediocrity and neither can you.

Preparation involves creating your plan, practicing that plan, and having plan B to fall back on. Just keep repeating this process until you get it right. You can never prepare enough for what life lessons or tests you will encounter, but you can always try to be prepared for the unknown.

#4—Setting Your Goals

Think back to when you had to set your very first goals. We get the message early in life that giving and persevering 100 percent is the key to accomplishment. Goals are always measurable. This has remained true from kindergarten to adulthood. But often we lose track of the clarity of mind needed to achieve our goals. The following are some key tips to help us refocus:

Program for Goal Setting

1. Make a list of all the things you would like to see in your life. Write down every thought that comes into your mind. It can be happiness, athletic achievements, professional and personal goals, travel, the respect of others…use your imagination.
2. Begin to develop your goals. Know that there are two things you need to be successful: figuring out exactly what you *want* and figuring out what you *need* to get there. As you write out your goals, divide them into two columns: Personal and Professional.
3. As you begin to set your goals let your imagination soar and project into the future. Visualize where you desire to be personally and professionally, including income range, geographic location, health and fitness, relationships and friends, and spirituality.

4. Put a time frame on each goal. Set your intentions in daily, weekly, and monthly increments. Include where you want to be in three months, six months, nine months, one year, two years, three years and five years.

5. Determine your top ten goals for this year. Write them down, read them daily and keep them with you.

6. Focus on today. Be positive and grateful for all you have now. Know what motivates you and commit to your priorities. Own your passion and spirituality.

For some people, the word "success" sounds just too intimidating. In other words, they see themselves as someone who could never really be successful. A successful life is developed and accomplished by building one success upon another.

#5—Embracing Personal Growth

The good news is that you can change your world, your environment, and your situation. Whatever you desire to change in your life starts with your own thoughts. It is in changing your thoughts that you will change your condition, your situation, and your circumstances. Know that the choice is always yours.

The secret to achieving success is the willingness to change. This willingness will make you fluid enough to achieve great personal evolution. Keep in mind that change is a continuous process; you will never reach one static finish line, but you will cross a lot of finish lines along the way. Exhibit by example among your peers the joy of a commitment to evolve.

Regardless of whether you fear failure or success, it is important to keep in mind that people tend to put obstacles in their own path that prevent rising to new levels both professionally and personally. Look at tomorrow with eager anticipation rather than fear. Feel that the world is full of possibilities—not that the workplace is oppressive and will prevent you from achieving your goals or dreams. To do that, you must understand the difference between pressure and fear.

Feeling fear is inevitable, but it's how you choose to view it that determines if it's good or bad. You can see it as stimulating and exciting, something you can use as your ally, or you can allow it to hobble your performance. Ultimately it's up to you. When I am experiencing adversity, the one thing I always remember is that there are just two kinds of people: those who say "I can" and those who say "I can't." And then I ask myself which one I am.

Learn to trust yourself and your instincts. Trust is part of the goal. Initially, feelings of discomfort, fear, and uncertainty will arise. Remember, this is a healthy sign. Consider it a test of your will. It's a test to see just how deep you can really dig. It's a test to see if you have heart and the will to persevere.

#6—Execution

Nike™ said it best: "Just do it!" Women's suffrage activist Nellie McClung put it this way: "Get the thing done and let them howl." The five steps before this one will allow you to build yourself up to the point where the execution of your goal is the next logical step.

> *The world can only be grasped by action, not by contemplation.*
> Jacob Bronowski, *The Ascent of Man*

#7—The Journey

Being on this journey is the greatest reward of all. This is where you learn who you are as a person. You will learn to be very grateful for everything in your life that you may previously have taken for granted. As motivational speaker Grace Cirocco says, "We are human becomings, not just human beings."

For an athlete, the journey produces a new threshold for pain, a new stamina, a new personal best. In our professional careers, the journey of persistence, long hours, and never-ending effort produces personal growth and development. There are many correlations between running a marathon and the world of business and work. One inevitable truth of both is that you can't ultimate enjoy the reward without appreciating the numerous personal sacrifices you have made during your journey. The bottom line is that there is no reward or sense of accomplishment without sacrifice.

Running a marathon, there is the ultimate reward: CROSSING THAT FINISH LINE! What an incredible sense of jubilation. It will be by far the most exhilarating feeling when you complete the 26.2 miles! Many who cross that line become very emotional because they have trained and prepared for months. For many it seems impossible that they have just graduated from being a leisure runner to being a marathoner.

Keeping a journal is a great way to chronicle your triumphs, breakthroughs, and turning points. It's a great way to go back and reflect on your thoughts, your emotions, your victories, how you were able to overcome an obstacle, and how you felt. It's also a great way to reflect on monumental and pivotal moments that you imagined were unobtainable. Those impossible goals were actually met; your journal proves it. What a great feeling to know you can achieve anything!

#8—Contributing to Society

What type of role model or mentor you would like to be to others? What issues do you find yourself debating, discussing, or arguing about? How are you perceived as a person in your local community and with your peers or superiors?

To become an exemplary individual in all aspects of your personal or professional life is the greatest contribution that you can make to society, and it's part of being a whole and successful person. Why? Because you are being a leader rather than a follower and setting an example of what people can accomplish.

You can give back by volunteering your time at the local community center, church, or charitable organization. Look around, many community organizations need volunteers—for example, becoming a Big Sister or Big Brother—as well as financial donations. There is nothing more gratifying and personally strengthening than knowing you made a difference in someone's life.

#9—Your Legacy

» Mike was appointed President and CEO of one of the largest health care organizations in Southern California. Under his leadership the organization dedicated itself to transforming the health care experience for employees, physicians, and their clients. The focus was clearly placed on purpose, worthwhile work, and making a difference.

Employee, physician, and patient satisfaction increased while loyalty and outcomes were enhanced as the organization moved towards its vision of becoming the best place to work, practice medicine, and receive care.

Today, in addition to overseeing the organization's 14,000 plus employees, Mike is actively involved as a member and supporter of several community-based health and social service organizations. He has created a legacy and will always be remembered for setting a new standard for best practices. **

Have you ever thought about how you would like to be remembered? Have you thought about what kind of legacy you would like to leave? Or do you view your level of success by the level of your happiness or peace of mind, or by how good you feel about yourself and your own world?

Remember your legacy isn't comprised of just one day or one moment—it's an entire collection of the good, the bad, and the ugly experiences that either enhanced your life or changed you for the better. Know that you are where you are in life for a reason—and sometimes your journey includes a few detours. Remember too that every person who crosses your path is a gift. Experiencing this is part of your legacy as well.

Crossing the Finish Line

Through these nine key points, you've been given a model and a process to achieve personal and professional excellence. Keep the following pointers in mind as you work through this process:

Be open minded to making mistakes. In order to build character, you have to learn from failures and mistakes.

Never look back and have regrets. Look at past events as opportunities that got you where you are today.

Never lose your sense of humor. Change usually offers plenty of reasons to be upset, worried, and confused. You can choose to cry, or you can choose to laugh at the craziness of it all.

Don't let your strengths become your weaknesses. Read constantly and update your skills. Examine where you are today and figure out what got you there. Keep sharpening the saw.

Change is inevitable so never give up. You never know what is around the next bend in the road.

Exercise, exercise, exercise. It is a proven fact that vigorous activity relieves stress and helps keep you healthy.

Ask for constructive criticism. Ask your colleagues and employees for constructive feedback. This is the only way a person can work on their weaknesses.

Be purposeful. Set those goals and work on your legacy.

Anticipate. Accept the past, focus on the future, and anticipate. Consider what's coming, what needs to happen, and how you can rise to the occasion in every aspect of your life.

> There is something that can happen to every athlete, every human being—it's the instinct to slack off, to give in to the pain, to give less than your best…the instinct to hope to win through luck or your opponents not doing their best, instead of going to the limit and past your limit, where victory is always to be found. Defeating those negative instincts that are out to defeat us is the difference between winning and losing, and we face that battle every day of our lives.
>
> Jesse Owens, Olympic track champion

Victoria M. Schlosser

Victoria Schlosser's impressive career spans over two decades of exceptional business success as well as an extensive career background that includes broadcast journalism, hotel sales and marketing, and convention planning. She is an entrepreneur, and a triathlete! With over thirty years of experience working with people, Victoria has developed unique and effective systems that increase human potential, put attitude into action, and assist organizations and individuals to redefine excellence.

During her career with Hyatt Hotels and Resorts as a sales professional, Victoria was lauded for her success and seven career moves, as well as being named Director of Sales of the Year. She was the first woman to be recognized as Pre-Opening Director of Sales & Marketing for a resort. She has coached, mentored, and trained some of the top sales professionals in the hospitality industry. During her tenure with Hyatt Hotels—coupled with her triathlon training—she proved that no goal is unobtainable.

Victoria is well known in the hospitality industry and across corporate America for her energetic, innovative presentations. Her polished style, enthusiasm, powerful message, and proven ability as a consummate business professional assure a top-notch engagement every time. Her positive energy and enthusiasm are contagious and after each presentation participants know that there isn't anything they can't accomplish. Her ultimate goal is to assist others as they discover and utilize her proven techniques of "Mind over Mind" combined with individual talents to meet challenges and persevere.

Business Name: Victoria M. Schlosser International
Address: 4020 Falcon St., Suite 488, San Diego, CA 92103
Telephone: 619-296-8674
Email: victoria@vschlosserintl.com
Web Address: www.vschlosserintl.com
Professional Affiliations: National Speakers Association

Tammy Robertson

WorkHeart Consulting

Energize Your Workplace...How Inspirational Leaders Wake People UP!

We must learn quickly now how to work and live together in ways that bring us back to life.

Margaret Wheatley, *Leadership and the New Science*

Are you committed to renewing your workplace, to breathing life into your culture and creating a place where people are inspired and excited about what they're up to? Many leaders today, facing the challenge of attracting and retaining good workers, are asking questions about how to lead in a more meaningful way.

Leaders who inspire and energize their employees have four common traits they consistently demonstrate:

1. They build meaningful connections;
2. They create positive energy;
3. They invest in relationships;
4. They know the value of fun!

#1—Inspiring Leaders Build Meaningful Connections

The pursuit of meaning is happening on a scale never before imagined. We are pre-occupied with a hunger for more purpose and passion in our work and life.

> *People have enough to live, but nothing to live for; they have*
> *the means but no meaning.*
>
> Viktor Frankl, *Man's Search for Meaning*

Today we want our work to add value. We want to make a difference. We want to make our time count. We also want to be able to act on our most important values. We yearn to be authentic. We don't want to wear a mask, or adopt ways of being and acting that feel incongruent with who we are.

"Show me the love" has become more important than "Show me the money" in our current culture. Do you remember that famous line from the movie *Jerry McGuire*? In one scene the agent (played by Tom Cruise) has a real conversation with Rod Tidwell, the athlete he's representing (played by Cuba Gooding Jr.), and he tells him, "You are only thinking about how much you get paid. You gotta remember why you got into this game in the first place. You've gotta get your heart in the game!" Real passion comes from knowing why you're doing what you're doing—from a clear commitment to the purpose of your work and understanding how you are contributing to something bigger.

How do organizations create this powerful and compelling sense of purpose and passion? One person at a time...one leader at a time. Every conversation, every question asked with real curiosity and interest, and every acknowledgment either builds deeper engagement or deeper disconnect. As a leader, it is time to assess how you show up, and to become more aware of the impact that you have on the people around you and the overall work environment. How do you sustain positive emotion, hope, and optimism as you continue to work hard, often under pressure and tight timelines with constant change? The answer to that question is now more important than ever. Inspiring others means, first of all, that you find ways to stay inspired yourself.

Are YOU an Inspirational Leader?

Leaders who inspire have the ability to connect authentically with the hearts and minds of others in pursuit of some common goal. They get a kick out of watching people grow and develop and add huge value. The best part of making it your intention to encourage and support others is that it feels great. Inspirational leaders know that the real juice—the fuel to keep going—comes from seeing other people light up around them.

> In everyone's life, at some time, our inner fire goes out. It is
> then burst into flame by an encounter with another human
> being. We should all be thankful for those people who rekindle
> the inner spirit.
>
> Albert Schweitzer

We are all leaders. We can choose to be inspirational leaders. The beauty of inspiration is that it transcends the next project or goal and encourages real engagement in life and work. Above all, inspiration once ignited fuels itself and doesn't rely on external sources to keep the fires burning.

Exercise: How Inspired Are You?

Answer the following questions using the following scale:

Rarely—1; Occasionally—2; About half the time—3; Often—4; Always—5

Score

I wake up most days "ready to go," eager, and excited to get to work.   _____

I am clear about how my contribution makes an impact to the success of my organization.   _____

I know and act on my values daily and work with colleagues who hold similar values.   _____

I am crystal clear about who I am, and what success means to me personally.   _____

I have friends and colleagues who believe in me and inspire me to reach my potential. _____

I have goals and dreams that I'm actively working towards and feel supported and encouraged by my supervisor and colleagues. _____

I provide regular recognition and appreciation to others for the work they do. _____

I trust my supervisor and have an open respectful relationship with him/her. _____

I speak up at work freely and easily without fear of judgment. _____

I am able to take action and make decisions in my work without constantly checking with someone higher up. _____

I don't feel as though I need to wear a mask at work or have to hide parts of myself in order to fit in. _____

I approach the day with optimism and a positive perspective even during difficult periods. _____

I have a life outside of work that is fulfilling and satisfying. _____

I have rituals and routines that help to keep me energized throughout the day _____

I feel relaxed and happy at work most of the time. _____

I have quiet time daily to be reflective about my life—this time allows me to plan proactively and prepare for each day. _____

I celebrate milestones. I do something to mark personal successes. _____

I take my work seriously and myself lightly. I look for the humor in life and laugh a lot. _____

I have chosen to learn from every work and life experience. I regularly ask myself, "What did I learn from that?" _____

I go to bed most nights feeling this was a well-lived day! _____

To determine your inspiration score add up your total score and divide by 10.

***If you scored as high as 9 or 10** you are turned on by life and work and probably feel fully alive and engaged with what you are up to! You can't wait to get up each morning and start the day. You are positive and inspiring to be around.*

***If you scored between 6 and 8** you are content with things, but you are probably feeling there is still more. You know that the land of fulfillment is just around the corner and you can't wait to take the steps to being even more satisfied with your life and leadership.*

***If you scored less than 6** your experience of life and work at the moment may be more of a struggle. You are definitely ready to take positive action, and even the smallest step will make a difference.*

Begin by reflecting on your score and then asking yourself the following questions:

- Does your test score reflect how alive you feel? Is it higher or lower?
- What questions did you score low on?
- What questions did you score high on?
- Which areas would you like to improve on?

Recognize that it is normal to feel up and down in life. If you are in a struggle today, know that it isn't a static condition. By adopting a new perspective on your contribution at work and in life you will feel more inspired and alive.

Ten Practical Applications for Inspiring Yourself and Others

1. Find two or three of the best people leaders in your organization and take them to lunch. Ask them to share with you some of the things that work for them. Be intentional about hanging out with people who lead well.

2. Identify one thing you are working on changing. Write down your commitment on a card and carry it for 90 days (the length of time it takes to change our habits).

3. Ask for feedback. Ask three people you work with to tell you what they think is your biggest opportunity for growth. Ask them about a gap they see in your leadership.

4. Write out questions you want to ask yourself each day. Commit to talk with a partner every week. Use the conversation as a check-in to reflect on your progress and growth as a leader.

5. Change your morning focus. Instead of asking, "I wonder what life will do for me today?" begin your day with a different question: "What can I give to life today?" or "How can I contribute today?"

6. Start your day with conscious intention. Recite your personal mission, play a theme song on the way to work, go for a walk, meditate…come up with your own ritual. It matters how you start your day.

7. Plan to take a break each day. Get up and get away from your desk. Do something that is a pleasure and completely unrelated to whatever you are working on.

8. Write out some personal policies you have about protecting and replenishing your time and energy. Renew your commitment by clearly stating the boundaries you intend to honor. For instance, "I will not check email in the evenings at home," or "I will not work on Saturdays."

9. For the next seven days practice gratitude. At the end of each day write about the three things in your day that made you smile.

10. Say thank you often, sincerely, and genuinely. Say thank you to the bus driver, to the cashier, to your colleagues, employees, and leaders…and look them in the eye while you say it with attention and appreciation. Notice the impact on them and on yourself.

2—Inspiring Leaders Create Positive Energy

The fundamental role of a leader is to prime good feelings in those they lead…

Daniel Goleman, *Primal Leadership*

Have you ever walked into the coffee room and, before anything specific has been said, you have known immediately it wasn't a good atmosphere? Whatever they were talking about was not uplifting and exciting…in fact, you got the sense that there was trouble ahead. We transmit energy, positive or negative, more powerfully through our body language and facial expressions than we do by the words we actually use.

In every conversation we have we leave people feeling better or worse as a result of the interaction. Negative stories are hard to bear. They zap our spirit and fuel anxiety. They throw us off stride. Emotions spread irresistibly whenever people are near one another, even when the contact is completely non-verbal. Smiles are the most contagious; they have an almost irresistible power to make others smile in return.

As a leader, it is essential that you take responsibility for your "emotional wake." Cynicism spreads quickly from person to person in short moments of contact. My findings are that within 15 minutes our physiological profile matches that of our colleagues. The emotional climate of a workplace determines if performance soars or if people are thrown off stride by anxiety.

Amplify the Positive

If you tend to remember and talk about the hassles, struggles, and frustrations in a day more than the positive events, you are not alone. It seems that unless we consciously choose to focus on what is good, we don't. Many of us have been trained to think critically. We are paid to notice and fix what isn't right. Leaders today need to become capable of shifting their perspective and making room to see and celebrate the successes and opportunities for good.

A. *Think about an experience you had in the last week that really stressed you out, something you were frustrated or angry about. Tell someone about it. Or record a few notes about it.*

B. *Now think about the same experience, but this time make it a happy story. Talk about what was good about it. Write down some positive things about the whole experience. What good came from it? Think hard and you will find something.*

Resilient leaders have this ability to amplify the positive details of a situation. This is not the same as wearing rose-colored glasses and believing the world is a fair and just place. It's not about becoming Pollyanna. It is simply looking at the situation and focusing your energy where you can make a difference.

Ten Tips to Create Positive Energy

1. Choose one day and notice the impact of brief conversations. After every encounter ask yourself if you left the person feeling better or worse.

2. Decide to have a full day where you don't say anything negative. Make it a challenge to see how long you can go without uttering a negative thought. When you are about to say something that isn't positive, ask yourself how you can make it a neutral observation or state the upside. Have fun with it!

3. Visit www.bucketbook.com and complete the positive impact assessment. This 15-question test will help you determine if you are providing enough recognition and having a positive impact. You will be able to see how your score compares to others, based on results from a Gallup Poll.

4. Become more conscious of your thoughts and notice what you are saying to yourself. Replace such negative thoughts as, "I have to go to work today," with "I get to go to work today." Instead of repeating to yourself "I don't have enough time," say, "I have all the time there is." Notice when you are falling into the land of struggle with thoughts like "This is too hard" or "I can't possibly do this."

5. The next time things feel difficult just take a breath, pause, and say, "How fascinating!" It might make you giggle. And then look at the possibilities. Who knows?

6. Get serious about not taking in negative information. Turn off the news. Don't listen to the radio in your car on the way to work. Instead choose to listen to a favorite CD. Either choose not to read the newspaper, or start from the back of the paper first and read the travel and entertainment sections. Read something inspirational and have positive conversations.

7. *"And what I like about your idea is..."* Try using this phrase more often. Eliminate "but" from your vocabulary. This simple phrase will help you focus on finding value and creating alignment with your team, your colleagues, and even your children.

8. Surround yourself with optimism, hope, and enthusiasm. Choose not to go to lunch or coffee with "constipated personalities." Practice creative avoidance.

9. When you're feeling terrific…notify your face. Remember to smile. A smile can put you at ease and lift your spirits, while a frown or stressed expression can create anxiety for both you and the people you greet.

10. Notice the impact of your greeting. In Tibetan the greeting is "Tashi Delek"—it means I honor the greatness in you. What do you say when you are greeted? When you greet people in an upbeat way you create positive energy around you. When someone asks, "How are you?" and you respond with, "not bad," "hanging in there," "getting by," "could be worse," "can't complain," "exhausted," or "well, I'm here aren't I?" you get the same low energy back. Try "fantastic," "awesome," "excellent," or "terrific" and see what happens.

#3—Inspiring Leaders Invest in Relationships

Are pretend conversations the norm in your workplace? When was the last time you had a real conversation? A real conversation is one that you enter into with fascination and curiosity. It is one where you don't know what the outcome will be. It is not strictly run by a rigid agenda. A real conversation occurs when you're not checking your watch. It happens when your main concern is discovering more about the person across from you and supporting them as they move towards their potential. You are truly present and fully engaged in the moment.

If you are wondering who in the world has time for those conversations, you are not alone. That is why they are so rare. The most inspirational leaders, though, know that people don't care how much you know, until they know how much you care. In other words, if you don't have a trusting relationship built on mutual understanding, care, and concern, you have no influence. As Susan Scott says in her book, *Fierce Conversations*, the conversation is the relationship. No conversation. No relationship.

> *The experience of being understood, versus interpreted,*
> *is so compelling, you can charge admission.*
>
> B. Joseph Pine II, *The Experience Economy*

Twelve Tools for Real Conversations

1. Ask people, "What makes you proud of working as a part of our organization?" Get curious. Ask people how they feel at the beginning of the workweek. How about at the end of the workweek?

2. Make brief interactions meaningful. Even when you have only a few minutes, sit down, show by your body language that you are interested, look the person in the eye, take a deep breath and be "present."

3. Practice "thank you therapy"—thank people for their efforts.

4. Take time to listen intently to people. Instead of listening to assess whether you agree or disagree, listen just to get to know more about what they think and feel.

5. Look for an opportunity to change your perspective. The next time you are in conflict with someone, ask yourself how you can attune yourself to them and move past the roadblock by being more curious and interested. Notice what is true that you hadn't considered and build real understanding.

6. Introduce people by name and how they add value to the organization—not by referring to title or status, and never by saying, "This is my employee" or, worse, "my subordinate."

7. Know and use people's names. Spell and pronounce their name correctly. Don't use shortened nicknames just because it is easier or more convenient for you to remember.

8. Hold an off-site team meeting and make hearing people's stories the agenda. Encourage team members to talk about what experience has shaped them, who has influenced them and how they came to be in their current positions. The leader goes first.

9. Encourage networking—ask people who they've had lunch with this week.

10. Ask questions that challenge people to contribute more, such as, "What's the most exceptional thing you did this week?" or "What are you most proud of in your work?"

11. Once a month, ask employees to name one thing they think they can do better, and one thing you as the leader could do better to help them succeed.

12. Whenever possible, instead of dispensing advice or telling people how to do something, ask them questions. Ask "How do you think that will work

out?" "Have you thought about...?" "How will you manage…?" Encourage people to do their own problem solving. Coach them towards developing their own effective solutions.

#4—Inspiring Leaders Know the Value of Fun!

I think work and business can be creative and exciting. A hoot. A growth experience. A journey of lifelong learning and constant surprise.

Tom Peters

Most people today are yearning for a lighter atmosphere at work...a place they can look forward to going to; where they can express themselves, laugh and smile, be creative, enjoy good leadership, and have pleasant people to work with.

Playfulness is an outlook characterized by humanness, warmth, and acceptance. It's about recognizing that "we're all in this together" and looking for opportunities to ease the way for others.

I am preoccupied with the spirit of play no matter what I do.

John Travolta

>> A middle-aged accountant who attended one of my seminars shared this story with me. He decided to "break the mold" of a typically serious meeting he had with his banker. He went to the meeting looking for a substantial loan. As he emptied his briefcase onto the boardroom table, he pretended he couldn't find some of the papers he was looking for. Seeming a little disorganized, he pulled out his cell phone, his organizer, some paper, then a yellow happy face ball, his rubber ducky...and continued reaching and searching for his document. The banker began laughing loudly and asked, "What's up with the duck?" Dennis responded, "Oh, I like to take him with me. It makes me feel good." Even he smiled at the absurdity of the idea. But, the ice was broken; they had a great meeting. <<

It's so refreshing when, as a client or a customer, we're taken beyond the ordinary...to something interesting, surprising, and memorable. When you are present and you've embraced a spirit of playfulness, it's easy to make someone's day. Just like the accountant who surprised his banker, we can easily create more fun moments in our day. Be on the lookout for opportunities to spread some positive energy.

Ten Practical Ways to Create Fun

1. Spend one day finding any reason you can to laugh. Notice the absurdity, revel in our common humanity...amuse yourself. Make noticing humor an intention for the day.

2. Inspiring leaders have a kid alive in them. They love their work. Their passion is infectious. Do something today that sparks your inner excitement. Keep a Hula Hoop in your office, and when you're feeling as though work has stopped being fun—get up and shake things up a little. Maybe invite an unsuspecting visitor to try it out. Bottom line: have something you can do that livens you up.

3. Keep a metaphor log. Carry a small notebook with you, and when you read or hear an amusing metaphor write it down. Entertain yourself with your new-found creativity.

4. Create an inspiration board. Use a bulletin board to post anything you find compelling or interesting relating to your current project—a picture, quote, invitation, sign.

5. Take a humor test. Measure your level of mirth by visiting www.tinyurl.com/6t7ff and see where you stand.

6. Create a humor file. Collect quotes, stories, cartoons, and pictures that make you giggle.

7. Take a four-day weekend. Use your holidays. Don't accumulate time off. Leaders are in serious need of renewal to manage the pressure and demands of the role.

8. Plan to take a break each day. Get up and get away from your desk. Do something that is a pleasure and completely unrelated to whatever you are working on. Go browse in a card shop or bookstore, sit down in a busy

place and people watch, get some exercise, have an ice cream cone, sit on a park bench…

9. Buy a box of inspirational cards and make it a practice to pull one out each day. Notice what the message is. Keep the thought and the card with you throughout the day. Keep a basket of them on your desk and make them available for visitors.

10. The best way to get in touch with your inner child is to take it out for some play. So go back to the playground and watch how the real kids play.

Inspirational leaders stand out. You never forget them. When you have had the privilege to be led by someone who is completely alive and engaged in their life and work, you remember. Their energy is galvanizing. They lead you closer to your full potential and ask for more passion and contribution than you know you have. They give you hope for a better tomorrow.

It is easy to begin. Decide to investigate what it means to be inspired. Ask yourself and others what makes work meaningful. Be more positive. Make connecting with others an important part of your workday. Know that conversation is a valued business activity. The percentage of time people feel good at work is the strongest predictor of whether they will stay or leave. Lighten up—expect work to be fun. When you adopt a playful perspective it transforms your experience.

The best part of experimenting with some of these ideas is that inspirational leadership is mostly a gift we give ourselves. Making a difference in the lives of others is such a turn-on. It is the juice that keeps us going, no matter what's going on!

Tammy Robertson

Tammy Robertson believes that the essence of our challenge today is captured in one simple message: *"Get Your Heart in the Game!"™* As a life coach, author, and professional speaker to audiences across North America, Tammy inspires and challenges others to step into their BIG life and be more purposeful and passionate. Her aim is to deliver effective and practical ideas to build environments that support a new level of individual and organizational success.

In the past year, Tammy has spoken to over 60 different business groups, organizations, and associations, creating ripples of positive change and renewed energy among their leaders. In the media, she is a frequent commentator on workplace wellness and culture. Tammy has a masters degree in Physical and Health Education from the University of Western Ontario, and with 20 years of corporate and entrepreneurial experience, she brings a keen understanding of current challenges to her audiences.

Tammy is committed to stimulating leadership potential at all levels of an organization and believes that the driving force behind great organizations is the "heart power" of people—their engaged passion for excellence. She believes the best leaders are paying attention and consciously creating a culture that supports and inspires people's best and mobilizes every person to higher levels of achievement and satisfaction. The question she asks is, "What impact are you having?"

Tammy is the author of *Get Your Heart in the Game!™* a hands-on manual for holding yourself accountable to what matters. Tammy also contributed to *Expert Women Who Speak…Speak Out, Volume 6 (Life and Success Strategies by Women, for Women).*

Business Name: WorkHeart Consulting
Address: Calgary, AB
Telephone: 403-547-5344
Email: tammyrobertson@telus.net
Web Address: www.tammyrobertson.com
Speaking Affiliations: Canadian Association of Professional Speakers

Rhonda Victoor

Incite Coaching

Little Lies That Keep Us Gloriously Average at Work

Do you ever stand in front of your client or boss appearing calm, while your mind wrestles with doubt over your ability to really step up? They want answers, results, and excellence...and you haven't done what it takes to reach that. In this moment all the internal cheerleading in the world can't mask the fact that you are not as well prepared as you could be.

Each time that happens to me, I beat myself up over it...then go right back to procrastinating the next day. I think "If I had *chosen* to start earlier, I *could have* done better. It's just that I *chose* not to." Can you spot the self-deception? The rationalizing? Sound familiar?

> **Every time we procrastinate on important tasks, we lie**
> **to ourselves. We make other things, like "busy work" or**
> **being perfect, more important than getting the job done.**

Do you know that those lies erode our self-trust? And the same is true each time we make a decision that goes against our gut reaction or core values. We disconnect our heart from our head and continue down a path of being gloriously average. We rob ourselves of the chance to truly give our best—to really achieve excellence.

Imagine for a moment that you could give your *best* effort, rather than your *perfect* effort, and in doing so, learn to trust your decisions and your skill. Imagine you could stop lying to yourself through procrastination and actually start those important tasks early, and in doing so, create your true-best work. Imagine if you could replace the whirling rush of decision-making doubt with a sense of calm and deep satisfaction. And imagine that you already have everything within you that you need to achieve that ultimate state. Imagine!

The Procrasti-Lie

Can you relate to any of these "confessions of a procrastinator"?

> » I work best under pressure! Well, actually I've never tried to work any other way. I usually plan things so I have "just enough time" to get them done, but then other urgent tasks pop up, throwing me off schedule. Usually I schmooze my way out of any repercussions. But a few weeks ago I put off some marketing work and by the time it was launched I'd missed the window of opportunity: I didn't attract the number of clients I could have. Once in awhile I procrastinate on something because I'm nervous about the result: I had to do damage control with a client who hadn't received great service. I put it off, stressing over how hard it would be. And in the end, when I finally phoned him, it wasn't nearly as bad as I'd made it out to be. I could have saved myself a lot of stress! «

And so it goes. We build a habit of procrastinating: lying to ourselves about priorities and outcomes. Most of us began to procrastinate early in life. As young school children we learn that we can put off the work, cram it in at the last minute, and still pass. So why start early?

After 10 years of study on the topic, industrial psychologist Piers Steel of the University of Calgary (www.procrastinus.com) has become an expert on procrastination. His definition: *To procrastinate is to voluntarily delay an intended course of action despite expecting to be worse-off for the delay.* So if we know we'll be worse off, what makes us procrastinate?

According to Steel, it's not fear of failure or fear of success, as you might guess.

He says those fears explain why we avoid a task completely, but not why we put one off temporarily. Instead, he boils it all down to the components found in this mathematical formula called the **Temporal Motivation Theory** where:

$$\textbf{Utility} \text{ (desire to complete the task)} = \frac{E \times V}{G \times D}$$

According to Steel, we prefer large and immediate rewards, so we'll choose a task with a higher utility number even if we know that task is actually a "temptation" and not an important priority goal. He concludes that:

E = Expectation of success. People with low self-efficacy, that is low feelings of competence, are more likely to procrastinate.

V = Value of completion. If we see a task as unpleasant we are more likely to put it off.

G = Personal sensitivity to delay. People who are more distractible, impulsive, and have less self-control tend to procrastinate more.

D = Delay of payoff. The closer we are to realizing a goal the harder we work at it.

Do you see these components combining to create procrastination in your work? We don't calculate a mathematical equation each time we select one task over another; we are often unconscious of our habits. So let's bring them to a conscious level; check each box that applies to you, and be VERY honest:

☐ Deep down I know it's important to start early, but I downplay it in my mind and minimize the time estimated to complete it well.

☐ When I face a challenging task my negative self-talk kicks in: *this will be hard, I can't do it, this won't be fun.*

☐ At the office I need a mental break, so I succumb to "busy work" that isn't truly important but provides a jolt of accomplishment.

☐ When I schedule time for it, I don't allow any room for emergencies or factor in the time it will take to communicate information back and forth with people.

☐ I create an IF clause: *IF I get my office tidied up I'll start the project*, or *IF there is time at the end of the day then I'll start it.*

- [ ] I pass control to someone else. For instance, I leave a message for a colleague and wait for them to call me back before starting, when really I could start on my own.
- [ ] I tell myself other tasks are more important or urgent, when I know that's a lie.
- [ ] I know afternoons (or some other time of the day or week) are the worst time for me to work on a project like this, yet I schedule it into those times anyway.
- [ ] I know I'm easily distracted, yet I work in locations filled with "temptations."
- [ ] I rationalize that I work best under pressure, when really I've never tried to work any other way.
- [ ] Other patterns: _____

_____

_____

If this is your procrastination pattern, what do you get out of it? I see at least three common payoffs in the people I coach. As you read these, think of your own procrastination payoffs:

Payoff #1: We get to **ignore the emotion and fear** behind the procrastination, that nagging self-talk that whispers, *"This is going to be hard. Who do you think you are to tackle this?"* We don't really trust our ability to do it well. That's hard to swallow, so we avoid it all together.

Payoff #2: We get a **little rush of accomplishment** by checking off small tasks on a to-do list or answering a few emails. It's a short-lived and shallow victory, but it tempts us every time.

Payoff #3: We get an **internal alibi**. If we put it off and end up doing a mediocre job, we always have the excuse that if we'd started earlier, we would have nailed it. But we *chose* not to.

Other payoffs: _____

_____

Are these payoffs worth it? Are they serving you well? All three of my procrastination payoffs boil down to outright lying to myself. If you deceived a friend this way, you would feel crummy, he wouldn't trust you, and it could seriously jeopardize the relationship. The same is true when you tell yourself these things—only the effect is doubled because you're the one lying *and* being lied to. Over time it's difficult to trust yourself at work…or anywhere.

Lie Remedy #1: Oust the Procrasti-Lie

Your relationship with yourself can be salvaged. Be honest with yourself, follow through, and build that trust back bit by bit. When you see one of your patterns emerging, stop! Call it what it is. I actually stand up in my office and ask, *"What are you doing?"* While I don't advise talking to yourself out loud if you share an office space (you may get some peculiar looks), I do encourage you to answer that question honestly. As soon as we name the habit it begins to diminish. It moves into the light and we can apply strategies to it. When you're ready to truly give your best, try these five sure-fire tips to oust the procrasti-lie:

1. Ditch the distraction. Turn off your email notification function. Put away that pile of reading material. Turn off the television. Book a quiet boardroom for a morning. Eliminate those things you know will tempt you away from the important task at hand.

2. Employ a rah-rah technique. If you think a task is too hard, find a way to remind yourself of how competent you really are. Call a friend or colleague for a pep talk. Look back on positive feedback you received in the past. I keep congrats and thank you email messages in a folder for easy access. YOU are the only one that can *feel* competent. And once you feel it, that emotion will build and your confidence will grow!

3. Chunk it. If it seems too daunting as one big project or the deadline is too far away to create urgency, break it into chunks. Choose three steps that you can tackle independently of each other. And be sure to schedule them into specific time slots with their own deadlines. If this is truly important make it a priority—schedule it first in the day and early in the week.

4. Work while energy is high. No one has solid willpower 24 hours a day. Determine when your most focused hours are and do the toughest work then. If it's first thing in the morning, don't waste an hour sifting through unimportant email…dive into your tough project straight away.

5. Use the 10-minute rule. Set a timer for 10 minutes and start! Commit to focus for that short 10-minute span and let the ticking of the timer create urgency. At the end of 10 minutes you'll have overcome the barrier of starting and you'll be "into it." Keep on going. This works particularly well for folks who are easily distracted.

Think about the other ways you've ousted procrastination in the past. Those strategies work for you—no need to reinvent the wheel. Swap your old procrasti-lies for the deeper payoff of creating the time you need to truly give your best. In the process you will build meaningful trust in your skills and abilities.

Lie Remedy #2: Connect With the Decision Triangle

I've been rehashing the pros and cons of each side for days. I'm stuck! I need to make a decision. Sound familiar? We make dozens of decisions every day from choosing a restaurant to choosing a career. With all that practice it should be a breeze. But instead we get stuck in doubt.

Look around your workplace. Are you the only one doubting yourself? Chances are, some of your colleagues appear successful and confident, yet they struggle with indecision. We've all worn a mask of confidence while doubt swirls beneath. To build real self-trust we must connect all three points in the decision triangle. We must align our head, heart, and voice. If just one of these disconnects from the others, we will doubt our abilities and distrust our decisions. Take this example of someone who recently applied for, and won, a new position within the company she works for:

» It all looked great on paper. In my head I lined up the pros and cons and this new role was definitely a step up. *The pay will be better, I'm supervising more people, and my colleagues tell me it's a good move.* But the whole time I had a nagging feeling in my gut that it wasn't the right fit for me. Whenever I talked about it I bounced back and forth, trying to defend the decision to myself but not really believing it. So I went for it...and I got it. That was four months ago—four long stressful months. This isn't the right role for me. I should have listened to my gut. **«**

Have you ever made a decision like this? One that feels disconnected? Perhaps, like this woman, you diligently made a pro and con list...but failed to listen to your heart? Or maybe you followed your intuition, but every time you spoke to others you became defensive and uncertain. As you examine the decision triangle below, which point has become disconnected in your work and your life?

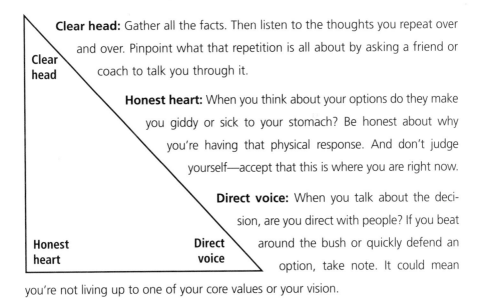

Clear head: Gather all the facts. Then listen to the thoughts you repeat over and over. Pinpoint what that repetition is all about by asking a friend or coach to talk you through it.

Honest heart: When you think about your options do they make you giddy or sick to your stomach? Be honest about why you're having that physical response. And don't judge yourself—accept that this is where you are right now.

Direct voice: When you talk about the decision, are you direct with people? If you beat around the bush or quickly defend an option, take note. It could mean you're not living up to one of your core values or your vision.

The decision triangle can be used for big life decisions, such as moving, accepting a promotion, or pursuing a relationship. But it can also be used with more "everyday" decisions, such as which invitation to accept, what recommendation to give my boss, or which committee to volunteer with.

Think about a decision that is weighing on you right now. What is the core message coming from your head, heart, and voice? How aligned are these three elements for you? Be honest, clear, and direct with yourself to make the BEST decision you can today. Draw the decision triangle and post it by your desk, in your car, or next to your bed for frequent reference. Whenever you are stuck in making a decision, check into those three points. Once they are connected you will trust your decision and truly give your personal best!

Lie Remedy #3: Wash Away Perfectionism

Picture it: your report was done three days ago, but the polishing, polishing, polishing has consumed hours of your time that could have been better spent elsewhere. Does shooting for perfection really create your best work?

If there was a 12-step program for perfectionists I'd be a lifetime member. Just watch me host a dinner party and you'll see all the signs: Each napkin is perfectly aligned. Each glass shines at the carefully set up "drink-pouring-station." And I buzz around like a wild woman doing everything myself—because only I can do it just right. I'm exhausted by the end of the night, I've had no decent conversations, and everyone is just wishing they could help.

Perhaps you can relate? People come by it honestly. You can look around and see a lot of very successful people who are perfectionists. So one would assume such tendencies create success. Wrong. Very successful people achieve success despite, not because of, perfectionist habits.

This diagram captures the principle that weaknesses are below average and strengths are above average. To achieve excellence we must grow our strengths, not just improve weak areas. Gurus build expertise in one strength area, becoming known for that.

So where does perfection fit? It does not exist above excellence. Perfection resides on another page, in another room, in a building across town. And that building is dark: it's out of reach, out of sight, intangible, and unattainable. When we shoot for something so undefined and far away, there is no way we will ever reach it. We set ourselves up for constant disappointment.

By attempting to be perfect we really become gloriously average at everything. We spread our energy so thin that we can never truly commit to excel in one area.

Excellence, not perfection, is your true target. To achieve excellence you need to discover and grow your core strength—that unique gift you bring to the world. With that core strength at the root you can create a vision for personal excellence. A vision with concrete steps attached. And when you hold yourself accountable to achieve those steps, you'll do your very best.

Think about one area where you seek perfection right now. Is it serving you well? Or is it keeping you stuck in gloriously average? Think about replacing that target of perfection with a target of excellence. What would a personal best look like here? If you don't know, ask a boss or colleague to clarify their expectation or brainstorm with a friend. What result would make you proud without allotting more time than this task is really worth? This is your new target for excellence!

When we succumb to perfectionism or procrastination (both of which are lying to ourselves) we set ourselves up for a gloriously average career and perpetual disappointment. You deserve far more than gloriously average. You deserve to find and grow your strength. You deserve to feel that rush of satisfaction from knowing you've done your best and made the decision that fits.

Pull the Plug on the Whirlpool of Lies

Most of us swim in a whirlpool of procrastination, perfectionism, and decision-doubt...each one feeding the next. They develop into such a way of life that we come to expect that stress sensation. What if we actually pulled the plug on those lies? What might we achieve? Years ago I had a glimpse of deep honesty in my work, and the result was amazing!

> **»** I can't believe I made it here to Ecuador! I'm about to walk on stage to compete for The Americas Effective Speaking Championship. Fifteen intimidating competitors are jammed into this tiny glass room while hundreds of conference delegates wander past to peer in at us. We're like fish in a tank. This "fishbowl" moment has all the makings of self-doubt and stress. So why am I so calm?

Six months prior to stepping into the fishbowl, I was given my topic for the competition. I had six months to prepare for six minutes on stage. Talk about a recipe for procrastination. And that had always been my routine: cramming my writing and rehearsals in at the last minute and nervously waiting backstage not sure if I would remember everything. I was on the path to gloriously average.

But this time, I was determined things would be different. No Canadian had won on South American soil in decades. I knew that if I was really going to step up and give my best work, for the first time in my life I had to start early. I had to stop lying to myself.

I called my coach and set up an appointment! I was committed. Week after week I practiced and honed my presentation and delivery. And as the competition date neared, a strange calm came over me. I was no longer frantically rehearsing every spare moment. I realized my speech would not be perfect. But it would be mine—the speech I was meant to give. I owned it. That self-trust calmed me like nothing else. And it forever changed how I approached my work.

When I was finally released from that fishbowl in Ecuador, I stepped on the stage trusting ME. It was a beautiful and peaceful sensation like none I had ever felt before. And, two days later, when they handed me the trophy, it was amazing validation. I had achieved excellence. But it felt a little anticlimactic: I'd already won the internal victory. **«**

Were there bumps along the way? Sure! Did I want to skip out on practice? Yes, and I *did* on a few occasions. But somewhere along the way I realized that trusting myself is like trusting other people. Once we've lost trust in someone, they have to work really hard to earn it back. They have to stop lying—point blank. And they have to consistently follow through when they say they will. It's like we're collecting quarters in the accountability piggy bank: once they've banked a certain amount of credibility, they earn back our trust.

Self-Assessment Exercise

When we procrastinate or make a disconnected decision, we let ourselves down. The lies erode trust with ourselves. To build it back up we need to continuously drop quarters into the accountability piggy bank. So what are you waiting for? Start dropping in those quarters to leap over gloriously average and achieve excellence! It's time to pull the plug on the lies you tell yourself.

Look back over each of the strategies explored in this chapter. Which habits are holding you back at work, for example, procrastination, perfectionism, or disconnected decisions? Note clear and specific examples.

_____

_____

_____

How does it make you feel when you succumb to these habits? And how are these behaviors negatively impacting your BIG career and life goals? Be very honest with yourself.

_____

_____

_____

Now…are you ready to make a change? You CAN leap from the gloriously average path to the path of excellence! What strategy do you commit to put into place in the next 48 hours?

_____

_____

_____

Terrific! This is an excellent start. If you want to hold yourself really accountable, tell a colleague, friend, boss, or coach about your commitment. This is just the first step. Go to your calendar right now and record (into precise time slots) the other specific steps you want to take; these will provide visual reminders of the shift you want to make. You can do this!

Swim Off Into the Sunset

It would be a "fairy-tale ending" to say that, after my fishbowl speaking experience in Ecuador, I never procrastinated again or doubted a decision. But that would be a lie. I didn't swim off into the sunset, leaving self-doubt in the wake. No! My self-trust and focus on priorities ebbs and flows like the tide. I put off important tasks every week or so. And every few months I let my head take over and totally disregard my heart and voice. Each time I do I end up with an enormous neck kink as a result. With that big warning sign I step back and reconnect to my decision triangle.

Yet, the percentage of time that I procrastinate is now one-fifth of what it was. It is mind-boggling the amount that I accomplish now and how much more energy I have.

Know that along the way there will be great victories when you feel that rush of confidence and peace that comes with letting go of procrastination. And there will be other times when you fall on our face, pick yourself up, and rebuild self-trust.

The journey toward excellence, and away from being gloriously average, is akin to what author Karen Armstrong describes in *The Spiral Staircase: My Climb Out of Darkness*. We're each climbing a spiral staircase. With each step we learn about ourselves and grow. And just when we think we've overcome a big challenge such as self-doubt, we look over the banister and see it staring back at us. It can feel as though we've learned nothing, made no progress at all. But we have. We're a full flight higher on our staircase. That issue is a little lower down on the landscape. But on each loop of the staircase we'll face it again. And each time it will become smaller.

So remember the tools you've already jammed into your tool belt. If you connect the points of your decision triangle (your head, heart, and voice) you can trust your decisions and your skill. Stop lying to yourself through procrastination and perfectionism. Fess up. Self-trust will build with honesty. And remember…you already have everything within you that you need to succeed.

Rhonda Victoor

Rhonda Victoor challenges audience members to *stop lying to yourself!* She coaches entrepreneurs to *explode* business growth, salespeople to *niche their network*, and teams to connect on their *path to guru-dom*. Don't blink; you might miss a signature high-kick or a *hush-falls-over-the-crowd* story.

Coach Victoor speaks around the world, and in 2004 she was named The World Effective Speaking Champion. She won the title in Japan—less than 2 weeks after giving birth to her first child—at an event attracting over 10,000 leaders, including Stephen Covey.

Rhonda studied at the University of Plymouth, England, and earned a Bachelor of Commerce with Distinction from the University of Alberta. She wrote *Out with Schmoozing—Keys to Successful Networking* and is a contributing author to *Expert Women Who Speak—Speak Out, Volume 4*.

Business Name:	Incite Coaching
Address:	1331 Bartlett Place
	Kelowna, BC V1Y 6W8
Telephone:	250-712-0085
Email:	Rhonda@InciteCoaching.com
Web Address:	www.InciteCoaching.com
Professional Affiliations:	Professional Member, Canadian Association of Professional Speakers and International Coaching Federation; Past Executive, Junior Chamber International

Favorite Quote:
Try not. Do. Or do not. There is no try!
YODA, *Star Wars* character

If every person takes responsibility to live and work totally aligned with who they really are, and each plays their chosen role, the results will be enlightened organizations that are the outcome of the people in them.

Beryl Allport, *Awakening the Workplace, Volume 1*

Heather Colquhoun

Kaleidoscopic Training, Consulting & Facilitation Services Inc.

Managing the MultiGen Mix

**"I'll have someone from my generation get in
touch with someone from your generation!"**

Talking to someone from another generation can feel at times as though you are speaking two different languages. At best, people walk away shaking their head; at worst, they pitch a tent on their "side" and settle into mutual misunderstanding and conflict. Today's reality of up to four generations working together within an organization certainly presents challenges. However, by learning how to communicate more effectively with each generation you can decrease conflict and improve your working relationships and your productivity. In fact, effective multi-generational workplaces increase workplace productivity overall, given that managers spend up to 20 percent of their time handling conflict. Whether you are a manager or a colleague that is a full day per week, or two and a half months per year, that you likely agree could be put to better use!

Generational diversity is perhaps most pronounced with the most recent cohort to enter the workforce, the Millennials. It is already apparent how differently the Millennials view and approach work. These differences can be understood as a function of the generation to which they belong. We will examine how generations are defined and what shaped each generation. We will consider what each generation brings to the workplace, how best to manage each generation, and tips for employee engagement and retention.

Generational Theory

Generational cohorts are based on a combination of birth rates (demographers) and a shared experience of socio-historic events while growing up or "coming of age" (sociologists). However, demographers differ on precisely where to draw the beginning and end point for each generation. The variance is typically several years in either direction. The result is that readers may not agree with the generation to which they have been "assigned" by this author. This potential disagreement exists when any label is applied to a group. The solution is to choose the generation with which you most closely identify.

Generation	Veterans	Boomers	Xers	Millennials
Birth Years	1922-1945	1946-1964	1965-1980	1981-2000

For example, if you were born in 1947, you fall into the Boomer category as defined above. If, however, upon learning more about the experiences and attributes of the Veteran generation, you feel a closer tie to that cohort, you could choose to identify as a Veteran instead.

Other than year of birth, a generational cohort shares experiences as a result of coming of age during the same time period. These shared, significant social history events, trends, or icons are called "defining moments" because most members of that cohort are likely to recall them. While each generation may vividly recall the details surrounding such significant experiences, a defining event, trend, or icon has the greatest overall influence in shaping the views and characteristics of those individuals who are still forming their world view during the time of the event.

For example, while the Challenger explosion had a great impact on Veterans, Boomers, and Xers, its impact was greatest on the youngest generation at the time, the Xers. Many of them watched this defining *event* on television in their classrooms.

A defining *trend* for Xers was environmentalism. They grew up with the 3Rs: Reduce, Reuse, and Recycle. Though all generations may subscribe to the 3R mantra, it shaped the way Xers look at their planet.

For an example of a defining *icon*, look to the Boomer years. Martin Luther King Jr., Pierre Elliott Trudeau, Betty Friedan, and many others influenced the way an entire generation would look at civil rights and liberties.

The goal here is to provide you with an understanding of the four generations in today's workplace in order to promote effective and productive workplace relationships. Although it is useful to examine general information, statistics, and trends to gain understanding and new ideas, it is also important to be aware of the uniqueness of individuals within each generation.

A Snapshot of Each Generation

**To do justice to understanding individual categories,
we isolate them; to apply wisdom from any one category,
we must combine them.**

While some defining moments cross continents, such as the World Wars, we'll look at this from a Western experience. Globally, generational cohorts are defined slightly differently both with respect to birth years and defining moments. Interestingly, with the Digital Age in full swing, many current events are experienced simultaneously to some degree by individuals thousands of miles apart, such as the devastating tsunami in the Indian Ocean in December 2005.

Defining Moments

Question: What do the following eight items all have in common?

- JFK Assassination
- School Violence
- Digital Age
- Downsizing

- Women's Movement
- World War II
- Environmentalism
- Influence of the Silver Screen

Answer: They were defining moments for one of the four generations in the workplace today.

Veterans

- Influence of the Silver Screen
- World War II

Born between 1922 and 1945, in 2007 the Veterans are between 62 and 85 years old. A number of the individuals in this cohort are still contributing to the workplace through traditional positions within a company, or as consultants, members of Boards of Directors, or volunteers. They continue to make up five percent of the Canadian workforce. Characteristics associated with this generation include hard working, dedicated, and respectful of authority. Growing up, their world was shaped by tragic events, including the Great Depression and World War II, as well as by the economic upswing and optimism following the end of the war. For this cohort, work was a welcome opportunity. As an individual worker, you did what had to be done, and when you had served well and long enough, rewards were forthcoming. Promotion was primarily based on length of service. Loyalty and dedication were highly valued. If you worked hard, there was a sense of security; the employer would take care of you. Organizations were set up using a hierarchical system, and respect for authority was an important component in maintaining this structure. Employees did not challenge the status quo or question the system; they worked within it.

Boomers

- JFK Assassination
- Women's Movement

Boomers received their moniker because of their numbers. They are the children of the post-war baby boom. Born between 1946 and 1964, today they are 43 to 61 years old. Incidentally, Australia, Canada, New Zealand, and the United States each had similar birth rates during this period. Boomers came of age during the economic upswing following World War II. Their Veteran parents worked hard to provide their children with opportunities that they themselves had not had. Boomers learned about a world full of opportunity, not only from their parents but also through the television that was available in homes for the first time. Their experiences gave them a largely optimistic outlook. Boomers were raised in the era of interpersonal communication, a need that they took with them to the workplace.

By sheer volume, boomers form the majority of today's workforce. However, this generation can be divided into two groups based on their experience entering the workplace. For the older Boomers, the workplace expanded and "flattened out" to accommodate their numbers as they entered the labor market. On one hand, there was a lot of opportunity, and on the other, it was imperative to make a mark for yourself in order to keep your place and to get ahead. For those on the tail end of this generation, the ranks were full. Companies could no longer swell to accommodate them. The satiated workplace suddenly became competitive; during the late 1980s and early 1990s downsizing became a reality. Boomers were not only affected in great numbers, but they were also caught unawares because of the stability of the workplace that they and their parents had experienced to date. Couple these realities with the fact that the message from parents was "work hard and you will be rewarded" and the Boomer "live to work" philosophy is not difficult to grasp.

Xers

- Environmentalism
- Downsizing

Xers were born between 1965 and 1980, making them between 27 and 42 years old in 2007. This is a cautious, sometimes even cynical generation, and with good reason. Xers were the first generation en masse to have both parents working outside the home. They were "latchkey" kids, letting themselves into the house and microwaving dinner for themselves and their siblings. This generation was required very early on to be independent and resourceful. This cohort saw their parents downsized, right-sized, and generally surprised as the shift from "employer looking out for you" to "cost-cutting, lean workplace" took place.

When the Xers began looking for work, they discovered two difficult things about following a generation called "Boomer" into the labor market. The first was that, with so much downsizing, jobs were competitive and not necessarily stable. Resourcefulness and independence serve Xers well in this case; every job hunter for herself. However, their cynicism was only reinforced: when another opportunity comes along outside your current company, take it. After all, your employer would not think twice about letting you go if necessary.

The second was the Boomer philosophy of "live to work." Xers examined this philosophy in light of downsizing, lack of job security, and interests outside of work, including family, and essentially turned the philosophy on its head. Xers "work to live." Work–life balance is important. Older generations have judged Xers to lack loyalty, dedication, and the ability to work hard. However, their resourcefulness, coupled with the climate of the workplace when they arrived, has translated into Xers managing their career paths much differently than the generations before them.

Millennials

- School Violence
- Digital Age

Born between 1981 and 2000 to younger Boomers and older Xers, this generation is the newest to enter the workforce. The youngest of them are just starting elementary school at six years old, while the oldest are 26 years old. Thanks to birth control, this generation is the most planned-for generation in history. Their parents are highly involved and team-oriented. In the home, this means that Millennials often have input into family decisions. From a very early age, they have been encouraged to communicate and collaborate. It is no wonder that they are bringing these skills to the workplace. However, for Veteran and Boomer managers who have built the workplace around hierarchies, the Millennials' desire to contribute actively regardless of rank and file is often misinterpreted as overstepping their bounds.

Like the Boomers, this generation may still be split into two groups, though it is too early to tell just yet. The divide will likely be between those old enough to recall their experience pre-September 11, 2001 and those too young to remember this defining moment. Regardless of the division, most Millennials will not even recall a time without stringent airport security, including removing shoes at security checkpoints. News reports about national security and the war on terrorism is their norm. Indeed, in a 2002 poll conducted in the United States cited in *When Generations Collide*, Millennials named personal safety as their number one workplace concern.

Another division is due to advances in technology, dubbed the Digital Age. For this cohort, the divide between "have" and "have not" is once again pronounced. Those who "have" are privy to technology at a much earlier age than any generation prior. Those who do not have a computer in the home are at a distinct disadvantage during their school years and, of course, once they enter the world of work.

If you have ever watched a commercial aimed at a Millennial (and you are not a member of this generation), you may have experienced dizziness, nausea, or blurred vision. Due to the speed with which Millennials receive information via the Internet and television, they have the ability to process information simultaneously. This skill means they are great multi-taskers, but also that they need stimulation or they will become bored. Information travels so quickly that this generation is also the most informed generation to date. No more waiting for Mom or Dad to take you to the library to research a project.

Millennials turn to the Internet to seek answers. In fact, they may already have a friend in the country that they are researching, so an instant message or text message to the friend and they are directly linked to real-time current events. This generation has a much more global view of the world than did previous generations. These young people are open-minded; diversity is a part of the fabric of their world.

Millennials have taken seriously the "work to live" mantra. To employers, Millennials appear even less loyal than the Xers. They may even leave a job for travel or volunteer positions overseas. Across all industries, the retention and management of this generation are among the more costly human resource challenges today.

Understanding Current Workplace Structure

The Veterans and Boomers are at the helm of the majority of companies today. Initially, when Boomers entered the workplace, Veterans and Boomers struggled to converge their two styles. The Veteran style was groomed with a strong military influence due to experiences during World War II. Automatic respect was given to those in positions of authority. In the workplace, Veterans got ahead by listening and executing, not by challenging the status quo.

When the Boomers descended upon the workplace, the top-down approach felt institutional and uncommunicative. While they were raised in households where respect for authority was valued and instilled, their respect for authority fluctuated based on various defining moments, such as the Vietnam War. Boomers learned by experience that not all respect given was well-deserved and they questioned it, openly and collectively. Paradoxically, with time and experience behind them, today Boomers comfortably occupy positions of power and authority.

Boomers were not satisfied with the provision of information on a need-to-know basis. They sought to change the militaristic-centered management approach and, again because of their numbers, workplaces began to flatten out. Additional layers of management were added in many companies, thereby decreasing control by a few leaders at the top and increasing the flow of information.

Despite these seemingly divergent views on management styles, one thing that the Boomers did share with the Veterans was a belief in attaining promotions and other rewards by paying your dues. Both generations were, therefore, committed and loyal to an employer, and trusted that the employer would subsequently reward their years of service and experience.

Boomers' commitment to working in teams, with a common set of values and a shared goal, began to influence the workplace. Today many organizations speak about working in teams. However, a key factor for Boomer teams is to maintain group cohesion. Indeed, in the mid-1950s, conflict in the workplace was seen as abnormal and was pinned on troublemakers. While it is clearer today that conflict can be healthy and constructive, existing team structures and processes often discourage conflict by focusing on the appearance of cohesion rather than on completing a shared task. Switching this focus would allow team members to disagree with one another and to work differently and independently from the group while still accomplishing the task, and would have greater appeal to both Xers and Millennials.

For those Xers in managerial roles where Veterans or Boomers report to them, the above information provides a perspective of the type of values and assumptions under which these employees may be operating. As manager, these gaps can be bridged with an effective cross-generational management style.

Managing Xers and Millennials

The corporate downsizing trend that began in the 1980s had a great impact on the Xer trust in employer rewards, as described earlier. They competed for jobs not only against their own cohort but in the shadow of a boom generation and of downsizing. Boomers seemed to retain their optimism and continue to judge Xers and Millennials for what they view as lack of loyalty.

Xers

The book *Bridging the Boomer-Xer Gap*, by Hank Karp, cites a study done where the common myth of Xers being out for themselves was effectively dispelled. In fact, Xers were revealed to be significantly more committed to teamwork than Boomers, while at the same time remaining more individualistic. Xers do not automatically give respect based on an individual's job title. It may again be an effect of downsizing and their built-in caution mechanism, or because their generation saw widely publicized scandals by public figures, including Ben Johnson and Bill Clinton. To gain respect from an Xer, the person in authority must "walk the talk"; they must do what they commit to do. Xers are not intimidated by those in authority roles. Not only do they not fear the senior vice-presidents, they welcome an opportunity to discuss their ideas them.

Xers were the first generation to be raised on the information highway, which includes television, the Internet, and personal computers in the home. Growing up, they developed resiliency, self-assurance, and adaptability to change. In the workplace, they want to contribute from early on. When a manager undervalues an Xer, the latter's caution flag is raised and the individual does not feel a drive to complete his or her best work since it is clearly not valued. The result is a reinforcement of skepticism about loyalty to a company. The key for managers is to value Xers' contributions. When a manager not only values the work, but also provides opportunities for the individual to make lasting, visible contributions to the organization, engagement and loyalty increase. The more autonomy one can give the Xer, the more creative and innovative their work will be. Micromanaging will not get results from an Xer; autonomy will.

Millennials

It is critical to manage Millennials' expectations. They are used to having things come relatively easily to them, as their parents have been very involved in their lives. In fact, this involvement does not seem to cease as the Millennial prepares to enter the workforce; human resources departments have received follow-up phone calls from the applicant's parents inquiring on their child's behalf. Boomer and Xer managers are expressing frustration at the amount of input and guidance that this generation seems to need. However, knowing the level of parental involvement and understanding that Millennials are natural collaborators, gives managers insight into the coaching needs to set this generation up for future success.

Tips for Workplace Success

Regardless of the generational composition of your team, the potential for misunderstanding exists. To increase the likelihood of success, consider the following additional tips:

1. Ensure any deliberate competition is focused *outside* the team. Any win/lose scenarios, such as sales representatives striving to beat one another's targets, decreases trust. Coupled with other differences, including generational ones, this competition can destroy a team.

2. Beware of making performance comparisons, particularly across generations. This tip may sound obvious to some. Consider, however, that even subtle comparisons can plant the seeds of competition and mistrust among team members. For example, consider the ramifications during a Boomer's performance review if it is suggested that the individual consult a younger, more technologically savvy Xer or Millennial colleague to improve skills in that area. While the manager conducting the performance review may have intended it as a helpful suggestion, the comment may not be received as such.

3. Personality and temperament theories tell us that one's behavior is not an indicator of how one would like to be treated. Thus, the so-called Golden

Rule of "Treat others as you would like to be treated" is rewritten as the Platinum Rule of "Treat others the way *they* would like to be treated." The final tip is, therefore, to use the information gleaned about each generation to determine the best approach for each person based not on your own generational style, but on theirs.

Retention

Retaining any generation of employee is about plugging into whatever drives that generation's engagement. In short, retention is about satisfying the needs and values of the employee so that he or she will remain productive and committed to the organization. When employees become bored, there is a generational divide in their response. The older generations tend to quit and stay ("presenteeism") while the younger generations tend to quit and leave. Which of these two responses is more damaging is still up for debate. In either case, retention is not merely about keeping employees inside the organization, it is also about keeping them engaged in their work. Know that the type of work that each will find interesting varies not only by generation but also by individual. Therefore, wherever possible, permit direct managers to assign projects based on each individual's interests and skills.

Veterans and Boomers

Due in part to labor shortages and increased longevity, Veterans and Boomers are continuing to participate in the workplace beyond retirement. A Canadian survey sponsored by Desjardins Credit Union in August 2006 found that among workers over 40, only 39 percent intended to cease working completely at retirement, while 56 percent planned a gradual transition to full-retirement. The majority identify personal preference as the primary motivator for continuing to work. This news is a relief to employers who need to retain Veterans and Boomers. Their participation is critical from a knowledge management standpoint. Opportunities to successfully re-engage retired employees may be in the form of part-time or project-based work. According to a 2004 Statistics Canada report, workers over 65 opt for self-employment four times more often than those aged 15 to 64. Armed with this knowledge, employers can consider restructuring their human resource requirements to capitalize on these willing, if non-traditional, contributions to the workplace.

Retaining Younger Workers

Employers are frustrated by existing myths about both Xers and Millennials. Myths about Xers suggest that they are only looking out for themselves and have no company loyalty. For the Xers, long-term job security and promotions are simply no longer a reality that they feel they can count on. They seek shorter-term rewards. Xers also need opportunities for skill development and professional growth. Employers can meet these needs through such retention strategies as tuition reimbursement, internal mentoring and coaching programs, stretch assignments, and collaboratively mapping their career path.

Myths about Millennials' lack of commitment have employers doubting they will even see a return on their investment in training this generation. Providing training and learning opportunities are excellent retention strategies for Millennials; one human resources manager for a national rental company observed that calls seeking the next professional development opportunity come in the day after a Millennial attends a course. They are eager to learn and participate in the workplace. Millennials want and expect to collaborate in real time with colleagues across time zones. One global logistics company in particular has recognized this and installed software enabling real-time communication and collaboration on projects regardless of the employee's geographic location.

Both Xers and Millennials want to make an impact on the workplace, to see their contribution to the overall outcome. They are most engaged when they can participate fully, meaning with more context, information, and access to decision makers than Veterans and Boomers typically think is appropriate. As a retention strategy, therefore, examine current practices with respect to younger generations' participation on projects and exposure to company decision makers. Provide opportunities that stretch or challenge them, and offer them that exposure, such as having an Xer team member make the presentation to the Board.

Taking the CAR Approach

The differences between the generations offer much opportunity for misunderstanding and conflict. However, with a greater knowledge of some of the socio-historic factors behind each generation's characteristics, you can examine these differences using a different lens.

The value of a greater understanding of this layer of diversity is the ability to tailor your expectations and approach in order to build more rewarding, productive, and effective relationships with people from all generations. Think of it as using the CAR approach:

- Consider your intentions;
- Apply insights;
- Reap the rewards.

Consider your intentions in your own interactions with other generations. Take the insights gleaned from this chapter and apply them to those interactions to inject new understanding and perspective on team differences. Reap the rewards of improved working relationships between generations. Whether you are a manager or a colleague, interact with all four generations at work with more tact, understanding, and openness.

Heather Colquhoun

Heather Colquhoun is the owner and Director of Training & Development for Kaleidoscopic Training, Consulting & Facilitation Services Inc. Her company specializes in elevating organizations to peak performance through conflict management, diversity awareness, and team building. Her strong belief in and commitment to "positivity" (or the act of being positive) informs her approach to all projects.

Heather has passion for supporting and fostering effective communication, particularly in diverse environments. She is an experienced trainer, facilitator, mediator, and speaker with an enthusiastic, facilitative approach to developing participants' existing skills. Her speaking experience includes keynote speeches at national and regional conferences and for not-for-profit annual general meetings.

As a trainer, Heather develops and delivers energized programs in corporate, not-for-profit, and educational settings, as well as facilitates interpersonal mediations and multi-party conflicts. Clients include Ontario March of Dimes, The Jennifer Ashleigh Foundation, Unilever Canada, World Wildlife Federation Canada, and York University. Heather is a certified trainer in True Colors® and Personality Dimensions™.

Business Name:	Kaleidoscopic Training, Consulting & Facilitation Services Inc.
Address:	157 Adelaide Street West, Suite 143, Toronto, ON M5H 4E7
Telephone:	416-238-7454
Email:	Heather@kscopic.ca
Web Address:	www.kscopic.ca
Professional Affiliations:	Canadian Society for Training & Development; Conflict Resolution Network Canada; Member of Halton Region Diversity Advisory Committee

Favorite Quote:
Whether you think you can or you can't, you're right.

Henry Ford

Deri Latimer

Deri J. Latimer Professional Speaking & Consulting

Building Resilience in a S.N.A.P.

Resilience...when you see or hear the word, do you find yourself thinking *What is it?* or *How can I get some of that?* The word conjures up incredible images of strength and flexibility, of being adaptable, of possessing the ability to bounce back from the challenges of life.

According to the Oxford Dictionary, to be "resilient" is to be "able to recoil or spring back into shape after bending, stretching, or being compressed; able to recover quickly from difficult conditions." When thinking about this definition and the images the word conjures up—such as an elastic band or a bouncing ball—I decided that most people would likely agree that "resilience" is something that is useful in all parts of life—both personally and at work. You have likely felt from time to time that you have been stretched, compressed, and bent out of shape. Being able to recoil and spring back into shape quickly is a definite asset! The feedback I've received from individuals and organizations alike indicates that resilience is a key requirement in workplaces today, more so than ever before.

The following is a definition I've found that fits people's needs in an awakened workplace:

Resilience is the ability to absorb high levels of change while maintaining personal resourcefulness. Personal resourcefulness is akin to wellness and effectiveness;

**when you are personally resourceful, you are confident,
healthy, and can perform to your highest capability.**

It is important to note that this chapter is about *building* resilience. In your work experience, I'll bet you have been trained to "manage stress," "control costs," "eliminate waste," and "solve problems." In the next few pages, you are going to explore how to "build" something that you want, rather than learning how to "manage," "control," "eliminate" or "solve" something that you do not want. You will be more inspired and energized to build something positive, than you would be to control or eliminate something negative. And, an awakened workplace certainly requires inspired and energized individuals!

While there is much written about the resilience of economies and sports teams, there appears to be little written about resilience of human beings and resilience in the workplace. After researching and teaching resilience with hundreds of organizations and thousands of individuals over the past eight years, I've discovered some tools and techniques to make building resilience a "snap." In turn, I have used this word as the acronym for the model being shared with you now. Here is what each of the letters mean, and the pages that follow will explore each letter further:

> **S**—See yourself;
>
> **N**—Navigate a path;
>
> **A**—Assume control;
>
> **P**—Press on!

You can develop and enhance your personal resilience throughout your life. Organizations can, likewise, build resilient cultures using the same approach. The acronym S.N.A.P. works nicely because it implies a sense of ease and speed, which works well in our rapid, complex techno-world. Although resilience is about achieving a long-term destination, like many journeys, you know that achieving long-term success depends entirely on the short-term choices you make along the way.

> *Perseverance is not a long race; it is many short races, one after the other.*
> Walter Elliott, American Catholic priest and writer

In addition to being a great reminder of the meaning of resilience, the word "snap" is also a wonderfully sensory word. You can *hear* a snap; you can *see* something snapping back into shape after it has been stressed; you can even *feel* a snap, whether the snap of your fingers or the snap of an elastic band on your skin. You've likely heard the expression "snap to it" as a reminder to move into action. In building personal resilience, we are going to learn how to "snap *through* it" (as well as "snap to it") as a reminder to use the strategies outlined below to move you through your life and all of the challenges it presents, with ease and speed.

S.N.A.P. through it!

S—See Yourself

Who are you? and *What do you want?* These two questions address the essence of the first step in S.N.A.P. They are both vitally important questions. Answering these questions allows you to remain focused on your personal vision of yourself; to remain focused on your picture of yourself as an adaptable, flexible, resilient person.

What words come to mind when you think of these questions? *Who are you?* provides the context for your life. Think about the roles in which you find yourself. *What do you want?* helps you to identify the resources that are most useful to you in those various contexts. The following are examples of answers that might come to mind for you:

Who are you?	What do you want?
Team leader	Energy, wisdom
Parent	Caring, calm, happiness
Peer	Practicality, flexibility

Complete the chart below for yourself. What are the contexts (roles) in which you find yourself? What resources are most useful to you in each context?

Who are you?	What do you want?

This first step (**S**—See yourself) helps you to formulate the vision of yourself as a resilient person. Having a clear vision of yourself allows you to be more aware of the experience that you desire, and to be more aware of the people, resources, and information you need to move you toward your desired vision. Without having a clear vision, you might just miss out on the opportunities that present themselves to you every day. As an illustration, consider this story about the last time I bought a car, a silver Ford Taurus. I imagine you can relate to this story, as you likely have had an experience very much like this one:

» While driving out of the car lot on Pembina Highway in Winnipeg, I felt proud of my shiny new car, and maybe a little apprehensive at what I had spent for it. After driving for awhile, I looked around and noticed something…every second car was a silver Ford Taurus! Have you ever had an experience like that? I remember thinking, "Was there a sale on silver Ford Tauruses that I didn't know about?" Well, what do you think? Is that what happened? Of course not! You know that those silver Ford Tauruses were there the day before I bought my car; I just wasn't looking for them so I drove right past them without noticing them. «

This little story reinforces the power of vision and of selective perception. You already do select what you notice in the world around you; there is simply too much stimulation in the universe for you to attend to it all. You know that there are times when you can be very aware of someone else's voice in the room (when you hear your name being spoken, for example) and you also know that there are times when you are not at all aware of another person's voice or even presence in a room (when you are focused on completing the project in front of you). You are programmed to be selective. What's interesting is that the program is written entirely by you! The program includes your needs, interests, beliefs, values, expectations, objectives, and so on. These different personal programs account for how two people can experience the same thing (a new staff member, for example) and notice entirely different things about that experience. These personal programs can also explain how two people can work in the same organization and yet have very different impressions of the organization.

What you need is out there and available for you to perceive.

When you have a clear vision of what you want, you will notice (selectively perceive) the people, resources, and information you need in order to achieve your vision. And, you will not notice (because your attention is focused elsewhere) those things that will move you away from your vision. What you need is out there and available for you to perceive. A clear vision means you will notice it; and you will not miss the opportunity by "driving right past it." So, see yourself (**S**) having the resources you need to be the resilient person you desire to be.

Think about how powerful this can be in the workplace. Imagine that you have an important presentation to make as a project leader (the context) and you are feeling nervous. You decide that one of the resources you want for the presentation is "confidence." Rather than focusing on managing or eliminating the nervousness, you are focused on creating or building "confidence."

N—Navigate a Path

The second step involves navigating a path to your vision. You can choose strategies that help you to continually move toward how you "see yourself" (**S**). For example, if you want "confidence" you can begin to think about what "confidence" means to you. What is "confidence"? How does it feel? What does it look like? What does it sound like? What are the behaviors of "confidence"? When you are specific about what it is that you desire, in a sensory way, you can ensure that you notice the sights, sounds, feelings, and behaviors of that state when they are present. When you notice those sights, sounds, feelings, and behaviors, you will be able to enjoy the full experience of that desired state. You will, indeed, create the experience of confidence!

Let's look at an example. Notice how easily you can begin navigating your path:

What do you want?

I want confidence in delivering my presentation.

How will you know you have "confidence"? What will you see? What will you hear? What will you feel?

I will see others looking at me, nodding and smiling; I will hear people laughing and asking questions; I will hear myself saying "you'll be great"; I will feel light and tall; I will feel my breathing at a regular rate; I will feel myself smiling.

What will others notice when you have "confidence"? (How will you behave?)

They will see me walking briskly and in an upright fashion; they will see me making eye contact and shaking their hand when I arrive; they will hear my voice loud and clear; they will see me smiling and looking at them frequently.

What are you willing to do to have "confidence"?

I will visualize a great presentation before I leave for work in the morning; I will remind myself of my expertise in the subject matter; I will prepare at length and know my material well; I will anticipate audience questions and prepare responses; I will exercise to loosen and relax my body; I will get a good night's sleep before the presentation day; I will rise early and read over my notes; I will drink water to keep hydrated.

What are willing to stop doing so that you can have "confidence"?

I will stop believing that "I am a terrible presenter"; I will stop telling myself that other people want to judge me and want to see me fail; I will stop waiting until the last minute to prepare for my presentation.

Awakening the Workplace

In the space provided below, answer these questions for something that you want. When you think about what you want, make sure that you state it positively. For example, let's imagine that you want to be less anxious at meetings with your manager. If you word it that way, it is negative (it is about having less of something that is not positive, anxiety). To state this more positively, ask yourself, "If I had less anxiety, what would I have instead?" You might respond that you will have "calm," "peace," or "control." Then use the positive description as you navigate your path.

What do you want? (Make sure it is stated positively.)

_____

_____

_____

How will you know you have _____? What will you see? What will you hear? What will you feel?

_____

_____

_____

What will others notice when you have _____?

_____

_____

_____

What are you willing to do to have _____?

_____

_____

_____

What are willing to stop doing so that you can have _____?

_____

_____

_____

Trust yourself. You know more than you think you do.
Benjamin Spock, pediatrician and author

Now, go to your calendar and make a note about what you will do in order to get what you want; what actions you will take. Set a timeline to check in with yourself and see how you are doing. Are you doing what you said you will do? Have you stopped doing those things that are getting in your way? Have you taken notice of those sights, sounds, feelings, and behaviors that you desire? When you see yourself and navigate a path, you are well on your way to building your resilience.

A—Assume Control

This third step is about assuming control of your work and life experience. We human beings seem to do less well (and, likewise, resist change more) when we believe that the things that are happening around us are out of our control. The challenge in this step is to *assume* you have control.

Of course, there are things that have happened in your life over which you have had no control. There will continue to be things that happen in your life that you did not choose, and that you wish did not happen. This step is about assuming control over the only real thing you do control in this life: yourself and your behaviors and reactions.

By being proactive and continually moving toward your vision (**S**—See yourself) and by focusing on your behaviors and reactions (**N**—Navigate a path), you will already be more in control of your life and your experience. When you are focused on assuming control, you will be less distracted and less likely to become a victim to your circumstances (the "S.N.A.P.ee"); you will, instead, be the one in charge (the "S.N.A.P.er").

This step can be as easy as it sounds. Make sure you complete **S** and **N**; those first two steps help you to be proactive in building your resilience. Then, when something comes your way that you weren't expecting and didn't plan for, *assume control* (**A**). Ask yourself "So, what can I do? What are my options? What do I want?" When you are in action, you cannot be a victim. When you are in action, you are not waiting for someone else, or something else (outside of you) to solve your problem or to provide you with the answers. You are relying on the only real source of "the answers," yourself.

> *The antidote to stress and anxiety is action.*
>
> Dr. Wayne Dyer

Assuming control also means increasing your awareness of the indicators of distress (a lack of personal resourcefulness and a lack of resilience) that are true for you. The lists below present some common signs of distress. Place a check mark beside the *physical* signals that you notice when you are experiencing distress:

_____   Fatigue/lack of energy

_____   Insomnia/restlessness

_____   Dizziness/light-headedness

_____   Headaches/migraines

_____   Nausea/digestive-tract problems

_____   Allergies/breathing difficulties

_____   Skin problems/irritations

_____   Recurring colds/flu/infections

_____   Muscle aches/back pain

Now, place a check mark beside the self-talk (internal dialogue) that you hear in your mind when you experience distress:

_____   "It's not fair."

_____   "Nobody listens to me."

_____   "They're picking on me."

_____   "I feel all alone."

_____   "I can't count on anyone."

_____   "Nobody cares what I think."

_____   "Nobody understands."

_____   "I don't like being bossed around."

_____   "I can't keep up; I can't do it."

Being aware of distress signals that are true for you, means that you can notice them early (before they become too big, like a headache that is so bad you have to stay home from work) and then make choices to manage them well. For instance, if you tune in and notice that you are saying "Nobody cares what I think" prior to your presentation, you are likely feeling a low level of energy and control. You can "assume control" by asking yourself: "So, what can I do?" "What are my options?" "What do I want?" Your answers will likely show that you can *decide* that most people DO care about what you think. Your *options* are to do the presentation feeling confident or to do the presentation feeling as though no one cares what you think; and *what you want* is to deliver an excellent presentation with confidence. When you are *navigating* and moving toward creating the experience you want, rather than being stuck in an experience you do not want, you will become more resilient and more effective.

P—Press On!

This last step "press on" is really about being persistent and moving forward (not being stuck in the present or the past). This step helps you to increase your level of optimism, about yourself, your work, and your life. Optimists are inherently more persistent than pessimists, because they see setbacks as temporary occasions that can be moved through. Optimism is not about a "just be happy," "rose-colored glasses" perspective on life; optimism is about having a realistic and hopeful perspective on life today and in the future. Not only does an optimistic perspective feel more pleasant to experience, having optimism can actually impact your health positively. Martin Seligman, in his bestseller *Learned Optimism: How to Change Your Mind and Your Life,* noted that physical health is something over which we can have far greater personal control than we probably suspect. Seligman maintains that how we think changes our health, that optimists catch fewer infectious diseases than pessimists do, and that our immune system may work better when we are optimistic.

So…what is your perspective on life? When you experience a setback, what do you say to yourself? When you identify a pessimistic message from your self-talk, ask yourself: "Is this really true? Could there be another explanation? Is this kind of thinking useful for me?" Let's look at an example:

>> Jim and Jane are co-workers. They often go for lunch together and

enjoy sharing stories and catching up on what's happening at the office. Today at 11:55 a.m., Jim notices Jane walk past his cubicle with Sally. Jane and Sally are heading out the door together; they are laughing and chatting as they head toward the elevator. Jim is furious. He says to himself, "Jane is so rude! How could she not let me know that she planned to go for lunch with someone else! She completely lacks respect for my time; now it's too late for me to make other arrangements." Jim had been expecting to go for lunch with Jane; now he has to have lunch alone. Jim decides not to talk to Jane for the rest of the day. **«**

Before Jim proceeds with his day, ignoring Jane and potentially permanently affecting his relationship with her, he could ask himself: "Is this really true? Could there be another explanation? Is this kind of thinking useful for me?" Once he thought about it, he might come to the following conclusions:

- Jane is a great friend and I have no evidence that she would intentionally hurt me;
- Perhaps Jane thought she told me about her plans to have lunch with Sally today;
- I will enjoy my lunch break. When I get back to work, I will approach Jane and will ask her about what happened before I make any assumptions about it.

When Jim thinks this way, he demonstrates optimism and is better able to "press on" (**P**). He will likely find that there is, indeed, an alternative explanation for the lunch mix-up. Even if he finds out that Jane did want to purposely hurt him by leaving him out of her lunch plans, Jim will be in a better emotional place to be able to have the dialogue he needs to have with Jane in order to sort out their interpersonal difficulty. Jim will know that what he decides to focus on, and to spend time thinking about, will affect what he experiences.

We find that people's beliefs about their efficacy affect the sorts of choices they make in very significant ways. In particular, it affects their levels of motivation and perseverance in the face of obstacles. Most success requires persistent effort, so low self-efficacy becomes a self-limiting process. In order to succeed, people need a sense of self-efficacy, strung together with resilience to meet the inevitable obstacles and inequities of life.

Albert Bandura, psychologist

Think about the example we have been using of you making a presentation. Imagine that an audience member asks a tough question for which you were not prepared. You begin feeling anxious and thinking that he is trying to make you look incompetent in front of your peers. Before responding and behaving as though that were the case, you can ask yourself: "Is this really true? Could there be another explanation? Is this kind of thinking useful for me?" Answering these questions you could decide that:

- You really do not really know this person's intention in asking the question;
- Another explanation is that the person was so inspired by your presentation that it really got him thinking about the subject;
- The most useful thinking for you is that no one expects you to have answers for every possible question, and that you will appear most confident by saying, "That's a great question! I will research it after the presentation and get back to you tomorrow with an answer."

When you do this, you can press on (**P**) and move toward achieving your vision of completing an excellent presentation with confidence!

An awakened workplace is one that is full of resilient individuals. So, how can you *get some of that*? Remember to build personal resilience in a S.N.A.P.! "**S**ee yourself" as a resourceful, resilient person; "**N**avigate a path" to achieve your vision of yourself; "**A**ssume control" of your experience at work and elsewhere; and "**P**ress on," as you move forward. Also, remember the S.N.A.P. acronym because you know that "**S**uccess **N**eeds **A** **P**rocess." When you can follow a proven process, you can awaken yourself to be more personally resilient, and more effective, happy and successful overall.

S.N.A.P. to It!

Begin building personal resilience right now. Don't wait for something or someone outside of you to get you what you want. There is no time like the present to begin to take action!

> *People who want milk should not seat themselves in the middle of a field in the hope that a cow will back up into them.*
>
> Elbert Hubbard, writer and philosopher

S.N.A.P. Through It!

Use these strategies regularly. It took a long time to develop some of your present personal programs, habits, and perspectives, so remind yourself that it will take time to learn new ones. You can take small steps each day to increase your overall adaptability and effectiveness.

> *The person with the most flexibility in thinking and behaving has the best chance of succeeding.*
>
> Sue Knight, speaker and author

S.N.A.P. Out of It!

Pay attention to your distress indicators. When you find yourself on a downward spiral, feeling low energy and experiencing negative self-talk, remember to S.N.A.P. yourself out of it.

> *Our bodies communicate to us clearly and specifically if we are willing to listen to them.*
>
> Shakti Gawain, personal development author

S.N.A.P. Into...

SNAP into effectiveness! SNAP into happiness! SNAP into an awakened workplace! SNAP into success by building personal resilience throughout your life.

> ...everything can be taken from us but one thing; the last of human freedoms—to choose one's attitude in any given set of circumstances—to choose one's own way.
>
> Dr. Viktor Frankl, noted psychiatrist
> and Holocaust Survivor

Deri Latimer

Deri Latimer is a professional speaker, trainer, consultant, and author who combines a business degree with 19 years of human resource development experience. Deri's areas of expertise include personal resilience, group resourcefulness, leadership, and organizational development. She is a dynamic and engaging speaker, with a warm and enthusiastic style. Deri is a model of personal resilience, practicing what she preaches in how she chooses to live her life.

She is a certified practitioner of the Bar-On EQi® (Emotional Intelligence Indicator), the MBTI (Myers-Briggs Personality Type Indicator), and NLP (Neuro-linguistic programming). Deri has a reputation of being a credible and valuable resource to a wide range of organizations from various industries and business sectors. Her client list includes an impressive array of progressive local and international organizations.

Deri was a contributor to *Expert Women Who Speak...Speak Out!* Volume 5. She currently resides in Winnipeg with her husband and two children.

Business Name:	Deri J. Latimer Professional Speaking and Consulting
Address:	27 Exbury Place, Winnipeg, MB R3Y 1C2
Telephone:	204-269-5630
Email:	deri@derilatimer.com
Web Address:	http://www.derilatimer.com
Professional Affiliations:	Canadian Association of Professional Speakers; The Satir Institute

Favorite Quote:

See yourself, and what you see you will become.

—Aristotle

Learn to awaken a work attitude so vital that falling asleep at your desk would be as unconscionable as sleeping through your favorite dessert. Learn to have an attitude so delicious that everyone will want some.

Paul Huschilt, *Awakening the Workplace, Volume 1*

Bob Parker

Robert A. Parker & Associates Inc

Better Teams, Better Meetings

Why do we have meetings? On the surface, this might sound like a silly question, but meetings have become such a staple in the workplace environment that some might just consider them a necessity without really understanding why we have them at all. Meetings have been around since the beginning of time, ever since Eve got the idea to eat an apple and shared it at a meeting with Adam. Since then, meetings have provided a structured format to help team members contribute their ideas, get updates, understand challenges, ask questions for clarification, find solutions, develop recommendations, and from time to time even make decisions. With new communication technologies, such as software, the Internet, and email, there might seem to be justification for dispelling with meetings altogether. Work can be accomplished without the need for people to get together—right?

Not so fast! The one element that demands we continue to have meetings in spite of all our technological advances is the same reason we often fail to have productive ones. It is all about relationships and teaming, which, at their heart, rest on the basis of trust, risk, and reward.

Our need to get face-to-face with our co-workers is rooted in building those attributes that are essential for productive execution. These include trust, relationships, developing context, and understanding risk and rewards. These are difficult to do when you've never sat face-to-face with your co-worker. This is not to say you can't do it, it just takes a long time. When done properly, meetings can help to build all those productive attributes in a timely manner; done poorly, and you can destroy them even quicker.

Consider that those who attend a meeting are a team, whether a temporary one for a single project, or a long-term one, such as a department. Building a productive meeting is very similar in structure to building a strong team, and that will be the focus of this chapter.

Question: How do you have more productive meetings?
Answer: Create more productive teams.

Remember a time you left a meeting and wished you could have those few hours back? Did you feel as though you were on a train bound for nowhere, and it was off track, gaining speed, and looking for a place to crash all at the same time?

There are so many dynamics at play in meetings—from the participants to the location, from the topic to the urgency—that covering the subject in its entirety might require volumes of reading. The intention of this chapter is to focus clearly on the people component of meetings and to provide some tools to help structure your meetings around this complex variable. The people in the meeting room can vary in behavioral styles, personalities, expertise, authority, capabilities, energy, engagement, politics, loyalties, and emotions, just to name a few. Attempting to rush into a meeting without some foundation is an exercise for fools, and will no doubt lead to greater problems in the workplace down the road.

How effective a group is at working together
is a function of teaming.

Stages of Teams

Team development occurs in stages. Bruce Tuckman, in his book *Stages of Small Group Development Revisited* (1977), provided us with one of the most commonly accepted models for the process of team development. He demonstrated that all groups go through identifiable stages as they continue to engage. The following is an adapted interpretation of the stages of his model:

Forming Stage	Team forms or a new member joins
Storming Stage	Defining roles; who will lead?
Norming Stage	Agreeing on values and objectives and buying in
Performing Stage	Execution; team functions well
Mourning Stage	Project ends or a group member leaves

Teams begin in the forming stage where new teams are created for a project or department. Once formed, the group starts to define roles within the team and determines who will take on certain responsibilities. A good, functioning team will agree on values and objectives before moving any further into performance where the team will make decisions and execute their work. The final stage is that of mourning, where groups need to grieve or celebrate the end of the project. It can also involve a member leaving while the group remains functional. Teams find themselves having to move back to the forming stage again when a new member arrives and roles have to be redefined.

It may appear that this model happens naturally on its own, but without some leadership, groups can possibly get stuck at a lower level and never make it to performing. Arguments about, "who did what," or "when something should have been done," tend to keep teams in the storming stage, making meetings drag on and on without achieving results. If a team is going to have effective results, it must work its way through the model without skipping steps.

For most groups, deciding who should be in the room, and who will do what, is the easy part. Let's consider some of the components of teamwork during the "norming" stage of team development that need to play out in meetings. These are:

1. Understanding objectives;
2. Values;
3. Attributes (rules of engagement);
4. Developing context at meetings;
5. Making decisions;
6. Groupthink;
7. Resolving conflict.

In your workplace, some or all of these might be a component of your meeting, yet few are done well enough to provide encouraging results. Let's discuss each of these and see how they interact to ultimately produce great results for your time and effort in meetings.

#1—Understanding Objectives

What are the objectives of your project or team? Start at the beginning, and don't move on until the objectives are clearly understood by everyone around in the room. Too often projects get off track and meetings derail because team members move to solutions before they clearly understand the problem or task at hand. Everyone has to have buy-in and agreement on the objectives well before solutions can be approached. This aspect of teaming is the common goal stage. Without everyone starting on the same page at the beginning, the door is open for personal agendas to take the stage.

The meeting facilitator must help the group clearly articulate the team's objective. Is this a short-term project with a clearly defined end, or an ongoing project to be maintained over time? Either way, the objective must be defined well enough so that in the future, as new members join the team, they can easily understand what needs to be accomplished.

Sometimes the objective is provided for the team from some higher, strategic level in the organization; other times it must be developed to solve a specific problem. In either case, the objective needs to be articulated in a way that describes the desired future for the organization. What would we like the organization to look like in the future?

Examples of Objectives

Systems Department:

    Poor Objective: "Fix the server support network."

    Better Objective: "Have an efficient support network for internal sales staff."

Marketing Department:

> *Poor Objective:* "Create an advertising campaign for new product."
> *Better Objective:* "Retain a sustainable market for new 'techno-widget.'"

Objectives need to be stated in the present perfect tense as if they have already been accomplished and you are enjoying the benefits. Notice how the better objectives above are more future-oriented, while the poor objectives are more immediate.

Once the objectives are understood and you have buy-in, you can move into the next stage in developing your team. And no, it is not trying to brainstorm for solutions—yet.

#2—Values

What values will guide your decisions to help you know you are on the right track in solving your problems and developing your strategies? This is often the most ignored aspect of teaming and implementation, and yet it offers the best opportunity to improve decisions and resolve conflicts more effectively.

Many organizations have "guiding" or "corporate" values that are used to make decisions; however, many workers admit that they don't know how to implement these "organizational values" into their day-to-day work. The key is to create the relationship between objectives and values at every meeting and use them as the guiding force.

The values for your team or "project" need to be determined after your objective and before you start to solve the problem. What do we mean by values? What should they look like?

Examples of Values

Customer Focus: We ensure that customer needs are our primary focus in developing and implementing products and services.

Safety: We maintain a safe and healthy environment for all our stakeholders.

Quality: Products and services are delivered with the highest standards.

Too many values can hinder rather than help. Consider three values as a good starting place, and five as a maximum. Having more than five values can be difficult to manage as they may begin to compete with each other.

#3—Attributes (Rules of Engagement)

The difference between values and attributes is that values are principles and attributes are behaviors. The value is the intended result of the action or behavior.

Value	Attribute
Quality	Diligence, accuracy
Safety	Accountability, patience
Diversity	Respect, acceptance, understanding

Attributes are the "rules of engagement" for your team—the guidelines for behavior during your meetings or any other interaction. These are different from values, but definitely the two should be aligned with each other.

Examples of useful attributes would be behaviors such as respect, accountability, and openness. The tricky thing about values and attributes is that some values can be attributes and vice versa. It is important that you distinguish between the "desire" of the organization (values) and the "behaviors" (attributes) of your people that are needed to get there.

As a leader, you may suggest to your group some attributes that you have developed prior to the meeting, or have the team create these during initial discussions.

Guidelines for Meetings

The following are some guidelines or attributes that you can use for meetings:

1. **Respect:** Everyone has a right to their opinions and feelings;
2. **Listening:** One person speaks at a time;
3. **Openness:** Everyone has the opportunity to state their opinion;
4. **Clarity:** Ask if you don't understand;
5. **Support:** Reinforce others' ideas when you can;

6. **Challenge:** Don't be afraid to offer opposing views, but state them as such, and explain why you feel that way;

7. **Solutions:** Don't criticize, condemn, or complain—instead, offer solutions by attacking issues and problems, not people.

Putting It All Together

Everyone needs to understand the objectives and have buy-in, values need to be established at the beginning, and the "rules of engagement" need to be clear. Then, and only then, can you attack the business portion of your meeting and move into the "performance" stage. This might seem like a lot of extra work and perhaps even trivial, but putting it all together will help keep meetings on track, and save you from making poor decisions later.

You now have three tools to keep your meeting on track. If the topic gets side-tracked, someone can use the objective to bring it back on track; if the focus turns off the values, you can realign; and if behaviors are an issue, you have the rules of engagement to help everyone be mindful.

#4—Developing Context at Meetings

One factor that derails meetings and teams are the assumptions that members have about the project or team. We find ourselves telling others not to make assumptions, but we all keep doing it. Making assumptions is a part of our human nature and it is how we are hard-wired, but we can protect against making the wrong assumptions if we learn to help build the right context at meetings—or maybe even before people get there.

Everyone has their own context about the way they see the world. Some might call this a "mindset," others a "paradigm." Regardless of what we call it, it is important to realize that everyone sees the world just a little bit differently and this helps to make up their own unique context. Those differences can be a strength in making good decisions, yet if we don't address them, they can keep us from making any decision.

An individual's context is made up of all their perceptions about a subject over a long period of time. As new information comes along, that context is either rein-forced by the new information, or the context is challenged and maybe weakened. If this is a long-held belief, the individual might discard the data if it is in conflict, or feel affirmed if the data supports their context. People are always looking for data that supports their individual context, and will challenge data that goes against it. This makes changing a person's context very difficult. Instead of trying to change someone's context, we should be trying to understand it, while at the same time we help should them understand ours.

Active Inquiry is a process of asking questions to help everyone understand each individual's context and even that of the situation. Opinions expressed during a meeting are rooted in the individual's context—somewhere they picked up some data to come to this conclusion. Using Active Inquiry, we can ask questions to help get at the root data ensuring everyone has the same context.

Example of Active Inquiry

Group Leader: "Everyone, we need to get new customers, what should we do?"

Bill: "Customers only buy based on price! We should lower our prices."

Group Leader: "Bill, that's a strong assertion, and you may be right. What evidence have you seen to support that claim?"

Bill: "I get a lot of phone calls where people complain about price and they say they can get our product cheaper."

Group Leader: "They can get it cheaper, we know that. We do have a good client base, however, so why do you think other customers stay with us in spite of price?"

Bill: "We do have leading-edge technology that everyone wants."

Group Leader: "What technology do you think is our competitive advantage?"

Bill: "No one else has our updated software and hardware combination."

Group Leader: "So is that worth something to our customers, like a premium price?"

Bill: "Perhaps some people will pay it, but not everyone."

Group Leader: "Fair. Bill, can you help us figure out the "some people," so we can develop a strategy?"

Bill: "I'll do my best."

Active Inquiry helps us to get to the root of the team member's context so we can ensure we are developing the right data in making decisions.

You can help build the right context before people come to the meeting by sending them the "assumptions" of the meeting before they arrive. These are often the reasons for why the meeting was called in the first place. People should know the type of meeting they are attending, and its purpose. By labeling these assumptions, it gives us permission to change our context as new data becomes available.

Types of Meetings

Your meetings might be unique from other organizations; however, for the most part, they will fall into these four typical categories:

- **Team update meeting:** Update on progress or info sharing;
- **Idea meeting:** Brainstorming and idea generation;
- **Strategy meeting:** Recommendations and decisions;
- **Sell meeting:** Presentation.

It is quite possible that during a specific time period (or meeting) many of these types of meetings may occur. For example, the weekly team update meeting might uncover a problem that needs a solution. After a mini-idea meeting, and some ideas hit the table, someone might jump into a mini-sell meeting to try and sell their ideas to the group to get buy-in. This is all well and good and not necessarily dysfunctional, but group members, and specifically group leaders, should have some sense of appropriate behavior at each of these stages during a meeting.

#5—Making Decisions

If a meeting is going to derail, it will more than likely happen when members are trying to make a decision about something important to the team. Much research has been done about group decision making that could fill volumes of texts; however, we will explore some key themes that have significant impact on how our meetings operate.

Hierarchy Teams vs. Flat Teams

A hierarchy team is one where there are defined levels of responsibility within the group. Group members have specific roles and decisions are ultimately made by the highest level of the team.

Conversely, a flat team may also involve different levels of responsibility, yet leaders for the team emerge as needed during discussions and implementation based on skill, talent, and experience. Participants on a flat team would suggest that no one individual is their group leader and that various members take the role from time to time as skill and experience dictate.

The flat team model is becoming more popular as organizations are learning to become more agile and responsive to the market. Hierarchies can take too long to make decisions, and the impact of the leader can have a negative influence on the group, depending on their style and the type of meeting they are operating.

Closed Leader vs. Open Leader

There are many styles of leaders; however, let's simplify these by looking at two main attributes for how leaders run meetings. A closed leader expresses his or her opinion early during a meeting and often wants to get consensus from the team as quickly as possible. An open leader is one who does not express their opinion too early and is more interested in encouraging discussion and hearing new ideas from the group.

Leader influence on a group cannot be discounted. Modern research of group dynamics suggests that team members tend to want to please the leader of the group by their behavior. This is more prevalent in hierarchy teams with a closed leader where groups go with the suggestion that the leader proposed in order to satisfy some sort of risk/reward at play outside the meeting's context.

Flat teams are not without their challenges either. An open leader on a flat team may never get to a decision, or the group's desire to maintain or reach consensus can lead to "groupthink" (see #6 on next page) if we are not careful to look at our decisions carefully. Ultimately, decisions need to be made by looking at values and objectives. Be wary of consensus, and look to the experience in the group over its opinion.

The following table indicates the type of meeting and structure that works best for decision making in various situations:

Types of Meetings and Structures:

Idea meeting	Open leader Flat team
Sell meeting	Closed leader Hierarchy team
Team update Meeting	Closed or open leader Hierarchy or flat team
Strategy meeting	Open leader Flat team

#6—Groupthink

An idea surfaces during a meeting, there is evidence to support the claim, and the group buys in. Everyone thinks the idea will work, and has complete faith in the leader and the team. They believe they can't fail because everything has worked before. This context with no conflict is called "groupthink." Coined by Irving Janis in the early 1970s around political and military decisions, his work helps us understand much about group dynamics.

In the early to mid-1970s, the Ford Pinto was an affordable hatchback with a unique design that appealed to many after an earlier oil crisis. It had one problem: the gas tank was prone to exploding if the car was hit from behind. This design flaw was calculated after crash tests, yet even though Ford engineers had a fix, it would mean the cost of the car would go over the $2000 cost limit set by Lee Iacocca. The Pinto sold very well in its first few years, and the costs to recall and fix the gas tank would have been astronomical. Ford's leadership decided during a team meeting that it would be cheaper to pay out the wrongful death/injury lawsuit claims than recall all the cars. This idea was supported by the available data, and Ford agreed not to recall the cars. Their data was flawed, however, as more injuries were reported than anticipated. Eventually the government demanded a recall and Ford conceded. This was a perfect example of groupthink in that the engineers chose not to challenge the leader, who had a very closed style. Groupthink develops when we don't take into account our values when making decisions, nor allow for some conflict on our teams.

In 1982 someone put drugs in a Tylenol bottle that didn't belong there, and the result was the death of some innocent victims who unknowingly took these tainted drugs. This was a real challenge for Johnson & Johnson and the entire drug industry. One way to demonstrate to consumers that the company was serious about resolving this problem was to remove all the drugs from shelves at the cost of over $100 million dollars in lost product and revenue. This decision would nearly cripple the company while leaving it with no revenue until they could ensure this would not happen again. There was no question about their action, however, since their values were clear and demanded the appropriate action. To this day, Tylenol still enjoys some of the strongest brand loyalty and recognition among consumers.

#7—Resolving Conflict

This may sound like a contradiction, but conflict is the healthiest aspect of any great team. There must be conflict for a group to develop meaningful ideas and avoid groupthink. If there was no conflict, and everyone always agreed on ideas, you could develop an illusion of being invulnerable, and quite possibly take risks that are too great—otherwise defined as the beginning of failure.

Your team needs to develop some mechanisms to deal with conflict when it arises and even instill some from time to time. First of all, make sure that the conflict is focused on the task at hand and does not involve the desire to "just talk about something else." Here you can utilize a time-tested visual resolution tool— the **Parking Lot**. On a whiteboard or flip chart, label one corner "Parking Lot" and move anything to the parking lot that does not have an impact on the current issue facing the group. Always ensure you get the group's permission to move something to the lot. The parking lot, however, is not a trash can for ideas; instead, it keeps the ideas alive until the group can deal with them at the appropriate time. This means you must revisit the idea at some point.

To resolve conflicting issues on your team, always go back to values and objectives. Use Active Inquiry to make sure people see these points.

Example

Group Leader: "Lisa, you seem very strong about this different point of view. What value is driving this idea for you?" or, "How do you think this helps us meet our objective of…?"

At the end of the day, a good long discussion may be what is needed, or even breaking the meeting, and letting the informal discussions continue to resolve the ideas. If the conflict does not involve the entire team, take it off-line before it eventually does. If you rarely have conflict on your team, find some.

To instill some conflict try the **Devil's Advocate**. Assign someone during a meeting to play the role of devil's advocate so there is an opportunity to "rethink" and challenge any idea before it is finalized. At any time, this person may take the opposite point of view for the group to consider or challenge the integrity of the idea. For the integrity and cohesiveness of the team, this should not always be the same person at every meeting.

Try this idea: Assign one person to be the "devil's advocate," yet only the group leader knows who this is at any particular meeting. This may encourage others to feel comfortable about taking a contrary stand on an issue to enhance the conversation.

Remember it should always be about the "good of the decision," and not the "good of the team." Silence invokes complacency, making fools of us all.

Dropping the Bomb

Perhaps you have a meeting that you've scheduled where you need to share some information with your team that is more than likely not going to go over well. When you drop the "bomb" there is a good chance the meeting will go awry and you may lose control. Try the "30-second side conversation" technique. It is quite simple. When you notice your team members starting to lose focus, and it seems they want to share their feelings with others, actually give them permission to take 30 seconds for a side conversation with someone near them. You can time it if you feel you need to, but the most important part is the permission to have a side conversation when it might otherwise seem inappropriate. When you begin to talk again, they will want to know more.

Conclusion

If you take the effort to build it well at the beginning, your team can weather challenging events, and stand the tests of time. Effective leadership in meetings involves knowing which style will help move things forward and which styles may hold you back. Remember, an immediately consensual team is not necessarily a strong one, nor is it the cradle of good decision making.

This may seem like a lot of extra effort. Many people will not want to spend the time on developing their team; instead, they hope that maybe they'll just get lucky and things will work out. Chances are they won't. Remember, start with a strong foundation and the building goes up easily, and weathers the storms—rush the foundation, and collapse it will, over and over, causing frustration, infighting, and lack of results. Build the team well by ensuring strong values and context, and meetings will be shorter and more productive.

Bob Parker

Bob Parker is an expert at helping teams overcome their hidden challenges to performance. As a speaker, trainer, and facilitator for almost 20 years, he has developed unique programs to challenge the way individuals and groups see themselves. This awareness has led them to take action for improvement and greater fulfillment. Bob's signature keynote, "Walk on Wet Paint," addresses the corners we paint ourselves into and struggle to get out of.

In 2001, Bob created "The Pit Crew Challenge," an innovative development program teaching executives the impact of collaboration and teaming by having them become a "real" NASCAR-type pit crew. Activities such as changing the tires under the clock, benchmarking their time, and working toward improvement, have introduced working insights to many teams within Fortune 500 organizations. He is affiliated with Duke Corporate Education in North Carolina and the University of Toronto's Rotman School of Business—Executive Programs.

Bob's book *The Pit Crew Challenge: Winning Customers Through Teaming* (ISBN 978-0-9782221-3-0 www.pitcrew.ca) is scheduled for release in the Fall of 2007. This book explores the many unique learnings from over 20,000 changed tires.

Business Name:	Robert A. Parker & Associates Inc.
Address:	P.O. Box 3491, London, ON N6A 4K8
Telephone:	519-438-3555 or
	1-877-438-3555 (toll free North America)
Email:	Bob@walkonwetpaint.com
Web Addresses:	www.walkonwetpaint.com and www.pitcrew.ca
Professional Affiliations:	Professional Member, Canadian Association of Professional Speakers

Kathy Glover Scott, M.S.W.

Kathy Glover Scott is the mastery guru. As a keynote speaker and facilitator, she weaves together best business practices with advanced energy work to help attain powerful results. As an executive and business coach, Kahty teaches mastery and how to live optimally each day. In addition to being the co-publisher of this internationally best-selling book series, Kathy is the author of the acclaimed *Esteem!*, and *The Successful Woman* (also published in Europe and Asia). She is in demand as a cutting-edge keynote speaker and leader in innovative energy practices.

Kathy is one of only three people in North America accepted to teach Reiki to the 21st degree, as well as other advanced energy-based courses. Visit her website for speaking topics, online courses and upcoming programs in your area.

Kathy is currently working on two writing projects focusing on mastery and shifting consciousness.

Books and CDs by Kathy Glover Scott:
- The Successful Woman
- Esteem! A Powerful Guide to Living the Life You Deserve!
- The Craft of Writing for Speakers (CD)

Experts Who Speak Books (co-publisher):
- Expert Women Who Speak...Speak Out! Volumes 1–6
- Sales Gurus Speak Out
- Awakening the Workplace, Volumes 1 and 2

Business Name:	Kathy Glover Scott & Associates
Address:	P.O. Box 72073, Kanata North RPO
	Kanata, ON K2K 2P4
Telephone:	613-271-8636
E-mail:	Kathy@kathygloverscott.com
Web Address:	www.kathygloverscott.com
Professional Affiliations:	International Federation of Professional Speakers, Canadian Association of Professional Speakers (Ottawa Chapter)

Adele Alfano

Canada's Diamond Coach **Adele Alfano** is renowned as an expert in personal effectiveness and excellence, and change management. She has earned the reputation of being a "mining" expert in professional potential and personal empowerment. Nominated for Canada's 100 Most Powerful Women, Adele has been acclaimed for her energetic and content-rich keynotes and informative seminars. She has been described as a skillful and entertaining presenter who combines charm, wit, heart and passion.

As an award-winning professional and inspirational speaker since 1998, Adele has been a sought-after opening and closing conference keynoter, luncheon speaker, employee/volunteer recognition awards speaker, and seminar leader. Renowned for her proven techniques, she is privileged to have an extensive client list that includes large national associations, leading corporations, government, school boards, and the health care industry. Adele consistently receives rave reviews and standing ovations from audience members who find her presentations valuable, touching and informative.

Canada's Diamond Coach is the co-author, co-editor/ publisher of the *first ever* series of collaborative books by experts and speakers, entitled Experts Who Speak Books— www.expertswhospeakbooks.com.

Business Name:	Diamond Within Resources: Speaking and Consulting
Address:	P.O. Box 60511, Mountain Plaza Postal Outlet
	Hamilton ON L9C 7N7
Telephone:	905-578-6687
E-mail:	adele@diamondwithin.com
Web Address:	www.diamondwithin.com
	www.kissmytiara.ca
Professional Affiliations:	International Federation of Professional Speakers, Professional Member of the Canadian Association of Professional Speakers

Notes